T0271175

Econometric Modelling

Macroeconomic modelling has been one of the most important and influential areas of economic research. This book brings together contributions from the leading researchers working in the area. The papers combine a description of the latest techniques used in modelling the economy with an account of the way that models can be used for purposes of policy analysis. The book will be of interest to students and professional economists who want a better understanding of the questions that macroeconomic models can address and the techniques used to address them.

SEAN HOLLY is Deputy Director of the Department of Applied Economics at the University of Cambridge. He worked on policy design at Imperial College and on modelling at the London Business School before taking a Chair in Sheffield and then moving to Cambridge.

MARTIN WEALE is the Director of the National Institute of Economic and Social Research. He began his career on the Cambridge Growth Project directed by Sir Richard Stone and then worked with James Meade on economic policy design.

Econometric Modelling
Techniques and Applications

Edited by

SEAN HOLLY and MARTIN WEALE

CAMBRIDGE
UNIVERSITY PRESS

CAMBRIDGE UNIVERSITY PRESS
Cambridge, New York, Melbourne, Madrid, Cape Town, Singapore, São Paulo

Cambridge University Press
The Edinburgh Building, Cambridge CB2 2RU, UK

Published in the United States of America by Cambridge University Press, New York

www.cambridge.org
Information on this title: www.cambridge.org/9780521650694

First published 2000
Reprinted 2001

A catalogue record for this publication is available from the British Library

ISBN-13 978-0-521-65069-4 hardback
ISBN-10 0-521-65069-0 hardback

Transferred to digital printing 2006

Contents

viii   Contents

Contributors

Keshab Raj Bhattarai *Department of Economics, University of Warwick*

Andrew P. Blake *National Institute of Economic and Social Research*

Keith B. Church *University of Warwick*

Michael P. Clements *Department of Economics, University of Warwick*

Steven Cook *Department of Applied Economics, University of Cambridge*

Ray C. Fair *Harvard University*

Paul Fisher *Bank of England*

Anthony Garratt *Department of Applied Economics, University of Cambridge*

Jennifer V. Greenslade *Bank of England*

Stephen G. Hall *Imperial College and Centre for Economic Forecasting, London Business School*

David Hendry *Nuffield College, Oxford*

S.G. Brian Henry *Centre for Economic Forecasting, London Business School*

Sean Holly *Department of Applied Economics, University of Cambridge*

Kevin Lee *Department of Economics, University of Leicester*

Campbell B. Leith *Department of Economics, University of Glasgow*

Chris Melliss *HM Treasury*

Peter R. Mitchell *Bank of England*

James Nixon *Centre for Economic Forecasting, London Business School*

M. Hashem Pesaran *Trinity College, Cambridge*

Joanne E. Sault *University of Warwick*

Yongcheol Shin *Department of Economics, University of Edinburgh*

Paul Turner *Department of Applied Economics, University of Cambridge*
Kenneth F. Wallis *University of Warwick*
Martin Weale *National Institute of Economic and Social Research*
John Whalley *Department of Economics, University of Warwick*
John Whitley *Bank of England*
Rod Whittaker *HM Treasury*
Simon Wren-Lewis *Department of Economics, University of Exeter*
Garry Young *National Institute of Economic and Social Research*

1　Introduction

SEAN HOLLY and MARTIN WEALE

In this book we bring together papers prepared by many of the groups supported by the ESRC's UK Macroeconomic Modelling Consortium, together with a number of other contributions. The papers span the issues of forecasting and macroeconomic policy analysis as well as discussing new developments in modelling itself.

One of the puzzles of macroeconomic forecasting is why 'bad' forecasters, i.e. those with no coherent and properly articulated view of the functioning of the macroeconomy, do so well. Clements and Hendry (chapter 2) provide an explanation of this: the assumption that the future will be like the past may, in normal circumstances, provide a reasonably good means of forecasting. But it is obviously useless as a means of understanding either the effects of policy or of macroeconomic shocks on the economy. Their study is a cautionary tale against judging the quality of an economist from the performance of forecasts and, implicitly, a criticism of the argument that a theory can be assessed purely from its explanatory power.

Serious forecasters, like HM Treasury, nevertheless keep a careful eye on their record. Their finding, like that of other researchers, is that forecasts constructed with proper macroeconomic models do perform better than the naïve models of the sort that Clements and Hendry describe. An interesting twist which emerges from the Treasury paper (chapter 3) is that the forecasts presented in the Spring, which are mostly budget forecasts[1] and therefore the Chancellor of the Exchequer's rather than the Treasury's have, between 1986 and 1995, a record worse than those for which the Civil Servants take responsibility.

The middle section of the book deals with modelling itself. Bhattarai and Whalley set out a general equilibrium model and describe its use to look at tax issues. Like many general equilibrium models of this sort, it is purely static. As dynamic models of this type develop, so the existing gap between these and 'traditional' macroeconomic models is likely to become increasing blurred. Nevertheless, as the Bank of England explains, a number of different models is needed in order to ensure that the right tools are available to address the full range of policy issues.

Garratt *et al.* set out an alternative means of reconciling short-term dynamics with economic theory. They take the view that theory has more to say about long-run relations in the economy than about the short run; they set out a multivariate system in which long-term cointegrating relationships between variables are taken from economic theory (with the theory being tested and not always accepted) while the short term is driven by a vector autoregression. Their approach should be expected to provide a model which has the good forecasting properties that Clements and Hendry find in very simple models, but at the same time has the constraints of economic theory and a role for policy variables which should make it robust to the criticism of simple time-series models.

The received, but poorly defended logic that macroeconomic policy is to do with monetary policy, is reflected in the section on economic policy (chapters 8–12). All of the papers focus on monetary rather than on fiscal issues. All five papers in this section also consider the conduct of monetary policy in the context of econometric models. Moreover, they all evaluate monetary policy with the use of a variety of *rules*, both simple or 'handcrafted', and/or optimal (Blake, Weale and Young). Finally all but the contribution of Fair incorporate forward-looking expectations as a matter of course.

Note

1 The budget moved to November in 1993 and returned to March in 1998.

2 Economic forecasting in the face of structural breaks

DAVID F. HENDRY and MICHAEL P. CLEMENTS[1]

1. Introduction

The 'conventional' approach to the theory of economic forecasting is based on the well-established result that the conditional expectation given the available information delivers the minimum mean-square forecast error, so forecasts formed in this way should be unbiased, with independent (non-systematic) errors that have the smallest attainable variances: see *inter alia* Clements and Hendry (1994). The practical experience is very different: econometric model-based forecasts are usually modified by their proprietors, and are often systematically wrong with and without adjustments. Conversely, simple, extrapolative predictors often win forecasting competitions (see, for example, Fildes and Makridakis, 1995). This chapter seeks to explain why such outcomes emerge, and what implications should be drawn.

We have established definitions of the fundamental concepts (unpredictability and forecastability), and explored their properties when forecasting in a non-stationary, evolving economy subject to structural breaks, using mis-specified, data-based models. That has enabled us to clarify the role of 'causal' variables, and enunciate a taxonomy of forecast errors to elucidate the determinants of forecast failure: see Clements and Hendry (1998b). The taxonomy reveals that forecast-period shifts in deterministic factors are the dominant source of systematic failure. Model mis-specification, poor data, collinearity, a lack of parsimony, changes in parameters of zero-mean variables, and even inconsistent estimation do not by themselves induce systematic forecast failure. However, these can all interact with structural changes in deterministic factors to

3

exacerbate failure: see Hendry and Doornik (1997) and Clements and Hendry (1998a).

When forecasting in the face of structural breaks, therefore, the key aim is to avoid systematic forecasting errors due to deterministic shifts. Various approaches are possible, including intercept corrections, differencing, co-breaking and regime-switching models. We are currently examining their properties empirically and in simulation studies, emphasising the distinction between equilibrium correction (based on cointegration) and error correction (automatically offsetting past errors).

Of the many ways of making economic forecasts (including guessing; 'informal models'; extrapolation; surveys; leading indicators – see Emerson and Hendry, 1996; time-series models; and econometric systems), we will only consider time-series and econometric models. There is a vast literature on both, and we merely note some key publications on the former by Kalman (1960), Box and Jenkins (1976), and Harvey and Shephard (1992). The autoregressive integrated moving-average model (ARIMA) is a dominant class, based on the Wold (1938) decomposition theorem; the corresponding multivariate time-series form is the vector autoregression (VAR: see for example, Doan, Litterman and Sims, 1984). Economic forecasting based on econometric models of multivariate time-series will be our primary focus, since such systems consolidate empirical and theoretical knowledge of how economies function, provide a framework for a progressive research strategy, and help explain their own failures, as well as provide forecasts relevant to policy analyses.

However, the likely success of any model-based forecasts depends upon there being regularities which are informative about the future, which the proposed method captures without being swamped by non-regularities. The characteristics of the economic system determine the former so only the last two are under the control of the forecaster. The history of economic forecasting in the UK shows some regularities informative about future events, but also major irregularities as well (see for example, Burns, 1986, Wallis, 1989, Pain and Britton, 1992, and Cook, 1995). The dynamic, cointegrated systems with intermittent structural breaks that are formalised below are consistent with such evidence. Capturing regularities without suffering from non-regularities motivates a different interpretation of parsimony and collinearity, as well as a re-examination of the role of causal information when forecasting models are mis-specified. Several results transpire to be misleading once model mis-specification interacts with non-stationary data (denoting thereby the general sense of processes whose first two moments are not constant over time). Conversely, it becomes feasible to account for the empirical success of procedures that difference data, or use intercept corrections (see for example, Theil, 1961, Klein, 1971, and Wallis and Whitley, 1991), although these methods have no rationale when models are correctly specified. Many potential routes to improving model-based forecasts merit investigation: here, methods of robustifying forecasts by intercept corrections and co-breaking are considered, although we also note pooling devices related to forecast encompassing, and non-linear (regime-switching) models.

The plan of the chapter is as follows. Sections 2 and 3 review and contrast some of the results we have obtained for forecasting in cointegrated-stationary processes, and processes subject to breaks, respectively. We then discuss models and generating mechanisms, before developing a taxonomy of forecast errors in section 4 to highlight the impact of shifts in deterministic terms. Section 5 demonstrates why differencing can be an effective strategy for avoiding systematic forecast failure when deterministic shifts occur in cointegrated time series. Section 6 considers the removal of regime-shift non-stationarity by co-breaking, namely the cancellation of breaks across linear combinations of variables, analogous to cointegration removing unit roots. Such an outcome would allow a subset of variables to be forecast as anticipated despite a break occurring. Finally, section 7 concludes.

2. Forecasting in cointegrated-stationary processes

In Clements and Hendry (1998b), we expound a theory of forecasting applicable to economic time series that can be transformed to stationarity by differencing and cointegration. A general theory of macroeconomic forecasting must allow for non-stationary processes which are subject to intermittent structural breaks, using models that do not coincide with the mechanism that generated the data, and that are selected from (possibly inaccurate) data evidence. Nevertheless, many useful insights come from an analysis of the cointegrated-stationary case, even though it will transpire that there are also important differences when there are breaks. In this section, we review some of the main results for the cointegrated-stationary case, before reporting on the structural-break case in section 3.

The 'conventional' approach

We begin at a high level of abstraction – the theory of economic forecasting assuming that the econometric model coincides with the mechanism generating the data in a (difference) stationary world: see, for example, Klein (1971) and Granger and Newbold (1986). The economic system consists of an n-dimensional stochastic process x_t with density $D_{x_t}(x_t|X_{t-1}, \theta)$ for $\theta \in \Theta \subseteq^k$, which is a function of past information $X_{t-1} = (\dots x_1 \dots x_{t-1})$. A statistical forecast $\tilde{x}_{T+h}$ for period $T+h$, conditional on information up to period T is given by $\tilde{x}_{T+h} = f_T(X_T)$, where $f_T(\cdot)$ indicates that a prior estimate of θ may be needed (simpler still would be to assume θ is known). Forecasts calculated as the conditional expectation $\hat{x}_{T+h} = E[x_{T+h}|X_T]$ are unbiased, and no other predictor conditional on only X_T has a smaller mean-square forecast error (MSFE) matrix:

$$M[\hat{x}_{T+h} \mid X_T] = E[(x_{T+h} - \hat{x}_{T+h})(x_{T+h} - \hat{x}_{T+h})' \mid X_T].$$

However, the relevance of this result is suspect when the model is mis-specified for the mechanism in an unknown way, and requires both selection and estimation from available data generated by a non-stationary economy subject to unanticipated structural breaks. In such a setting, not only is it difficult to correctly model the underlying processes – the costs of failing to do so can be large. Consequently, we consider what can be established, based on research reported in Clements and Hendry (1995b, 1996a, 1996b) and Hendry and Clements (1994a, 1994b).

Conceptual basis

It is helpful to draw a distinction between two basic concepts which are often used interchangeably – (un)predictability and (un)forecastability. Unpredictability refers to the relationship between a random variable and an information set – a variable is unpredictable if the conditional distribution (given that information set) coincides with the unconditional distribution. Predictability is necessary but not sufficient for forecastability: for the latter, we require a systematic relationship, and also need to know the form of the conditional density of the variable, namely, how the information set enters the data generation process (DGP). Thus, although the conditional expectation delivers the minimum mean-square forecast error, its optimality properties are not a useful basis for forecasting when the *form* of the conditional expectation is either unknown or changes over time.

Non-causal variables may be more relevant than (previously) causally-relevant variables if the model is mis-specified for the DGP and the DGP undergoes structural breaks. This result will be reviewed below given its importance in explaining the roles of practical procedures that would otherwise seem unjustifiable. Since a non-constant DGP, and a misspecified model thereof, may occur regularly in economics, forecasting with an empirical model may be fundamentally different from predicting using the DGP.

That we cannot forecast the unpredictable is a truism. But the scope and applicability of this statement is often not appreciated: more aspects of reality may be unpredictable than just the stochastic error on postulated equations, which is all that forecast-error variance formulae sometimes reflect. Rather, the regular occurrence of forecast failure reveals that other unanticipated changes do occur over the forecast horizon, a theme explored in Hendry and Doornik (1997).

Measuring forecast accuracy

Forecast accuracy can only be assessed once a metric is agreed, and the choice of metric may have a greater influence on the success or failure of a forecasting exercise than is often imagined. Although context-specific cost functions defining mappings between forecast errors and the costs of making those errors may exist in some instances, **MSFE**-based measures have been the dominant criteria for assessing forecast accuracy in macroeconomic forecasting. However, for multi-step forecasts or multivariate models, such measures are not invariant to non-singular, scale-preserving linear transforms, even though linear models are. Further, unpredictability is not invariant under intertemporal transforms, so uniquely acceptable measures of predictability do not exist. Consequently, different rankings across models, methods or horizons can be obtained from various measures by choosing alternative yet isomorphic representations of a given model. Thus, **MSFE** rankings can be an artefact of the transformation selected. A generalised forecast-error second moment criterion (denoted **GFESM**) is invariant, but cannot resolve all problems relating to model choice across different forecast horizons (see Clements and Hendry, 1993), particularly for asymmetric loss functions. Although it is desirable that forecasts be unbiased and efficient, in practice, performance relative to rival forecasts determines the worth of any forecasting procedure.

Forecasts and their confidence intervals derived from linear autoregressive models depend crucially on the time-series properties of the variables. In practice, it may be difficult to discriminate between a trend-stationary and difference-stationary DGP, although the implications of the two for how accurately the process can be forecast are quite different in terms of the 'limit to forecastability' (the horizon up to which forecasts are informative).

Forecasting with systems of integrated (I(1)) variables is a non-trivial extension of the univariate analysis of forecasting with an integrated variable because of cointegration, whereby a linear combination of individually integrated variables may be non-integrated (I(0)). We have established representations of integrated-cointegrated systems relevant for forecasting, derived asymptotic forecast-error variances for multi-step forecasts (which transpire to be useful guides to the finite-sample outcomes), and addressed the implications for forecast accuracy of small-sample parameter estimation uncertainty: see Clements and Hendry (1995a). In bivariate systems, imposing too few cointegration vectors seemed to impose greater costs in forecast accuracy than including levels terms which did not cointegrate. Why this might be the case can be seen by comparing forecasts from a correctly-specified model with those from a model specified solely in differences (the DV model), where we abstract from parameter-estimation uncertainty. The correctly-specified model is the limiting case (infinite sample) of imposing too many levels terms and the DV model imposes too few. Figure 2.1 (reproduced from Clements and Hendry, 1993) plots the ratio of the trace **MSFE** (**TMSFE**) for the DV to that for the correctly-specified model, against the forecast horizon. The models are compared in terms of their ability to predict the levels of the variables (the solid line in the figure), their first-differences (the line with squares), and a cointegrating combination (the line with circles). It is apparent that the size of the forecast gains to allowing cointegration depend on the transformation selected, and moreover, for levels and differences evaluation, these gains are greater at short, rather than long, horizons. In fact, whether cointegration is imposed or not makes no difference to the rate at which the **MSFE**s (or forecast confidence intervals) increase in the forecast horizon. For the levels of the variables these are $O(h)$ in the horizon, h, and for the differences and cointegrating combination they are $O(1)$, for both models. The **GFESM** (not shown) unambiguously indicates gains to imposing cointegration. However, when breaks occur, differencing (in the sense of imposing too few cointegration vectors) may play a 'robustifying role', as discussed below, potentially reversing the above implications, and instead leading to the strategy of imposing too few cointegration vectors being preferred.

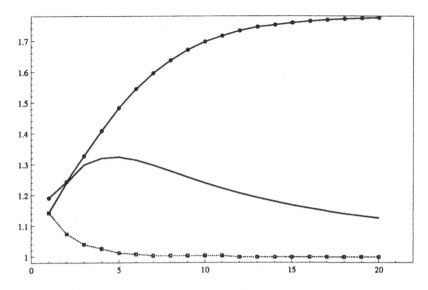

Figure 2.1 *Ratio of* **TMSFE** *of the DV model to the correctly-specified case. The solid line is for the levels of the* I(1) *data, the line with squares their first differences, and the line with circles an* I(0) *transform (a difference and the cointegrating combination).*

Model adjustments

Forecasts from large-scale macroeconometric models usually reflect adjustments made by their proprietors, and the value-added of such adjustments has long been recognised. We have developed in Hendry and Clements (1994b) a general framework for analysing the adjustments typically made to model-based forecasts, based on the relationships between the DGP, the estimated econometric model, the mechanics of the forecasting technique, the data accuracy, and any information about future events held at the beginning of the forecast period. This suggested various rationales for intercept corrections (non-zero values for a model's error terms over the forecast period), which dove-tail with the sources of forecast error in the taxonomy of Clements and Hendry (1994). Intercept corrections were shown to offer some protection against structural breaks (see Clements and Hendry, 1996b), a point to which we return below. A number of taxonomies of forecast errors can be developed as organising tools for analysing forecasts from large-scale macroeconometric models (see for example, Hendry, 1997, and section 4 below). Generally, we decompose forecast errors into five major categories: parameter non-constancy, model mis-specification, sampling variability, variable mis-measurement, and error uncertainty. Subsequent investigations have suggested that parameter change may have been responsible for many of the more dramatic historical episodes of forecast failure, and that research is the focus of section 3.

Forecast combinations

A combination of forecasts may be superior (on **MSFE**) to each of the constituents. However, forecast combination runs counter to encompassing: a test for forecast encompassing is the same as that for whether there is any benefit to combination. When models do not draw on a common information pool, so are of an essentially different type, or are differentially susceptible to structural breaks, then a case can be made for combination. Nevertheless, if the aim of an econometric modelling exercise is discovering forecasting models that can be used reliably, then combination is at best a stop-gap measure.

Non-linear models

Two well-known classes of non-linear model which have been used to model (univariate) economic time series are SETAR (self-exciting threshold autoregression: see for example, Tong, 1983) and MS-AR (Markov-switching autoregression: see for example, Hamilton, 1989): Krolzig (1997) provides an overview. The SETAR model is an example of a piece-wise linear model, in that the model is linear within a regime but moves between regimes depending upon the realised value of the process a number of periods previously. The MS-AR model is also linear, conditional upon the regime that the process is in, but now the regime-determining variable is an unobservable variable assumed to follow a Markov chain.

   While such models may possess some attractive features for characterising the history of economic processes, their forecast performance is not clearly superior: see, for example, Clements and Smith (1997b, 1999), Clements and Krolzig (1998). The linear autoregressive model is a relatively robust forecasting device against a range of non-linear DGPs. The ability to exploit non-linearities for forecasting may turn on whether forecasts are evaluated conditional upon the regime, reflecting the ability of non-linear models to forecast well in certain states of nature, but not always sufficiently well to score better than linear models on average (across all states of nature). Moreover, non-linear models may be favoured by qualitative measures of forecast performance, again raising the question of the appropriate way to evaluate forecasts of variables subject to regime shifts.

Multi-step estimation

We have also evaluated multi-step (or dynamic) estimation (DE) strategies (see Clements and Hendry, 1996c). When a model is mis-specified, minimisation of 1-step errors may not deliver reliable forecasts at longer lead times, so that estimation by minimising the in-sample counterpart of the desired step-ahead horizon may be advantageous. We showed that model mis-specification was necessary but not sufficient to justify DE, which could alter the implicit model class, and conversely. Thus, DE may accommodate incorrectly-specified models as the forecast lead alters, improving forecast performance for some mis-specifications, such as estimating a unit root in the presence of a neglected negative moving-average (MA) error. A drawback of DE is its lack of invariance to linear transformations so different decisions could result for levels versus first differences. In stationary processes, the gains typically fade rapidly in the forecast horizon. When the process contains unit roots, large negative MA errors exacerbate the downward bias of OLS, and a Monte Carlo showed somewhat improved forecast accuracy from DE, although other solutions existed. Even so, we found a relatively small impact of parameter-estimation uncertainty on forecast-error distributions, so the need for robustness to deterministic shifts, discussed below, seems likely to dominate over estimation considerations in model selection.

Parsimony

Some forecasters believe that parsimony is important for multi-step forecasting despite the lack of a formal theory other than model-selection criteria. We have considered decisions based on the t-test for a coefficient being zero in stationary processes, and related the outcome to the result on non-monotonic forecast confidence intervals in Chong and Hendry (1986) – see Clements and Hendry (1998b, chapter 12). However, as powers of a matrix greatly affect the importance of individual coefficients, that result does not generalise usefully to vector processes. We also established that collinearity between regressors could not justify parsimony for linear models of stationary processes, as the forecasts from such models are invariant to orthogonal transforms. Thus, a strong justification for parsimony, or 'tightly parameterised models', when forecasting must depend on the implications of structural shifts in collinear or over-parameterised models.

Finally, tests of predictive failure based on 1-step forecast errors are invariant to linear transformations, in contrast to multi-period forecast accuracy comparisons based on MSFE-measures. 'Structural stability' can be tested by checking whether a model is constant across different sub-samples, or whether estimates over one period provide adequate forecasts over a subsequent period. However, if deterministic shifts are the dominant cause of predictive failure, then a better testing strategy may be based on only testing the non-constancy of the unconditional means.

We conclude that although many important insights have been developed by careful analysis of forecasting in cointegrated-stationary processes, and the majority of tools have derived from that setting, it is essential to tackle the additional problems ensuing from structural breaks impinging on incomplete models of economic processes, where such models may be data-based using poor evidence and inappropriate estimators.

3. Forecasting in processes subject to structural breaks

The results summarised in the previous section mainly relate to aspects of economic forecasting in processes that are reducible to stationarity after differencing or cointegration transforms. It explicitly allowed for the model to be a mis-specified representation of the data generation process, and for the evaluation of forecast accuracy by MSFEs to depend on which isomorphic representation of the model is used. This section extends the analysis to processes that are subject to structural breaks, where many results will in fact change radically.

Causal information

When there are structural breaks in the data generating mechanism the usefulness of causal information for forecasting, the role of parsimony, and the impact of collinearity need to be re-worked. When the model and mechanism differ in a world subject to structural breaks, Hendry (1997) shows that it is impossible to establish the primacy for forecasting of causal information over non-causal variables. In such circumstances, time-series models may outperform econometric models that contain 'causal variables'. While both parsimony and collinearity appear to have only a small effect on forecast accuracy in constant-parameter worlds, the impact of changing collinearity can be detrimental to forecast accuracy, so parsimony may have a justification in non-constant processes.

Equilibrium correction and error correction

Structural breaks show up an important distinction between two notions that are often conflated: equilibrium correction and error correction. Some breaks have a differential impact on models with and without cointegration feedbacks, whereby models with cointegration will continue to equilibrium correct, but may not error correct between equilibria. As a consequence, Box–Jenkins methods, or time-series VARs, which impose differencing and neglect 'levels equilibria' might outperform econometric models in forecasting, even when the latter are the DGP within sample. Such results point towards a 'forecasting *versus* policy' dilemma: the econometric model provides the better guide to policy, but may not forecast as well as a 'robustified' extrapolative predictor, as we show below.

Leading indicators

The same analytic tools can be applied to explain why leading-indicator systems are frequently altered. The framework for index analysis in Emerson and Hendry (1996) was applied to the UK longer-leading indicator, considering issues of cointegration within the indices, and between their components and macroeconomic variables. Since economic relationships alter over time, composite leading indicators (CLIs) suffer forecast failure just like econometric models. CLIs may be less robust than differenced-data models, and to the extent that they capture chance associations between variables rather than causal relations, they may fare worse than econometric models. While it is impossible to prove that causal information is superior to non-causal information when the model is mis-specified for the DGP and the DGP is non-constant, a case can be made for causal information on the grounds of capturing persistent relationships between variables: the notion of co-breaking discussed below relies on such causal links. The effects of adding CLIs to macro models were considered, and the evidence confirmed that they are at best an adjunct to, and not a substitute for, econometric modelling.

Before setting out the forecast-error taxonomy, we need to introduce notation, and define the classes of models and generating-mechanisms which we explicitly analyse.

The data generation process

The data generation process (DGP) is defined over the period $t = 1, \ldots,$ T by a first-order vector autoregressive process (VAR) in the n variables $\mathbf{x}_t$:

$$\mathbf{x}_t = \tau + \Upsilon \mathbf{x}_{t-1} + v_t \quad \text{where} \quad v_t \sim \mathsf{IN}_n[\mathbf{0}, \Omega], \tag{2.1}$$

denoting an independent normal error with expectation $\mathsf{E}[v_t] = \mathbf{0}$ and variance matrix $\mathsf{V}[v_t] = \Omega$. The DGP is integrated of order unity (I(1)), and satisfies $r < n$ cointegration relations such that:

$$\Upsilon = \mathbf{I}_n + \alpha\beta', \tag{2.2}$$

where α and β are $n \times r$ matrices of rank r. None of the roots of $|\mathbf{I}_n - \Upsilon L|$ $= 0$ lies inside the unit circle (where L is the lag operator defined by $L^k \mathbf{x}_t = \mathbf{x}_{t-k}$), and $\alpha'_\perp \Upsilon \beta_\perp$ is full rank, where $\alpha_\perp$ and $\beta_\perp$ are full column rank $n \times (n - r)$ matrices such that $\alpha'\alpha_\perp = \beta'\beta_\perp = \mathbf{0}$, so the time series $\mathbf{x}_t$ are not integrated of order 2.

Then (2.1) can be reparameterised as the vector equilibrium-correction model (VEqCM):

$$\Delta\mathbf{x}_t = \tau + \alpha\beta'\mathbf{x}_{t-1} + v_t, \tag{2.3}$$

where $\Delta\mathbf{x}_t$ and $\beta'\mathbf{x}_t$ are I(0) but may have non-zero means. Let:

$$\tau = \zeta - \alpha\mu, \tag{2.4}$$

where μ is $r \times 1$ and $\beta'\zeta = \mathbf{0}$, with $\zeta = \beta_\perp(\alpha'_\perp\beta_\perp)^{-1}\alpha'_\perp\tau$. The decomposition using $\tau = \zeta - \alpha\mu$ is not orthogonal since $\zeta'\alpha\mu \neq \mathbf{0}$, but as a DGP, (2.5) is isomorphic to (2.3). Thus, in deviations about means:

$$(\Delta\mathbf{x}_t - \zeta) = \alpha(\beta'\mathbf{x}_{t-1} - \mu) + v_t \tag{2.5}$$

where the system grows at the unconditional rate $\mathsf{E}[\Delta\mathbf{x}_t] = \zeta$ with long-run solution $\mathsf{E}[\beta'\mathbf{x}_t] = \mu$.

The model class

The form of the model coincides with (2.1) as a linear representation of $\mathbf{x}_t$, but is potentially mis-specified:

$$\mathbf{x}_t = \tau_p + \Upsilon_p \mathbf{x}_{t-1} + \mathbf{u}_t, \tag{2.6}$$

where the parameter estimates $(\hat{\tau} : \hat{\Upsilon} : \hat{\Omega})$ are possibly inconsistent, with $\tau_p \neq \tau$ and $\Upsilon_p \neq \Upsilon$. Empirical econometric models like (2.6) are not numerically calibrated theoretical models, but have error processes which are derived, and so are not autonomous: see Gilbert (1986), Hendry (1995a), and Spanos (1986) *inter alia*. The theory of reduction explains the origin and status of such empirical models in terms of the implied information reductions relative to the process that generated the data. Some reductions, such as invalid marginalisation, affect forecast accuracy directly, whereas others, such as aggregation, may primarily serve to define the object of interest.

Three specific models considered below are defined by $(\tau_p = \tau, \Upsilon_p = \Upsilon)$, $(\tau_p = \zeta, \Upsilon_p = \mathbf{I}_n)$ and $(\tau_p = \mathbf{0}, \Upsilon_p = \mathbf{I}_n)$ with the extra term $\Delta \mathbf{x}_{t-1}$ having a coefficient of $\mathbf{I}_n$. The first model is the DGP in sample. Although empirical econometric models are invariably not facsimiles of the DGP, they could match the data evidence in all measurable respects – that is, be congruent; but as we allow for forecast-period structural change, the model will not coincide with the DGP in the forecast period. The second model is a VAR in the differences of the variables (DV):

$$\Delta \mathbf{x}_t = \zeta + \xi_t, \tag{2.7}$$

so is correctly specified only when $\alpha = \mathbf{0}$ in (2.5), in which case $\xi_t = \nu_t$. Otherwise, it is mis-specified by omitting the cointegrating vectors, and hence omits causal information. The third model we examine is a DV in the differences of the variables (DDV):

$$\Delta^2 \mathbf{x}_t = \eta_t \text{ or } \mathbf{x}_t = \mathbf{x}_{t-1} + \Delta \mathbf{x}_{t-1} + \eta_t. \tag{2.8}$$

Intercept corrections

Intercept corrections (ICs) are non-zero values for a model's error terms added over a forecast period to adjust a model-generated forecast to prior beliefs, allow for anticipated future events that are not explicitly incorporated in a model, or 'fix-up' a model for perceived mis-specification over the past: see, for example, Wallis and Whitley (1991). A general theory of the role of intercept corrections in macroeconometric forecasting is provided in Hendry and Clements (1994b): here we establish the effects of one commonly-used IC following Clements and Hendry (1996b).

A typical IC for a 1-step ahead forecast is to add in the residual from the final sample observation to the first period forecast value. To see the consequences, consider the simple example of a stationary first-order autoregressive process:

$$y_t = \rho y_{t-1} + \epsilon_t \quad \text{where} \quad \epsilon_t \sim \text{IN}\left[0, \sigma_v^2\right] \qquad (2.9)$$

and $|\rho| < 1$. Let $\hat{\rho}$ denote the estimate of ρ, then the conventional forecast of period $T + 1$ given T is:

$$\hat{y}_{T+1} = \hat{\rho} y_T,$$

with forecast error:

$$\hat{\epsilon}_{T+1} = y_{T+1} - \hat{y}_{T+1} = (\rho - \hat{\rho})y_T + \epsilon_{T+1}.$$

The intercept-correcting forecast is:

$$\hat{y}_{\iota,T+1} = \hat{y}_{T+1} + \hat{\epsilon}_T = \hat{\rho}y_T + \hat{\epsilon}_T,$$

with a forecast error $\hat{\epsilon}_{\iota,T+1}$ given by

$$\hat{\epsilon}_{\iota,T+1} = y_{T+1} - \hat{y}_{\iota,T+1} = (\rho - \hat{\rho})y_T + \epsilon_{T+1} - \hat{\epsilon}_T = \Delta\hat{\epsilon}_{T+1},$$

so that the IC differences the original forecast error. Thus, ICs can help correct for forecast biases arising from unanticipated structural breaks, and the next section develops this implication.

4. A taxonomy of forecast errors

To clarify the impact of structural breaks on forecasting, we reconsider the taxonomy of forecast errors in Clements and Hendry (1994). Despite allowing general structural change in the forecast period, the model and DGP to differ over the sample period in any way, the parameters of the model to be estimated (perhaps inconsistently) from the data, and the forecasts to commence from initial conditions (denoted by $\hat{\mathbf{x}}_T$) which may differ from the 'true' values $\mathbf{x}_T$, nevertheless some useful results can be established. The present analysis will highlight the role of changes in deterministic factors, confirming the apt naming of intercept corrections, and illustrating the efficacy of differencing.

Write the closed system (1) in I(0) space using the n variables $\mathbf{y}_t$ (r of which are $\boldsymbol{\beta}'\mathbf{x}_{t-1}$ and $n - r$ are $\Delta\mathbf{x}_t$) as:[2]

$$\mathbf{y}_t = \boldsymbol{\phi} + \mathbf{\Pi}\mathbf{y}_{t-1} + \boldsymbol{\epsilon}_t \quad \text{with} \quad \boldsymbol{\epsilon}_t \sim \text{IN}_n[\mathbf{0}, \mathbf{\Omega}_\epsilon], \qquad (2.10)$$

so that the unconditional mean of $\mathbf{y}_t$ is:

$$E[\mathbf{y}_t] = (\mathbf{I}_n - \mathbf{\Pi})^{-1}\boldsymbol{\phi} = \boldsymbol{\varphi} \tag{2.11}$$

and hence, in deviations:

$$\mathbf{y}_t - \boldsymbol{\varphi} = \mathbf{\Pi}(\mathbf{y}_{t-1} - \boldsymbol{\varphi}) + \boldsymbol{\epsilon}_t.$$

Distinguishing between changes which induce biased forecasts, and those which do not, is important below. However, we only consider shifts in the unconditional mean $E[\mathbf{y}_t]$, and do not allow changes in trends. Changes in trends would magnify the types of effect we delineate below (at considerably increased complexity in the algebra), but the simpler case suffices for the present exposition. As a contemporaneous example of a mean shift, we note the changes to the savings ratio following the financial deregulation of the 1980s (see for example, Muellbauer, 1994, and Hendry, 1994), and the potential changes that might ensue now the UK government has eschewed blanket state coverage for ill health in old age.

The h-step ahead forecasts at time T for $h = 1, \ldots, H$ can be written as:

$$\hat{\mathbf{y}}_{T+h} - \hat{\boldsymbol{\varphi}} = \hat{\mathbf{\Pi}}(\hat{\mathbf{y}}_{T+h-1} - \hat{\boldsymbol{\varphi}}) = \hat{\mathbf{\Pi}}^h(\hat{\mathbf{y}}_T - \hat{\boldsymbol{\varphi}}), \tag{2.12}$$

where $\hat{\boldsymbol{\varphi}} = (\mathbf{I}_n - \hat{\mathbf{\Pi}})^{-1}\hat{\boldsymbol{\phi}}$, and '^'s denote estimates on parameters, and forecasts on random variables. Although initial conditions are unknown in practice, we assume $E[\hat{\mathbf{y}}_T] = \boldsymbol{\varphi}$ here, so that on average no systematic bias results.

After the forecasts at time t have been made, we allow $(\boldsymbol{\phi} : \mathbf{\Pi})$ to change to $(\boldsymbol{\phi}^* : \mathbf{\Pi}^*)$ where $\mathbf{\Pi}^*$ still has all its eigenvalues less than unity in absolute value, so that the process remains $I(0)$. However, from $T + 1$ onwards, the data are generated by:

$$\mathbf{y}_{T+1} = \boldsymbol{\phi}^* + \mathbf{\Pi}^*\mathbf{y}_T + \boldsymbol{\epsilon}_{T+1}.$$

Letting $\boldsymbol{\phi}^* = (\mathbf{I}_n - \mathbf{\Pi}^*)\boldsymbol{\varphi}^*$:

$$\mathbf{y}_{T+h} - \boldsymbol{\varphi}^* = \mathbf{\Pi}^*(\mathbf{y}_{T+h-1} - \boldsymbol{\varphi}^*) + \boldsymbol{\epsilon}_{T+h}$$

$$= (\mathbf{\Pi}^*)^h(\mathbf{y}_T - \boldsymbol{\varphi}^*) + \sum_{i=0}^{h-1}(\mathbf{\Pi}^*)^i\boldsymbol{\epsilon}_{T+h-i}. \tag{2.13}$$

Consequently, from (2.12) and (2.13), the h-step ahead forecast error made from T, and denoted $\hat{\boldsymbol{\epsilon}}_{T+h|T} = \mathbf{y}_{T+h} - \hat{\mathbf{y}}_{T+h}$ is:

$$\hat{\epsilon}_{T+h|T} = \varphi^* - \hat{\varphi} + (\Pi^*)^h (\mathbf{y}_T - \varphi^*) - \hat{\Pi}^h (\hat{\mathbf{y}}_T - \hat{\varphi}) + \sum_{i=0}^{h-1} (\Pi^*)^i \epsilon_{T+h-i}.$$

(2.14)

Following the findings in Hendry and Doornik (1997) that deterministic shifts are the main determinant of systematic forecast failure, we have designed the taxonomy to highlight their impact. Of course, many factors could induce serious forecast errors: possible examples include large blips resulting from pre-announced tax changes (as in 1968(1)–(2) for consumers' expenditure in the UK), but we construe the first blip to be the above change in the mean, followed by a second shift superimposed thereon.

We denote deviations between sample estimates and population parameters by $\delta_{\varphi} = \hat{\varphi} - \varphi_p$ (where $\varphi_p = (\mathbf{I}_n - \Pi_p)^{-1}\phi$) and $\delta_{\Pi} = \hat{\Pi} - \Pi_p$, and let $(\hat{\mathbf{y}}_T - \mathbf{y}_T) = \delta_y$. Since parameter estimation effects are relative to their probability limits, and all additional inconsistencies are accounted for by centring on Π_p and ϕ_p, then $\mathsf{E}[\delta_{\Pi}^v]$ and $\mathsf{E}[\delta_{\varphi}]$ are non-zero only because of finite-sample biases. However, we use the result in Hendry (1997) that forecasts are approximately unbiased even when based on biased estimates of Π in (2.10). Thus, despite the system being a dynamic process, parameter-estimation biases do not necessarily bias forecasts: although this result is inexact and relies on symmetry arguments, it nevertheless suggests that finite-sample forecast-error biases are not the most serious problem confronting macroeconomic forecasters.

To obtain a clearer interpretation of the various sources of forecast errors, we ignore powers and cross-products in the δs for parameters, but not those involving parameters interacting with initial conditions. Appendix A2 details the mathematical derivation, and defines $\mathbf{C}_h$ and $\mathbf{F}_h$. Table 2.1 combines all the sources of forecast errors that arise from the above decompositions, and expresses them in interpretable components with distinct impacts on forecast failure. Each effect is treated in isolation: some could offset others by chance in any given instance, but we neglect such interactions and focus on the primary effects.

In the present formulation, the second and fourth rows are the only source of biases, whereas the remaining rows just affect forecast-error variances, albeit that both will influence the conventionally-calculated MSFE. The role of econometrics in reducing these sources of forecast error is discussed in Clements and Hendry (1994) and Hendry and Clements (1994a); however, we are mainly concerned here with the consequences of deterministic breaks.

To establish the overall forecast-error bias, take expectations of every term in table 2.1, using (2.11) with $\mathsf{E}[\delta_y] = \mathbf{0}$, and neglect finite-sample biases in parameter estimation as just argued (so $\mathsf{E}[\delta_\Pi^v] = \mathbf{0}$ and $\mathsf{E}[\delta_\varphi] = \mathbf{0}$), to obtain:

$$\mathsf{E}\left[\hat{\epsilon}_{T+h|T}\right] = \left(\mathbf{I}_n - (\mathbf{\Pi}^*)^h\right)(\varphi^* - \varphi) + \left(\mathbf{I}_n - \mathbf{\Pi}_p^h\right)\left(\varphi - \varphi_p\right). \qquad (2.15)$$

Thus, forecasts will be biased when the long-run mean: (a) is inconsistently estimated; or (b) shifts from its in-sample value. In both cases, the impact increases over time as $\mathbf{\Pi}_p^h$ or $(\mathbf{\Pi}^*)^h$ respectively tends to zero, eventually converging on $(\varphi^* - \varphi_p)$. The main causes of $\varphi \neq \varphi_p$ are omitting an intercept, or having suffered a previous, unmodelled, deterministic shift. The first of these is easily remedied, but the second illustrates the potential dangers of inadequate in-sample diagnostic testing, and is a powerful argument for using congruent models in econometrics. Again, by chance, φ_p may be closer to φ^* than is φ, but that is not a reliable basis for forecasting. The main cause of $\varphi^* \neq \varphi$ is obviously a shift in the unconditional mean after making a forecast. Assuming investigators always include intercepts, then past or current changes in the unconditional means of the I(0) components are the main sources of systematic forecast failures, so we analyse these in more detail below, in the context of real-time forecasting for the three models above.

First, we consider several of the salient cases discussed in Hendry and Doornik (1997). An important result is that the forecast-error bias in

Table 2.1 *Forecast error taxonomy*

$$\hat{\epsilon}_{T+h|T} \simeq \left((\mathbf{\Pi}^*)^h - \mathbf{\Pi}^h\right)(\mathbf{y}_T - \varphi) \qquad \text{(ia) slope change}$$

$$+ \left(\mathbf{I}_n - (\mathbf{\Pi}^*)^h\right)(\varphi^* - \varphi) \qquad \text{(ib) equilibrium-mean change}$$

$$+ \left(\mathbf{\Pi}^h - \mathbf{\Pi}_p^h\right)(\mathbf{y}_T - \varphi) \qquad \text{(iia) slope mis-specification}$$

$$+ \left(\mathbf{I}_n - \mathbf{\Pi}_p^h\right)\left(\varphi - \varphi_p\right) \qquad \text{(iib) equilibrium-mean mis-specification}$$

$$- \mathbf{F}_h \delta_\Pi^v \qquad \text{(iiia) slope estimation}$$

$$- \left(\mathbf{I}_n - \mathbf{\Pi}_p^h\right)\delta_\varphi \qquad \text{(iiib) equilibrium-mean estimation}$$

$$- \left(\mathbf{\Pi}_p^h + \mathbf{C}_h\right)\delta_y \qquad \text{(iv) initial condition uncertainty}$$

$$+ \sum_{i=0}^{h-1} (\mathbf{\Pi}^*)^i \epsilon_{T+h-i} \qquad \text{(v) error accumulation.}$$

(2.15) is zero in mean-zero processes (that is, when $\varphi_p = \varphi = \varphi^* = 0$). This suggests that non-congruent models which are deliberately designed to have zero means (for example, by differencing the data sufficiently often) might also avoid systematic forecast failures, and that is precisely the motivation for analysing (2.7) and (2.8). Alternatively, one can view their 'random walk' property (for levels or differences) as ensuring they get 'back on track' rapidly. Next, from table 2.1, if $y_T = \varphi$, then the first and third rows also vanish. Thus, if a forecast commences at a point of long-run equilibrium (or close to such a point), then changes to the dynamics will have no noticeable effects on forecast errors. Conversely, the impact of a change in Π will be more marked the further the economy is from equilibrium. Such interactions may be important at times when legislative changes follow large shocks (such as the oil crises, or joining EMU). Finally, forecast-error biases are also zero if shifts in ϕ^* offset those in Π^* to leave φ unaffected (that is, $\varphi^* = \varphi = \varphi_p$). This is the most startling case in Hendry and Doornik (1997): major changes in the processes that we model may have undetectable effects on the econometric models used, given the sample sizes available in macroeconomics. In other words, both parameter-constancy and forecast-failure tests lack power to detect such changes in conventional sample sizes. The obverse is that we need not worry about such changes: only direct, or induced, shifts in the deterministic factors lead to serious forecast biases.

There are variance effects as well, which are detrimental on a MSFE basis, and Hendry and Doornik (1997) document how large these can be in collinear models which experience a change in collinearity. Also, $V[\delta_\Pi^v]$ and $V[\delta_\varphi]$ could potentially be large in small samples, or in processes treated as stationary but where estimates induce another near unit-root. However, the results on parsimony reported in both Hendry (1997) and Hendry and Doornik (1997), and those on the effects of parameter estimation uncertainty on forecast-error variances in Chong and Hendry (1986) and Clements and Hendry (1996c) suggest these problems may be dominated by mean-shift structural breaks. Finally, if models are misspecified or changes occur, the *ex ante* forecast-error variance estimates will mis-estimate those ruling *ex post*, which could lead to rejection of such models when uncertainty is seriously underestimated, reaching the right conclusion for the wrong reason. Although non-linearities, asymmetric errors, or roots moving onto the unit circle could generate more complicated outcomes, these basic findings indicate the main causes of, and remedial action for alleviating, systematic forecast-error biases.

In a seasonal context, the results are analogous, but considerably more complicated (see Clements and Hendry, 1997). It is also less clear how to offset seasonal deterministic shifts, and this may be why several investigators are finding apparent seasonal unit roots (compare the impact of breaks inducing apparent unit roots in scalar processes in for example, Hendry and Neale, 1991) or periodic variation in model parameters (see, for example, Clement and Smith, 1997a).

5. Forecast errors under structural breaks

The generality of the forecast-error taxonomy may hide its detailed implications for different model types, so in this section we explore in greater detail how (2.5), (2.7), and (2.8) perform when forecasting both before and after deterministic shifts. We consider 1- and 2-step ahead forecasts, made before and after a break at time T. The model in (2.5) coincides with the DGP in sample, but nevertheless performs badly in the face of structural breaks: it is highly non-robust to such changes, despite embodying all the available causal information and cointegration relations. By way of contrast, the non-congruent specification in (2.8), which embodies no causal information and relies on variables that do not even enter the DGP in (2.1), is highly robust, and generally outperforms the other models at the short horizons considered here. These outcomes are predictable from the above analysis of the forecast biases in table 2.1. Moreover, they have important implications for forecasting in macroeconomics where deterministic structural shifts introduced by sudden legislative, policy, technological, or behavioural changes seem to have been all too common historically.

Forecasting models: VEqCM, DV and DDV

In terms of (2.1), the 1-step forecasts from (2.5), (2.7), and (2.8) respectively at time T are:

$$\Delta\hat{\mathbf{x}}_{T+1|T} = \zeta + \alpha(\beta'\mathbf{x}_T - \mu) \tag{2.16}$$

$$\Delta\tilde{\mathbf{x}}_{T+1|T} = \zeta, \tag{2.17}$$

and:

$$\Delta^2\overline{\mathbf{x}}_{T+1|T} = \mathbf{0},$$

or:

$$\Delta\overline{\mathbf{x}}_{T+1|T} = \Delta\mathbf{x}_T. \tag{2.18}$$

The corresponding 2-step forecasts are:

$$\hat{x}_{T+2|T} = \Upsilon\hat{x}_{T+1} + \zeta - \alpha\mu = \Upsilon^2 x_T + (I_n + \Upsilon)(\zeta - \alpha\mu); \qquad (2.19)$$

$$\tilde{x}_{T+2|T} = x_T + 2\zeta; \qquad (2.20)$$

and:

$$\bar{x}_{T+2|T} = \bar{x}_{T+1} + \Delta\bar{x}_{T+1} = x_T + 2\Delta x_T, \qquad (2.21)$$

from (2.18). Similar expressions, updated by the time subscripts, hold for forecasting in later periods.

There could be changes in any or all of α, β, ζ, or μ, but here β will be held constant. We will consider the effects on the VEqCM, DV and DDV, both 1-step and 2-periods ahead. Thus, after time T, the data are in fact generated by:

$$\Delta x_{T+1} = \zeta^* + \alpha^*(\beta' x_T - \mu^*) + \nu_{T+1}. \qquad (2.22)$$

We consider 1 and 2-step ahead forecasts from the pre-break origin T (so T to $T+1$, T to $T+2$) and from the post-break origin $T+1$ ($T+1$ to $T+2$, $T+1$ to $T+3$) where the latter are prepared in ignorance of the break. When a break occurs, its timing matters greatly relative to the forecast origin, and we consider this pattern of pre- and post-break forecasts to mimic real-time economic forecasting, where eventually forecasts will be made after a break. Throughout, we assume the parameter values are known; estimation would add sampling uncertainty, and model selection could introduce additional biases. We also ignore model revision in the light of forecast failure. Model revision will move the outcomes toward the no-break scenario, but unless this is wholesale, and all the pre-break observations are discarded, the results below will hold approximately.

From T to $T+1$

The 1-step forecast errors of the three models in terms of the levels are as follows. From (2.16), letting $\hat{e}_{T+1|T} = x_{T+1} - \hat{x}_{T+1|T}$:

$$\hat{e}_{T+1|T} = \zeta^* - \zeta + \alpha^*(\beta' x_T - \mu^*) - \alpha(\beta' x_T - \mu) + \nu_{T+1}. \qquad (2.23)$$

From (2.17), and (2.18) respectively:

$$\tilde{e}_{T+1|T} = x_{T+1} - \tilde{x}_{T+1|T} = \zeta^* - \zeta + \alpha^*(\beta' x_T - \mu^*) + \nu_{T+1}, \qquad (2.24)$$

and:

$$\bar{e}_{T+1|T} = x_{T+1} - \bar{x}_{T+1|T} = \zeta^* + \alpha^*\left(\beta' x_T - \mu^*\right) + v_{T+1} - \Delta x_T.$$

(2.25)

One can distinguish conditional and unconditional forecast biases, and additional variance effects, but here we focus on the unconditional biases, using $E[\beta' x_T] = \mu$:

$$E[\hat{e}_{T+1|T}] = \zeta^* - \zeta + \alpha^*(\mu - \mu^*),$$ (2.26)

$$E[\tilde{e}_{T+1|T}] = \zeta^* - \zeta + \alpha^*(\mu - \mu^*),$$ (2.27)

and as $E[\Delta x_T] = \zeta$:

$$E[\bar{e}_{T+1|T}] = \zeta^* - \zeta + \alpha^*(\mu - \mu^*).$$ (2.28)

Thus, forecasting from T to $T+1$ when an unknown break occurs at T after the forecast is made, the three forecasting procedures deliver identical unconditional biases. The conditional biases only differ to the extent that $\beta' x_T \neq \mu$ and $\Delta x_T \neq \zeta$, so could attenuate or exacerbate the misprediction on any given occasion.

From $T+1$ to $T+2$

Here the outcome is remarkably different, in that all three predictors now deliver distinct outcomes. All the terms have to be tracked, as the unconditional expectations are altering along the adjustment path, and must be time dated due to the non-stationarity induced by the breaks. First, and assuming that no additional changes occur at time $T+1$, the DGP produces:

$$\Delta x_{T+2} = \zeta^* + \alpha^*\left(\beta' x_{T+1} - \mu^*\right) + v_{T+2}$$ (2.29)

and as:

$$x_{T+1} = x_T + \zeta^* + \alpha^*\left(\beta' x_T - \mu^*\right) + v_{T+1},$$

then:

$$\beta' x_{T+1} = \beta' x_T + \beta' \zeta^* + \beta' \alpha^*\left(\beta' x_T - \mu^*\right) + \beta' v_{T+1},$$

and consequently:

$$E[\beta' x_{T+1}] = \mu + \beta' \zeta^* + \beta' \alpha^*(\mu - \mu^*) = \mu^* - \Lambda^*(\mu^* - \mu) + \beta' \zeta^*,$$

(2.30)

where $\Lambda^* = (I_r + \beta'\alpha^*)$ has all its eigenvalues inside the unit circle. Further, letting $\Upsilon^* = (I_n + \alpha^*\beta')$, then:

$$x_{T+2} = x_{T+1} + \zeta^* + \alpha^*(\beta'x_{T+1} - \mu^*) + v_{T+2}$$
$$= x_T + (I_n + \Upsilon^*)[\zeta^* + \alpha^*(\beta'x_T - \mu^*)] + \Upsilon^*v_{T+1} + v_{T+2} \quad (2.31)$$

hence, as $\beta'\Upsilon^* = \beta'(I_n + \alpha^*\beta') = (I_r + \beta'\alpha^*)\beta' = \Lambda^*\beta'$:

$$\beta'x_{T+2} = \beta'x_T + \beta'(I_n + \Upsilon^*)[\zeta^* + \alpha^*(\beta'x_T - \mu^*)] + \beta'\Upsilon^*v_{T+1} + \beta'v_{T+2}$$
$$= \beta'x_T + (I_r + \Lambda^*)\beta'[\zeta^* + \alpha^*(\beta'x_T - \mu^*)] + \Lambda^*\beta'v_{T+1} + \beta'v_{T+2},$$

and so:

$$E[\beta'x_{T+2}] = \mu + (I_r + \Lambda^*)[\beta'\alpha^*(\mu - \mu^*) + \beta'\zeta^*]$$
$$= \mu^* - (\Lambda^*)^2(\mu^* - \mu) + (I_r + \Lambda^*)\beta'\zeta^*. \quad (2.32)$$

In the limit:

$$E[\beta'x_{T+h}] \overset{h\to\infty}{\to} \mu^* + (I_r - \Lambda^*)^{-1}\beta'\zeta^* = \mu^* \text{ if } \beta'\zeta^* = 0,$$

so the new growth rate remains orthogonal to the cointegration vector. Below, we impose that requirement, as otherwise the new growth rate will depend on all the changed parameters, since:

$$E[\Delta x_{T+h}] = (\Upsilon^*)^{h-1}(\zeta^* - \alpha^*(\mu^* - \mu))$$
$$\overset{h\to\infty}{\to} \left(\Upsilon^* + \alpha^*\Lambda^*(I_r - \Lambda^*)^{-1}\beta'\right)(\zeta^* - \alpha^*(\mu^* - \mu)).$$

By setting $\beta'\zeta^* = 0$ we obtain:

$$E[\Delta x_{T+h}] = \zeta^* - \alpha^*(\Lambda^*)^{h-1}(\mu^* - \mu) \overset{h\to\infty}{\to} \zeta^*$$

The three 1-step forecasts are just:

$$\Delta\hat{x}_{T+2|T+1} = \zeta + \alpha(\beta'x_{T+1} - \mu) \quad (2.33)$$

$$\Delta\tilde{x}_{T+2|T+1} = \zeta, \quad (2.34)$$

and:

$$\Delta\bar{x}_{T+2|T+1} = \Delta x_{T+1}, \quad (2.35)$$

with corresponding 1-step forecast errors:

$$\hat{e}_{T+2|T+1} = \zeta^* - \zeta + \alpha^*(\beta'x_{T+1} - \mu^*) - \alpha(\beta'x_{T+1} - \mu) + v_{T+2} \quad (2.36)$$

$$\tilde{e}_{T+2|T+1} = \zeta^* - \zeta + \alpha^*(\beta'x_{T+1} - \mu^*) + v_{T+2} \quad (2.37)$$

and:

$$\bar{e}_{T+2|T+1} = \zeta^* + \alpha^*(\beta' x_{T+1} - \mu^*) + v_{T+2} - \Delta x_{T+1}. \tag{2.38}$$

Using (2.30), the unconditional biases are (since $\alpha^* \Lambda^* = \Upsilon^* \alpha^*$):

$$\begin{aligned}
\mathsf{E}[\hat{e}_{T+2|T+1}] &= (\zeta^* - \zeta) - (\Upsilon^* - \alpha\beta')\alpha^*(\mu^* - \mu) \\
&= \mathsf{E}[\hat{e}_{T+1|T}] - (\alpha^* - \alpha)\beta'\alpha^*(\mu^* - \mu)
\end{aligned} \tag{2.39}$$

$$\begin{aligned}
\mathsf{E}[\tilde{e}_{T+2|T+1}] &= (\zeta^* - \zeta) - \alpha^*\Lambda^*(\mu^* - \mu) \\
&= \mathsf{E}[\tilde{e}_{T+1|T}] - \alpha^*\beta'\alpha^*(\mu^* - \mu)
\end{aligned} \tag{2.40}$$

and:

$$\mathsf{E}[\bar{e}_{T+2|T+1}] = -\alpha^*\beta'\alpha^*(\mu^* - \mu), \tag{2.41}$$

as $\mathsf{E}[\Delta x_{T+1}] = \zeta^* - \alpha^*(\mu^* - \mu)$. Consequently, the VEqCM and the DV differ depending on the relative size of $(\alpha^* - \alpha)$ compared to α^*, but the DDV shows considerable 'error-correction' behaviour at this post-break 1-step ahead horizon, completely removing $\mathsf{E}[\bar{e}_{T+1|T}]$. In particular, when $\alpha^* = \alpha$, so only deterministic terms change, then:

$$\begin{aligned}
\mathsf{E}[\hat{e}_{T+2|T+1}] &= (\zeta^* - \zeta) - \alpha(\mu^* - \mu) \\
\mathsf{E}[\tilde{e}_{T+2|T+1}] &= (\zeta^* - \zeta) - \alpha\Lambda(\mu^* - \mu) \\
\mathsf{E}[\bar{e}_{T+2|T+1}] &= -\alpha(\beta'\alpha)(\mu^* - \mu).
\end{aligned} \tag{2.42}$$

As anticipated, second differencing has removed any impact from the growth rate changing, and as $\beta'\alpha$ corresponds to the roots inside the unit circle, dampened the effect of shifts in the equilibrium mean. First differencing has not removed the impact of changes in growth, and only partly attenuated the effect of shifts in μ.

From T to T + 2

This comprises 2-steps ahead forecasts made prior to the break, to illustrate how the results change for multi-step forecasts. From (2.31):

$$x_{T+2} = (\Upsilon^*)^2 x_T + (I_n + \Upsilon^*)(\zeta^* - \alpha^*\mu^*) + \Upsilon^* v_{T+1} + v_{T+2} \tag{2.43}$$

as:

$$x_{T+1} = \Upsilon^* x_T + (\zeta^* - \alpha^*\mu^*) + v_{T+1}. \tag{2.44}$$

Thus, the corresponding 2-step ahead forecast error biases are, after some simplification (using $\Upsilon\zeta = \zeta$):

$$E[\hat{e}_{T+2|T}] = (I_n + \Upsilon^*)(\zeta^* - \alpha^*[\mu^* - \mu]) - 2\zeta$$
$$= 2(\zeta^* - \zeta) - \alpha^*(I_r + \Lambda^*)(\mu^* - \mu) \qquad (2.45)$$

$$E[\tilde{e}_{T+2|T}] = 2(\zeta^* - \zeta) - \alpha^*(I_r + \Lambda^*)(\mu^* - \mu) \qquad (2.46)$$

$$E[\bar{e}_{T+2|T}] = 2(\zeta^* - \zeta) - \alpha^*(I_r + \Lambda^*)(\mu^* - \mu). \qquad (2.47)$$

Thus, all suffer from the same impact of a change in the equilibrium mean or from a growth-rate shift.

From T + 1 to T + 3

First:

$$x_{T+3} = (\Upsilon^*)^2 x_{T+1} + (I_n + \Upsilon^*)(\zeta^* - \alpha^* \mu^*) + \Upsilon^* v_{T+2} + v_{T+3} \qquad (2.48)$$

whereas the forecasting rules are just time-index shifted versions of (2.19)–(2.21). However, again, the expectations are changing.

$$\beta' x_{T+2} = (I_r + 2\beta'\alpha^* + \beta'\alpha^*\beta'\alpha^*)\beta' x_T + \beta'(I_n + \Upsilon^*)(\zeta^* - \alpha^*\mu^*) \qquad (2.49)$$

$$\beta' x_{T+3} = (I_r + 2\beta'\alpha^* + \beta'\alpha^*\beta'\alpha^*)\beta' x_{T+1} + \beta'(I_n + \Upsilon^*)(\zeta^* - \alpha^*\mu^*) \qquad (2.50)$$

with:

$$\hat{x}_{T+3} = \Upsilon^2 x_{T+1} + (I_n + \Upsilon)(\zeta - \alpha\mu) \qquad (2.51)$$

$$\tilde{x}_{T+3} = x_{T+1} + 2\zeta, \qquad (2.52)$$

and:

$$\bar{x}_{T+3} = x_{T+1} + 2\Delta x_{T+1}. \qquad (2.53)$$

The difference of practical importance lies in the changed expectations of the variables, $\beta' x_{T+1}$ in (2.32) and Δx_{T+1}:

$$E[\hat{e}_{T+3|T+1}] = [(I_n + \Upsilon^*)\Upsilon^* - (I_n + \Upsilon)\Upsilon](\zeta^* - \alpha^*[\mu^* - \mu])$$
$$+ (I_n + \Upsilon)([\zeta^* - \zeta] - \alpha^*[\mu^* - \mu])$$
$$= 2(\zeta^* - \zeta) - [\alpha^*(I_r + \Lambda^*)\Lambda^* - \alpha(I_r + \Lambda)\beta'\alpha^*](\mu^* - \mu).$$

In the special case that α is constant:

$$E[\hat{e}_{T+3|T+1}] = 2(\zeta^* - \zeta) - \alpha(I_r + \Lambda)(\mu^* - \mu). \qquad (2.54)$$

Next:

$$\mathsf{E}\big[\tilde{\mathbf{e}}_{T+3|T+1}\big] = 2(\zeta^* - \zeta) - \boldsymbol{\alpha}^*\boldsymbol{\Lambda}^*(\mathbf{I}_r + \boldsymbol{\Lambda}^*)(\boldsymbol{\mu}^* - \boldsymbol{\mu}),$$

so, if $\boldsymbol{\alpha}$ is constant:

$$\mathsf{E}\big[\tilde{\mathbf{e}}_{T+3|T+1}\big] = 2(\zeta^* - \zeta) - \boldsymbol{\alpha}\boldsymbol{\Lambda}(\mathbf{I}_r + \boldsymbol{\Lambda})(\boldsymbol{\mu}^* - \boldsymbol{\mu}). \qquad (2.55)$$

Finally, we can write the DDV forecast-error bias as:

$$\mathsf{E}\big[\bar{\mathbf{e}}_{T+3|T+1}\big] = (\mathbf{I}_n + \boldsymbol{\Upsilon}^*)(\zeta^* + \boldsymbol{\alpha}^*(\mathsf{E}[\boldsymbol{\beta}'\mathbf{x}_{T+1}] - \boldsymbol{\mu}^*)) - 2\mathsf{E}\big[\Delta\mathbf{x}_{T+1}\big],$$

which clarifies that it will converge on zero when $\mathsf{E}[\boldsymbol{\beta}'\mathbf{x}] = \boldsymbol{\mu}^*$ and $\mathsf{E}[\Delta\mathbf{x}] = \zeta^*$; or as:

$$\mathsf{E}\big[\bar{\mathbf{e}}_{T+3|T+1}\big] = -\boldsymbol{\alpha}^*(2\mathbf{I}_r + \boldsymbol{\Lambda}^*)\boldsymbol{\beta}'\boldsymbol{\alpha}^*(\boldsymbol{\mu}^* - \boldsymbol{\mu}).$$

Consequently, if $\boldsymbol{\alpha}$ is constant:

$$\mathsf{E}\big[\bar{\mathbf{e}}_{T+3|T+1}\big] = -\boldsymbol{\alpha}(2\mathbf{I}_r + \boldsymbol{\Lambda})\boldsymbol{\beta}'\boldsymbol{\alpha}(\boldsymbol{\mu}^* - \boldsymbol{\mu}). \qquad (2.56)$$

These comparisons clarify why the DDV does so well in a Norges Bank study comparing the *ex ante* forecast performance of their macroeconometric model with the equivalents of the DV and DDV above (see Eitrheim, Husebø and Nymoen, 1999). Once a break has happened, which could be any time over their 12 quarter 'post-estimation sample', the DDV is unaffected by growth-rate changes, $\boldsymbol{\beta}'\boldsymbol{\alpha}$ delivers the 'stable roots', $\boldsymbol{\Lambda}$ has all its eigenroots inside the unit circle, and the biases are dampened by the feedback coefficient $\boldsymbol{\alpha}$. The additional biases in (2.54) over (2.55), and (2.55) over (2.56) are:

$$-\boldsymbol{\alpha}\Big(\mathbf{I}_r - \boldsymbol{\Lambda}^2\Big)(\boldsymbol{\mu}^* - \boldsymbol{\mu}) \quad \text{and} \quad 2(\zeta^* - \zeta) - 2\boldsymbol{\alpha}(\boldsymbol{\mu}^* - \boldsymbol{\mu}).$$

Overview

The bias calculations are summarised in table 2.2 to aid comparison, where $\mathbf{B} = \mathbf{I}_r + \boldsymbol{\Lambda}$, $\boldsymbol{\delta}_{\mu} = \boldsymbol{\mu} - \boldsymbol{\mu}^*$ and $\boldsymbol{\delta}_{\zeta} = \zeta^* - \zeta$.

When the parameter change occurs, forecasts will be incorrect from almost any statistical procedure, so a key question is how quickly the model adapts to the changed environment. The results of the previous analysis allow us to give a reasonably comprehensive answer to this question for the three models considered. The VEqCM is alone in having the same pre- and post-break biases for changes in μ and ζ. The DV has the same pre- and post-break biases for changes in ζ, but has begun to 'error-correct' post-break for the change in μ, while the DDV eliminates

Table 2.2 *Forecast-error biases at 1 and 2-steps pre and post break*

	VEqCM	DV	DDV	VEqCM	DV	DDV
	Forecasting before break			Forecasting post break		
	1-step forecasts					
$\mu \to \mu^*$	$\alpha\delta_\mu$	$\alpha\delta_\mu$	$\alpha\delta_\mu$	$\alpha\delta_\mu$	$\alpha\Lambda\delta_\mu$	$\alpha\beta'\alpha\delta_\mu$
$\zeta \to \zeta^*$	δ_ζ	δ_ζ	δ_ζ	δ_ζ	δ_ζ	0
$\alpha \to \alpha^*$	0	0	0	0	0	0
	2-step forecasts					
$\mu \to \mu^*$	$\alpha\mathbf{B}\delta_\mu$	$\alpha\mathbf{B}\delta_\mu$	$\alpha\mathbf{B}\delta_\mu$	$\alpha\mathbf{B}\delta_\mu$	$\alpha\Lambda\mathbf{B}\delta_\mu$	$\alpha(\mathbf{I}_r + \mathbf{B})\beta'\alpha\delta_\mu$
$\zeta \to \zeta^*$	$2\delta_\zeta$	$2\delta_\zeta$	$2\delta_\zeta$	$2\delta_\zeta$	$2\delta_\zeta$	0
$\alpha \to \alpha^*$	0	0	0	0	0	0

changes in ζ post-break and had begun to error-correct for changes in μ. Precisely because the VEqCM biases are the same pre- and post-break a constant adjustment (that is, an intercept correction) to its forecasts would dramatically reduce the bias when forecasting after the break.

The DV, and particularly the DDV model, are 'non-causal' in comparison to the 'causal' VEqCM, and serve as an illustration of the proposition that non-causal infomation can dominate causal on some forecast-accuracy measures (here, bias).

The differences between the alternative procedures, their relative susceptibility to the three forms of structural break, and the changes from forecasting pre-break to post-break are all very marked. The 1-step to 2-step effects are more natural, and suggest little will be gained by extending the analysis to h-steps after a break. However, a more complete treatment would need to allow for combinations of breaks before and after forecasting if long-horizon forecast comparisons are to be understood: for example, a 4-step forecast where one break occurred before forecasting (helpful to DV and DDV relative to the VEqCM), and another after 2 periods.

Clements and Hendry (1996b) examine the VEqCM and DV models in some detail, and allow for trends in the data. The DDV model seems robust to many of the shifts, but may 'over-insure' by not predicting any developments of interest, merely 'tracking' by never being badly wrong. Moreover, we have considered forecast bias reduction but not the impact on forecast error variances. While some robustness of the VEqCM model to regime shifts can be obtained by intercept corrections that carry forward the shift, the cost in terms of increased forecast-error variance may be large: see Clements and Hendry (1996b, 1998a).

Although differencing and intercept correcting can improve forecast accuracy, especially on bias measures, they entail nothing about the usefulness for other purposes of the forecasting model. Even if the resulting forecast is more accurate than that from (2.12), this does not imply choosing the 'robustified' model for policy, or later modelling exercises. If any policy changes were implemented on the basis of mechanistic forecasts, the latter would have the odd property of continuing to predict the same outcome however large the policy response. Thus, there may be benefits to pooling robust predictors with forecasts from econometric systems in the policy context, and this is a hypothesis to consider if encompassing fails: see Hendry and Mizon (2000).

6. Co-breaking

We define structural breaks as 'permanent large shifts' that occur intermittently, as against 'permanent small shifts' occurring frequently, which generate I(1) effects. Nevertheless, these two forms of non-stationarity due to unit roots and structural breaks are closely related (see Rappoport and Reichlin, 1989), can be hard to discriminate empirically (see Perron, 1989, and Hendry and Neale, 1991), and have similar solutions (for example, being 'removed' by differencing: see Clements and Hendry, 1998b). Since cointegration also removes unit roots in I(1) systems, but by taking linear combinations of variables (see Engle and Granger, 1987), it is natural to introduce a similar notion for systems with structural breaks: co-breaking is the removal of structural breaks by taking linear combinations of variables (see Hendry, 1995c). As changes in deterministic factors are an important source of forecast biases (see Clements and Hendry, 1998b, 1999, and Hendry and Doornik, 1997), we focus on those.

Consider the n-dimensional vector stochastic process $\{x_t\}$, where there are well-defined unconditional expectations around an initial parameterisation ϱ (at $t = 0$ say):

$$E[x_t - \varrho] = \mu_t \in \mathbb{R}^n \; \forall t > 0 \tag{2.57}$$

where $|\mu_t| < \infty$ but otherwise is unrestricted. When any $\mu_t \neq 0$, a deterministic structural break occurs. Co-breaking is defined as the cancellation of such deterministic breaks in time series across linear combinations of variables.[3]

Definition 2.1. *The $n \times m$ matrix Φ of rank m $(n > m > 0)$ is said to be contemporaneous mean co-breaking of order m (CMC(m)) for $\{x_t\}$ in (57) if $\Phi' \mu_t = 0 \; \forall t \in \mathcal{T}$.*

From which it follows that in (2.57):

$$\mathrm{E}\left[\Phi' x_t - \Phi' \varrho\right] = \Phi' \mu_t = 0 \qquad (2.58)$$

so that the parameterisation of the reduced set of m linear transforms $\Phi' x_t$ is independent of the deterministic shifts.

Mean co-breaking may seem unlikely when the $\{\mu_t\}$ can change in any way from period to period, since a fixed matrix Φ is required to annihilate all such changes. Nevertheless, there are many cases where co-breaking can occur in principle even though no $\mu_{i,t}$ is constant. Let $M_T^1 = (\mu_1 \; \mu_2 \cdots \mu_T)$ where $T > n$ (otherwise CMC($n - T$) is automatic) then $\Phi' \mu_t = 0$ $\forall t \in \mathcal{T}$ entails $\Phi' M_T^1 = 0'$, so:

Theorem 2.1. *A necessary and sufficient condition for $\Phi' \mu_t = 0 \; \forall t \in \mathcal{T}$ is that:*

$$rank\left[M_T^1\right] \leq n - m. \qquad (2.59)$$

The theorem follows immediately from the equivalence of reduced rank and linear dependence. Thus:

Corollary 2.1. *The nullity of M_T^1, denoted $nul\left(M_T^1\right) \geq m$, determines the order of CMC(m) and requires $rank(\Phi) = m < n$.*

Further CMC(m) implies CMC($m - 1$); and in corollary 2.1 if H is any $m \times m$ non-singular matrix, then $\Phi' M_T^1 = 0$ implies that $H\Phi' M_T^1 = 0$ as well. An important practical case is where breaks are related across variables:

Theorem 2.2. *If $\mu_t = \alpha \lambda_t \; \forall t$ where α is $n \times k$ of rank $k < n$ and λ_t is $k \times 1$, then CMC occurs for at least order $m = n - k$.*

Proof. Let $L_T^1 = (\lambda_1 \; \lambda_2 \cdots \lambda_T)$ then:

$$rank\left(M_T^1\right) = rank(\alpha \lambda_1 \; \alpha \lambda_2 \cdots \alpha \lambda_T) = rank\left(\alpha L_T^1\right) \leq k.$$

Alternatively, consider the $n \times (n - k)$ matrix $\alpha_\perp$ of rank $n - k$ such that $(\alpha : \alpha_\perp)$ is rank n and $\alpha'_\perp \alpha = 0$. Then for $\Phi = \alpha_\perp$:

$$\alpha'_\perp \mu_t = \alpha'_\perp \alpha \lambda_t = 0 \; \forall t.$$

Thus, co-breaking is possible, and as will be seen below, necessary for invariant policy effects. As discussed in Hendry (1997), cointegration vectors and common trends are also co-breaking vectors for specific shifts in deterministic terms.

Consider breaks in ζ or μ in a VEqCM, focusing on one-off shifts (so Υ stays constant). The relevant regime shifts are denoted $\mu^* = \mu + \nabla\mu$ and $\zeta^* = \zeta + \nabla\zeta$ where:

$$\Delta x_{T+1} = \zeta^* + \alpha(\beta' x_T - \mu^*) + v_{T+1}. \tag{2.60}$$

Then from (2.60):

$$\Delta x_{T+1} = \left[\zeta + \alpha(\beta' x_T - \mu) + v_{T+1}\right] + [\nabla\zeta - \alpha\nabla\mu]$$
$$= \widetilde{\Delta x_{T+1}} + [\nabla\zeta - \alpha\nabla\mu]. \tag{2.61}$$

The first term is the constant-parameter value of Δx_{T+1} and the second term is the composite intercept shift. Form the m linear combinations $\phi' \Delta x_{T+1}$:

$$\phi' \Delta x_{T+1} = \phi' \widetilde{\Delta x_{T+1}} + \phi'[\nabla\zeta - \alpha\nabla\mu]. \tag{2.62}$$

Then m-dimensional equilibrium-mean co-breaking requires that $\phi'\alpha\nabla\mu = 0$; whereas q-dimensional drift co-breaking requires $\phi'\nabla\zeta = 0$. 'Common trends' are equilibrium-mean co-breaking, since $\alpha'_\perp \alpha = 0$, when $\nabla\zeta = 0$:

$$\alpha'_\perp \Delta x_{T+1} = \alpha'_\perp \zeta + \alpha'_\perp v_{T+1}. \tag{2.63}$$

Thus, the $n - r$ dimensional subset $\alpha'_\perp \Delta x_{T+1}$ is unaffected by the shift in the equilibrium mean. This helps explain the effectiveness of differencing as a 'solution' to intercept shifts. Also, cointegrating vectors are drift co-breaking when they are trend free (that is, $\beta'\zeta = \beta'\zeta^* = 0$). Premultiply (2.60) by β' when $\nabla\mu = 0$:

$$\beta' \Delta x_{T+1} = \beta'\alpha(\beta' x_T - \mu) + \beta' v_{T+1}, \tag{2.64}$$

thereby eliminating the shift in the drift parameter. Providing $\beta'\alpha \neq 0$, the resulting subsystem is unaffected by changes in the trend rates of growth in the economy. Conversely, a vector that eliminated such breaks would look like a cointegration vector, so discrimination between cointegration and co-breaking may not be easy (and may be unnecessary). Thus, a subset of equations remains constant despite the break: if these were really 'structural' (see for example, Hendry, 1995b) they would continue to be constant across further breaks. The remaining variables to be forecast would need extra differencing or intercept corrections pending further theoretical developments.

Consequently, econometric systems may yet prove a superior vehicle even in the forecasting context.

7. Conclusion

Given that most results for forecasting from constant-parameter, cointegrated-stationary processes do not apply in realistic settings, we conclude that a formal theory of forecasting for mis-specified models under irregular and substantive structural breaks is an essential development. Despite the formidable technical obstacles to be overcome, only by doing so will we obtain a theory of economic forecasting relevant to the real world. We have established a basis for understanding systematic predictive failure, and hence for avoiding it. Nevertheless, improved procedures are undoubtedly possible, and await further exploration.

In Clements and Hendry (1998a), we applied our theories to forecasting a scalar economic process, namely UK consumers' expenditure, comparing extrapolative and adaptive devices with the equilibrium correction approach in Davidson, Hendry, Srba and Yeo (1978). The empirical findings matched the theory predictions closely, and while the context is simple, that outcome is promising. Clements and Hendry (1996b) was a multivariate application to the model of wages, prices and unemployment of Mizon (1995). Because of the apparent shift in the long-run equilibrium in the 1980s, forecasts from a DV were superior to those from a vector equilibrium-correction model, as expected, and intercept-correcting reduced the biases in the latter. The only large-scale trial of which we are aware, using the Norges Bank model in Eitrheim *et al.* (1999) as discussed above, showed that a specially developed DV performed well relative to the econometric system despite the latter taking all the non-modelled variables at their outcome values. At the shortest horizons, however, their analogue of the DDV tended to be best on **MSFE**. Moreover, that adaptive predictors tend to perform well in forecasting competitions, as noted in the introduction, supports our stance that deterministic shifts are pernicious, relatively common, and that methods which are robust to them fail less badly. We also emphasised how other parameter changes may be less relevant, suggesting the value of direct tests for changes in equilibrium means, as we are currently developing.

We are currently completing the second volume of our text on economic forecasting, Clements and Hendry (1999), which focuses on forecasting in the face of structural breaks. This will integrate the available research on that problem, propose practical procedures that can help offset the effects of large unanticipated deterministic shifts, and thereby robustify econometric models to match other forecasting methods.

Appendix A2: Taxonomy derivation for table 2.1

First, we make the approximation:

$$\hat{\Pi}^h = (\Pi_p + \delta_\Pi)^h \simeq \Pi_p^h + \sum_{i=0}^{h-1} \Pi_p^i \delta_\Pi \Pi_p^{h-i-1} \doteq \Pi_p^h + C_h. \qquad (2.65)$$

Also, using (2.65), letting $(\cdot)^v$ denote forming a vector and $\otimes$ a Kronecker product:

$$C_h\left(\mathbf{y}_T - \boldsymbol{\varphi}_p\right) = \left(C_h\left(\mathbf{y}_T - \boldsymbol{\varphi}_p\right)\right)^v$$

$$= \left(\sum_{i=0}^{h-1} \Pi_p^i \otimes \left(\mathbf{y}_T - \boldsymbol{\varphi}_p\right)' \Pi_p^{h-i-1\prime}\right) \delta_\Pi^v \doteq \mathbf{F}_h \delta_\Pi^v.$$

To highlight components due to different effects (parameter change, estimation inconsistency, and estimation uncertainty), we decompose the terms $(\Pi^*)^h(\mathbf{y}_T - \boldsymbol{\varphi}^*)$ and $\hat{\Pi}^h(\hat{\mathbf{y}}_T - \hat{\boldsymbol{\varphi}})$ in (2.14) into:

$$(\Pi^*)^h\left(\mathbf{y}_T - \boldsymbol{\varphi}^*\right) = (\Pi^*)^h\left(\mathbf{y}_T - \boldsymbol{\varphi}\right) + (\Pi^*)^h(\boldsymbol{\varphi} - \boldsymbol{\varphi}^*)$$

and:

$$\hat{\Pi}^h\left(\hat{\mathbf{y}}_T - \hat{\boldsymbol{\varphi}}\right)$$

$$= \left(\Pi_p^h + C_h\right)\delta_y - \left(\hat{\boldsymbol{\varphi}} - \boldsymbol{\varphi}_p\right) + \left(\mathbf{y}_T - \boldsymbol{\varphi}_p\right)$$

$$= \left(\Pi_p^h + C_h\right)\delta_y - \left(\Pi_p^h + C_h\right)\delta_\varphi + \left(\Pi_p^h + C_h\right)\left(\mathbf{y}_T - \boldsymbol{\varphi}_p\right)$$

$$= \left(\Pi_p^h + C_h\right)\delta_y - \left(\Pi_p^h + C_h\right)\delta_\varphi + \mathbf{F}_h\delta_\Pi^v + \Pi_p^h\left(\mathbf{y}_T - \boldsymbol{\varphi}\right) - \Pi_p^h\left(\boldsymbol{\varphi}_p - \boldsymbol{\varphi}\right)$$

so $(\Pi^*)^h(\mathbf{y}_T - \boldsymbol{\varphi}^*) - \hat{\Pi}^h(\hat{\mathbf{y}}_T - \hat{\boldsymbol{\varphi}})$ yields:

$$\left((\Pi^*)^h - \Pi_p^h\right)\left(\mathbf{y}_T - \boldsymbol{\varphi}\right) - \mathbf{F}_h\delta_\Pi^v - \left(\Pi_p^h + C_h\right)\delta_y$$

$$- (\Pi^*)^h(\boldsymbol{\varphi}^* - \boldsymbol{\varphi}) + \Pi_p^h\left(\boldsymbol{\varphi}_p - \boldsymbol{\varphi}\right) + \left(\Pi_p^h + C_h\right)\delta_\varphi. \qquad (2.66)$$

The interaction $C_h\delta_\varphi$ is like a 'covariance', but is omitted from the table. Hence (2.66) becomes:

$$\left((\Pi^*)^b - \Pi^b\right)(y_T - \varphi) + \left(\Pi^b - \Pi_p^b\right)(y_T - \varphi)$$
$$- (\Pi^*)^b(\varphi^* - \varphi) + \Pi_p^b\left(\varphi_p - \varphi\right)$$
$$- \left(\Pi_p^b + C_b\right)\delta_y - F_b\delta_\Pi^v + \Pi_p^b\delta_\varphi.$$

The first and third rows have expectations of zero, so the second row collects the 'non-central' terms.

Finally, for the term $\varphi^* - \hat{\varphi}$ in (14), we have (on the same principle):

$$(\varphi^* - \varphi) + \left(\varphi - \varphi_p\right) - \delta_\varphi.$$

Notes

1   Nuffield College, Oxford and Economics Department, Warwick University. Financial support from the U.K. Economic and Social Research Council under grant L116251015 is gratefully acknowledged by both authors.

2   The identities determining the future values of the cointegrating vectors are omitted for simplicity: see Hendry and Doornik (1994). The analysis is conditional on assuming such vectors remain unchanged, so the transformed system remains I(0) after the structural change.

3   Contemporaneous mean co-breaking of order m could be defined for subvectors by partitioning, and for higher moments (for example, variance co-breaking). Similarly, it extends to functions of non-stationary processes which have well-defined expectations, such as Δx_t or $\beta' x_t$ (cointegrated combinations). Finally, the class of processes $\{x_t\}$ in (2.57) may be extended to conditional functions of past variables, so co-breaking could be defined for common shifts in other parameters.

References

Box, G.E.P. and Jenkins, G.M. (1976), *Time Series Analysis, Forecasting and Control*, San Francisco, Holden-Day. First published, 1970.

Burns, T. (1986), 'The interpretation and use of economic predictions', in *Proceedings of the Royal Society*, No. A407, pp. 103–125.

Chong, Y.Y. and Hendry, D.F. (1986), 'Econometric evaluation of linear macroeconomic models', *Review of Economic Studies*, 53, pp. 671–90. Reprinted in Granger, C.W.J. (ed.) (1990), *Modelling Economic Series*, Oxford, Clarendon Press.

Clements, M.P. and Hendry, D.F. (1993), 'On the limitations of comparing mean squared forecast errors', *Journal of Forecasting*, 12, pp. 617–37. With discussion.

(1994), 'Towards a theory of economic forecasting', in Hargreaves, C. (ed.), *Non-stationary Time-series Analysis and Cointegration*, pp. 9–52. Oxford, Oxford University Press.

(1995a), 'Forecasting in cointegrated systems', *Journal of Applied Econometrics*, 10, pp. 127–46.

(1995b) 'Macro-economic forecasting and modelling' *Economic Journal*, 105, pp. 1001–13.

(1996a), 'Forecasting in macro-economics', in Cox, D.R., Hinkley, D.V. and Barndorff-Nielsen, O.E. (eds.), *Time Series Models: In econometrics, finance and other fields*, London, Chapman and Hall.

(1996b), 'Intercept corrections and structural change', *Journal of Applied Econometrics*, 11, pp. 475–94.

(1996c), 'Multi-step estimation for forecasting', *Oxford Bulletin of Economics and Statistics*, 58, pp. 657–84.

(1997), 'An empirical study of seasonal unit roots in forecasting', *International Journal of Forecasting*, 13, pp. 341–55.

(1998a), 'Forecasting economic processes', *International Journal of Forecasting*. With discussion. 14, 111–131.

(1998b), *Forecasting Economic Time Series*, Cambridge, Cambridge University Press, The Marshall Lectures on Economic Forecasting.

(1999), *The Zeuthen Lectures on Economic Forecasting*, Cambridge, Mass., MIT Press.

Clements, M.P. and Krolzig, H.M. (1998), 'A comparison of the forecast performance of Markov-switching and threshold authoregressive models of US GNP', *Econometrics Journal*, 1, pp. 1–27.

(1997a), 'Forecasting seasonal UK consumption components', Warwick Economic Research Papers, no. 487, Department of Economics, University of Warwick.

(1997b), 'The performance of alternative forecasting methods for SETAR models', *International Journal of Forecasting*, 13, pp. 463–75.

Clements, M.P. and Smith, J. (1999), 'A Monte Carlo study of the forecasting performance of empirical SETAR models', *Journal of Applied Econometrics*, 14, 124–141.

Cook, S. (1995), 'Treasury economic forecasting', Mimeo, Institute of Economics and Statistics, University of Oxford.

Davidson, J.E.H., Hendry, D.F., Srba, F. and Yeo, J.S. (1978), 'Econometric modelling of the aggregate time-series relationship between consumers' expenditure and income in the United Kingdom', *Economic Journal*, 88, pp. 661–92. Reprinted in Hendry, D.F. (1993), *Econometrics: Alchemy or Science?*, Oxford, Blackwell Publishers.

Doan, T., Litterman, R. and Sims, C.A. (1984), 'Forecasting and conditional projection using realistic prior distributions', *Econometric Reviews*, 3, pp. 1–100.

Eitrheim, Ø., Husebø, T.A. and Nymoen, R. (1999), 'Equilibrium-correction versus differencing in macroeconometric forecasting', *Economic Modelling*, 16, 515–544.

Emerson, R.A. and Hendry, D.F. (1996), 'An evaluation of forecasting using leading indicators', *Journal of Forecasting*, 15, pp. 271–91.

Engle, R.F. and Granger, C.W.J. (1987), 'Cointegration and error correction: Representation, estimation and testing', *Econometrica*, 55, pp. 251–76.

Fildes, R. and Makridakis, S. (1995), 'The impact of empirical accuracy studies on time series analysis and forecasting', *International Statistical Review*, 63, pp. 289–308.

Gilbert, C.L. (1986), 'Professor Hendry's econometric methodology', *Oxford Bulletin of Economics and Statistics*, 48, pp. 283–307. Reprinted in Granger, C.W.J. (ed.) (1990), *Modelling Economic Series*, Oxford, Clarendon Press.

Granger, C.W.J. and Newbold, P. (1986), *Forecasting Economic Time Series*, 2nd edn, New York, Academic Press.

Hamilton, J.D. (1989), 'A new approach to the economic analysis of nonstationary time series and the business cycle', *Econometrica*, 57, pp. 357–84.

Harvey, A.C. and Shephard, N. (1992), 'Structural time series models', in Maddala, G.S., Rao, C.R. and Vinod, H.D. (eds.), *Handbook of Statistics*, Vol. 11. Amsterdam, North-Holland.

Hendry, D.F. (1994), 'HUS revisited', *Oxford Review of Econometric Policy*, 10, pp. 86–106.

(1995a), *Dynamic Econometrics*, Oxford, Oxford University Press.

(1995b), 'Econometrics and business cycle empirics', *Economic Journal*, 105, pp. 1622–36.

(1995c), 'A theory of co-breaking, Mimeo', Nuffield College, University of Oxford.

(1997), 'The econometrics of macro-economic forecasting', *Economic Journal*, 107, pp. 1330–57.

Hendry, D.F. and Clements, M.P. (1994a), 'Can econometrics improve economic forecasting?', *Swiss Journal of Economics and Statistics*, 130, pp. 267–98.

(1994b), 'On a theory of intercept corrections in macro-economic forecasting', in Holly, S. (ed.), *Money, Inflation and Employment: Essays in Honour of James Ball*, pp. 160–82. Aldershot, Edward Elgar.

Hendry, D.F. and Doornik, J.A. (1994), 'Modelling linear dynamic econometric systems', *Scottish Journal of Political Economy*, 41, pp. 1–33.

(1997), 'The implications for econometric modelling of forecast failure', *Scottish Journal of Political Economy*, 44, pp. 437–61. Special Issue.

Hendry, D.F. and Mizon, G.E. (2000), 'On selecting policy models by forecast accuracy', in Atkinson, A.B., Glennerster, H. and Stern, N. (eds.) 'Putting Economics to Work': Volume in Honour of Michio Morhshima, STICERD, London School of Economics. pp. 71–113.

Hendry, D.F. and Neale, A.J. (1991), 'A Monte Carlo study of the effects of structural breaks on tests for unit roots', in Hackl, P. and Westlund, A.H. (eds.), *Economic Structural Change, Analysis and Forecasting*, pp. 95–119. Berlin, Springer-Verlag.

Kalman, R.E. (1960), 'A new approach to linear filtering and prediction problems', *Journal of Basic Engineering*, 82, pp. 35–45.

Klein, L.R. (1971), *An Essay on the Theory of Economic Prediction*, Chicago, Markham Publishing Company.

Krolzig, H.-M. (1997), *Markov Switching Vector Autoregressions: Modelling, Statistical Inference and Application to Business Cycle Analysis*, Lecture Notes in Economics and Mathematical Systems, 454, Berlin, Springer-Verlag.

Mizon, G.E. (1995), 'Progressive modelling of macroeconomic time series: The LSE methodology', in Hoover, K.D. (ed.) *Macroeconometrics: Developments, Tensions and Prospects*. Dordrecht: Kluwer Academic Press, pp. 107–169.

Muellbauer, J.N.J. (1994), 'The assessment: Consumer expenditure', *Oxford Review of Economic Policy*, 10, pp. 1–41.

Pain, N. and Britton, A. (1992), 'The recent experience of economic forecasting in Britain: some lessons from National Institute forecasts', Discussion paper (new series) 20, London, National Institute of Economic and Social Research.

Perron, P. (1989), 'The great crash, the oil price shock and the unit root hypothesis', *Econometrica*, 57, pp. 1361–401.

Rappoport, P. and Reichlin, L. (1989), 'Segmented trends and non-stationary time series', *Economic Journal*, 99, pp. 168–77.

Spanos, A. (1986), *Statistical Foundations of Econometric Modelling*, Cambridge, Cambridge University Press.

Theil, H. (1961), *Economic Forecasts and Policy*, 2nd edn. Amsterdam, North-Holland Publishing Company.

Tong, H. (1983), *Threshold Models in Non-Linear Time Series Analysis*, Springer-Verlag, New York.

Wallis, K.F. (1989), 'Macroeconomic forecasting: A survey', *Economic Journal*, 99, pp. 28–61.

Wallis, K.F. and Whitley, J.D. (1991), 'Sources of error in forecasts and expectations: U.K. economic models 1984–8', *Journal of Forecasting*, 10, pp. 231–53.

Wold, H.O.A. (1938), *A Study in The Analysis of Stationary Time Series*, Stockholm, Almqvist and Wicksell.

3 The Treasury's forecasts of GDP and the RPI: how have they changed and what are the uncertainties?

CHRIS MELLISS and ROD WHITTAKER[1]

1. Introduction

Techniques of forecast evaluation continue to develop, as recent contributions by Blake (1996), Poulizac *et al.* (1996) and Pain (1994) show. Hendry (1997) gives an overview from a theoretical standpoint. However the main questions of interest remain the same as in Theil (1966): are the forecasts efficient in the sense of using optimally the information available at the time when the forecast is made, and how large are the error bands associated with the point forecasts? The Treasury first published error margins in 1977, and there has been a series of papers describing the forecast record, in terms of both descriptive statistics and formal tests of rationality, the latest of which was Melliss (1997).

This chapter extends the data sample for GDP and the RPI used earlier by including the fourteen forecasts made between January 1993 and May 1996, with the results described in sections 2 and 4 respectively. Some alternative tests of forecast efficiency are applied in sections 3 and 5. In section 6 we demonstrate how probabilistic error bands may be calculated, apply the method to Treasury forecasts of GDP and the RPI and discuss how they might be used to help assess the risks to the forecasts. This exercise also gives information on how the forecast horizon and accuracy interact. The relationship between errors on GDP and RPI forecasts is examined in section 7 to see whether observable information could have been used to improve forecast accuracy. Section 8 looks at the relationship between GDP growth and inflation and inflation surprises as proxied by the errors in Treasury forecasts of the RPI. Section 9 concludes.

The 1997 study examined the eighty-seven forecasts for seventeen quarterly and two annual variables made between January 1971 and October

38

Table 3.1 *Forecasts and outturns*

Pre unified budget	Latest outturn	First forecast
January	$Q3_{t-1}$	$Q4_{t-1}$
FSBR (March)	$Q4_{t-1}$	$Q1_t$
June	$Q1_t$	$Q2_t$
September/October	$Q2_t$	$Q3_t$
Post unified budget		
Unified budget (November)	$Q3_{t-1}$	$Q4_{t-1}$
May	$Q4_{t-1}$	$Q1_t$
Summer	$Q1_t$	$Q2_t$
October	$Q2_t$	$Q3_t$

Note: For the RPI the outturn data is one quarter later. The FSBR, unified budget and Summer forecasts are published.

1992. There have been eighteen forecasts since, of which fourteen, up to the summer forecast in 1996, are included here. The timing of forecasts changed with the first unified budget in November 1993, as table 3.1 shows.

The irregular pattern through the year implies that, especially where there are monthly data as with the RPI, the timing of the latest data in relation to the forecast differs slightly depending on which is considered. With the pre-November 1993 January forecasts and the post unified budget May forecasts, the lags between the outturn data and the construction of the forecast are longer than for the others. For this chapter the main focus is on GDP and the RPI, with RPI excluding mortgage interest payments (RPI ex MIPs) given a brief mention. We also focus exclusively on the four and eight step ahead forecasts for GDP and the four step and year 2 forecasts for the RPI.[2]

The earlier study found that for GDP, the null hypotheses of unbiasedness could be rejected for the 1979–85 sub-period, but not for other periods. However there was evidence that the three, four and eight step ahead forecasts were inefficient from 1979 onwards, with the coefficient on the forecast being significantly greater than unity. By including past information, some of which would have been available at the time of the forecast, errors might have been reduced, especially at longer horizons. Past outturns of GDP growth and the rate of change of growth and, for RPI forecasts, CBI capacity utilisation and lagged GDP forecast errors, were elements in the extended information sets found to be significant when added to forecast efficiency or bias equations, especially with 4 and 8 step or year 2 forecasts. These relationships were not robust across sub-periods of the full sample, and this probably explains why they have not been exploited in Treasury forecasts. GDP forecasts one year ahead had a standard error of 2.0 per cent for the whole period 1971–92, falling to 1.67 per cent after 1985. The root mean squared errors (RMSEs) for GDP forecasts were especially high in the 1970s. RPI forecasts were accurate at short horizons; inefficient and biased at some horizons. Theil statistics showed that, with the exception of the RPI on a year 2 basis, both GDP and RPI forecasts comfortably outperformed naïve extrapolations for the sample as a whole and in all sub-periods. There appeared to be no discernible trend in RPI forecast accuracy within the sample on this measure. The earlier study found that forecasts of GDP were generally more accurate than for its main components. The RPI ex MIPs forecasts had lower standard errors than other nominal variables, including the RPI. The one year ahead standard error from 1985–92 was 1.08 per cent compared with 1.71 per cent for the RPI.[3]

2. GDP forecasts

The main descriptive statistics for GDP growth are shown in table 3.2. An unusual feature of the most recent data is their exceptionally low variability. Some of this may be ascribed to revised methods used by the CSO/ONS which involve alignment adjustment of the income and expenditure measures of GDP with the smoother output measure, ONS (1997). This is reflected in the outturn standard deviations, which have been lower since the new method was introduced in 1993, and the Theil statistics which are close to unity at all horizons.[4] The tendency for data to be revised upwards between the first available measure of the outturn, denoted the A series, and the latest outturn, the B series, which was apparent in the period from 1985–92, has continued. However, in the 1985–92 sub-period, the forecasts were about equally accurate on both measures. Since 1992 the errors have been smaller when measured against the first outturn, as the error statistics in table 3.2 clearly show. The positive average errors, even with the A series, suggest that the forecasts have tended to underestimate the strength of the recent recovery.

Forecast accuracy has changed over time, but not systematically. Table 3.3 shows for four and eight quarter horizons the RMSE statistics by sub-period. Accuracy deteriorated between 1979–85 and 1990–92. (Although not shown in the tables here, the four quarter average error and average absolute error were equal from 1990–92, indicating that these forecasts were also biased). As figure 3.1 demonstrates, there was no clear warning

Table 3.2 *GDP growth: summary statistics*

Dates[a]	Forecast horizon	Outturn[b] Mean	Outturn[b] SD	Average[b] error	Average[b] absolute error	RMSE[b,c]	Theil[d]
71Q1–96Q2	One	0.51	1.11	0.19	0.68	4.85	1.09
	Two	1.03	1.67	0.06	0.95	2.91	0.87
	Three	1.56	2.14	–0.10	1.19	2.16	0.76
	Four	2.10	2.60	–0.03	1.45	1.89	0.73
	Eight[e]	4.25	4.06	0.02	2.65	1.62	0.80
	Twelve[f]	7.17	5.27	1.20	4.18	1.59	0.90
85Q3–92Q4	One	0.51	0.81	–0.04	0.47	2.27	0.79
	Two	0.97	1.39	–0.06	0.56	1.41	0.62
	Three	1.45	2.02	–0.01	0.99	1.53	0.72
	Four	1.92	2.60	–0.02	1.50	1.67	0.83
	Eight[e]	3.76	4.72	–0.55	0.73	1.67	0.73
	Twelve[f]	5.18	6.50	–1.53	0.63	1.98	0.63
93Q1–96Q2	One A)	0.54	0.29	0.05	0.14	0.79	0.71
	B)	0.73	0.36	0.24	0.35	1.78	1.14
	Two A)	1.19	0.50	0.08	0.36	0.89	0.91
	B)	1.46	0.65	0.35	0.58	1.43	0.99
	Three A)	1.91	0.69	0.12	0.50	0.82	0.87
	B)	2.20	0.86	0.41	0.71	1.26	0.96
	Four A)	2.69	0.80	0.22	0.69	0.80	0.90
	B)	2.98	0.99	0.51	0.87	1.09	0.91
	Eight[e] A)	5.76	0.94	0.67	1.15	0.69	0.90
	B)	6.39	1.18	1.30	1.54	0.98	0.90

Notes:
[a]Dates refer to date of forecast.
[b]Statistics are calculated using latest (October 1997) estimates of outturns, except rows marked A which use first estimate of outturn. Note that the RMSE and Theil statistics only are on annualised data for all horizons; others based on actual per cent change.
[c]Root mean squared error $= \sqrt{\Sigma (A-F)^2/n}$ where $(A-F)$ is expressed at an annual rate.
[d]Theil $= RMSE/\Sigma (A-A^{*})^2/n$ is the error from an extrapolative forecast growth rate of 2.25 per cent. A value of 1 implies that the forecast was no better than assuming unchanged growth or levels.
[e]To 1995Q2.
[f]To 1994Q3.

in the forecasts of the 1990–91 recession, in contrast to 1980, when the timing, duration and extent of the recession were foreseen, even in the eight quarter ahead forecast.

Four quarters ahead

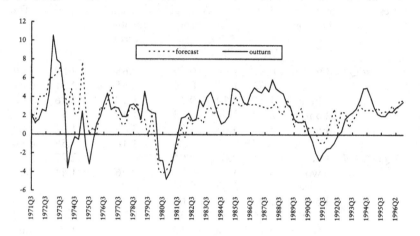

Eight quarters ahead

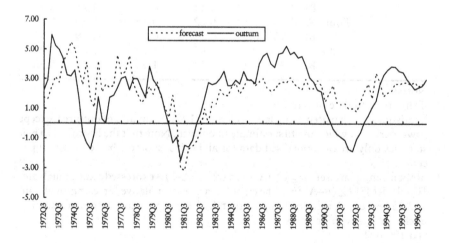

Figure 3.1 *GDP growth four and eight quarters ahead*
Notes: Dates refer to outturns. Latest available outturns used.

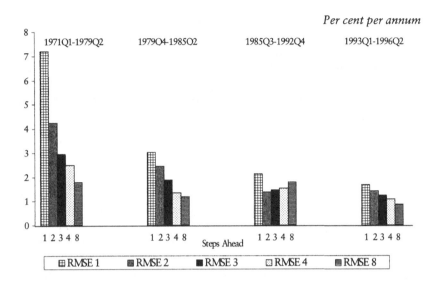

Figure 3.2 *GDP forecasts: root mean squared errors*
[a]The root mean squared error for eight steps ahead is for 1993Q1–1995Q3.

Table 3.3 GDP: RMSE by sub-period[a]

Period[b]	4 step ahead	8 step ahead
1971Q1–1979Q2	2.50	1.79
1979Q4–1985Q2	1.34	1.19
1985Q3–1989Q4	1.53	1.78
1990Q1–1992Q4	1.91	2.10
1993Q1–1996Q2	1.09	0.98[c]

Notes:

[a]Uses B series data. The RMSE figures are expressed at an annual rate, see table 3.2, note c.
[b] Dates refer to data of forecast.
[c]1993Q1–1995Q2.

The variance of GDP in the first two sub-periods was about equal, so the large reductions in RMSEs suggest an unconditional improvement in forecast accuracy. The variance of GDP was lower from 1993–6 than at any other time in the sample, and there was a smooth upward trend. This helps to explain the lower RMSEs seen in this period.

Table 3.2 gives information on how forecast errors evolve with forecast horizon, and this is also summarised in figure 3.2, which shows the RMSEs expressed at an annual rate in a particular sample period at a given horizon. One might expect forecast accuracy to fall as the horizon lengthens, but in the first two sub-periods accuracy improved as the horizon was extended. After 1985 this pattern was reversed, although the one step errors remain proportionately large.

3. GDP forecast efficiency

Holden and Peel (1985) apply regression tests of weak efficiency or rationality to the National Institute forecasts from 1975 to 1980.[5] Theirs has become the standard framework, used by Britton and Pain (1992), for example.

Representative regression tests of forecast efficiency and unbiasedness are given in tables 3.4–3.6. For both the whole sample and the two sub-samples shown, GDP forecasts are unbiased at the four and eight step horizons with the constant term insignificantly different from zero (tables 3.4 and 3.5). For the two sub-periods, the null that the forecast errors are distributed normally cannot be rejected at the 95 per cent level. Table 3.6, however, shows that for the full sample, a chi-squared test accepts the null hypothesis that forecasts were weakly efficient, although with the post-1985 samples the relevant restrictions are rejected at the 95 per cent level. To get a measure of how much of the variance of GDP was explained by the forecasts, the full sample equations in table 3.6 were re-estimated without the event, seasonal or shift dummies. The R-bar squared statistics were 0.47 and 0.30 for the four and eight step ahead forecasts respectively.[6]

A number of alternative tests of forecast efficiency have been proposed. For a fixed event forecast, say of the level of GDP in 1996Q4, Clements (1995) shows that weak efficiency implies that successive forecast revisions are uncorrelated, so that $_{t-i}F_T - _{t-i-1}F_T = R_t$ where $t-i$ and $t-i-1$ are forecast horizons of length i and $i-1$, and R_{it} is the forecast revision made at time t with horizon i. If the forecast revisions are independent, R_i is white noise, and the sequence of forecasts of an event at T will follow a random walk. The intuition is that, if successive forecast revisions have a particular structure, then they are predictable, so the forecast would not be using efficiently the available information. A test of first or higher order autoregression of the forecast revisions against the null of no autoregression therefore provides a test of weak efficiency.[7]

We are able to consider only five forecasts for any particular fixed event, whereas Clements in his empirical application uses 26, based on quarterly

Table 3.4 *GDP growth: tests of forecast bias: A series*
Estimate of equation $A_t - {}_{t-i}F_t = a + c_i D_{it} + u_t$

Sample	Forecast horizon	Constant	Event[a] dummies	Seasonal, shift dummies[a]	Normality[c]	Q[d]	$\overline{R}^2$
71Q1–96Q2	Four	0.18 (0.4)	D2,D8 D79	K1,K3	X		0.29
	Eight[b]	0.13 (0.08)	D79	K3	Y	*	0.25
85Q3–96Q2	Four	−0.59 (−0.9)			Y	*	0.05
	Eight[b]	−1.33 (−0.8)			Y	*	−0.03
92Q1–96Q2	Four	0.23 (0.4)			Y		−0.18
	Eight[b]	0.64 (0.8)			Y	*	−0.22

Notes:
[a]D_{it} represents the *i*th dummy variable. For GDP equations the event dummies included cover the 1972 dock strike (D1), the 1974 3-day week (D2), the 1979 winter strike (D3) and the 1984–5 miners' strike (D8). D79 is a dummy for the June 1979 forecast. The three shift dummies K1, K2, K3 cover the periods 1971Q1–1978Q4, 1979Q1–1985Q2 and 1990Q1–1992Q4 respectively. Shift dummies were only included in full sample estimates. Dummies only shown where |t>2|.
[b]To 95Q2.
[c]Normality test of skewness and kurtosis: if either is significant at 5 per cent level the residuals are given as not normal (X).
[d]Lagrange multiplier test for serial correlation of residuals:
** significant at 90% level, * significant at 95 per cent level.
A series is first available estimate of outturn.

forecasts made at monthly intervals with a maximum horizon of 2½ years. With only five forecasts and four revisions, our sample is too small to test for independence this way. Taking up an idea in Clements (1997), we apply the test to pooled data which combines fixed, that is, successive forecasts of the same data point, with rolling forecasts, that is, data of the same horizon but from successive forecasts.

Regressions of the following form were estimated:

$$E_{1t} = a_0 + a_1 R_{1t} + a_2 R_{2t} + a_3 R_{3t} + a_4 R_{4t} + u_t \qquad\qquad t = 1 \dots T \quad (3.1)$$

Table 3.5 *GDP growth: tests of forecast bias: B series*
Estimate of equation $A_t - {}_{t-i} F_t = a + c_i D_{it} + u_t$

Sample	Forecast horizon	Constant	Event[a] dummies	Seasonal, shift dummies[a]	Normality[c]	Q^d		$\overline{R}^2$
71Q1–96Q2	Four	0.76	D2,D3	S1,K3	X		*	0.31
		(1.6)	D8,D79					
	Eight[b]	1.02	D79	K3	X		*	0.20
		(0.5)						
85Q3–96Q2	Four	−0.09			Y		*	−0.03
		(-0.1)						
	Eight[b]	−0.63			Y		*	−0.05
		(−0.3)						
92Q1–96Q2	Four	0.55			Y			−0.18
		(0.7)						
	Eight[b]	1.25			Y		*	−0.22
		(1.1)						

Note: B series is latest (October 1997) estimate of outturn. Other definitions and notes as for table 3.4.

$$R_{1t} = b_0 + b_1 R_{2t} + b_2 R_{3t} + b_3 R_{4t} + u_t \qquad\qquad t = 1 \ldots\ldots T \quad (3.2)$$

where E_{1t} is the one step error for the forecast for GDP or the RPI made at t. Table 3.7 reports individually significant coefficients from these regressions for GDP, and a χ^2 test for joint significance.[8] There is a consistent pattern to the results. After 1985 the t statistics in both equations are lower, although the coefficients remain jointly significant. There is clear evidence of autoregression with equation 3.1, less so with equation 3.2 and only for the post-1985 period.

The coefficient estimates for equation 3.2, although not significant, suggests that up to 1985, when GDP forecasts were revised at the shortest horizon, this was associated with revisions in the opposite direction or no revision at longer forecast horizons. The equation 3.1 results suggest that positive one-step errors were generally associated with positive revisions in previous periods suggesting that the revisions were not carried through to a sufficient extent.

The information used in constructing the forecast error statistics discussed in section 6 below can also be used to provide another test forecast rationality. For each of the eight horizons, simple forecast efficiency equations were estimated over the sample January 1982 to October 1995.

Table 3.6 *GDP growth: test of forecast efficiency: B series*
Estimate of equation $A_t = a + b_{t-i} F_t + c_i D_{it} + u_t$

Sample	Forecast horizon	Constant	Forecast	Dummies[a]	X_2^{2b}	Seasonal shift dummies[a]	Normality	Q	$\bar{R}^2$
71Q1–96Q2	Four	0.86 (1.5)	0.96 (7.1)	D2,D3 D8,D79	2.7	S1,K3	X	*	0.63
		0.24 (0.7)	0.87 (6.6)	–	1.0	–	X	*	0.47
	Eight[c]	1.63 (0.8)	0.88 (6.6)	D79	1.0	K3	Y	*	0.43
		0.86 (0.8)	0.78 (5.1)	–	2.1	–	Y	*	0.30
85Q3–96Q2	Four	–1.16 (-1.8)	1.53 (7.6)		7.3**		Y	*	0.59
	Eight[c]	–7.16 (2.6)	2.4 (4.0)		6.6*		Y	*	0.46
92Q1–96Q2	Four	1.59 (12.3)	0.55 (1.7)		192.0*		Y	*	–0.21
	Eight[c]	7.9 (16.3)	–0.35 (–1.6)		8.9**		Y	*	–0.33

Notes:[a]Dummies only shown where t>2. [b]Wald tests of hypothesis $a = 0$, $b = 1$. **
denotes rejection at the 95 per cent level; * denotes rejection at the 99 per cent level.
[c]Estimated to 1995Q2. See table 3.4 for other definitions.

Table 3.7 *GDP forecasts: regression test of forecast revisions*

Equation (1) E_{it}	a_0	a_1	a_2	a_3	a_4	χ^2 Test[a]
71Q1–95Q2	–	0.17	0.13	–		70.1*
71Q1–85Q2	–	0.17	0.14	–	–	63.8*
85Q3–95Q2	–	0.18	–	–	–	11.4**

Equation (2) R_{it}	b_0	b_1	b_2	b_3		
71Q1–95Q2	–	–	–	–		3.3
71Q1–85Q2	1.17	–	–	–		4.7
85Q3–95Q2	–	–	0.87	–		10.2**

Notes: Individual coefficients shown only when significant at 95 per cent level
or higher. [a]χ^2 test of joint significance of regressors other than the constant:
*rejection of null at 99 per cent.
**rejection of null at 95 per cent.

Table 3.8 *GDP forecasts: rationality and normality*

		Rationality[a]	Normality[a]
Year ahead	January	0.06	0.99
	FSBR	2.90	0.90
	June	0.12	0.85
	October	1.41	1.21
Current year	January	1.86	3.77
	FSBR	0.74	1.26
	June	1.18	4.83**
	October	27.60*	0.41

Notes:
[a]Chi-squared 2 test
* Significant at 95 per cent level.
** Significant at 90 per cent level.

The results are summarised in table 3.8, where the results of the Wald test of the null that $a = 0$; $b = 1$ in the regression $A_t = a + b\ F_t$ are given, using the Newey-West adjusted variance covariance matrix as before. They support the hypotheses that the forecast residuals are normally distributed and efficient.

4. RPI inflation forecasts

The headline inflation indicators, the RPI and RPI ex MIPs, are available monthly 1–2 working weeks after the end of the month to which the latest data refer. Compared with the timing of GDP forecasts shown in table 3.1, the first forecast and latest outturn are one quarter later, so that, for example, in the January forecast the latest outturn is the fourth quarter of the previous year. To the extent that there is timely within-quarter data available, RPI forecasts at short horizons might be expected to be more accurate than GDP forecasts. The four step and year 2 forecasts are illustrated in figure 3.3. The tendency for the forecasts to understate inflation volatility is apparent.

The Theil statistics in table 3.9 show that while the forecasts generally outperform a naïve 'no change inflation' projection, they are especially accurate one step ahead. Table 3.9 and figure 3.4 also show that, except for the most recent period, the RMSE increases with the forecast horizon, as expected. The Theil statistics for 1971–9 (not shown) were about the same as in 1985–92, except at one step ahead, which were much higher in the

Table 3.9 *RPI inflation: summary statistics*

Dates	Forecast horizon	Outturn[a]		Average error	SD	Average absolute error	RMSE[c]	Theil[d]
		Mean	SD					
71Q1–	One	2.08	1.70	−0.05	0.48	0.34	1.92	0.31
96Q2	Two	4.19	3.09	0.11	1.09	0.79	2.19	0.41
	Three	6.33	4.50	0.48	1.80	1.36	2.49	0.53
	Four	8.52	5.91	0.71	2.64	1.95	2.72	0.60
	Eight[b]	18.32	12.15	3.31	7.64	5.47	3.98	0.69
	Year 2	8.56	6.02	2.23	5.03	3.51	5.48	1.19
85Q3–	One	1.29	0.99	0.07	0.29	0.25	1.18	0.21
92Q4	Two	2.57	1.54	0.19	0.83	0.70	1.67	0.45
	Three	3.90	2.14	0.30	1.34	1.11	1.81	0.54
	Four	5.24	2.58	0.44	1.68	1.37	1.71	0.62
	Eight	10.66	4.84	1.72	3.92	3.33	2.08	0.59
	Year 2	5.11	2.70	1.18	2.62	2.09	2.83	1.11
93Q1–	One	0.65	0.73	−0.06	0.19	0.13	0.76	0.17
96Q2	Two	1.36	0.72	−0.18	0.31	0.28	0.79	0.25
	Three	2.01	0.72	−0.33	0.45	0.43	0.72	0.41
	Four	2.68	0.57	−0.45	0.68	0.65	0.80	0.80
	Eight[b]	5.74	0.57	−1.04	0.61	1.04	0.60	0.74
	Year 2[b]	2.87	0.53	−0.31	0.34	0.36	0.45	0.46

Notes:
[a]Dates refer to forecast, but note that for the RPI the first forecast quarter is the one in which the forecast takes place, that is, Q1 for the January forecast, Q2 for the FSBR forecast and so on, one quarter later than for all other variables. RPI figures are not revised; latest estimate of outturn used throughout.
[b]To 1995Q2. Year 2 defined as inflation from Q4 to Q8 ahead.
[c]See note c of table 3.2. [d]As note d of table 3.2, with the extrapolated growth rate t periods ahead set equal to that in the previous t periods.

Table 3.10 *RPI ex MIPS inflation: summary statistics*

Dates	Forecast horizon	Outturn		Average error	SD	Average absolute error	RMSE[c]	Theil[d]
		Mean	SD					
88Q4–	One	1.14	0.92	0.00	0.24	0.18	0.95	0.17
96Q	Two	2.16	1.07	0.11	0.69	0.55	1.38	0.39
	Three	3.22	1.42	0.16	0.98	0.74	1.31	0.52
	Four	4.18	1.55	0.26	1.19	0.90	1.20	0.72
	Eight	8.28	2.40	0.75	2.72	1.96	1.37	0.54
	Year 2	3.63	0.94	0.51	1.74	1.12	1.78	0.76

Note: See tables 3.2 and 3.9 for explanations.

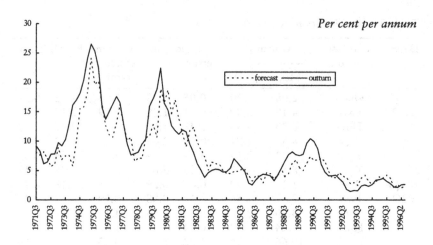

Figure 3.3a *Retail price inflation – four quarters ahead*[a]
Notes: Latest annual outturns. [a]Dates refer to outturns.

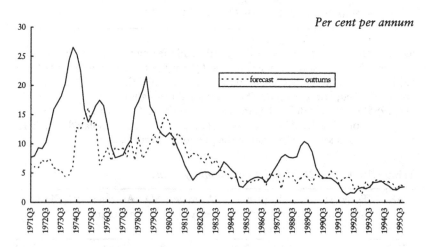

Figure 3.3b *Retail price inflation – year 2*[a] *forecasts*
Notes: Latest annual outturns. [a]The second year refers to the forecast four to
eight years ahead.

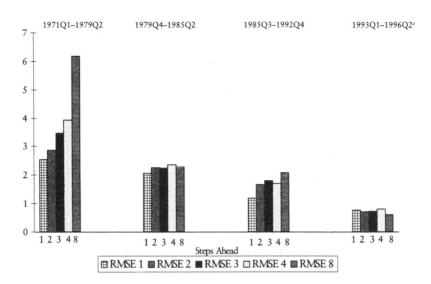

Figure 3.4 *RPI inflation forecasts: root mean squared errors*
[a]The root mean squared error for eight steps ahead is for 1993Q1–1995Q3.

earlier period. From autumn 1992, when inflation targeting started, inflation has been exceptionally low compared with the rest of our sample, and this is clearly reflected in both the low variance of the RPI data and RMSE figures. The one year ahead forecast standard error from 1993Q1 to 1996Q2 was 0.8 per cent, compared with 1.7 per cent from 1985Q3 to 1992Q4. The Theil statistics improved only for the 2 step and year 2 horizons. Unlike the previous twenty years when there was a tendency for the forecasts to under-predict, there is evidence of upward bias in the most recent forecasts. (This is apparent from the negative average errors.)

Forecasts of RPI ex MIPs have been produced since 1988. The summary statistics are shown in table 3.10. There appears to be little difference in forecast accuracy of the RPI and RPI ex MIPs as shown in the Theil statistics. This is not surprising given that the only difference between the two series is mortgage interest payments, which, while volatile, currently have a weight of only 0.042.

Table 3.11 *RPI inflation forecast: test of forecast bias*
Estimate of equation $A_t - {}_{t-i}F_t = a + c_i D_{it} + u_t$

Sample	Forecast horizon	Constant	Event[a] dummies	Seasonal, shift dummies[a]	Normality[c]	Q	$\overline{R}^2$
71Q1–96Q2	Four	0.63 (0.9)	D7	S2,K3 K4	X	*	0.28
	Year 2[b]	2.04 (1.9)		K3 K2,K3,	X	*	0.37
85Q3–96Q2	Four	0.42 (0.6)		K4	Y	*	0.03
	Year 2[b]	0.86 (0.7)	D7		Y	*	0.13
92Q1–96Q2	Four	−0.51 (−1.9)			Y		0.00
	Year 2[b]	−0.36 (−0.9)			Y		−0.24

Notes:
[a]For RPI and RPI ex MIPs the event dummies are for the 1979 VAT rise (D6) and the 1990 community charge (D7). Seasonal and shift dummies as for GDP, see notes to table 3.4 for further explanation.
[b]To 1995 Q2.

5. RPI forecast efficiency

Tables 3.11 and 3.12 give the results of the tests of forecast bias and efficiency. The null of weak efficiency is rejected for the post-1992 period and for the year 2 forecasts throughout. The significant negative constant term in the post-1992 bias equations reflects the large average error at the four-quarter horizon shown in the summary statistics. The estimates imply that the four step forecasts predicted about 80 per cent of the variance in inflation.

We repeated the error revision test with the RPI data with the result shown in table 3.13.

There is only one significant effect with the equation 1 version of the test – shown in the top half of the table. In the lower half of the table, where the difference between the first and second error is the dependent variable, forecast revisions are jointly significant. An interesting feature of these equa-

Table 3.12 *RPI forecast: test of forecast efficiency: B series*
Estimate of equation $A_t = a + b_{t-i} F_t + c_i D_{it} + u_t$

Sample	Forecast horizon	Constant	Forecast	Dummies[a]	X_2^{2b}	Seasonal shift dummies[a]	Normality	Q	$\bar{R}^2$
71Q1– 96Q2	Four	0.95 (1.1)	0.94 (8.1)	D7	1.2	S2,K3 K4	X	*	0.86
	Four	–0.09 (–0.1)	1.10 (11.2)	–	2.1	–	X	*	0.80
	Year 2[c]	4.76 (2.9)	0.37 (1.8)		10.0*	K1,K3 K4	X	*	0.64
	Year 2[c]	2.59 (1.7)	0.95 (5.0)	–	4.2	–	X	*	0.30
85Q3– 96Q2	Four	–2.12 (-1.7)	1.56 (5.7)		4.9		Y	*	0.69
	Year 2[c]	1.96 (1.5)	0.72 (10.1)		16.4*		Y	*	0.24
92Q1– 96Q2	Four	1.23 (2.0)	0.40 (2.4)		18.8*		Y	*	0.14
	Year 2[c]	1.08 (5.2)	0.54 (11.4)		11.1*		Y		0.36

Notes:
[a]For RPI the event dummies are for the 1979 VAT rise (D6) and the 1990 community charge (D7). Seasonal and shift dummies as for GDP, see table 3.4 for further explanations.
[b]Chi-squared test of hypotheses $a = 0$, $b = 1$. ** denotes rejection at the 95 per cent level; * denotes rejection at the 99 per cent level.
[c]To 1995Q2.

tion 2 results is that, in contrast to GDP, there is a preponderance of positive coefficients, suggesting that positive (negative) errors and revisions are associated with positive (negative) revisions at longer horizons. In other words, an adjustment at one horizon is associated with an adjustment in the same direction at other horizons.

Table 3.14 presents the tests of rationality and normality for the RPI based on the forecast error statistics. For the January year ahead forecasts, the longest horizon, the errors are not normally distributed, and this is probably linked to the forecast errors associated with the introduction of the community charge in 1990, further evidence for which is given in the regressions in tables 3.11 and 3.12.

Table 3.13 *RPI inflation: regression tests of revisions to forecasts*

Equation (1) E_{it}	a_0	a_1	a_2	a_3	a_4	χ^2 Test[a]
71Q1–95Q2	–	–	–	–		5.5
71Q1–85Q2	–	–	–	–	–	5.6
85Q3–95Q2	–	–	–	–	–0.17	9.2*
Equation (2) R_{it}	b_0	b_1	b_2	b_3		
71Q1–95Q2	–	–	–	–		7.1
71Q1–85Q2	–	0.56	–	–		6.8
85Q3–95Q2	–	–	–	–		5.8

Notes: Individual coefficients shown only when significant at 95 per cent level or higher.
[a] χ^2 test of joint significance of regressors other than the constant term: *rejection of null at 95 per cent level.

Table 3.14 *RPI forecasts: rationality and normality*

		Rationality[a]	Normality[a]
Year ahead	January	1.37	7.20*
	FSBR	4.11	2.89
	June	0.15	1.57
	October	4.19	0.43
Current Year	January	1.38	0.80
	FSBR	3.01	0.30
	June	2.05	1.04
	October	0.63	0.54

Notes: [a]Chi-squared 2 test. * Significant at 95 per cent level. ** Significant at 90 per cent level.

6. Forecast error bands

Published Treasury forecasts have since 1977 reported average absolute errors for fifteen key variables, including GDP and its main components, the RPI, PSBR and current account. There have also been a number of other Treasury studies giving a more comprehensive range of statistics (HM Treasury, 1994). A drawback of these descriptive statistics is that they do not readily convey the risks and uncertainties surrounding the point forecasts. For this, confidence intervals, perhaps based on the past distribution of errors, are needed.

A number of approaches have recently been suggested in the literature. Blake (1996) uses a stochastic simulation approach with the National Institute model. This involves running the model a large number of times with each replication involving a set of shocks based on the estimated equation residuals and, in the case of exogenous variables, residuals drawn from time series models. Such a model based approach can incorporate explicitly changes in the policy framework, and different expectational assumptions, which procedures based on historical forecast errors are unable to do. This is a potentially important weakness when a new regime such as inflation targeting has been introduced within the period used to calculate the forecast errors. In the Bank of England's *Inflation Report*, error bands for the forecasts of RPI ex MIPs are given which represent probabilistic confidence intervals around a central forecast. These allow for possible skewness and heteroscedasticity in the error distribution, and subjective views of future uncertainty; see Britton *et al.* (1998). The Bank's work may be seen as an approach which represents 'a subjective distribution for its inflation projection based on economic analysis and the judgement of the Monetary Policy Committee'. Yet another way of conveying forecast uncertainty is scenario analysis. This is exemplified by the GDP forecasts given in Appendix A of the 1997 Pre-Budget Report, HM Treasury (1997), where two GDP forecasts are given, based on alternative assumptions about the degree of supply side improvement to be expected.

Using a classical approach, Poulizac *et al.* (1996) have shown how, with information about the distribution and magnitude of past forecast errors, probabilistic confidence intervals around forecasts into the future can be made. The procedure is transparent and, compared with stochastic simulations or scenario analysis, is based on the record of forecast errors, which reflects both the judgements of the forecasters and the underlying model. A possible weakness is that it is difficult to take account of structural or regime changes. The favourable effects of inflation targeting may therefore be given insufficient weight when the procedure is used to give confidence intervals to forecasts currently being made. Over the sample period that we use, the evidence supports the hypothesis that errors were normally distributed, tables 3.4, 3.8, 3.11 and 3.14. GDP and RPI forecasts made from January 1986 to October 1995, a sample of 38 forecasts, were used to calculate the error variances. The results are presented in tables 3.15 and 3.16 respectively.

Table 3.15 *GDP forecast errors*

	Variance of forecast	Correlation forecast and outturn	Variance of error	Correlation forecast and error
Year ahead				
January	0.09	0.41	4.95	0.29
FSBR	0.18	0.45	5.34	−0.11
June	0.15	0.48	4.72	0.34
October	1.14	0.72	3.00	0.34
Current year				
January	1.52	0.91	1.69	0.69
FSBR	2.43	0.80	2.08	0.21
June	3.47	0.94	0.74	0.38
October	4.18	0.97	0.35	0.38

Notes: Forecasts covered were made between January 1986 and October 1995. The year ahead forecast for January 1986 is annual growth from 1986Q3 to 1987Q3; the current year forecast for the same forecast is from 1985Q3 to 1986Q3, where 1985Q3 is the latest outturn available.

GDP confidence intervals

So that probabilities can be assigned to particular forecast horizons, the sample of forecasts is partitioned. So for the eight step ahead forecast we take successive January forecasts, for which the latest outturn is Q3 of year $t–1$, and calculate the forecast annual growth rate between Q3 of the current year t and Q3 of the year $t+1$. The variance of the forecast is then calculated from the ten forecasts for each horizon. The figure of 0.09 in column 1, row 1 in table 3.15, indicates that there has been little variation in the eight step *forecasts*, whereas the variance of actual GDP growth over this horizon – not shown – was 7.1, and the variance of the errors was 4.95. As the forecast horizon falls the forecasts become more accurate. This is reflected in increasing forecast variance, diminishing error variance and a rise in the correlation between forecasts and outturn. The correlations between forecast and errors shown in the final column are insignificantly different from zero, except the January forecast for the current year, implying that the forecasts were efficient.

The error variances shown in this table are used to calculate confidence intervals for each horizon.[9] Figure 3.5 gives the calculated confidence intervals for four step ahead GDP forecasts alongside actual GDP. The interquartile range, within which one could be confident that a GDP forecast would fall with a probability of more than 50 per cent, was ±0.9 per

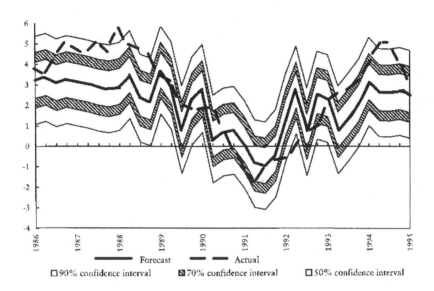

Figure 3.5 *GDP confidence intervals with forecast*

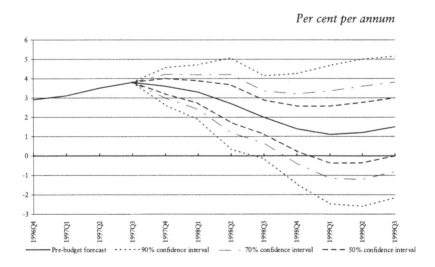

Figure 3.6 *GDP growth confidence intervals for HM Treasury Pre-Budget Forecast*

cent. This implies that with a four step ahead forecast growth rate of 2 per cent, there is a probability of 50 per cent that growth would lie between 1.1 per cent and 2.9 per cent. The corresponding 90 per cent confidence interval is ±2.1 per cent, implying that there is a 90 per cent probability of growth between –0.1 per cent and 4.1 per cent. An important reason for this large error band is that the sample used includes the 1990–91 recession, which was not foreseen clearly (figure 3.1). The average absolute errors, quoted in published Treasury forecasts, correspond approximately to the 70 per cent confidence interval. From figure 3.5 one may infer that the outturn was outside this 90 per cent error band on three occasions – in 1988, 1992 and 1994 – about the frequency expected with a sample of 38 forecasts.

To give a practical example of the procedure, we have taken the GDP forecast published in the Pre-Budget Report (1997) which assumes no supply side improvement and applied confidence intervals derived for steps one to eight.[10] The result is shown in figure 3.6. As the forecast horizon lengthens, the degree of uncertainty in the forecasts increases, although not monotonically. From this figure one can infer, for example, that the probability that GDP growth will be higher than at its peak in 1997 within the forecast period is about 15 per cent. Within the forecast period the probability that GDP growth will fall below zero is, on the basis of these historic errors, about 25 per cent, with zero growth within the interquartile range in 1999.

Confidence intervals for RPI forecasts

Table 3.16 gives the statistics necessary to construct the confidence intervals.

For this sample period the confidence intervals at most horizons are narrower than for the corresponding GDP forecasts. Also, the correlations between forecast and outturns are generally higher than for GDP. However, the unconditional variance of the outturn was higher for the RPI than for GDP; compare tables 3.2 and 3.9, indicating that the RPI series is not inherently easier to forecast because it is less volatile. This suggests that for this sample the RPI may be more forecastable than GDP. Recent forecasts have been well within the 70 per cent band. This may reflect an improvement in forecasters' skill. Alternatively, and perhaps more plausibly, stable and low inflation may be easier to forecast.

The confidence intervals at the four step horizon around past forecasts are shown in figure 3.7. For the pre-Budget forecast we assumed that the published RPI ex MIPs forecast would also hold for the RPI, a not unreasonable assumption for the medium term. Applying the confidence intervals for the RPI to this forecast gives the error bands shown in figure 3.8.

Table 3.16 *RPI forecast errors*

	Variance of forecast	Correlation forecast and outturn	Variance of error	Correlation forecast and error
Year ahead				
January	0.74	0.72	4.52	0.50
FSBR	0.31	0.01	7.36	−0.19
June	1.51	0.73	3.84	0.36
October	1.74	0.87	2.71	0.61
Current year				
January	2.06	0.86	2.60	0.53
FSBR	2.26	0.93	1.87	0.72
June	4.79	0.98	0.45	0.63
October	7.08	0.99	0.08	−0.05

Notes: Forecasts cover the period from January 1986 to October 1995. The year ahead forecast for January 1986 is the annual growth 1986Q4 to 1987Q4; the current year forecast for the same forecast is 1985Q4 on 1986Q4, where 1985Q4 is the latest outturn available.

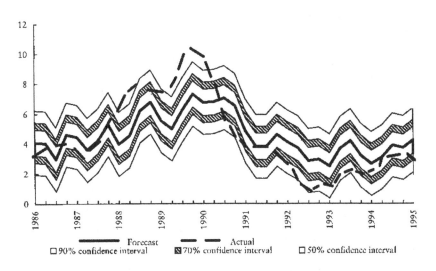

Figure 3.7 *RPI confidence interval with forecast*

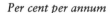

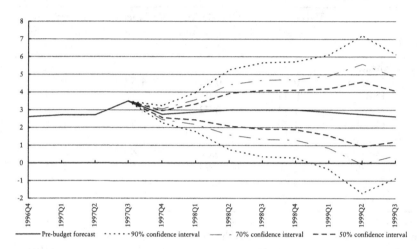

Figure 3.8 *RPI confidence intervals for HM Treasury Pre-Budget Forecast*

7. The relationship between errors in GDP and RPI forecasts

In Melliss (1997), the information set used in the GDP forecast equations
was extended by the addition of past forecast errors. Significant effects were
found at the four or eight step horizons for some samples. The 'revision'
regressions presented in tables 3.7 and 3.13 also suggest that forecasts may
not have made efficient use of all the available information. Another approach is to estimate a VAR model of the errors on the RPI and GDP
forecasts. An unrestricted estimate of a two equation VAR in the two forecast error series provides a test of whether the forecasts use efficiently all
the information in past errors. A possible specification might be:-

$$Dy^{er}_t = k + \sum_{t=i}^{n} \alpha_i Dp^{er}_{t-i} + \sum_{t=i}^{n} \beta_i Dy^{er}_{t-i} + u_t \qquad (3.3a)$$

$$Dp^{er}_t = k + \sum_{t=i}^{n} \gamma_i Dy^{er}_{t-i} + \sum_{t=i}^{n} \delta_i Dp^{er}_{t-i} + v_t \qquad (3.3b)$$

where Dy^{er}, Dp^{er} are the errors in GDP and RPI forecasts respectively.
  For one step errors the structure of the information set available to the
forecaster is clear: at each forecast there is information about the one step
error made in the previous forecast.[11] However for longer horizons some
lagged errors may not be part of the information set available to forecast-

Table 3.17 *Summary of error deletion tests*

Sample	1973Q1–1996Q2		1974Q1–1995Q2	
Horizon	four step		eight step	
Variable deleted	GDP	RPI	GDP	RPI
Dependent variable: GDP errors				
Wald Test[a]	1.0	15.1*	8.4	10.0**
Dependent variable: RPI errors				
Wald Test[a]	0.47	7.8	11.4**	16.4*

Notes: [a]Chi-squared 5; * significant at 95%; ** significant at 90%.

ers. For example, with the four step forecasts there is a four quarter delay before the four step error made in the immediately preceding forecast is known. Both OLS and Seemingly Unrelated Regression estimates (SURE) of equations 3.3(a) and 3.3(b) were made taking account of the timing of known errors.[12] Table 3.17 summarises the results of the variable deletion tests. It is clear that lagged errors which could have been observed contain statistically significant information.

In particular, RPI forecast errors are significant at both horizons in the GDP error equations, while lagged RPI errors are highly significant in the eight step RPI equations. Observable errors in GDP forecasts appeared to have no explanatory power in the equations for GDP errors, corroborating the regression evidence on forecast efficiency. In the equation for the eight step RPI errors, the finding that past errors in GDP growth forecasts had a significant effect at the 90 per cent level is consistent with earlier evidence that pressure of demand effects may not have been adequately captured in inflation forecasts.

8. Inflation surprises

An obvious extension of this work on forecast errors is to use the forecast errors for inflation as proxies for the unanticipated component of inflation. Official forecasts have not been significantly or consistently different from those of other forecasting groups, Britton and Pain (1992), so they therefore provide one possible indicator of the inflationary expectations of forecasters in general.

There is a large literature on the issue of whether inflation surprises have effects on the real economy. There are three main strands. The first concentrates on the role of misperceptions about relative prices, and is due to

Lucas (1973). The second is the result seen in some 'growth regressions' where high and variable inflation leads to generally poor economic performance, via a mechanism which is not precisely specified although high inflation is generally associated with high inflation uncertainty, Barro (1995). A third view is that the main transmission mechanism is an aggregate price effect working through real interest rates. In the Lucas 'islands' story, agents supplying output misidentify a part of any positive aggregate price surprise as a reduction in the relative price of their own output and therefore reduce supply. In the third hypothesis, the main effect is monetary. An unexpected increase in inflation reduces real interest rates *ex post*, so that a positive output effect response may be expected. However, if the monetary authorities react, or if higher inflation persists and agents revise their expectations upwards, then any real effects may be short-lived, Barro (1978). These stories generally assume that the fully anticipated component of inflation has no real effects.

A number of empirical approaches have been applied to the problem. For a recent survey of the literature see Hasiag (1997), and for an earlier example with a time series model, Jansen (1989). We have tested the general hypothesis in an autoregressive model of output growth augmented with RPI inflation and RPI inflation forecast errors:-

$$Dy_t = \phi Dy_{t-1} + \eta Dp_{t-1}^{er} + \rho Dp_{t-1} + u_t \qquad (3.4)$$

where Dp^{er} is the forecast error and Dp the actual rate of inflation. Wald tests for the exclusion of the forecast errors and actual inflation were conducted to test for the real effects of inflation surprises. This can be seen as being in the spirit of the of the Barro growth regressions, although by omitting such factors as the capital stock, both human and physical, it is clearly mis-specified. Also, estimates may suffer from simultaneity bias.

Equation (3.4) was estimated with one step, four step and year two RPI forecast errors and actuals. For example, with the equation for the four quarter growth in GDP, the lagged dependent variable, four quarter inflation and inflation errors, both lagged by one period, are used as regressors. Thus the inflation errors have not been entered in such a way as to reflect when the errors data becomes available. We justify this by assuming that forecast errors reflect general inflation uncertainty in this context, rather than information of potential value to forecasters. Because of the overlapping nature of successive forecasts, the equations were estimated with the Newey-West covariance correction.

The equation estimates are summarised in table 3.18, where the coefficients on the RPI and RPI error terms are shown, together with the Wald tests for exclusion.

Table 3.18 *Summary of inflation surprise equations*

1971Q2–1996Q2	Inflation	Inflation error
1[a]	–0.16 (6.1*)	0.22 (0.9)
4	–0.07 (2.2)	0.00 (0.0)
Year 2[b]	–0.02 (0.1)	–0.08 (2.8)
8[b]	0.00 (0.0)	–0.07 (16.5*)
1979Q1–1996Q2		
1[a]	–0.17 (5.3**)	0.06 (0.1)
4	–0.12 (6.8*)	0.00 (0.0)
Year 2[b]	–0.14 (13.1*)	–0.08 (2.0)
8[b]	–0.05 (22.8*)	–0.08 (10.2*)
1985Q2–1996Q2		
1[a]	–0.03 (0.1)	0.09 (0.1)
4	–0.18 (4.8**)	–0.01 (0.0)
Year 2[b]	–0.48 (32.0*)	0.26 (21.3*)
8[b]	–0.23 (21.6*)	0.09 (7.1*)

Notes: Figures in brackets are Wald test statistics, chi -square (1).
[a]OLS estimate
[b]Estimated to 1995Q2
* significant at 99% level; ** significant at 95% level.

In all the estimates there is a highly significant lagged dependent variable, with a coefficient typically between 0.8 and 0.9. This implies that the long-run effects of inflation on growth are larger than the short-run.[13]

For the full sample, the Wald test for the restriction that the coefficients on either inflation or the forecast error is significant in two cases, the one step, inflation, and eight step, inflation error, both with the expected negative sign. For the 1979Q1–1996Q2 and 1985Q2–1996Q2 sub-periods, inflation has a negative effect, and the Wald test is significant in seven of the eight regressions. For the inflation error terms, results are mixed. Only with the eight step estimate over the 1979Q1–1995Q2 period is there a negative and significant effect as suggested by theory.

These results suggest that any relationship between GDP growth and inflation or inflation errors as measured by Treasury forecasts in the last 25 years has not been stable. Comparing the estimates over the full sample with those on the 1979Q1–1996Q2 period suggests that any relationship was insignificant or unstable in the 1971Q1–1979Q1 period, or that it changed around 1979. Separate estimates, not reported, for the period 1971Q1–1979Q1 gave coefficients on the inflation and inflation error terms which were significant in only one out of eight cases. This suggests either that there was no underlying relationship, or that the presence of special factors, see the list of dummy variables in table 3.3, has made it difficult to identify.

9. Conclusions

There is no easy answer to the question of how the Treasury's GDP and RPI forecasts have changed over the last 25 years. The greater volatility of the data, especially of the RPI, in the 1970s, and the various criteria of forecast performance, which can and do give results which are not fully consistent, make it difficult to compare forecasts across different time periods. Moreover, the preferences of the forecast user also contribute to this ambiguity. For example, is a forecast which correctly warns of falling output especially useful even though it has a standard error no smaller than average?

With a steady upward trend in GDP and subdued but steady inflation, the data over the last three years appear to have been comparatively easy to forecast. In this period, GDP errors were smaller with the first available rather than the latest outturn data, a feature which was not apparent previously. However the forecasts on both sets of data appear to be unbiased but not efficient.

For the whole sample from 1971–96 the four step forecasts explain about half, and the eight step about 30 per cent, of the variance in GDP. As a generalisation GDP forecasts made in the 1970s suffered from the noisy data, and there was a marked improvement, on most measures, in the first half of the 1980s. But this was not sustained into the second half of the decade and early 1990s largely due to a failure to predict the extent of the boom and subsequent recession.

Evaluating how RPI forecasts have changed is complicated by the changes in inflation volatility within the sample, the most recent data showing the lowest volatility. This has been reflected in the RMSE statistics which have also tended to be on a declining trend. However, the Theil statistics have shown no discernible trend.

We have investigated a number of alternative ways of testing for forecast efficiency, all of which have been applied elsewhere in the literature. The tests do not give fully consistent results, although the caveat has to be made that the samples used in each case did not match precisely and previous work had shown that test results are known to be sample sensitive. In the standard regression framework, for GDP the null of unbiasedness could not be rejected, although the forecasts were found to be inefficient in recent years. For the RPI, the year 2 forecasts were both biased and inefficient for the full sample. Our application of a forecast revision method which pools fixed and rolling event data showed that there was some structure in the pattern of revisions to both GDP, prior to 1979, and RPI forecasts. On this basis the forecasts are not efficient since the revisions follow an identifiable pattern. However the method suggested by Poulizac *et al.*, which we applied to Treasury forecasts of GDP and the RPI from 1982–96, suggested that the forecasts were generally rational. This is not surprising, since their method is very similar to the standard regression tests.

The calculation of forecast error bands revealed wide intervals at conventional probability levels; the 90 per cent interval for a four step ahead forecast of GDP is ±2.1 percentage points, and ±1 percentage point for the RPI. The outturns fell outside the 95 per cent bands on about four occasions in the sample, as expected. Estimates of forecast confidence intervals clearly give additional information on forecast uncertainty over and above that given by average absolute errors, provided that the underlying distribution is known and stable.

In the penultimate section of the chapter we asked whether forecast accuracy might have been improved by incorporating observable information on past errors. Taking care to consider only those errors which could actually have been observed, we found evidence that errors in inflation forecasts especially had significant effects both on RPI errors, and also, at long horizons, GDP errors. This last might be explained by policy reaction, with positive inflation surprises leading to a tighter policy stance. The role of GDP errors in inflation forecasts is more easily explained as a pressure of demand effect.

An obvious extension of this is to ask whether the errors in forecasts of inflation, which may be considered a proxy for inflation uncertainty, are linked to GDP growth, as theory and empirical work have suggested. Using a simple framework relating output growth to both inflation and inflation forecast errors, evidence was found for a significant negative relationship with inflation, but not with the errors on inflation forecasts. This may be indicative of the underlying relationship, or that the errors in Treasury inflation forecasts are a poor proxy for the unanticipated component.

Notes

1 HM Treasury. The views expressed, errors and omissions are the sole responsibility of the authors. They are grateful for comments on an earlier version of this chapter from Charlie Bean, Andrew Britton, Michael Clements, Andrew Gurney, Chris Kelly, David Maude, and participants at the ESRC conference on Macroeconomic Modelling and Economic Policy organised by NIESR, especially the discussant, Nigel Pain. The chapter is © Crown Copyright 1999, published by permission of Her Majesty's Stationery Office.

2 The year 2 forecast is defined as the annual rate of growth between 4 and 8 steps ahead.

3 This estimate uses actual and forecast values of the Consumers' Expenditure Deflator from 1985Q3 to 1988 Q3, before forecasts of the RPI ex MIPs were made.

4 The Theil statistics for GDP are here based on a constant growth rate of 2.25 per cent a year. This was the trend growth rate approved by the NAO as a reasonable assumption, in its recent assessment of Treasury assumptions, having regard to past experience.

5 A necessary condition for the forecast to be weakly rational is: $E(A_t - _{t-i}F_t|I_t)=0$ which implies a test $A_t - _{t-i}F_t=A+u_t$ with the null H_0: $a=0$. As Holden and Peel (1990) show, this is both a necessary and sufficient condition for weak rationality and is referred to as the test for unbiasedness here. Rejection of this null implies that the forecasts are both biased and inefficient. We also test for (weak) efficiency by implementing $A_t=a+b_{t-i}F_t+u_t$ with the null H_0: $a=0$; $b=1$, which is the sufficient, but not necessary, test of weak rationality.

6 The t statistics and Wald tests reported in regressions in this chapter are based on estimates of the variance covariance matrix corrected for third and seventh order moving average error process using Newey-West adjustment with equal weights.

7 If the series being forecast follow, for example, a first order autoregressive component, it can be shown that the forecast errors followed a first order process, but that successive revisions are independent. So the same test procedure can be applied.

8 The equations were estimated using GLS to correct for possible heteroscedasticity, see Clements (1997).

9 The x per cent confidence interval for horizon $T = \sqrt{\text{var}_T} . Z_x$ where var_T is the forecast variance for horizon T, and Z_x is the value of the normal density function within which the forecast will fall x per cent of the time.

10 We interpolated the published half yearly forecasts to obtain a quarterly profile.

11 This is an approximation if the forecasts are spread unevenly through the year. Also, the one step ahead forecasts of GDP may be made with the actual change in the RPI available.

12 The decision to use SURE estimates as well as OLS was indicated by the structure of equations 3.3a and 3.3b which is such that the system variance–

covariance matrix has possibly significant non-diagonal elements. The log-likelihood statistic tests suggested that for both the four and eight step systems the hypothesis that the error covariance matrix is diagonal could not be rejected. Nevertheless, the Wald tests in table 3.17 use the SURE estimates.

13 For example the long-run effect of inflation in the four step equation for the 1979Q1–1996Q2 period is –0.65, the coefficient on the lagged dependent variable being 0.82.

References

Barro, R.J. (1978), 'Unanticipated money, output, and the price level in the United States', *Journal of Political Economy*, 86, pp. 549–80.

(1995), 'Inflation and economic growth', National Bureau of Economic Research Working Paper 5326.

Blake, A.P. (1996), 'Forecast error bounds by stochastic simulation', *National Institute Economic Review*, 156, pp. 72–9.

Britton, A. and Pain, N. (1992), *Economic Forecasting in Britain*, National Institute Report no. 4.

Britton, E., Fisher P. and Whitley, J. (1998), 'The *Inflation Report* projections: understanding the fan chart', *Bank of England Quarterly Bulletin*, February, pp. 30–37.

Clements, M.P. (1995), 'Rationality and the role of judgement in macroeconomic forecasting', *Economic Journal*, 105, pp. 510–20.

(1997), 'Evaluating the rationality of fixed-event forecasts', *Journal of Forecasting*, 16, pp. 225–39.

Hasiag, J. (1997), 'Output, growth, welfare and inflation: a survey', *Federal Reserve Bank of Dallas Economic Review*, second quarter.

Hendry, D.F. (1997), 'The econometrics of macroeconomic forecasting', *Economic Journal*, 107, pp. 1330–57.

HM Treasury (1994), *Memorandum on Official Economic Forecasting*, House of Commons Paper 532(i), session 1990–91. Reprinted as GES Working Paper no. 121.

(1997), *The Economy and Public Finances: Supplementary Material*, Pre-Budget Report Publications, November.

Holden, K. and Peel, D.A. (1985), 'An evaluation of quarterly National Institute forecasts', *Journal of Forecasting*, 4, pp. 227–34.

(1990), 'On testing for unbiasedness and efficiency of forecasts', *The Manchester School*, 58, 2, pp. 120–27.

Jansen, D.W. (1989), 'Does inflation uncertainty affect output growth? Further evidence', *The Federal Reserve Bank of St Louis Review*, July/August 1989.

Lucas, R.E. (1973), 'Some international evidence on output–inflation trade-offs', *American Economic Review*, 68, pp. 326–34.

Melliss, C. (1997), 'The Treasury forecasting record: an evaluation', ESRC Macroeconomic Modelling Bureau Discussion Paper no. 47, August.

Office for National Statistics (ONS) (1997), 'Quarterly alignment adjustments in the UK National Accounts', *Economic Trends*, November.

Pain, N. (1994), 'Cointegration and forecast evaluation: some lessons from National Institute forecasts', *Journal of Forecasting*, 13, pp. 481–94.

Poulizac, D., Weale, M. and Young, G. (1996), 'The performance of National Institute economic forecasts', *National Institute Economic Review*, 156, pp. 55–62.

Theil H. (1966), *Applied Economic Forecasting*, Amsterdam, North-Holland Publishing.

4 General equilibrium modelling of UK tax policy

KESHAB BHATTARAI and JOHN WHALLEY

1. Introduction

This chapter summarises activity thus far in the general equilibrium tax modelling area undertaken at Warwick University as part of a wider project on 'General Equilibrium Analysis of UK Policy Issues' supported by the ESRC Macromodelling Consortium. Some of this work has been undertaken jointly with the Research Division of the Inland Revenue, to whom we are indebted for collaborative support on the data front.

We set out the basic approach, summarise a standard general equilibrium tax model for the UK providing some initial results, and indicate some extensions to the approach which have been undertaken in stand alone research papers.[1]

2. General equilibrium tax models[2]

Broad approach

In a traditional general equilibrium model of either the tax or non-tax variety, a number of consumers are identified, each with an initial endowment of commodities and preferences. Under optimisation, the latter yield household demand functions for each commodity, with market demands given by the sum of the individual consumer's demands. Market demands depend on all prices, are continuous, non-negative, homogeneous of degree zero (that is, there is no money illusion), and satisfy Walras' law (that is, that at any set of prices the total value of consumer expenditures equals consumer incomes). The production side of such models incorporates technology described by either constant-returns-to-scale activities or non-increasing returns-to-scale production functions, and has producers maximise profits.

An equilibrium is characterised by a set of relative prices and levels of production by each industry such that market demand equals supply for all commodities (including disposals if any commodity is a free good). Since producers are assumed to maximise profits, this implies that in the constant-returns-to-scale case no one does any better than break even at the equilibrium prices. The zero homogeneity of demand functions and linear homogeneity of profits in prices (that is, doubling all prices doubles money profits) implies that only relative prices are of any significance in this model; the absolute price level has no impact on the equilibrium outcome.

Taxes typically appear in these models in *ad valorem* form (see Shoven and Whalley, 1973; Shoven, 1974), either as producer taxes on inputs or consumer taxes on incomes or expenditures, revenues either being redistributed to consumers or used to finance publicly provided goods and services. The taxes that characterise modern tax systems (personal, corporate, sales, excise, property, social security, resource, and other taxes) are usually represented in model-equivalent *ad valorem* form. The equilibrium behaviour of the model can be investigated as taxes change and, on that basis, policy evaluations made.

A numerical example

A numerical example is a good way to illustrate this approach; although, in representing actual economies, much more specificity is required than the general form of the model usually admits. Particular functional forms for production and demand functions need to be chosen and parameter values selected. The tax policy instruments to be analysed need to be incorporated, and the treatment (or model closure) of the various items such as foreign trade, savings, and public goods all need to be settled.

A simple numerical example of a tax-policy-oriented general equilibrium model is presented by Shoven and Whalley (1984). In this example, there are two final goods (manufacturing and non-manufacturing), two factors of production (capital and labour), and two classes of consumers (a 'rich' consumer group that owns all the capital and a 'poor' group that owns all the labour). There are no consumer demands for factors (that is, there is no labour–leisure choice). Each consumer group generates demands by maximising a constant elasticity of substitution (CES) utility function subject to its budget constraint. CES production functions are assumed.

The CES utility functions are

Table 4.1 *Production and demand parameters and endowments used by Shoven and Whalley (1984) for their two-sector general equilibrium numerical example*

	ϕ_i	δ_i	σ_i
Production parameters			
Manufacturing	1.5	0.6	2.0
Non-manufacturing	2.0	0.7	0.5
Demand parameters			
Rich consumers	Poor consumers		

a^1_1,	a^1_2,	σ_1,	α^2_1,	α^2_2	σ_2
0.5	0.5	1.5	0.3	0.7	0.75
Endowments					

	K	L
Rich households	25	0
Poor households	0	60

$$U^c = \left[\sum_{i=1}^{2} \left(a_i^c \right)^{1/\sigma_c} \left(X_i^c \right)^{\left(\sigma_c - 1 \right)/\sigma_c} \right]^{\sigma_c/(\sigma_c - 1)} \tag{4.1}$$

where X^c_i is the quantity of good i demanded by the cth consumer, a_i^c are share parameters, and σ_c is the substitution elasticity in consumer c's CES utility function. The consumer's budget constraint is $P_1 X_1^c + P_2 X_2^c \leq P_L W_L^c + P_K^c W_K^c = I^c$, where P_1 and P_2 are the consumer prices for the two goods, W^c_L and W^c_K are consumer c's endowment of labour and capital, and I^c is the income of consumer c.

Maximising this utility function subject to the budget constraint yields the commodity demands

$$X_i^c = \frac{a_i^c I^c}{P_i^{\sigma_c} \left(a_i^c P_1^{(1-\sigma_c)} + a_2^c P_2^{(1-\sigma_c)} \right)} \qquad i = 1, 2; \, c = 1, 2 \tag{4.2}$$

The production functions are

$$Q_i = \phi_i \left[\delta_i L_i^{(\sigma_i - 1)/\sigma_i} + (1 - \delta_i) K_i^{(\sigma_i - 1)/\sigma_i} \right]^{\sigma_i/(\sigma_i - 1)} \qquad i = 1, 2 \tag{4.3}$$

where Q_i denotes output of the ith industry, ϕ_i is a scale or unit parameter, δ_i is a distribution parameter, K_i and L_i are capital and labour factor inputs, and σ_i is the elasticity of factor substitution in industry i.

This example has six production function parameters (that is, ϕ_i, δ_i, and σ_i for $i = 1, 2$), six utility function parameters (that is, a_1^1, a_2^1, a_1^2, a_2^2, σ_1 and σ_2, and four exogenous variables (the endowment of labour (W_L) and capital (W_K) for each of the two consumers).

An equilibrium for the model is given by the four prices P_1, P_2, P_L, and P_K and eight quantities x_1^1, x_1^2, x_2^1, x_2^2, and K_1, K_2, L_1, and L_2, which meet the equilibrium conditions that market demand equals market supply for all inputs and outputs and that zero profits apply in each industry. Once the parameters are specified and the factor endowments are known, a complete general equilibrium model is available. Tax and other policy variables can then be added as desired.

Table 4.1 presents the values for the parameters and the exogenous variables used by Shoven and Whalley in their example. The equilibrium solution is reported in table 4.2 for a case where a 50 per cent input tax applies to the use of capital in manufacturing. Only relative prices are relevant in this model and, somewhat arbitrarily, labour is chosen as the numeraire. At the equilibrium prices, total demand for each output equals production, and producer revenues equal costs. Labour and capital endowments are fully employed, and consumer incomes from sale of factors plus transfers equal consumer expenditures. Because of the assumption of constant returns to scale, the per-unit costs in each industry equal producer selling prices, meaning that economic profits are zero. Expenditures by each household exhaust its income. Shoven and Whalley illustrate how this general equilibrium model can be adapted for policy evaluation work by comparing the with-tax equilibrium solution reported in table 4.2 to the no-tax equilibrium solution to obtain measures of the welfare costs of such a tax.

Empirical implementation and model structure

The differences between the model actually used to analyse tax policy proposals and the numerical example above lie in their dimensionality (that is, the number of sectors and consumer types modelled), their parameter specification procedures and use of data, and their inclusion of more complex policy regimes than a simple tax on one factor in one sector.

Although the appropriate general equilibrium model for any particular policy analysis varies with the issue, most tax models are variants of static, two-factor models, that have long been employed in public finance and international trade. Most involve more than two goods even though fac-

Table 4.2 *Equilibrium solution for Shoven and Whalley's example with a 50 per cent input tax on capital in manufacturing*

Equilibrium prices

Manufacturing output	1.47
Non-manufacturing output	1.01
Capital	1.13
Labour	1.00

Production side: Outputs

	Quantity	Revenue
Manufacturing	22.39	32.83
Non-manufacturing	57.31	57.64

Inputs	Capital	Capital cost (incl. tax)	Labour	Labour cost	Total cost	Cost per unit output
Manufacturing	4.04	6.83	1.00	26.00	32.83	1.47
Non-manufacturing	20.96	23.64	34.00	34.00	57.60	1.00

Demand side

	Manufacturing	Non-manufacturing	Expenditure
Rich households	8.94	15.83	29.10
Poor households	13.40	41.48	61.37

	Labour income	Capital income	Transfers	Total income
Rich households	0	28.19	0.91	29.10
Poor households	60.00	0	1.37	61.37

tors of production are classified into two broad categories of capital and labour services. In some models these are further disaggregated into subgroups (for instance, labour may be identified as skilled or unskilled). Intermediate transactions are usually incorporated either through fixed or flexible input–output coefficients.

The rationale for proceeding this way is that tax and policy issues are frequently analysed using a general equilibrium theoretical framework, and it is natural to retain the same basic structure in applied work. This is especially the case if the major contribution of the numerical work is to advance from qualitative to quantitative analysis. Also, most data on which the numerical specifications of tax models are based come in a form consistent with the two-sector approach. National accounts data, for instance, identify wages and salaries and operating surplus as major cost components. Input–output data provide intermediate transaction data, with value added broken down in a similar way. This all suggests a model in which capital and labour are identified as the principal factor inputs.

The partition between goods and factors in two-sector models is used in tax models to simplify computation. By using factor prices to generate cost-covering goods prices, consumer demands can be calculated and the derived demands for factors that meet consumer demands evaluated. Thus, even a model with a large number of goods can be solved by working only with the implicit system of excess factor demands.

There are a range of more specific model design issues that are also encountered with tax models, including the treatment of investment, foreign trade, and government expenditures. Where there are no international capital flows, the level of investment in the model reflects household saving decisions (broadly defined to include corporate retentions). These are based on constant-savings propensities in static models and on explicit intertemporal utility maximisation in dynamic models. Government expenditures usually reflect transfers and real expenditures, with the latter frequently determined from assumed utility-maximising behaviour for the government. In this approach, the government is treated as a separate consumption-side agent that buys public goods and services. In a few cases (such as Piggott and Whalley 1985), tax models have been used with public goods explicitly appearing in household utility functions, although this complicates the basic approach.

As regards the treatment of time, some of the static equilibrium tax models have been sequenced through time to reflect changes in the economy's capital stock due to net saving. Models such as those due to Summers (1981), Auerbach, Kotlikoff, and Skinner (1983), and Fullerton, Shoven, and Whalley (1983) have been used to analyse intertemporal issues in tax policy, such as whether a move from an income tax to a consumption tax (under which saving is less heavily taxed) is desirable. This approach links a series of single-period equilibria through saving decisions that change the capital stock of the economy. Saving, in turn, is based on maximisation of a utility function defined over current and expected future consumption. Myopic expectations (that is, expected future rates of return on assets are assumed equal to current rates of return) are often used to simplify computation. Saving in the period augments the capital stock in all future periods. The general equilibrium computed for each period has all markets clearing, including that for newly produced capital goods. The economy passes through a sequence of single-period equilibria in which the capital stock grows. Tax changes that encourage higher savings typically cause lowered consumption in initial years and eventually higher consumption due to the larger capital stock.

Functional forms

When building a tax model to represent an actual economy, in addition to selecting the model structure one also has to choose particular functional forms. Typically the major constraint on the choice of demand and production functions is that they be consistent with the theory and are analytically tractable. This involves choosing functions that satisfy the usual demand- and production-side restrictions assumed in general equilibrium models, such as Walras' law. It also requires that excess-demand responses be easy to evaluate for any price vector considered as a candidate equilibrium solution for the model.

The choice of a specific functional form by any given modeller usually depends on how elasticities are to be used in the model. The general approach is one of selecting a functional form that best allows key parameter values (for example, income and price elasticities) to be incorporated while retaining tractability. This largely explains why the functional forms used in general equilibrium tax models are so often drawn from the family of 'convenient' forms (Cobb-Douglas, CES, linear expenditure system (LES), and translog, generalised Leontief, or other flexible functional forms).

Demands from Cobb-Douglas utility functions are easy to work with but have unitary income and uncompensated own-price elasticities and zero cross-price elasticities; restrictions are typically implausible. If all expenditure shares for CES functions are small, compensated own-price elasticities equal the elasticity of substitution in preferences. It may thus be unacceptable to model all commodities as having essentially the same compensated own-price elasticities. One alternative is to use hierarchical or nested CES functions, although here the issues that arise are the global properties of these more flexible functional forms, such as concavity. Unitary income elasticities implied by Cobb-Douglas or CES functions can be relaxed by using LES functions with a displaced origin, but the origin displacements need to be specified.

On the production side, where only two primary factors enter the model, CES value-added functions are usually assumed. If more than two factors are used, hierarchical CES functions or translog cost functions are again used. Intermediate requirements functions may be modelled as fixed coefficients, or intermediate substitutability may be introduced.

Choice of parameter values

Parameter values for the functions used in tax models are crucial in determining the results of simulations for various tax policies. The procedure
most commonly used in these models has come to be labelled 'calibration'
(Mansur and Whalley, 1984). Under this approach, the economy under consideration is assumed to be in equilibrium in the presence of existing tax
policies, that is, at a so-called benchmark equilibrium. Parameters for the
model are then calculated such that the model can reproduce the equilibrium data as a model solution.

A feature of this calibration procedure that has both attracted interest
and raised concerns is that there is no statistical test of the resulting model
specification implied by calibration. The procedure for calibrating parameter values from a constructed equilibrium observation is deterministic. This
typically involves the key assumption that the benchmark data represent
an equilibrium for the economy under investigation, and required parameter values are then calculated using the model equilibrium conditions. If
the equilibrium conditions are not sufficient to identify the model, additional parameter values (typically elasticities) are exogenously specified until
the model is identified. These are usually based on a literature search or,
less frequently, on separate estimation. In contrast to econometric work that
often simplifies the structure of the economic portion of models to allow
for substantial richness in statistical specification, the procedure in these
models is the opposite. The richness of the economic structure only allows
for a crude statistical model that, in the case of calibration to a single year's
data, becomes deterministic.

If the widespread use of deterministic calibration in these models is trou-
bling, it is perhaps worthwhile outlining some of the reasons why this
calibration approach is so widely used. First, in some of the tax models,
several thousand parameters may be involved, and to simultaneously estimate all of the model parameters using time series methods requires either
unrealistically large numbers of observations or overly severe identifying
restrictions. Partitioning models into submodels (such as a demand and
production system) may reduce or overcome this problem, but partitioning does not fully incorporate the equilibrium restrictions that are
emphasised in calibration. Also, benchmark data sets are usually constructed in value terms, and their separation into price and quantity
observations with consistent units through time as would be required for
time series estimation. Finally, the dimensions used in these models make
the construction of benchmark equilibrium data sets a non-trivial exercise.
Some of the large-scale data sets have required upwards of eighteen months

work, so that if time series are to be constructed, the required workload may not be sustainable.

Calibration usually involves one year's data, or a single observation represented by an average over a number of years, and it is only in the Cobb-Douglas case that the benchmark data uniquely identify a set of parameter values. In other cases, the required values for the relevant elasticities needed to identify other parameters in the model are usually based on other sources. Typically, heavy reliance is placed on literature surveys of elasticities, and as other modellers have also observed, the literature on elasticity values is sparse (and sometimes contradictory). Also although this procedure might sound straightforward, it can be difficult because of differences among studies in estimates.

Elasticity values in these models specify the curvature of isoquants and indifference surfaces, with their position given by the benchmark equilibrium data. Because the curvature of CES indifference curves and isoquants cannot be inferred from the benchmark data, extraneous values of substitution elasticities are required. Similarly, for LES demand functions, income elasticities are needed upon which to base the origin coordinates for utility measurement.

In practice, data representing benchmark equilibria for use in calibration are constructed from national accounts and other government data sources. In these data, available information does not satisfy micro-consistency conditions (for example, payments to labour from firms will not equal labour income received by households), and a number of adjustments are needed to ensure that the equilibrium conditions of the models hold. In these, some data are taken as correct and others adjusted to reflect consistency. Tax-related data sets of this type are described in St-Hilaire and Whalley (1983), Piggott and Whalley (1985), and Ballard *et al.* (1985).

Because these benchmark data are usually produced in value terms, in using the data in a general equilibrium model units must be chosen for goods and factors so that separate price and quantity observations are obtained. A commonly used convention, originally adopted by Harberger (1962), is to assume units for both goods and factors such that they have a price of unity in the benchmark equilibrium.

Solving general equilibrium models

The early general equilibrium tax models typically used Scarf's algorithm for their solution (see Scarf, 1967; Scarf and Hansen, 1973). More recent models rely on optimisation software such as GAMS (the Generalised Algebraic Modelling System). In this latter approach, all equilibrium conditions are written as constraints for an optimisation problem with an arbitrary (or convenient) objective function. Any solution to the optimisation problem which lies in the contstraint set is, by construction, an equilibrium.

A GAMS model in this format essentially is a set of statements in GAMS syntax (Brook, Kendrick and Meeraus, 1992) which declare sets, data, parameters, variables, equations, and assigns model relationships in a natural way legible to any model user. A specific GAMS formulation, MPSGE, has also become popular for generating a specific set of large scale standard Arrow-Debreu applied general equilibrium models (Rutherford, 1997). This declares the full model equations in symbolic form. After models are generated, either in GAMS or MPSGE format, a one line command instructs solvers to solve the declared models. It is possible to declare a number of models consisting of different equations in the same file, and include statements to solve these models sequentially with loops over time or counterfactual experiments. The class of these models can reflect linear, non-linear, mixed complementarity, integer or discrete programming problems. Optimisation solvers (MINOS5 and CONOPT) are the most popular for solving non-linear and linear programming problems in GAMS, while PATH is a more powerful solver for mixed complementarity problems (Dirkse and Ferris, 1995). At the end of the GAMS program file, a series of reporting statements are included to handle the report. In recent versions of GAMS a user has more control over the output generated from the model; the results of desired variables can be displayed, put in tabular spreadsheet format, or plotted directly at the end of the model execution.

Evaluating impacts of policy changes

Theoretical literature on welfare economics is usually followed in making comparisons between equilibria in order to arrive at policy evaluation based on these tax models. For welfare impacts, Hicksian compensating (CV) and equivalent variations (EV) are commonly used as summary measures of welfare impact by agent. Economywide welfare measures are often computed by aggregating CVs or EVs over consumer groups. Although this is consistent with practice in the cost–benefit literature, the theoretical short-comings in using the sum of CVs or EVs as an aggregate welfare criterion are well known.

Models also provide a detailed evaluation of who gains, who loses, and by how much as a result of a policy change. No single summary measure need be chosen if the policy analyst is interested only in the detailed impacts of any policy change. In some tax models, new (policy change) equilibria are computed under the restriction that government revenues remain constant. In these models, this usually implies replacing one set of taxes with another, but with new tax rates endogenously determined to preserve revenues. In other models government revenues change, but where this occurs the welfare impact from changes in the amount of public service needs to be factored into any economywide welfare measure.

In addition to welfare impacts, other impacts of tax changes can be investigated, such as income distribution effects using Lorenz curves or Gini coefficients. Alternative income concepts (for example, gross of tax or net of tax) can also be used in such calculations. Changes in relative prices can be evaluated, as can changes in the use of factors of production across industries or changes in the product composition of consumer demands.

Uniqueness of equilibrium

One final point to keep in mind is that the applied general equilibrium approach to tax policy may not be particularly instructive if the equilibrium solution in any model is not unique for any particular tax policy. Uniqueness, or lack of it, has been a long-standing interest of general equilibrium theorists (see Kehoe (1980)). There is, however, no theoretical argument that guarantees uniqueness in the tax models currently in use. With some of the models, researchers have conducted *ad hoc* numerical experimentation (approaching equilibria from different directions and at different speeds) but have yet to find a case of nonuniqueness. In the case of the US tax model due to Ballard, Fullerton, Shoven, and Whalley (1985), uniqueness has been numerically demonstrated by Kehoe and Whalley (1985). The current working hypothesis adopted by most tax modellers seems to be that uniqueness can be presumed in the models discussed here until a clear case of nonuniqueness is found.

3. A UK tax model

We next discuss a simple version of a UK tax model built under project support. This is a single household model with a variety of tax instruments (sales, income and VAT taxes) similar to that considered earlier by Piggott and Whalley (1985), with a labour–leisure choice component to the model. For this model, we briefly discuss the specification of preferences and technology and then describe the construction of micro-consistent data sets required for model calibration We discuss the methods used for calibration and choice of the elasticity parameters in preferences and production functions. Since the models replicate a base year economy in the presence of taxes, we can solve for a counterfactual equilibrium without taxes in order to evaluate the welfare costs of tax distortions.

The data for this model draw on input–output tables for the UK economy (ONS, 1995).[3] We discuss a model for the one household case, with the same sectoral disaggregation as available in the 1990 UK input–woutput table (ONS, 1995). Model parameters are inferred from a fully micro-consistent UK data set for 1990, constructed using these data, and supplemented by literature based estimates of behavioural elasticities. The flexibility of the modelling format allows parameters to be calibrated to later years as and when relevant information becomes available.

Demands

The household maximises a CES utility function defined over commodities and leisure, subject to a budget constraint. This utility function can be written as

$$U_h = \left(\sum_i \alpha_{i,h} C_{i,h}^{\rho_h} + \beta_h L_h^{\rho_h} \right)^{\frac{1}{\rho_h}}$$
(4.4)

where U_h is the utility of household h, $C_{i,h}$ is the consumption of good i by household h, L_h is the leisure taken by household h, $\alpha_{i,h}$ is the share of income of household h spent on consumption of good i, β_h is the share of full income spent on leisure, and ρ_h is the elasticity parameter in the utility function, the elasticity of substitution between goods (and leisure) being equal to $\sigma = \frac{1}{1-\rho_h}$ (Varian, 1992). In versions of the model in which leisure does not appear $\beta_h = 0$.

Households receive income from capital and labour endowments, and transfers from the government. They pay taxes on household and capital income. The disposable income of a households is given by

$$I_h = r(1 - t_k)\overline{K}_h + (1 - t_l^h)w\overline{L}_h + TR_h$$
(4.5)

where I_h is the full income of the households, $\overline{K}_h$ is the endowment of capital, $\overline{L}_h$ is the endowment of labour, TR_h are the transfers received by the household h, r is the rental rate of capital, w is the wage rate, t^h_l is tax rate on household h's labour income,[4] and t_k is tax rate on capital income.

The demand functions for goods and leisure are obtained by maximising (4.4) with respect to (4.5), and take the following form

$$C_{i,h} = \left(\frac{\alpha_{i,h} I_h}{\left(P_i(1+t_i^v) \right)^{\sigma_h} \left(\sum_i \alpha_{i,h} \left(P_i(1+t_i^v) \right) \right)^{1-\sigma_h} + \beta_h \left(w(1-t_l^h) \right)^{1-\sigma_h}} \right) \quad (4.6)$$

where t_i^v is value added tax rate and t_l^h tax rate on labour income.
Consumption of leisure is given by

$$L_h = \left(\frac{\beta_h . I_h}{\left(w(1-t_l^h) \right)^{\sigma_h} \left(\sum_i \alpha_{i,h} \left(P_i(1+t_t^v) \right) \right)^{1-\sigma_h} + \beta_h \left(w(1-t_t^h) \right)^{1-\sigma_h}} \right). \quad (4.7)$$

In versions of the model where there is no demand for leisure households have demand functions only for goods. In that case equation (4.7) does not exist, and equation (4.6) is modified with the setting $\beta_h = 0$.

In the one household case, the labour supply of each household LS_h is given by the difference between the household labour endowment, and the demand for leisure, L_h:

$$LS_h = \overline{L}_h - L_h . \quad (4.8)$$

In equilibrium, this labour supply by household must be consistent with the total demand for labour derived from the profit maximisation behaviour of firms as set out in the following section.

Production

Producers use labour and capital in each of N sectors to yield value added according to CES functions.

$$Y_i = \Omega_i ((1-\delta_i)(K_i)^{\gamma_i} + \delta_i (LS_i)^{\gamma_i})^{\frac{1}{\gamma_i}} \quad (i = 1...N) \quad (4.9)$$

where Y_i is the value added of sector i, Ω_i is a shift parameter in the production function, K_i and LS_i are the amounts of capital and labour used in sector i, δ_i is the share parameter on labour in the CES function, and γ_i is the CES factor substitution parameter.

The gross output of each sector reflects the use of value added, Y_i and intermediate inputs. We assume fixed coefficients both among intermediate inputs, and between value added and intermediate inputs; M_{ij} is the intermediate use of good i in the production of good j and X_j is the gross output of sector j. At any set of prices, producers in each sector maximise profits subject to their technology constraint

$$\max \Pi_i = P_i X_i - w L_i - r K_i - \sum_j P_j M_{ji} \qquad (4.10)$$

where Π_i is the profit of sector i. In equilibrium, factor demands by sectors are determined where the value marginal product of factors equal factor prices, and there are no positive profits for producers.

Government budget

The government collects revenue from taxes on capital and labour income and value-added taxes. All the tax revenues collected are transferred to households in lump sum form; that is,

$$\sum_h TR_h = \sum_i t_k r K_i + \sum_h t_i^v P_i C_{i,h} + \sum_h t_l^h w L S_h \qquad (4.11)$$

where t_k is the tax rate on capital income, t_i^v is the *ad valorem* tax rate on final sales, t_l^h is the tax rate on labour income of the household.

These taxes, particularly when they are levied at different rates on different sectors and households, have distortionary impacts on the allocation of resources in the economy. These are captured by the model. Government budget balance is a property of an equilibrium.

Model equilibrium conditions

In this model a competitive equilibrium is given by prices of consumption goods, P_j; the prices of capital, P^k; a wage rate for labour, w and levels of gross output, Y_j; capital use, K_j; and sectoral use of labour, L_j; such that, given these,

i) markets for goods and services, labour and capital clear; and
ii) the government budget constraint is satisfied.
    More specifically the market clearing condition for the goods market is given by

$$X_i = C_i + \sum_{j=1}^N a_{ij} X_j \qquad (4.12)$$

where $C_i = \Sigma_h C_{ih}$ is household final consumption, and $\Sigma_j a_{ij} X_j$ the intermediate demand.

The capital market clearing condition implies

$$\sum_h \overline{K}_h = \sum_i K_i \tag{4.13}$$

and labour market clearing implies:

$$\sum_h LS_h = \sum_i LS_i \;. \tag{4.14}$$

Government budget balance is given by (4.12). When there are n different markets in the economy, relative prices that clear $n-1$ markets also clear the nth market as well.

Data sources and calibration

The implementation of the UK model begins with input–output data. Input–output information for 1990 is published in the ONS publication *Input–Output Tables for the United Kingdom*, and are available for up to 123 sectors. The breakdown of consumption spending and the distribution of income across households is limited in this source. We therefore take an eight-sector version of the input–output table (see table 4.3) to represent the intersectoral linkages in UK production. The input–output table shows the quantities of labour and capital services which producers purchase (see table 4.4). It also shows how commodities supplied by the various sectors are bought either by households for final consumption (see table 4.5), or by other sectors as intermediate inputs. The zero profit conditions for producers in the benchmark data are met in the input–output data for the various sectors of the economy. This essentially means that the value of output equals payments to labour and capital services and intermediate inputs.

We make two modifications to this input–output data for use in the model. First, in an initial closed economy formulation of the model we do not explicitly consider import and export functions. We modify the data such that exports and imports balance for the economy as a whole, and there are no foreign transfers in the model.[5]

The second modification relates to the treatment of final demand. We consider only one category of final demands and do not explicitly incorporate investment and government demands into the model. For simplicity, we also do not separate government consumption and investment.

This model is thus a closed economy single household static model, with

Table 4.3 *Aggregated input–output table of the UK economy, 1990 (£ millions)*

	Agri[a]	Energy[b]	Manuf[c]	Constr[d]	Distr[e]	Transp[f]	Bus serv[g]	Other serv[b]
Agri	2,853	0	9,059	3	536	32	0	88
Energy	550	22,203	5,377	598	2,670	2,241	1,824	694
Manuf	3,774	2,896	60,613	14,961	13,372	4,290	8,763	3,410
Constr	186		791	23,022	760	128	1,808	999
Distr	873	1,220	12,171	2,891	4,438	2,700	2,472	742
Transp	266	1,253	7,251	846	12,956	8,091	10,599	1,303
Bus serv	1,010	1,648	21,717	9,008	18,348	7,336	49,008	11,278
Other serv	375	331	3,518	403	1,118	949	3,314	6,059

Source: ONS (1995), *Input–Output Tables of the United Kingdom.*
Notes: [a]Agriculture, Forestry and Fishing (1–3). Numbers in parentheses in this and other notes refer to input–output classifications. [b]Coal, Oil, Gas, Electricity, Water supply (4–9). [c]All Manufacturing (10–90). [d]Construction (91). [e]Wholesale, Retail Services, Hotel and Entertainment (92–95) [f]Railways, Air, Road, Sea, Postal and Telecommunications (96–102). [g]Business Services, Banking, Insurance, Accountancy (103–114). [b]Other Services, Public Administration, Education, Health (115–123).

Table 4.4 *UK value added and indirect business taxes 1990 (£ millions)*

	Agri[a]	Energy[b]	Manuf[c]	Constr[d]	Distr[e]	Transp[f]	Bus serv[g]	Other serv[b]
Labour	2,966	7,918	69,787	16,703	50,599	22,953	52,776	88,656
Capital	5,228	14,255	29,176	16,923	19,175	16,365	23,047	42,359

Source: As table 4.3.
Notes: As table 4.3.

Table 4.5 *UK Final demands 1990 (£ millions)*

	Agri[a]	Energy[b]	Manuf[c]	Constr[d]	Distr[e]	Transp[f]	Bus serv[g]	Other serv[b]
Total								
FD	5,059	18,597	109,143	57,953	105,376	23,534	40,058	140,253
VAT	876	2,485	9,015	655	14,943	2,852	3,224	8,518

Source: As table 4.3.
Notes: As table 4.3.

Table 4.6 *Calibrated share parameters in production and consumption in UK tax model*

Sectors	Calibrated share parameter on capital inputs	Calibrated share parameter on labour inputs	Calibrated share parameters for household expenditures by product
Agriculture	0.638	0.362	0.006
Energy	0.643	0.357	0.023
Manufacturing	0.295	0.705	0.137
Construction	0.503	0.497	0.073
Distribution	0.275	0.725	0.132
Transport	0.416	0.584	0.030
Business services	0.304	0.696	0.050
Other services	0.323	0.677	0.176

Table 4.7 *Elasticity parameters used in the UK tax model*

Sectors	Elasticity of substitution in production functions	Central tendency values of own price elasticities of household demand functions
Agriculture	0.50	0.468
Energy	0.75	0.659
Manufacturing	0.45	0.592
Construction	0.50	0.250
Distribution	0.80	0.642
Transport	0.80	0.977
Business services	0.80	0.461
Other services	0.50	0.461

Source: Piggott and Whalley (1985).

the government collecting taxes and redistributing income by means of transfers to households. The government collects revenue from taxes on capital income, value-added taxes on commodities and taxes on household income. The value-added tax influences the composition of final demand. The household income tax and accompanying transfers influence the labour supply decisions of the household sector. Differences in tax rates on capital income across sectors distort the allocation of capital resources among various sectors. In a competitive environment, resources are diverted from heavily taxed sectors to less taxed sectors. Production taxes and subsidies paid to producers both apply, having the effect of reducing the selling price below the cost of production.

Parameters and elasticities

We use literature based estimates of elasticities of substitution between labour and capital in the production functions in calibration, and elasticities of substitution among various commodities (including leisure) that enter the utility function of households in the model are based on literature values reported in table 4.7. Data on input–output transactions, value-added, taxes and final demand as presented above are then used to calibrate parameters on the consumption and production sides of this model. Model parameters are chosen in such a way that its solution replicates base year quantities, when base year prices are given to the model with the calibrated parameters. The resulting calibrated parameters are shown in table 4.6.

The welfare costs of taxes

This basic model captures three different tax instruments: taxes on capital income, value-added taxes on sales of final goods and taxes on household labour income. Tax rates on capital income are taken from information in the UK input–output tables. Value added tax rates and tax rates on household labour income are calculated from the data on income and sales taxes contained in *Economic Trends* (ONS, 1995). (See tables 4.8 and 4.9.)

To assess the welfare impacts of alternative UK tax policies, the model computes compensating and equivalent variations based on consumers' money metric welfare associated with various tax changes. It also computes the marginal excess burdens involved when raising additional tax revenues from various sources.

Model results (table 4.10) indicate that the removal of all taxes in the UK model yields a gain equal to 1.762 per cent of the benchmark income. The largest welfare gain results from the removal of household labour income tax distortions which equal 1.132 per cent of benchmark income. Among the three tax measures, taxes on capital income show the lowest welfare cost, equal to 0.33 per cent of income in the benchmark equilibrium.

Table 4.10 also reports the marginal cost of public funds (MEB) for the three categories of taxes in this initial UK model. The marginal excess burden is 23 pence per pound of revenues raised from taxes on household income and 13 pence per pound if extra revenues are raised by means of VAT. However, revenues raised by capital taxes improve the welfare in the economy. This outcome is due to the distortionary nature of capital taxes in the base year, which partly reflects distortions elsewhere in sales and

Table 4.8 *Production side tax rates in the UK tax model*

Sectors[a]	Tax rate on capital income (%)	Value-added tax rates (%)
Agriculture	8.6	23
Energy	2.3	23
Manufacturing	6.0	23
Construction	1.7	23
Distribution	46.5	23
Transport	6.2	23
Business services	25.2	23
Other services	1.7	23

[a]See table 4.3 for a key to sectoral abbreviations.

Table 4.9 *Household tax rates in the UK tax model*

Household labour income tax rate	Transfers as fraction of household income
22%	0.273

Table 4.10 *Welfare effects of the removal of tax distortions in the UK model (EV as a % of GDP)*

	Removal of VAT	Removal of taxes on capital income	Removal of taxes on household labour income	Removal of all three taxes
Hicksian EV for representative household as % of GDP	1.002 VAT	0.33 Capital income	1.132 Household labour income	1.762 All taxes
MEB £1 of extra revenue when raised by taxes	0.132	−0.028	0.234	0.191

other taxes. In the model data, for instance, capital income from the distribution sector is taxed at 46.5 per cent, while capital income from construction and other sectors is subject only to 1.7 per cent tax rate on capital income.

4. Extensions to the basic approach

Disaggregation and elaboration

This basic UK model has already been expanded in several ways in the project. We have disaggregated the households sector into ten different categories so that we can analyse incidence effects of taxes. We use data reported in the *Family Expenditure Survey* and income distribution data published in *Economic Trends*. As data tables in the latter sources are presented for ten deciles ranked by household income, we have expanded the UK model set out above to capture ten household groups. In the model, households are grouped by income decile, each endowed with labour and capital. Households receive income by supplying labour and capital, and receive transfers from the government. Rich households have proportionately larger capital endowments, and are liable for higher rates of taxes than poor households. In turn, poor households receive larger transfers from the government than those received by rich households. The income distribution data in the model includes income on wages and salaries, income from investment, and transfers by decile.

We have also extended the model to include an international trade sector, using two different variants. One is a small open economy model of the UK and the other is a world trade model, including the UK. The latter can be used to analyse multilateral trade policy initiatives, such as the impacts of the Uruguay Round decisions in the WTO.

Discreteness of labour supply choices and tax distortions of labour supply

Bhattarai and Whalley (1997a) have also used this modelling approach to investigate the significance of discrete choice for calculations of the welfare cost of tax distortions of labour supply by constructing observationally equivalent discrete and continuous choice UK based labour supply models.[6] The discrete analogue models they use embody varying forms of agent heterogeneity (over share parameters in preferences, substitution elasticities, endowments), while maintaining equivalence to identical single agent continuous models through similar model generated aggregate uncompensated labour supply elasticities. Issues arise as to how discrete choice is modelled in the with-tax case, and they present two alternative formulations. In one, tax revenues are returned to those who pay the tax; no interagent redistribution occurs. In the other, households have proportional claims on revenues generated by the tax, and redistribution occurs. The discrete analogue forms both asymptotically approach the continuous case as the grid over which discrete choice occurs becomes everywhere dense.

Results from these exercises are striking. In simple numerical examples using their first discrete formulation (tax revenues recycled to those who pay the tax), the discrete choice model produces sharply lower welfare costs of taxes if model calibration is made to the same uncompensated labour supply elasticities in both discrete and continuous models. Welfare costs of similar *ad valorem* labour supply tax distortions differ between models by factors of around 5, being sharply lower in the discrete formulation. On the other hand, under their second discrete choice formulation, which maintains fixed shares of households in tax revenues, the discrete choice model produces sharply higher welfare cost estimates. This is because households who switch from high to low labour supply inflict a fiscal externality on those remaining in their original state, since revenues fall. For an individual close to indifferent between high and low discrete labour supply states, when switching to the low labour supply state they experience little or no gain, while all other individuals collectively experience a loss represented by the tax revenue foregone. The factors of proportionality in results between discrete and continuous models change as the form of discreteness changes (step size across uniform parameter distributions, numbers of individuals, model parameters used for the population distributions), but not markedly.

They also consider cases where there is discrete choice for one household member (the primary worker) and continuity of choice for the other (the secondary worker); and consider household rather than individual optimisation. Differences in results between mixed discrete-continuous choice models are smaller, but other insights also emerge. These include the influence of discreteness of choice for one household member over the labour supply behaviour of the other, with implications for the literature on labour supply elasticities for primary and secondary workers. They investigate differences in model results empirically using UK data and literature based parameter estimates instead of numerical examples. Results indicate slightly smaller but still significant factors of proportionality to those which occur in numerical examples. The conclusion is that discreteness in modelling labour supply behaviour matters, not only for labour supply estimation but also for the calculation of welfare costs of labour supply taxation. The formulation chosen also critically affects whether estimates are raised or lowered.

The redistributive effects of transfers

Bhattarai and Whalley (1997b) also use this modelling approach to investigate the redistributive effects of transfers in the UK. The point of departure in their analysis is the observation, seemingly not in the literature, that with voluntary participation in transfer programmes (with tax back or withdrawal provisions), the utility, or real income, value of transfers to participants is typically less than the cash transfers received. This is because individuals (or households) compare utility across two regimes; one with benefits and tax back arrangements, and the other with no benefits and no tax back, choosing the higher utility regime. A money metric utility comparison between the regimes (the real income difference) bears no direct relation to the net of tax back cash transfers actually received. Indeed, in an extreme case where an individual (or household) is indifferent between participating and not participating, if they were recorded as a benefit programme participant, the real income gain to them from participation in the transfer programme would be zero, despite the disbursement of public funds to the recipient. This analysis argues that, in general, and ignoring wage rate effects, the real income received by transfer recipients is smaller than the cash transfers actually made, since to the recipient the reference point for valuing them should be the reservation utility in the no benefit no tax back regime.

Given tax back rates, individuals (or households) will also not participate in transfer programmes until some threshold level of transfers is reached, raising utility under participation above that in the no participation regime. Tax back conditions in benefit programmes thus impose a form of real income entry fee on participation, which must be deducted when evaluating the redistributive effects of transfer programmes. Conditional on participation in transfer programmes, transfers shift recipients' budget constraints parallel. In the homothetic case, after the entry fee has been paid, marginal increases in transfers (for fixed tax back rates) provide recipients with corresponding marginal increases in real income in the fixed wage case. They also argue that an additional effect, also seemingly missing from existing literature, needs to enter analyses of the redistribution effects of transfers, namely that when the poor participate in a conditional transfer scheme, the associated withdrawal of low wage labour from the market place drives up the wage of low wage(skill) workers relative to high wage(skill) workers. Thus, with heterogeneous labour income(skill) range, the withdrawal of low wage labour due to high tax back conditional transfers to the poor raises their wage rate. This set-aside effect potentially substantially raises the welfare of the poor. Thus, conventional redistribution to the poor through transfers may be overestimated for the reasons given above, but induced redistribution via changes in the wage distribution can provide significant redistribution.

Bhattarai and Whalley use conditional choice general equilibrium models to assess the importance of these two effects. These models embody both endogenous participation decisions in transfer schemes by households, and heterogeneous labour in production (by income range or skill type). In such models, programme participation by low income households is endogenously determined in equilibrium, along with the wage distribution since wage rates change as transfer programmes characteristics (benefit levels, tax-back rates) change. The budget set for households is non-convex, presenting special computation problems not tackled, as far as we are aware, in existing general equilibrium tax computation literature. Commodity demands by households, including leisure, are no longer analytic, even for conventional CES or Cobb-Douglas utility functions. This means that household demands have to be evaluated numerically using optimisation techniques within a larger equilibrium structure, including the production side modelling of the economy. The larger model is itself solved through separate application of numerical optimisation methods; in essence optimisation embedded within a wider optimisation, since consumer demands are non-analytic.

The bottom line conclusion they offer is that assessing the redistributive effects of conditional transfers is neither as straightforward as it at first sight appears, nor is the real income value of such transfers seemingly so large as is implicitly assumed in the literature. Regime choice significantly affects such measures, and their general equilibrium effects through programme-induced low wage labour withdrawal need to be taken into account. These effects seem to be virtually ignored in available literature in the area, and are important because they can radically change perceptions as to the redistributive effects of transfers.

5. Concluding remarks

This chapter discusses applied general equilibrium tax modelling, and initial applications to UK policy issues under an ESRC supported research project on General Equilibrium Modelling of UK Policy Issues. Future activity on the project will reflect the objectives outlined in the original project proposal. Further work also remains to be done on model applications to the analysis of other UK policy issues (for example effects on the UK of the Uruguay Round of GATT negotiations, possible effects of a carbon tax on UK economic performance, and analysis of UK social security issues) through the development of other issue-driven modelling structures. The original project proposal set out a research agenda through the years

1998–9. Furthering the development of general equilibrium and dynamic modelling techniques and providing a better integration with other disciplines, including econometrics, while contributing to the dissemination of general equilibrium modelling techniques and relevant software tools will remain the focus of the remainder of project.

Notes

1 This chapter draws on an earlier presentation to a conference on Macroeconomic Modelling and Economic Policy organised by Cambridge University and the National Institute for Economic and Social Research, January 8/9, 1998. We are grateful to the Research Division of the Inland Revenue for their collaborative support of this work.
2 The discussion in this section draws on Whalley (1985).
3 We use data for 1990. Data for a later year was not available at construction stage, but 1995 data has since been released.
4 The effect of tax distortions on the labour leisure choice can be captured through a subsidy to the consumption of leisure at rate t_l^h.
5 Elaboration of this model to more fully include is to follow in the project.
6 See the discussion of the related but different issue of non-linear budget constraints and the welfare cost of taxes in Preston and Walker (1992).

References

Auerbach, A.J., Kotlikoff, L.J. and Skinner, J. (1983), 'The efficiency gains from dynamic tax reform', *International Economic Review*, 24, pp. 81–100.
Ballard, C., Fullerton, D., Shoven, J.B. and Whalley, J. (1985), *A General Equilibrium Model for Tax Policy Evaluation*, Chicago, University of Chicago Press.
Bhattarai, K. and Whalley, J. (1997a), 'Discreteness and the welfare cost of labour supply tax distortions', NBER Working Paper No. 6280, November.
(1997b), 'The redistrbutive effects of transfers', NBER Working Paper No. 6281, November.
Brook, A., Kendrick, D. and Meeraus, A. (1992), *GAMS: User's Guide*, release 2.25, San Francisco, Scientific Press.
Dirkse, S.P. and Ferris, M. (1995), 'The PATH solver: a non-monotone stabilization scheme for mixed complementarity problems', *Optimisation Mehods and Software*, 5, 123–56.
Fullerton, D., Shoven, J.B. and Whalley, J. (1983), 'Replacing the U.S. income tax with a progressive consumption tax. A sequenced general equilibrium approach',

Journal of Public Economics, 20, pp. 3–23.

Harberger, A.C. (1962), 'The incidence of the corporation income tax', *Journal of Political Economy*, 70, pp. 215–40.

Kehoe, T. (1980), 'An index theorem for general equilibrium models with production', *Econometrica*, 48, pp. 1211–32.

Kehoe, T. and Whalley, J. (1985), 'Uniqueness of equilibrium in a large scale numerical general equilibrium model', *Journal of Public Economics*, 28, pp. 247–54.

Mansur, A., and Whalley, J. (1984), 'Numerical specification of applied general equilibrium models: estimation, calibration and data', in Scarf, H. and Shoven, J. B. (Eds), *Applied General Equilibrium Analysis*, New York, Cambridge University Press.

Office of National Statistics (1995), *Economic Trends*.

Piggott, J.R. and Whalley, J. (1985), *Economic Effects of UK Tax-Subsidy Policies: A General Equilibrium Appraisal*, Cambridge, Cambridge University Press.

Preston, I. and Walker, I. (1992), 'Welfare measurement in labour supply models with non-linear budget constraints', Institute of Fiscal Studies, Working Paper No. 292/12, London.

Rutherford, T.F. (1997), *The GAMS/MPSGE and GAMS/MILES User Notes*, GAMS Development Corporation, Washington, DC.

St.-Hilaire, F. and Whalley, J. (1983), 'A microconsistent equilibrium data set for Canada for use in tax policy analysis', *Review of Income and Wealth*, June, pp. 175–204.

Scarf, H. E. (1967), 'On the computation of equilibrium prices', in Fellner, W.J. (ed.), *Ten Economic Studies in the Tradition of Irving Fisher*, New York, Wiley.

Scarf, H.E. and Hansen, T. (1973), *The Computation of Economic Equilibria*, New Haven, Conn., Yale University Press.

Shoven, J.B. (1974), 'A proof of the existence of general equilibrium with *ad valorem* commodity taxes', *Journal of Economic Theory*, 8, pp. 1–25.

Shoven and Whalley, J. (1973), 'General equilibrium with taxes: a computational procedure and an existence proof', *Review of Economic Studies*, 40, pp. 475–90.

(1984), 'Applied general equilibrium models of taxation and international trade', *Journal of Economic Literature*, September, pp. 1007–51.

Summers, L.H. (1981), 'Capital taxation and accumulation in a life cycle growth model', *American Economic Review*, 71, pp. 533–44.

Taylor, L. (ed.) (1990), *Socially Relevant Policy Analysis: Structuralist Computable General Equilibrium Models for the Developing World*, Cambridge, Mass., MIT Press.

Varian, H.R. (1992), *Microeconomic Analysis*, 3rd edn, New York, W.W. Norton and Company.

Whalley, J. (1985), *Trade Liberalization Among Major World Trading Areas*, Cambridge, Mass., MIT Press.

5   A structural cointegrating VAR approach to macroeconometric modelling

ANTHONY GARRATT, KEVIN LEE,
M. HASHEM PESARAN and YONGCHEOL SHIN

1. Introduction[1]

Macroeconometric modelling in the UK and elsewhere has undergone a number of important changes during the past two decades, largely in response to developments in economic and econometric theory as well as to changing economic circumstances. One important impetus in this process was Lucas' (1976) critique of macroeconometric policy evaluation, which resulted in widespread adoption of the rational expectations methodology in macroeconomic models. It also provoked considerable scepticism concerning the use of large-scale macroeconometric models in policy analysis and initiated the emergence of a new generation of econometric models explicitly based on dynamic intertemporal optimisation decisions by firms and households. In contrast, Sims' (1980) critique raised serious doubts about the traditional, Cowles Commission approach to identification of behavioural relations, which had been based on what Sims termed 'incredible' restrictions on the short-run dynamics of the model. This critique generated considerable interest in the use of vector autoregressive (VAR) models in macroeconometric analysis.[2] A third impetus for change in the way in which macroeconometric modelling has been undertaken came from the increased attention paid to the treatment of non-stationarity in macroeconomic variables. The classic study was that by Nelson and Plosser (1982), who showed that the null hypothesis of a unit root could not be rejected in a wide range of macroeconomic time series in the US. This resurrected the spectre of spurious regression noted originally by Yule (1926), Champernowne (1960), and more recently by Granger and Newbold (1974). Subsequently, the work of Engle and Granger (1987), Johansen (1991) and Phillips (1991) on cointegration showed possible ways of dealing with the spurious regression problem in the presence of unit root variables, with important consequences for macroeconometric modelling in particular.

Following these developments, the alternative approaches to macroeconometric modelling in the UK and elsewhere can be grouped under four broad categories. First, there are large-scale macroeconometric models such as HM Treasury's model of the UK economy, and the Federal Reserve Board's model of the US economy. Although these models have made many important innovations, by their very nature they have been slow to evolve and essentially follow the tradition of the Cowles Commission, making a distinction between exogenous and endogenous variables and imposing restrictions, often on the short-run dynamic properties of the model, in order to achieve identification. The parameters are typically estimated by least squares or by instrumental variables methods, and full information estimation of the model parameters is rarely attempted.

Secondly, following the methodology developed by Doan, Litterman and Sims (1984) and Litterman (1986), there are unrestricted, Bayesian, and structural VARs. These are frequently employed for forecasting but are of limited use in policy evaluation.[3] The structural VAR approach aims to provide the VAR framework with structural content through the imposition of restrictions on the covariance structure of various shocks.[4] However, this approach is typically employed to carry out impulse response analysis in a 'structurally' meaningful manner, and does not attempt to model the structure of the economy in the form of specific behavioural relationships.

The third approach is closely associated with the dynamic stochastic general equilibrium (DSGE) methodology employed in the real business cycle literature. This approach, developed following the seminal work of Kydland and Prescott (1982) and Long and Plosser (1983), provides an explicit intertemporal general equilibrium model of the economy based on optimising decisions of households and firms. Originally, the emphasis of these models was on real factors (for example, productivity shocks), but more recently the DSGE models have been extended in a number of directions aimed at allowing for nominal effects, adjustment costs, heterogeneity, and endogenous technological progress, for example.[5] In consequence, the differences between the DSGE and the traditional macroeconometric models have become less pronounced. Also many of the DSGE models can be approximated by restricted VAR models, which brings them more into line with other modelling approaches.[6]

The fourth approach, and the one which we aim to promote here, is the 'structural cointegrating VAR' approach. This approach is based on the desire to develop a macroeconometric model which has transparent theoretical foundations, providing insight into the behavioural relationships which underlie the functioning of the macroeconomy, and which has flexible dynamics that fit the historical time-series data well. The modelling approach advocated here is based on a log-linear VAR model estimated subject to long-run relationships obtained from economic theory. On the assumption that the individual macroeconomic series have a unit root, each of the long-run relationships derived from theory is associated with a cointegrating relationship between the variables, and the existence of these cointegrating relationships imposes restrictions on a VAR model of the variables. Hence, the approach provides an estimated structural model of the macroeconomy in which the only restrictions on the short-run dynamics of the model are those which are imposed through the decision to limit attention to log-linear VAR models with a specified maximum lag length. The work of King et al. (1991) and Mellander et al. (1992) is in this vein, but is limited in scope. The six-variable model of King et al. is a closed economy model not suitable for modelling a small open economy such as the UK. The four-variable model by Mellander et al. attempts to capture the open nature of the Swedish economy only by adding a terms of trade variable to the familiar consumption-investment-income model also analysed by King et al. In this chapter we use the recently developed core UK model by Garratt et al. (1998, 1999a) to illustrate the practical advantages of the structural cointegrating VAR approach to macroeconometric modelling of small open economies.

The structure of the remainder of the chapter is as follows. Section 2 gives a brief overview of the alternative macroeconometric modelling approaches. Section 3 provides a more detailed description of the structural cointegrating VAR approach. Section 4 illustrates the uses of the approach in impulse response analysis and probability forecasting. Section 5 concludes.

2. Alternative approaches to macroeconometric modelling

In this section we elaborate on three of the broad approaches to macroeconometric modelling raised in the introduction, focusing in particular on the implications of the different approaches for modelling the long run. The discussion considers the different ways that the long-run relations are modelled (whether explicitly or not) in large-scale simultaneous equation macroeconometric models, in unrestricted and structural VAR models and in DSGE models.

2.1 Large-scale simultaneous equation models

Recent developments

Large-scale simultaneous equation macroeconometric models (SEMs) can be traced back to the modelling approach of Tinbergen and Klein and its subsequent developments at the Cowles Commission. Prominent examples of such large-scale models include the first and second generation models developed at the Federal Reserve Board (see, for example, Ando and Modigliani, 1969, Brayton and Mauskopf, 1985, and Brayton and Tinsley, 1996), Fair's (1994) model of the US economy, Murphy's (1988, 1992) model for Australia, and the models constructed for the UK at the London Business School (LBS), the National Institute of Economic and Social Research (NIESR), HM Treasury (HMT), and until recently at the Bank of England (BE).[7]

The relatively poor forecasting performance of the large-scale models in the face of the stagflation of the 1970s, in conjunction with the advent of rational expectations and the critiques of Lucas (1976) on policy evaluation and Sims (1980) on identification, brought about a number of important changes in the development and the use of large-scale SEMs throughout the 1980s and 1990s. Important developments have taken place in three major areas.[8] First, in response to Sims' criticism of the use of 'incredible' identifying restrictions involving short-run dynamics, and under the influence of recent developments in cointegration analysis (for example, Engel and Granger, 1987), a consensus has formed that the important aspect of a structural model is its long-run relationships, which must be identified without having to restrict the model's short-run dynamics. Second, in response to the criticism that large-scale models paid insufficient attention to the micro foundations of the underlying relationships and the properties of the macroeconomic system considered as a whole, there is now a greater use made of economic theory in the specification of large-scale models. And third, in response to the criticisms of Lucas, considerable work has been undertaken to incorporate rational expectations (RE), or model-consistent expectations, into large-scale models.

Under the influence of these recent developments, the new generation of large-scale models share a number of important features. Invariably they comprise three basic building blocks: equilibrium conditions, expectations formation, and dynamic adjustments. The equilibrium conditions are typically derived from the steady state properties of a Walrasian general equilibrium model, and there seems to be clear evidence of a developing consensus on what constitutes the appropriate general equilibrium model for characterising the long-run relations. This consensus side-steps the Sims critique by focusing on the long-run and remaining agnostic on short-run dynamics. Britton and Westaway (1998) provide a good example of the nature of the consensus in the UK.[9] These authors use standard simulation methods to show that, broadly speaking, the NIESR model has the characteristics of a Walrasian general equilibrium system in the long-run. The steady state values of the key aggregates in the NIESR model (namely output, net investment overseas, domestic investment, and employment) are determined as outcomes of utility maximisation by households and profit maximisation by firms subject to appropriate budget and technological constraints. The relative prices (namely, the real wage, the relative price of domestic to foreign outputs, and the differential between domestic and foreign interest rates) are then determined to ensure market clearing and the neutrality of nominal magnitudes in the long run.

In a similar vein, Allen *et al.* (1994) describe the role of the supply side in determining the LBS model's long-run properties. The relations characterising the supply side in the LBS model are explicitly based on optimising models of firm and union behaviour, and consist of a system of factor demand and (relative) price equations (for labour, energy, imported inputs and capital). The relationships are estimated as a single system, imposing all the cross-equation restrictions suggested by cost minimisation on the part of firms. And finally, as a third illustration of the developing consensus, Murphy's macroeconometric model of the Australian economy is described in Murphy (1992) as sharing the main features of the intermediate-run version of the Dornbusch (1976) model, but in addition includes all balance sheet and flow of funds constraints applicable to households, firms, government and foreign sectors, and incorporates full neoclassical optimising behaviour in production in the steady state. Restrictions are also imposed to ensure that there is 'balanced growth' in the long run, where 'balanced growth' is taken to mean that real growth is driven by technical progress and population growth, the unemployment rate equals the NAIRU, and inflation is the difference between the monetary and the real output growths.

The need for transparency

Despite the progress made so far, and the growing consensus on what constitutes best practice in macroeconometric modelling, large-scale models continue to be viewed with some scepticism, in particular in the area of policy analysis.[10] Furthermore it can be argued that it is simply not possible for large-scale models to follow such a best practice approach because of their size and complexity. The complexity of the interactions of different parts of a large dynamic model means that the accumulated response of the macroeconomy to a particular shock, or to a change in a given exogenous variable, can be very difficult to interpret, particularly as far as their effects on the long-run relations are concerned. It is also difficult to identify and correct for misspecification in large-scale models, as attempts to fix one part of the model could have far reaching (and often unpredictable) consequences for the properties of the overall model. And as far as estimation is concerned, full information methods are often not even an option given the large size of these models. Generally speaking, large-scale models lack transparency, which often hinders interpretation of model properties and impedes communication on policy debate, and this might explain why both academics and policy makers have, on occasions, bypassed large models in debates on certain areas of policy formation.

The lack of transparency of large-scale models has resulted in the development of a number of innovative methods for characterising and summarising their short-run and long-run properties. The standard approach is through (stochastic) simulations. Sensitivity analysis is then undertaken, and dynamic multipliers derived, by simulating the model under alternative scenarios for the exogenous variables and/or parameters of interest.[11] However, such a numerical solution procedure for identification of the model's long-run properties, besides being computationally expensive, remains difficult to interpret. Further, it could be sensitive to particular realisations of the forcing variables used in the simulation analysis, especially when there are strong non-linear effects in the relationships between the endogenous and the forcing variables of the model.[12] But the fact that such methods are necessary is in itself an important indicator of the general lack of transparency of large-scale models with respect to their long-run properties.

Because of their size, theory-based restrictions are imposed in different parts of the large-scale models often in a piecemeal fashion. For example, restrictions might be imposed in one part of a model to ensure long-run consistency with economic theory, but there may be complicated feedbacks in another part of the model which are not fully taken into account and may result in the model as a whole being at variance with the theory in the long run. Such a possibility is clearly illustrated in the empirical exercise of Fisher et al. (1992), where attention is drawn to the differences between the models developed by NIESR, LBS, BE and HMT in terms of the reaction of the current account balance to nominal exchange rate changes.

A second illustration of the difficulties associated with the use of theory-based restrictions in large-scale SEMs relates to the choice of terminal conditions in the case of models involving forward-looking expectations. The long-run solution and the short-run dynamics of large-scale RE models can be very sensitive to the choice of terminal conditions. However, in the past, many large-scale models employed automatic rules to deal with the terminal conditions which were chosen relatively arbitrarily, with little regard to economic theory.[13] While the more recent generation of large-scale models have paid greater attention to the choice of terminal conditions, particularly as far as the long-run properties of these models are concerned, this provides a further example of the difficulties faced when attempts are made to incorporate theory-consistent long-run structures in large-scale models.[14]

To summarise, while important progress has been made in the construction and use of large-scale SEMs over the past two decades, it can still be argued that these models are subject to a number of limitations that arise primarily because of their large and complex structure. As Brayton *et al.* (1997) conclude: 'Large-scale macro models are by their nature slow to evolve'. Simultaneous estimation and evaluation of such models is currently computationally prohibitive, and given the available time series data may not be even feasible. A full integration of theory and measurement has proved elusive to large-scale model builders. Despite the imaginative attempts made over the past two decades, it remains a formidable undertaking to construct a large-scale macroeconometric theory-consistent model which has transparent long-run properties and which fits the data reasonably well.

2.2 Unrestricted and structural VARs

Unrestricted VARs

The various technical and methodological difficulties associated with the construction of large-scale models, and their highly labour and capital intensive nature has led many researchers to seek modelling strategies that are less demanding and more manageable. The unrestricted VAR approach, introduced into macroeconometrics by Sims (1980), stands at the other extreme to large-scale models. It focuses on fitting the model to the data at the expense of theoretical consistency, both from a short-run and a long-run perspective. Sims' objective was to investigate the dynamic response of the system to shocks (through impulse response functions) without having to rely on 'incredible' identifying restrictions, or potentially controversial restrictions from economic theory. This strategy eschews the need to impose long-run relationships on the model's variables, and relies exclusively on time-series observations to identify such relationships if they happen to exist.

The statistical basis of the unrestricted VAR modelling approach is the Wold decomposition theorem. According to this theorem, all covariance stationary processes can be written as the sum of a deterministic (perfectly predictable) component and a stationary process possessing an infinite order moving average (MA) representation. Restricting attention to 'invertible' processes,[15] one obtains a unique MA representation, also known as the 'fundamental' representation which fully characterises the sample autocorrelation coefficients. Such a fundamental representation can be approximated by a finite order vector autoregressive-moving average (VARMA) process. However, estimation of VARMA models poses important numerical problems, particularly when the number of variables in the VARMA model is relatively large. For this reason Sims chooses to work with a finite order VAR model which is much simpler to estimate, but involves further approximations. To perform impulse response analysis, Sims' approach then requires the use of a Choleski decomposition of the variance covariance matrix of the model's innovations/shocks. This enables the MA representation to be written in terms of orthogonalised innovations. It is the response of the macroeconomic variables to these orthogonalised shocks that are described in Sims' orthogonalised impulse responses.

This approach to modelling has been subject to a number of criticisms (see, for example, Pagan, 1987), some of which are worth noting here. First, the approach requires care in the initial stages in the choice of transformation of the data to achieve stationarity. In particular, it is important that economically meaningful, and statistically significant, relations are not excluded from the analysis at this stage by the choice of transformation. For example, a VAR model of the first-differences of I(1) variables is misspecified if there exists a cointegrating relationship between two or more of the I(1) variables. Second, care is needed in the choice of variables to be included in the VAR analysis, and it is difficult to imagine how this choice could be made without reference to some underlying economic theory. And third, since the choice of the Choleski decomposition is not unique, there are a number of alternative sets of orthogonalised impulse responses which can be obtained from any estimated VAR model. A particular choice of orthogonalisation might be suggested by economic theory, and Sims' own approach to choosing an orthogonalisation was to impose a causal ordering on the VAR. However, this requires recourse to economic theory (which defeats the object of this approach) and in general no such restrictions are available or acceptable. In the absence of such restrictions, the orthogonalised impulse responses are difficult to interpret economically, so that the estimated model gives few meaningful insights into the economic system that it represents.

Notwithstanding their weak theoretical underpinnings, due to their flexibility and ease of use, VAR models are used extensively in forecasting and as benchmarks for evaluation of large-scale and DSGE models. In order to increase the precision of forecasts based on VAR models, Doan, Litterman and Sims (1984) have also proposed Bayesian VARs (BVARs) which combine unrestricted VARs with Bayesian, or what has come to be known as 'Minnesota', priors. Other types of priors have also been considered in the literature. See, for example, DeJong et al. (1997) who combine a VAR(1) model with prior probabilities on its parameters derived from an RBC model.

Structural VARs

The structural VAR approach builds on Sims' approach but attempts to identify the impulse responses by imposing *a priori* restrictions on the covariance matrix of the structural errors and/or on long-run impulse responses themselves. This approach is developed by Bernanke (1986), Blanchard and Watson (1986) and Sims (1986) who considered *a priori* restrictions on contemporaneous effects of shocks, and more recently by Blanchard and Quah (1989), Clarida and Gali (1994) and Astley and Garratt (1996) who use restrictions on the long-run impact of shocks to identify the impulse responses. In contrast to the unrestricted VAR approach, structural VARs attempt explicitly to provide some economic rationale behind the covariance restrictions used, and thus aim to avoid the use of arbitrary or implicit identifying restrictions. However, while the use of 'theory-based' covariance restrictions in small systems allows the impulse responses to be identified under the structural VAR approach, such restrictions still do not enable identification of the long-run relationships among the variables.[16] Furthermore, even the covariance restrictions are not always easy to interpret or motivate from an economic perspective, particularly in the case of VAR models with more than two or three variables. The number of exactly identifying covariance restrictions required increases rapidly with the number of variables in the VAR. In a system involving m variables, the number of such restrictions is equal to $m(m - 1)/2$. For example, in the case of the model presented here the number of covariance restrictions required to identify exactly the impulse responses will be twenty-eight. It is not clear how these restrictions could be obtained, let alone motivated from an appropriate economic theory perspective.

There are also inherent difficulties with the interpretation that are given to the impulse responses obtained under the structural VAR approach. For example, in Blanchard and Quah (1989), a bivariate VAR model of unemployment and output growth is investigated by first solving the two variables in terms of two orthogonalised white-noise shocks, and then estimating impulse responses under the identifying assumption that one of the shocks has no long-run effects on output levels. They then duly refer to this shock as the 'demand' shock, and refer to the other shock as the 'supply' shock.[17] However, while it might be an interesting exercise to consider the effects on output and unemployment of the two different types of shock, and while it might be possible to elaborate a model of the macroeconomy in which demand shocks have the property assumed by Blanchard and Quah, there seems little rationale in referring to these innovations as 'demand' and 'supply' shocks in the context of the purely statistical model used by these authors. The different types of shock considered in this analysis are defined with reference to their statistical properties (i.e. whether or not they have a permanent effect on output levels) and not with reference to a model of how consumers and producers behave in a macroeconomy.[18]

2.3 Dynamic stochastic general equilibrium models

Unrestricted VARs, BVARs, or the structural VARs all make minimal use of economic theory, while the use of theory in large-scale models is modular, in the sense that the theory is used in a coherent manner only in specific modules or parts of the model. In contrast, the DSGE models develop a general equilibrium approach to modelling using stochastic intertemporal optimisation techniques applied to decision problems of households and firms.[19]

The DSGE model is expressed in terms of 'deep' structural parameters, namely the parameters that enter the preferences, production technologies and the probability distributions of taste and technology shocks. In practice, very simple forms are chosen for these functions (power utility functions and Cobb-Douglas production functions, for example). Nevertheless, the resultant optimal decision rules are complicated and typically are approximated around the deterministic steady-state values of the macroeconomic variables. The outcome for standard models typically is a highly restricted VAR(1) model.[20]

The proponents of the DSGE approach to macroeconomic modelling argue that this approach takes macroeconomic theory seriously in a way that the large-scale SEMs do not. In particular, it is argued that the use of a general equilibrium framework ensures that the DSGE models display stock equilibria, rather than the flow equilibria which are characteristic of the traditional approach to macroeconometric models. The derivation of the model's relationships as solutions to intertemporal optimisation problems of households and firms ensures that the model has an internal consistency and a relationship with economic theory that is lost in traditional large-scale models. However, we have already noted that the proponents of large-scale models have made considerable progress in relating the structure of their models to economic theory, particularly in relation to the long-run properties of the model. Indeed, we noted that there has developed a consensus on the appropriate theory for the characterisation of the long run, based on Walrasian general equilibrium theory, and that this has been adopted (at least in principle) in many of the current generation of large-scale models. In this respect, therefore, the differences in the theoretical underpinnings of the DSGE models and the large-scale models are less polarised than is sometimes argued.

However, there are important differences between the two approaches both in content and in emphasis. They differ significantly in their treatment of short-run dynamics. The DSGE models not only provide the form of relationships between economic variables that exist in the long run, but also provide an explicit statement of the dynamic evolution of the macroeconomy in response to shocks. It is argued (for example, in Plosser, 1989) that the foundations of typical Keynesian models are static in nature, and that the dynamics are introduced arbitrarily through accelerator mechanisms for investment and inventory behaviour, or through nominal rigidities in wage and price setting, or through partial adjustment mechanisms in various forms, for example. The lack of cohesion in the derivation of the long-run and dynamic properties in the large-scale models represents a fundamental shortcoming of the approach, according to this argument, encouraging the view that the long-run evolution of the macroeconomy can be considered independently of short- and medium-term fluctuations. In contrast, there are no dichotomies between the determinants of long-run growth and short-run fluctuations in DSGE models, though the long-run is of course often not modelled explicitly in its entirety, in that model and actual data are (arbitrarily) filtered before they are analysed.

While it is true that many DSGE models provide an integrated approach to the study of growth and fluctuations, it is acknowledged that the approach is in its infancy in terms of providing a satisfactory understanding of economic fluctuations. The current generation of DSGE models have extended the original models to incorporate features such as: adjustment costs (Kydland and Prescott, 1982, Christiano and Eichenbaum, 1992, and Cogley and Nason, 1995); signal extraction and learning (Kydland and Prescott, 1982, and Cooley and Hansen, 1995); aggregation (Christiano et al., 1991, on temporal aggregation, and Cooley et al., 1997, and Ríos-Rull, 1995, on cross-sectional aggregation); endogenous technological progress (Stadler, 1990, and Hercowitz and Sampson, 1991) and information heterogeneities (Kasa, 1995). However, it remains unclear whether a model could be developed that is capable of simultaneously dealing with all of these factors in a satisfactory manner and, even if it could, whether it would be any more transparent or easy to interpret than the currently available stock of large-scale models.

Three further points are worth making on the comparison of DSGE models and the large-scale SEMs in terms of their treatment of dynamics (elaborated in, for example, McCallum, 1989). First, while the recent literature on endogenous growth theory has begun to develop a theory of how economic fluctuations might influence technical progress, the extent to which technical progress is exogenously determined remains unclear. If it is believed that technical progress is actually taking place independently of the developments in the macroeconomy, then the emphasis on providing a single, internally-consistent model of growth and fluctuations is likely to be misplaced. Secondly, although the DSGE models place more emphasis on the mechanism by which shocks are propagated over time than the more traditional theories underlying the large-scale models, they are by no means incompatible with them. It is widely acknowledged, for example, that shocks generated by the signal extraction problem (and of a type which can be readily accommodated with a standard large-scale model) are likely to trigger the same type of dynamic response as the taste and technology shocks typically considered in DSGE models. Seen in this light, one might argue that the DSGE approach to dynamics is potentially over-restrictive, limiting attention to particular sources of dynamics. Indeed, when the models were confronted with the data, in Christiano and Eichenbaum (1992) or Kim and Pagan (1995), for example, the evidence suggests that this might be true.

A third important difference between the approaches taken in the construction of the large-scale SEMs and the DSGE models is in the emphasis placed on real (and especially technological) shocks as opposed to nominal shocks. For example, many proponents of the DSGE approach do not deny the potential importance of money in explaining economic fluctuations. Indeed, a considerable literature has developed to incorporate money in DSGE models (see, for example, Cooley and Hansen, 1989, 1995, and

Christiano *et al.*, 1998). However, one of the primary motivating arguments behind the DSGE research agenda was to establish that the dynamic responses of the macroeconomy are consistent with a model in which there are no market failures, in which the outcome is Pareto optimal, and in which intervention by a social planner to force agents to change their actions will be welfare-reducing. Consequently, the research agenda behind the development of the DSGE approach to modelling has, until recently, downplayed the potential role of monetary policy in generating economic fluctuations and instead has placed considerable emphasis on real shocks. Indeed, many of the calibration exercises undertaken in the DSGE literature have ignored the monetary sector altogether. In fact, in terms of explaining macroeconomic time series, it is unambiguously the case that the use of data on nominal magnitudes, including nominal interest rates and money stock data, improves the explanatory power of models of real magnitudes such as output or employment (see, for example, King *et al.*, 1991, and Litterman and Weiss, 1985). These results, and associated causality tests, do not provide a test of the relevance of the DSGE models versus the large-scale SEMs, but they emphasise the importance of incorporating a monetary sector in a macroeconomic model despite the difficulties perceived by some proponents of the DSGE approach in developing a convincing and coherent explanation of the monetary transmission mechanism.

3. The structural cointegrating VAR approach

The structural cointegrating VAR modelling strategy begins with an explicit statement of the long-run relationships between the variables of the model obtained from macroeconomic theory. These relationships will typically be based on stock-flow and accounting identities, arbitrage conditions, and long-run solvency requirements that ensure stationary asset–income ratios. The long-run relationships are approximated by log-linear equations, with disturbances that characterise the deviations of the long-run relations from their realised, short-run counterparts. These deviations are referred to as the 'long-run structural shocks'. Not all of the variables contained in the long-run relationships suggested by economic theory are observable, however, and in writing the long-run relationships in terms of observable variables, 'long-run reduced form shocks' are derived as functions of the long-run structural shocks. The long-run reduced form shocks are then embedded within an otherwise unrestricted log-linear VAR model of a given order in the variables of interest to obtain a cointegrating VAR model which incorporates the structural long-run relationships as its steady-state solution. In this way the cointegrating VAR model will embody the long-run theory restrictions in a transparent manner. The theory also imposes restrictions on the intercepts and/or the trend coefficients in the VAR, which play an important role in testing for cointegration as well as for testing restrictions on the long-run relations.[21]

This approach, however, differs from many applications of cointegration analysis, which start with an unrestricted VAR and then attempt to impose restrictions on the cointegrating relations, without a clear *a priori* view of the economy's structural relations. Such a strategy is likely to work when there exists only one long-run relationship among the macro variables. However, when the number of cointegrating relations are two or more, without a clear and comprehensive theoretical understanding of the long-run relations of the macroeconomy, identification of the cointegrating relations and the appropriate choice of intercepts/trends in the underlying VAR model will become a very difficult, if not an impossible, undertaking.

3.1 Comparisons with the three alternative approaches

Comparison with large-scale SEMs

As the discussion above makes clear, the structural cointegrating VAR approach to macroeconometric modelling begins by describing the relationships which define the long-run structure of the macroeconomy, and embeds these long-run relationships within an otherwise unrestricted VAR model of the macroeconomy. The number of variables chosen to include in the core model is selected to ensure that the system can be estimated simultaneously, taking into account all of the potential feedbacks between the variables captured by the short-run dynamics and suggested by the long-run economic relationships. One of the primary strengths of this approach, therefore, is that the model is developed and estimated in a way that ensures that the estimated model is consistent with, and is based on, a theoretically-coherent view of the long-run properties of the macroeconomy. Furthermore, this is accomplished without compromising empirical adequacy as an important criterion by which models must be judged. The transparency of the model's long-run properties will also be important for impulse response analysis and forecasting, particularly over the medium term.

Despite its advantages, the cointegrating VAR model is still highly restrictive and, given the available time-series data, it can deal with at most 8–10 variables simultaneously. This clearly precludes addressing many important issues, if we were to confine our analysis to a single cointegrating VAR model. Macroeconometric models are used for many different purposes by government, academic and corporate institutions, and no one model will be appropriate for all of these uses (see Whitley, 1997). However, traditional macroeconometric models tend to become large often in response to demands for more disaggregated analysis, and for addressing a wider range of policy questions. For example, a central bank may require a detailed model of the monetary sector; corporate institutions might require forecasts and analysis disaggregated by the main industrial sectors (energy, construction, agriculture, transportation and so on); and government agencies might be required to investigate the effects of a given policy on particular interest groups and/or markets. Our approach to meeting these model-specific requirements is through the development of appropriate satellite models. These are constructed using similar econometric techniques to those employed in the estimation of the core model, and are then linked up to the core model, with the core variables (and the associated error correction terms from the core model) influencing sectoral developments, but not vice versa (see Pesaran and Smith, 1997). In this chapter, we are only concerned with the core model of the macroeconomy, which can be dealt with independently of the satellites under the assumption that there are no feedbacks from the variables in the satellites into the core model. This assumption could be tested in principle. However, given the limited length of the time series available, and in the interest of transparency of the model's long-run properties and their theoretical coherency, we do not propose that such a test should be carried out. Insisting on two-way feedbacks between the core and the satellites would result in models that are too large for the application of the econometric techniques favoured here, and takes us back to the difficulties faced by the large-scale SEMs. In our approach, it is made explicit that the variables of the core macroeconomic model can be decoupled from any potential satellite to allow full information maximum likelihood estimation of the model under fairly general short-run dynamics, but restricted (to the extent supported by the data) to ensure cohesion with a long-run structural view of the macroeconomy.

Comparison with unrestricted and structural VAR modelling

One of the primary advantages of the structural cointegrating VAR approach to macroeconomic modelling is that it provides an explicit link between the estimated model residuals and the structural shocks of the underlying economic model. This explicit link indicates very clearly the restrictions that are required for identification of the effects of specific innovations to the model. In general, it is unlikely that such restrictions are available, and it is for this reason that a more general method of analysing impulse responses is required; i.e., one which does not rely on the use of identifying restrictions. The generalised impulse response (GIR) analysis, introduced in Koop *et al.* (1996) and developed in Pesaran and Shin (1998), provides such a method. The GIR analysis describes the effects of a shock to an equation in the model on all of the variables in the system without giving an economic interpretation to the shock. So long as the mapping between the structural shocks and the shocks to the equations of the model remains constant, the analysis of the shocks to the estimated equations provides insights into the response of the macroeconomic model to the underlying structural shocks, taking into account the contemporaneous effects that such shocks might have on the different variables in the model. While this analysis cannot provide an understanding of the response of the macroeconomy to specified structural shocks, therefore, it does provide a meaningful characterisation of the dynamic responses of the macroeconomy to 'realistic' shocks (meaning shocks of the type that are typically observed).

Comparison with DSGE modelling

In DSGE modelling, the derivation of the long-run, steady-state relations of the macro model starts with the inter-temporal optimisation problems faced by households and firms and then solves for the long-run relations using the Euler first-order conditions and the stock-flow constraints. Given the invariably non-linear nature of the Euler equations and the linear forms of the constraints, the resultant relations of the model economy are generally highly non-linear and are usually approximated by log-linear relations (the real business cycle literature follows this methodology). The long-run relations are then obtained by ignoring expectational errors and assuming that the model economy is stationary and ergodic in certain variables, such as growth rates, capital per effective worker and asset–income ratios. The structural cointegrating VAR approach, on the other hand, works directly with the arbitrage conditions which provide inter-temporal links between prices and asset returns in the economy as a whole. The arbitrage conditions, however, must be appropriately modified to allow for the risks associated with market uncertainties.

Clearly, the above two approaches are closely related and yield similar results as far as the long-run relations are concerned. The main difference between the two approaches lies in their treatment of short-run dynamics. The strength of the intertemporal optimisation approach lies in the explicit identification of macroeconomic disturbances as shocks to tastes and technology, rendered possible by the explicit statement on the form of the short-run dynamics. This is achieved, however, at the expense of often strong assumptions concerning the form of the underlying utility and cost functions, expectations formation, and the process of technological change. In contrast, the cointegrating VAR approach advanced here is silent on short-run dynamics, but is in line with the DSGE model as far as the long-run relations are concerned.

4. A core macroeconometric model of the UK economy

In this section, we illustrate the structural cointegrating VAR approach to macroeconometric modelling in the context of a small quarterly 'core' macroeconometric model of the UK, estimated over the period 1965Q1–95Q4, described in detail in Garratt *et al.* (1998, 1999a). The model is based on five long-run equilibrium relations derived from production, trade, arbitrage (in goods and capital markets), solvency and portfolio balance conditions. The model contains five domestic variables, whose developments are widely regarded as essential to a basic understanding of the behaviour of the UK macroeconomy; namely, output, the domestic price level, the nominal interest rate, the exchange rate and real money balances. It also contains four foreign variables; namely, foreign output, the foreign nominal interest rate, the foreign price level and oil prices. To simplify the analysis, and to avoid working with possibly I(2) price levels, the model is constructed in terms of domestic and foreign price variables measured relative to oil prices (in logs). As a result, there are only eight variables in the core model. The five long-run relationships are then embodied in a cointegrating VAR model with the relative foreign price variable treated as a weakly exogenous I(1) variable (see below for an elaboration). The order of the VAR model is chosen using familiar model selection criteria, otherwise its short-run dynamics are left unrestricted. In this way, we are able to capture the complicated dynamic relationships that exist between the domestic and foreign variables while at the same time maintaining a transparent and theoretically coherent long-run foundation.

4.1 The core macroeconomic model

The five long-run equilibrium relationships are given by:

Table 5.1 *List of variables and their descriptions in the core model*

y_t : natural logarithm of the UK real per capita GDP at market prices (1990 = 100).

p_t : natural logarithm of the UK Producer Price Index (1990 = 100).

r_t : is computed as $r_t = 0.25\ln(1 + R_t/100)$, where R_t is the 90-day Treasury Bill average discount rate per annum.

h_t : natural logarithm of UK real per capita M0 money stock (1990 = 100).

e_t : natural logarithm of the nominal sterling effective exchange rate (1990 = 100).

y_t^* : natural logarithm of the foreign (OECD) real per capita GDP at market prices (1990 = 100).

p_t^* : natural logarithm of the foreign price index (1990 = 100). Where the index is an import weighted average of 42 countries' price indices (where the countries are the OECD, oil producing and a number of other countries with relatively large values of imports and exports with the UK).

r_t^* : is computed as $r_t^* = 0.25\ln(1 + R_t^*/100)$, where R_t^* is the weighted average of 90-day interest rates per annum in the United States, Germany, Japan and France.

p_t^o : natural logarithm of oil prices, measured as the average price of crude oil.

t : time trend, taking the values 1, 2, 3, ..., in 1965Q1, 1965Q2, 1965Q3, ..., respectively.

Notes: For the data sources and a detailed description of the construction of foreign prices and interest rates see the Data Appendix in Garratt *et al.* (1999a).

$$(p_t - p_t^o) - (p_t^* - p_t^o) - e_t = a_{10} + a_{11}t + \beta_{18}(p_t^* - p_t^o) + \varepsilon_{1,t+1}, \qquad (5.1)$$

$$r_t - r_t^* = a_{20} + \varepsilon_{2,t+1}, \qquad (5.2)$$

$$y_t - y_t^* = a_{30} + \varepsilon_{3,t+1}, \qquad (5.3)$$

$$(p_t - p_t^o) - (p_t^* - p_t^o) - e_t = a_{40} + a_{41}t + \beta_{43}r_t + \beta_{45}y_t$$
$$+ \beta_{48}(p_t^* - p_t^o) + \varepsilon_{4,t+1}, \qquad (5.4)$$

$$h_t - y_t = a_{50} + a_{51}t + \beta_{53}r_t + \beta_{55}y_t + \varepsilon_{5,t+1}, \qquad (5.5)$$

where p_t is the logarithm of domestic prices, p_t^* is the logarithm of foreign prices, p_t^o, the logarithm of oil prices, e_t is the logarithm of nominal effective exchange (defined as the domestic price of a unit of foreign currency, so that an increase represents a depreciation of the home currency), y_t is the logarithm of real per capita domestic output, y_t^* is the logarithm of real per capita foreign output, r_t is the domestic nominal interest rate variable, r_t^* is the foreign nominal interest rate variable, h_t is the logarithm of the real per capita money stock, and the $\varepsilon_{i,t+1}$, $i = 1, 2, ..., 5$, are stationary reduced form errors (see table 5.1 for more details).

A complete description of the framework for long-run macromodelling, describing the economic theory that underlies the relationships in (5.1)–(5.5), is provided in Garratt *et al.* (1998b). In brief, we note here that the first relationship relates to a (modified) purchasing power parity (PPP) relationship, based on international goods market arbitrage, but modified to take into account the potential effects of oil prices on the measured relationship given the different baskets of commodities used to measure prices in different countries; equation (5.2) sets out the interest rate parity (IRP) relationship and is based on arbitrage between domestic and foreign bonds; (5.3) relates to an 'output gap' (OG) equation derived from a stochastic version of the Solow growth model in which there is common technological progress in production at home and abroad;[22] the fourth and fifth equations (5.4) and (5.5) relate to a trade balance (TB) and a real money balance (RMB) relationship, respectively, both of which are based on the condition that the economy must remain solvent in the long run. The relationships in (5.4) and (5.5) are obtained by modelling the equilibrium portfolio balance of private sector assets, which it is assumed can be held in the form of high-powered money, domestic bonds or foreign bonds, and augmenting the solvency condition with assumptions on the determinants of the demand for money and for foreign assets.

The five long-run relations of the core model, (5.1)–(5.5), can be written compactly as

$$\varepsilon_t = \beta' z_{t-1} - (a_0 - a_1) - a_1 t, \tag{5.6}$$

where

$$z_t = (p_t - p_t^o, e_t, r_t, r_t^*, y_t, y_t^*, h_t - y_t, p_t^* - p_t^o)',$$
$$a_0 = (a_{10}, a_{20}, a_{30}, a_{40}, a_{50})', a_1 = (a_{11}, 0, 0, a_{41}, a_{51}),$$
$$\varepsilon_t = (\varepsilon_{1t}, \varepsilon_{2t}, \varepsilon_{3t}, \varepsilon_{4t}, \varepsilon_{5t})',$$

and

$$\beta' = \begin{pmatrix} 1 & -1 & 0 & 0 & 0 & 0 & 0 & -(1+\beta_{18}) \\ 0 & 0 & 1 & -1 & 0 & 0 & 0 & 0 \\ 0 & 0 & 0 & 0 & 1 & -1 & 0 & 0 \\ 1 & -1 & -\beta_{43} & 0 & -\beta_{45} & 0 & 0 & -(1+\beta_{48}) \\ 0 & 0 & -\beta_{53} & 0 & -\beta_{55} & 0 & 1 & 0 \end{pmatrix}. \tag{5.7}$$

Our modelling strategy involves partitioning $z_t = (y'_t, p^*_t - p^o_t)'$, where $y_t = (p_t - p^o_t, e_t, r_t, r^*_t, y_t, y^*_t, h_t - y_t)'$ is treated as a vector of endogenous $I(1)$ variables, and $p^*_t - p^o_t$ as a weakly exogenous $I(1)$ variable, in the sense that changes in $p^*_t - p^o_t$ have a direct influence on y_t, but $p^*_t - p^o_t$ is not affected by error correction terms which measure the extent of disequilibria in the UK economy.[23] We then embody ε_t in an otherwise unrestricted $VAR(s-1)$ in Δy_t:

$$\Delta y_t = -\alpha \varepsilon_t + \sum_{i=1}^{s-1} \Gamma_i \Delta z_{t-i} + \psi \Delta (p^*_t - p^o_t) + u_t, \qquad (5.8)$$

where u_t is a 7 x 1 vector of serially uncorrelated shocks, α is a 7 x 5 matrix of error-correction coefficients, $\{\Gamma_i, i = 1, 2, \ldots, s-1\}$ are 7 x 8 matrices of short-run coefficients, and ψ is a 7 x 1 vector representing the impact effects of changes in the relative foreign price variable on Δy_t. Using equation (5.6) we have

$$\Delta y_t = \alpha(a_0 - a_1) + \alpha a_1 t - \alpha \xi_t + \sum_{i=1}^{s-1} \Gamma_i \Delta z_{t-i} + \psi \Delta (p^*_t - p^o_t) + u_t, \qquad (5.9)$$

where $\xi_t = \beta' z_{t-i}$ are the error correction terms. By construction, the above specification embodies the economic theory's long-run predictions, in contrast to the more usual approach where the starting point is an unrestricted VAR model, with some vague priors about the nature of the long-run relations.

Estimation of the parameters of the core model, (5.9), can be carried out using the long-run structural modelling approach described in Pesaran and Shin (1999) and Pesaran et al. (1999). Following this approach, having selected the order of the underlying VAR model (using model selection criteria such as the Akaike information criterion (AIC) or the Schwartz Bayesian criterion (SBC)), we first test for the number of cointegrating relations among the eight variables in z_t. When performing this task, and in all the subsequent empirical analysis, we work in the context of a VAR model with no restrictions on the intercept terms, $\alpha(a_0 - a_1)$, but with the trend coefficients restricted so that $\alpha a_1 = \Pi \gamma$, where $\Pi = \alpha \beta'$ and γ is an 8 x 1 vector of unknown coefficients. These restrictions ensure that the solution of the model in levels of z_t will not contain quadratic trends. We then compute maximum likelihood (ML) estimates of the model's parameters subject to exact and over-identifying restrictions on the long-run coefficients.[24] Assuming that there is empirical support for the existence of five long-run relationships, as suggested by theory, exact identification in our model requires five restrictions on each of the five cointegrating vectors (each row of β), or a total of twenty-five restrictions on β. These

Table 5.2 *Cointegration rank statistics for the core UK model – 1965Q1–95Q4* $(p_t - p_t^o, e_t, r_t, r_t^*, y_t, y_t^*, h_t - y_t, p_t^* - p_t^o)$

H_0	H_1	Trace			Max		
		Statistic	95% cv	90% cv	Statistic	95% cv	90% cv
$r = 0$	$r = 1$	231.74	163.01	157.02	61.73	52.62	49.70
$r \leq 1$	$r = 2$	170.02	128.79	123.33	43.51	46.97	44.01
$r \leq 2$	$r = 3$	126.50	97.83	93.13	40.62	40.89	37.92
$r \leq 3$	$r = 4$	85.88	72.10	68.04	38.20	34.70	32.12
$r \leq 4$	$r = 5$	47.69	49.36	46.00	26.64	28.72	26.10
$r \leq 5$	$r = 6$	21.05	30.77	27.96	13.19	22.16	19.79
$r \leq 6$	$r = 7$	7.87	15.44	13.31	7.87	15.44	13.31

Notes: The underlying VAR model is of order 2 and contains unrestricted intercepts and restricted trend coefficients, with $p_t^* - p_t^o$ treated as exogenous $I(1)$ variable. The statistics are computed using 124 observations for the period 1965Q1–95Q4. 'Trace' and 'Max' represent Johansen's log-likelihood-based trace and maximum eigenvalue statistics, respectively, and 'cv' stands for critical value of the tests, which are obtained from Pesaran *et al.* (1999).

represent only a subset of the restrictions suggested by economic theory as characterised in (5.7), however. Estimation of the model subject to all the (exact- and over-identifying) restrictions given in (5.7) enables a test of the validity of the over-identifying restrictions, and hence of the economic theory, to be carried out.

This entire exercise was conducted using UK data over the period 1965Q1–95Q4, and this is described in detail in Garratt *et al.* (1999a). Here, we provide a brief summary. Having first confirmed that a VAR(2) model is appropriate, the cointegration tests were carried out. The results of these tests are presented in table 5.2. These provide relatively good evidence to support the prediction of the theory that there are five cointegrating relationships among the eight variables. The model was then estimated, first subject to twenty-five restrictions which exactly identify the system, and then subject to a further fourteen over-identifying restrictions as suggested by the economic theory and contained in (5.7). The test of the over-identifying restriction produced a statistic of 39.78. The statistic is asymptotically distributed as a chi-squared variate with fourteen degrees of freedom, although the asymptotic result is unreliable in cases like this one, where the number of parameters of the underlying VAR model, and the number of restrictions, is large relative to the sample of data available. The extent of the small sample bias of the chi-squared tests

Table 5.3 *Error correction specification for the core UK model – 1965Q1–95Q4*

Equation	$\Delta(p_t - p_t^o)$	Δe_t	Δr_t	Δr_t^*	Δy_t	Δy_t^*	$\Delta(h_t - y_t)$
$\hat{\varepsilon}_{1,t}$	0.007	−0.019	−0.030[a]	−0.008[a]	0.029	0.017	−0.078[b]
	(0.020)	(0.085)	(0.006)	(0.003)	(0.026)	(0.012)	(0.041)
$\hat{\varepsilon}_{2,t}$	−0.631[a]	0.355	−0.019	0.067[b]	0.889[a]	0.616[a]	−0.236
	(0.242)	(1.050)	(0.080)	(0.038)	(0.315)	(0.155)	(0.507)
$\hat{\varepsilon}_{3,t}$	0.135[a]	−0.241	−0.017	−0.006	−0.134[a]	−0.016	0.096
	(0.034)	(0.145)	(0.011)	(0.005)	(0.044)	(0.021)	(0.070)
$\hat{\varepsilon}_{4,t}$	−0.063[a]	0.132	0.041[a]	0.015[a]	−0.043	−0.016	0.049
	(0.027)	(0.116)	(0.009)	(0.004)	(0.034)	(0.017)	(0.056)
$\hat{\varepsilon}_{5,t}$	0.009	0.001	0.006	0.005[a]	−0.081[a]	−0.045[a]	0.001
	(0.015)	(0.063)	(0.005)	(0.002)	(0.019)	(0.009)	(0.031)
$\Delta(p_{t-1} - p_{t-1}^o)$	0.405[a]	0.522	0.003	−0.007	0.015	0.051	−0.480[a]
	(0.090)	(0.391)	(0.030)	(0.014)	(0.118)	(0.058)	(0.189)
Δe_{t-1}	−0.013	0.268[a]	0.010	0.006	−0.004	−0.004	0.027
	(0.027)	(0.119)	(0.009)	(0.004)	(0.036)	(0.018)	(0.057)
Δr_{t-1}	0.123	−1.140	0.154	−0.083[b]	0.563	0.294	−0.534
	(0.306)	(1.320)	(0.101)	(0.048)	(0.398)	(0.195)	(0.639)
Δr_{t-1}^*	−0.405	2.300	0.312	0.297[a]	0.963	0.781[b]	−1.810
	(0.624)	(2.700)	(0.207)	(0.098)	(0.813)	(0.399)	(1.310)
Δy_{t-1}	0.095	−0.007	−0.029	−0.001	−0.063	−0.012	−0.190
	(0.094)	(0.408)	(0.031)	(0.015)	(0.123)	(0.060)	(0.198)
Δy_{t-1}^*	−0.162	−0.335	−0.022	0.076[a]	0.014	0.111	0.494
	(0.160)	(0.693)	(0.053)	(0.025)	(0.208)	(0.102)	(0.335)
$\Delta(h_{t-1} - y_{t-1})$	0.106[a]	0.264	0.012	0.010	0.082	−0.035	−0.187
	(0.053)	(0.231)	(0.018)	(0.008)	(0.070)	(0.034)	(0.112)
$\Delta(p_t^* - p_t^o)$	1.030[a]	0.019	−0.002	−0.001[b]	0.011[b]	0.003	−0.021[a]
	(0.004)	(0.019)	(0.001)	(0.0007)	(0.006)	(0.003)	(0.009)
$\Delta(p_{t-1}^* - p_{t-1}^o)$	−0.418[a]	−0.528	−0.001	0.006	−0.026	−0.057	0.521[a]
	(0.093)	(0.400)	(0.030)	(0.015)	(0.121)	(0.059)	(0.194)
$\overline{R}^2$	0.778[c]	0.030	0.225	0.363	0.212	0.374	0.142
$\hat{\sigma}$	0.007	0.032	0.002	0.001	0.010	0.005	0.015
$\chi_{SC}^2[4]$	1.25	3.47	5.08	10.6[a]	5.86	2.45	5.54
$\chi_{FF}^2[1]$	0.13	0.26	0.87	5.14[a]	0.07	0.12	0.09
$\chi_N^2[2]$	14.2[a]	20.7[a]	16.9[a]	18.5[a]	108.6[a]	10.0[a]	20.0[a]
$\chi_H^2[1]$	0.51	0.79	5.03[a]	9.82[a]	0.65	2.36	0.88

Notes: The five error correction terms are given by

$$\hat{\varepsilon}_{1,t+1} = p_t - p_t^* - e_t - 0.0856(p_t^o - p_t^*) - 4.6386,$$

$$\hat{\varepsilon}_{2,t+1} = r_t - r_t^* - 0.0050 \underset{(0.0336)}{,} \hat{\varepsilon}_{3,t+1} = y_t - y_t^* - 4.6091,$$

$$\hat{\varepsilon}_{4,t+1} = p_t - p_t^* - e_t - 11.5501 r_t + 1.5244 y_t - 0.0071t - 10.5992,$$

$$\hat{\varepsilon}_{5,t+1} = h_t - y_t + 20.3253 \underset{(4.3501)}{r_t} + 0.0102 \underset{(0.4541)}{t} + 0.5295 \underset{(0.0021)}{.}$$
$$\underset{(5.0024)}{} \underset{(0.0005)}{}$$

Standard errors are given in parenthesis. (a) indicates significance at the 5% level. (b) indicates significance at the 10% level. (c) refers to the Δp_t equation. The diagnostics are chi-squared statistics for serial correlation (SC), functional form (FF), normality (N) and heteroscedasticity (H).

in (small) cointegrating VAR models is illustrated, for example, by Gredenhoff and Jacobson (1998) who suggest the use of bootstrapped critical values. In our application the bootstrapped critical values were 54.21 and 59.26 at the 10 and the 5 per cent significance levels, respectively, so that there is no evidence with which to reject the validity of the theory restrictions incorporated in the core model. The estimated long-run relationships, and the associated error correction equations are summarised in table 5.3.

4.2 Impulse responses and forecasting

Having estimated our structural cointegrating VAR model, we are now in a position to use the model in the examination of the economy's short-run dynamic properties. To illustrate how we might use the model in this way, in what follows, we illustrate three (complementary) ways in which to characterise the model's properties; further details of the methods are provided in Garratt et al. (1999a). The first two make use of 'persistence profiles' and 'generalised impulse responses' to examine the effect of system wide shocks in causing deviations from the long-run equilibrium relations and the time profile of the model variables when subject to shocks to the core model equations, respectively. The third approach to characterising the model's properties involves out-of-sample forecasting, describing some probability forecasts, with which the uncertainties surrounding forecasts from a macroeconomic model can be conveyed in a straightforward manner.

In order to compute these measures, we first need to supplement the core model with equations for the exogenous variables. We therefore assume that both oil price changes and foreign price relative to the oil price changes are strictly exogenous. After some experimentation, we arrived at the following specification for Δp_t^o estimated over the period 1965Q1–95Q4:

$$\Delta p_t^o = 0.01678 + \hat{u}_t^o,$$
$$\underset{(0.0150)}{}$$
$$\hat{\sigma}_{u^o} = 0.1676, \chi_{SC}^2[4] = 1.58, \chi_N^2[2] = 6361.9.$$

To model $\Delta(p_t^* - p_t^o)$ over the same period, we estimated autoregressive distributive lag models, ARDL(s_1, s_2), in $\Delta(p_t^* - p_t^o)$ and Δp_t^o for all orders $s_1 \leq 4$ and $s_2 \leq 4$, and then selected s_1 and s_2 using the Akaike information criteria. The result was the following ARDL(2,2) specification:[25]

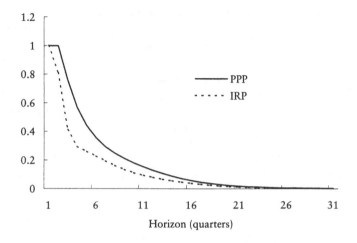

Figure 5.1 *Persistence profiles of the modified purchasing power parity (PPP) and interest parity relations (IRP) in the core model*

$$\Delta(p_t^* - p_t^o) = \underset{(0.0007)}{0.0022} + \underset{(0.0896)}{0.5848}\Delta(p_{t-1}^* - p_{t-1}^o) + \underset{(0.0853)}{0.2155}\Delta(p_{t-2}^* - p_{t-2}^o)$$
$$- \underset{(0.0023)}{0.9603}\Delta p_t^o + \underset{(0.0861)}{0.5737}\Delta p_{t-1}^o + \underset{(0.0827)}{0.2107}\Delta p_{t-2}^o + \hat{u}_t^*,$$

$$\overline{R}^2_{\Delta p^*} = 0.856, \hat{\sigma}_{u^*} = 0.0043, \chi^2_{SC}[4] = 3.86, \chi^2_{FF}[1] = 0.32,$$
$$\chi^2_N[2] = 386.4, \chi^2_H[1] = 0.042.$$

Persistence profiles

Persistence profiles (PP) provide information on the speed with which deviations from the long-run relations in the model, due to system-wide shocks, are eliminated. The profiles are constructed so that they take the value of unity on the impact of the shock and tend to zero as the time horizon tends to infinity, assuming that the long-run relationship in question is in fact cointegrating.

Figure 5.1 plots the PP of two of the five long-run relations of the model; namely, the (modified) *PPP* and *IRP* relations. In the case of the modified *PPP*, the profile shows a steady decline towards its equilibrium value, with

approximately 80 per cent of the adjustment taking place within seven
quarters, and the full adjustment taking about five years to complete.[26]
The fact that the persistence profile of the modified *PPP* relation tends to
zero is in line with our earlier conclusion (based on formal statistical tests)
that the modified *PPP* relationship is in fact cointegrating. The PP profile
of the *IRP* relationship shows a more rapid rate of adjustment towards
its long-run value, with approximately 80 per cent of the adjustment having been completed within three quarters and near full adjustment
occurring within three to four years. These results are consistent with those
found in the literature. Notice, however, that the speed of convergence of
the modified *PPP* towards its equilibrium is much faster than the ones reported in the literature for the *PPP* (unmodified). The existing results put
half life of deviations from *PPP* at about four years for the major industrialised countries (see, for example, Johansen and Juselius,1992, Pesaran
and Shin, 1996, or Rogoff, 1996), while for the modified *PPP* this figure
is much shorter.

Generalised impulse response: shocking the foreign output equation

The Generalised Impulse Response (GIR) functions describe the time profile of the effect of a unit shock to a *particular equation* on all the model's
endogenous variables. The dynamics which result from the shock will embody the contemporaneous interactions of all the endogenous variables
of the system, as captured by the elements of the estimated covariance matrix of the shocks to the endogenous variables, u_t . There are many issues
that could be analysed through the GIR analysis and here we focus on the
effects of shocks to the foreign output equation. We assume that the shock
(which can also be viewed as an intercept shift) is sufficiently small so that
it does not materially alter the parameters of the underlying VAR model.

In figures 5.2–5.4, we report the GIRs for a unit shock to the foreign
output equation, where the size of the shock is scaled so as to ensure that
foreign output rises by one standard error on impact; this corresponds to
a 1.9 per cent increase in foreign output per annum. Note that because of
the strict exogeneity of oil and foreign price changes, the particular specification of these two variables does not affect the GIRs.

Given the strong positive correlation that exists between foreign and
domestic output innovations, the effect of the foreign output shock is to
cause domestic output to increase by approximately 1.38 per cent (see figure 5.2).[27] These effects continue to persist over the subsequent quarters.
In the long run, the effect of a unit shock to the foreign output equation
is to increase both domestic and foreign output by 0.8 per cent above their

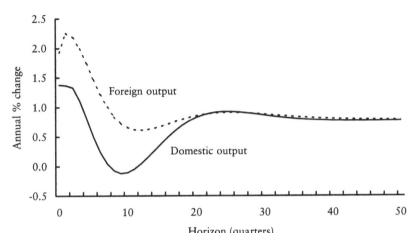

Figure 5.2 *Generalised impulse responses of domestic output and foreign output to a one SE shock to the* y_t^* *equation in the core model*

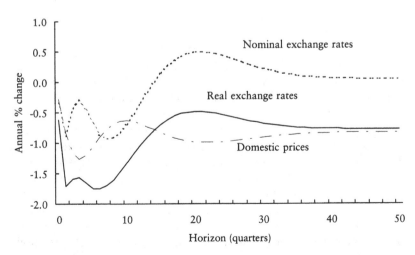

Figure 5.3 *Generalised impulse responses of domestic prices, real and nominal exchange rates to a one SE shock to the* y_t^* *equation in the core model*

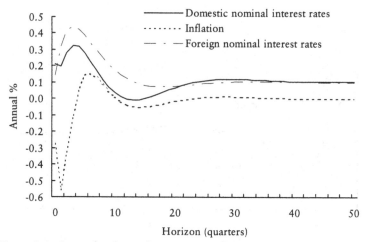

Figure 5.4 *Generalised impulse responses of domestic and foreign nominal interest rates and inflation to a one SE shock to the* y_t^* *equation in the core model*

baseline values, as predicted by equation (5.3). However, it is important to note that the gap between domestic and foreign output growth persists even after twenty quarters, with the foreign output growth exceeding domestic output growth often by as much as 1 per cent per annum.

The GIRs for the foreign output shock on the domestic price level, the nominal and the real exchange rates are displayed in figure 5.3. The shock initially reduces domestic prices by 0.28 per cent, appreciates the nominal exchange rate on impact by 0.62 per cent, and therefore causes a small appreciation of the real exchange rate of 0.34 per cent.

The effects of the shock on domestic inflation, domestic interest rate and foreign interest rates are displayed in figure 5.4. The initial response to the shock is to increase domestic and foreign interest rates by 21 and 14 basis points, respectively. Initially, the foreign interest rate rises above the domestic interest rate, but eventually this gap disappears, as predicted by the long-run interest parity relation embodied in the core model.

The initial effect of the foreign output shock on domestic inflation is to decrease the rate of inflation by 0.28 per cent, followed by a further fall over the next quarter. The reduction in inflation is reversed from this point onwards, with the inflation rate returning to its baseline value after about twelve quarters. In the long run, the effect of the foreign output shock on the domestic inflation rate is zero, so that the effects are purely temporary.

Probability forecasts

Recently, there have been a number of welcome developments in macroeconomic forecasting, the aim of which is to convey to the public the potentially large degree of uncertainty that is associated with central or point forecasts. For example, in the area of policymaking the Bank of England now produces a range of outcomes around its central forecasts for future inflation and output growth in its quarterly *Inflation Reports* (see Britton *et al.*, 1998). In academia, Fair (1993) was one of the first to compute probability forecasts, using a macroeconometric model of the US economy. The NIESR, using their large-scale SEM, now publish probability statements alongside their central forecasts (their methods are described in Blake, 1996, and Poulizac *et al.*, 1996), and in the financial sector, J.P. Morgan presents 'event risk indicators' in its analysis of foreign exchange markets.

In this section, we briefly report the probability forecasting exercise performed using our core UK model.[28] A probability forecast (PF) is a statement of the likelihood of a specified event taking place and can be estimated given a model specification and its underlying error assumptions. The event can be defined with respect to the values of a single variable or set of variables, measured at a particular point in time, over a sequence of time periods, or over particular time intervals in the future. Here we provide probability estimates of two separate events; namely, the probability of 4-quarter moving average inflation falling below 2.5 per cent per annum (the current inflation target in the UK) and the probability of 4-quarter moving average output growth falling below 0 per cent per annum over a number of forecast horizons.[29]

In this illustrative exercise, we use an updated version of the model presented in section 4.1, where the estimation period is extended to cover 1965Q1–98Q2.[30] The forecasts are then computed over the period 1998Q3–2004Q2, conditional on the oil price index being at their 1998Q2 level, and using an updated version of the relative foreign price equation given above to forecast the foreign price variable. In this application, we assume the form of the model is given, but allow for two sources of forecast uncertainties: future uncertainties due to unknown values of the future shocks and the uncertainties surrounding the model's parameter values. In order to take account of the parameter uncertainty on forecasts we undertake a bootstrap exercise which makes use of a non-parametric resampling technique. Accordingly, we estimate the short-run parameters of the model for each bootstrap sample. Then for each of these bootstraps, we repeatedly simulate the future values of z_t, for t = 1998Q3, 1998Q4,

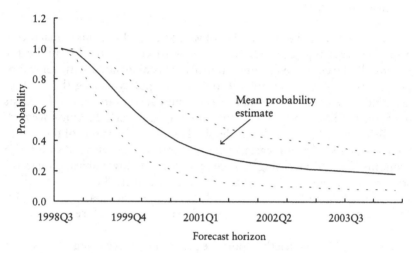

Figure 5.5 *Mean probability estimate and 90 per cent confidence intervals of 4-quarter average inflation (based on producer prices) falling below 2.5 per cent*

..., 2004Q2, by resampling from the past residuals of the estimated model. The probabilities plotted in figures 5.5 and 5.6 are the averages computed using all the bootstrap samples, and their associated 90 per cent confidence intervals. The computational details can be found in Garratt *et al.* (1999b).[31]

Inflation Figure 5.5 provides the estimated probabilities of the 4-quarter moving average of producer price inflation, $\pi_{t+h} = (p_{t+h} - p_{t+h-4})\,/\,4$, falling below 2.5 per cent over the horizon $t = 1998\text{Q}3, 1998\text{Q}4, ..., 2004\text{Q}2$. This figure shows the empirical mean of the bootstrapped probability forecasts and the associated 90 per cent confidence intervals. The results suggest the probability of the producer price inflation falling below the 2.5 per cent threshold value is very high during the second and the third quarters of 1998, but it starts to fall thereafter. The initial high probability of the producer price inflation hitting its target largely reflects the recent history. However, the probability of π_{t+h} falling below 2.5 per cent decreases as the forecast horizon is extended, reaching around 0.45 by the year 2000. In the long run, the probability that inflation is less than 2.5 per cent falls to 0.19. The uncertainty around this estimate is relatively large, covering the range 0.08 to 0.31.[32] Only at short forecast horizons are these 90 per cent confidence bands reasonably tight.

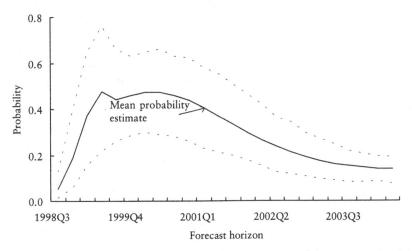

Figure 5.6 *Mean probability estimate and 90 per cent confidence intervals of 4-quarter average output growth falling below 0 per cent*

Output growth Focusing on 4-quarter moving average aggregate output growth, $g_{t+h} = (y^a_{t+h} - y^a_{t+h-4})/4$, where y^a_t is aggregate real output rather than per capita real output, we estimated the probability of output growth falling below 0 per cent over the forecast horizons $t = 1998Q3$, 1998Q4, ..., 2004Q2. These estimates together with their associated 90 per cent confidence bounds are displayed in figure 5.6. The probability that g_{t+h} falls below zero in 1998Q3 is 0.05, but this probability is estimated to rise to a peak of 0.48 by 1999Q2, and remains relatively high, at around 0.47 over the subsequent year, 1999Q3–2000Q2. It then gradually starts to fall to a long-run value of 0.14. The uncertainty associated with these probabilities again is relatively large, particularly over the short- to medium-term forecast horizons, but is reduced at the longer forecast horizon as output growth converges to its steady state value.

5. Concluding comments

In this chapter we discuss the structural cointegrating VAR approach to macroeconometric modelling and compare it with a number of alternative modelling approaches. We then illustrate the structural cointegrating VAR approach in the context of a model of the UK economy based on data covering the period 1965Q1–95Q4. In this exercise, the long-run relationships, derived from macroeconomic theory, are based on production, trade, arbitrage, solvency and portfolio balance conditions. This application, described in more detail in Garratt *et al.* (1998), constitutes the first attempt to make use of the structural cointegrating VAR approach in the context of a relatively comprehensive core macro model of a small open economy. This chapter also illustrates how a model of this type can be used for impulse response analysis and probability forecasting.

In practice, it is fully recognised that a model, or indeed a modelling approach, can only be judged in terms of its relevance to the question at hand. This has been a recurring theme in the literature on model comparison in economics (see, for example, Pesaran and Smith, 1985, 1995). A particular model or modelling approach might be more or less relevant for a given purpose, but it seems unlikely that one single model could be found to suit all purposes. The cointegrating VAR modelling approach advanced here should be viewed as one among many possible approaches that could be fruitfully employed. But it is hoped that the core model of the UK economy which is described here will motivate others to explore this approach to macroeconomic modelling (examining alternative economic frameworks, or through the development of satellite models for use with the core model, for example). In this way, its advantages and disadvantages will be more fully understood and its contribution to the already rich field of macroeconometric modelling will be more clearly defined.

Notes

1   An earlier version of this chapter was presented at the ESRC conference on Macro Modelling, NIESR, London, January 1998. We are grateful to Paul Fisher, Ron Smith, Adrian Pagan, Ken Wallis, and particularly Michael Binder for helpful comments. Financial support from the ESRC (grant no. L116251016) and from the Isaac Newton Trust of Trinity College Cambridge is gratefully acknowledged.

2   Sims' critique also extends to the identification of rational expectations models.

3   See, for example, Cooley and LeRoy (1985).

4   This approach has been used, for example, by Blanchard and Quah (1989).

5   See section 2.3 below for details.

6   See, for example, Kim and Pagan (1995) and Christiano *et al.* (1998).

7   Bodkin *et al.* (1991) provide a comprehensive survey of the history of macroeconometric model building. The evolution and the development of macroeconometric modelling at the Federal Reserve Board is reviewed by Brayton *et al.* (1997). For the UK these developments have been documented in a series of volumes produced by the ESRC Macroeconomic Modelling Bureau (see, for ex-

ample, Wallis *et al.*, 1987). Further reviews of the modelling in the UK and elsewhere can be found in Smith (1994), Wallis (1995) and Hall (1995).

8 A detailed discussion of these developments in the case of the UK practice can be found in Hall (1995). Similar arguments have also been advanced by Brayton *et al.* (1997) in the case of the US experience.

9 Brayton *et al.* (1997) also make similar observations with respect to the new FRB/US model which was officially adopted by the Federal Reserve Board in 1996.

10 See, for example, Whitley (1997).

11 For illustrations of this approach in the context of the analysis of the UK labour market, see, for example, Wallis *et al.* (1987), Turner (1991) and Wallis and Whitley (1987).

12 Other more effective methods for the analysis of the long-run properties of large macroeconometric models have been developed by Murphy (1992), Fisher *et al.* (1992), and Wren-Lewis *et al.* (1996).

13 The importance of the choice of terminal conditions in the context of the LBS, NIESR and the Liverpool models is illustrated in Fisher (1992).

14 Some of these difficulties concerning the choice of the terminal conditions have been addressed. See, for example, Minford *et al.* (1979) and, more recently, Fuhrer and Bleakley (1996) for a certainty equivalent solution method in the case of non-linear dynamic rational expectations models where the terminal conditions for the solution path are derived using the uniqueness and stability conditions of an associated linearised model.

15 Limiting attention to the fundamental Wold representation is not uncontentious: as shown in Hansen and Sargent (1991), for example, the MA representation that underlies the VAR model can be non-fundamental (in the sense that one or more of the roots of the MA process fall inside the unit circle) and at the same time be economically meaningful.

16 In this sense, it is a misnomer to refer to these models as *structural*.

17 Recall that since $m = 2$, one only needs one covariance restriction to identify the impulse responses.

18 For a more detailed critical evaluation of the structural VAR approach see Levtchenkova *et al.* (1998).

19 For a survey of recent developments in the literature on DSGE models see the contributions in the volume edited by Cooley (1995).

20 See, for example, Binder and Pesaran (1995), Kim and Pagan (1995) and Wickens (1995).

21 For a discussion of the relevant econometric issues involved in the analysis of cointegrating VARs see Johansen (1995), Pesaran *et al.* (1999), and Pesaran and Smith (1998).

22 Our use of the term 'output gap relationship' to describe (5.3) should not be confused with the more usual use of the term which relates more specifically to the difference between a country's real and potential output levels (although clearly the two uses of the term are related).

23 For details of the econometric formulation see Pesaran *et al.* (1999).

24 The computations were carried out using Microfit 4.0. See Pesaran and Pesaran

(1997).
25 The $\bar{R}^2$ for the $\Delta(p_t^* - p_t^0)$ equation is computed with respect to Δp_t^*. The diagnostics are chi-squared statistics for serial correlation (SC), functional form (FF), normality (N) and heteroscedasticity (H). See Pesaran and Pesaran (1997, pp. 349–52).
26 It is also possible to compute standard error bounds around the point estimates of the persistence profiles displayed in figure 5.1, but we found that their use does not materially alter our main conclusions. See Pesaran and Shin (1996) for further discussion.
27 All percentage changes quoted in this section are computed at annual rates.
28 The probability forecasts reported here were made in early August 1998 when a complete set of quarterly observations on output growth and inflation for the first quarter of 1998 became available.
29 The event of 4-quarter moving average output growth falling below 0 per cent per annum, is intended to represent a 'recession', although other definitions, such as quarterly output growth falling below 0 per cent in two successive quarters, have also been used.
30 The details of the analysis of the extended data set are reported in Garratt *et al.* (1999b).
31 In Garratt *et al.* (1999b), we consider a range of issues relating to forecasting the probability of an event. We also consider the various forms of uncertainty surrounding forecasts, including 'future uncertainty', 'parameter uncertainty' and 'model uncertainty', and discuss alternative ways of taking them into account.
32 It is worth noting that we could not reject the hypothesis that the difference between the producer and retail price inflation is stationary with a zero mean. Therefore, it is likely that the probability statements for producer price inflation will also apply to retail price inflation in the long run. However, persistent short-run deviations exist between the two inflation rates, and probability statements relating to the producer price inflation need not carry over to the retail price inflation in the short run.

References

Allen, C., Hall, S.G. and Nixon, J. (1994), 'The new London Business School model of the UK economy', Centre for Economic Forecasting Discussion Paper no. 18-94.
Ando, A. and Modigliani, F. (1969), 'Econometric evaluation of stabilisation policies', *American Economic Review*, 59, pp. 296–314.
Astley, M. and Garratt, A. (1996), 'Interpreting sterling exchange rate movements', *Bank of England Quarterly Bulletin*, 36, pp. 394–404.
Bernanke, B. (1986), *Alternative Explanations of the Money–Income Correlation*, Carnegie-Rochester Conference Series on Public Policy, 25, pp. 49–99.
Binder, M. and Pesaran, M.H. (1995), 'Multivariate rational expectations models

and macroeconometric modelling: a review and some new results', Chapter 3 in Pesaran, M.H. and Wickens, M. (eds), *Handbook of Applied Econometrics: Macroeconomics*, Oxford, Basil Blackwell.

Blake, A.P. (1996), 'Forecast error bounds by stochastic simulation', *National Institute Economic Review*, 156, pp. 72–9.

Blanchard, O.J. and Quah. D. (1989), 'The dynamic effects of aggregate demand and supply disturbances', *American Economic Review*, 79, pp. 655–73.

Blanchard, O.J. and Watson, M. (1986), 'Are all business cycles alike?' in Gordon, R.J. (ed.), *The American Business Cycle*, Chicago, University of Chicago Press, pp. 123–56.

Bodkin, R.G, Klein, L.R. and Marwah, K. (eds) (1991), *A History of Macroeconometric Model Building*, Aldershot, Edward Elgar.

Brayton, F., Levin, A., Tryon, R. and Williams, J.C. (1997), 'The evolution of macro models at the Federal Reserve Board' (http://www.bog.frb.fed.us/pubs/feds/1997).

Brayton, F. and Mauskopf, E. (1985), 'The Federal Reserve Board MPS quarterly econometric model of the US economy', *Economic Modelling*, 2, pp. 170–292.

Brayton, F. and Tinsley, P. (eds) (1996), *A Guide to FRB/US: A Macroeconomic Model of the United States*, Finance and Economics Discussion Series, 1996–42, Washington, Federal Reserve Board.

Britton, E., Fisher, P. and Whitley, J. (1998), 'The inflation report projections: understanding the fan chart', *Bank of England Quarterly Bulletin*, 38, 1, pp. 30–37.

Britton, A. and Westaway, P. (1998), 'On the equilibrium properties of macroeconomic models', in Begg, I. and Henry, B. (eds), *Applied Economics and Public Policy*, Cambridge, Cambridge University Press.

Champernowne, D.G. (1960), 'An experimental investigation of the robustness of certain procedures for estimating means and regressions coefficients', *Journal of the Royal Statistical Society*, Series A, 123, pp. 398–412.

Christiano, L.J. and Eichenbaum, M. (1992), 'Liquidity effects and the monetary transmission mechanism', *American Economic Review*, 82, pp. 346–53.

Christiano, L.J., Eichenbaum, M. and Evans, C.L. (1998), 'Modeling money?', NBER Working Paper no. 3916, 98/1.

Christiano, L.J., Eichenbaum, M. and Marshall, D. (1991), 'The permanent income hypothesis revisited', *Econometrica*, 59/2, pp. 397–423.

Clarida, R. and Gali, J. (1994), *Sources of Real Exchange Rate Fluctuations: How Important are Nominal Shocks?*, Carnegie-Rochester Series on Public Policy, 41, pp. 1–56.

Cogley, T. and Nason, J.M. (1995), 'Output dynamics in real business cycle models', *American Economic Review*, 85, pp. 492–511.

Cooley, T. F. (ed.) (1995), *Frontiers of Business Cycle Research*, Princeton, Princeton University Press.

Cooley, T.F., Greenwood, J. and Yorukoghu, M. (1997), 'The replacement problem', *Journal of Monetary Economics*, 40, pp. 457–99.

Cooley, T.F. and Hansen, G.D. (1989), 'The inflation tax in a real business cycle model', *American Economic Review*, 79, pp. 733–48.

(1995), 'Money and the business cycle', Chapter 4 in Cooley, T.F. (ed.), *Frontiers* of *Business Cycle Research*, Princeton, Princeton University Press.

Cooley, T. F. and LeRoy, S. (1985), 'Atheoretical macroeconometrics: a critique', *Journal of Monetary Economics*, 16, pp. 283–308.

DeJong, D.N., Ingram, B.F. and Whiteman, C.H. (1997), 'A Bayesian approach to macroeconomics' (http://www.biz.uiowa.edu/faculty/cwhiteman).

Doan, T., Litterman, R. and Sims, C. (1984), 'Forecasting and conditional projections using realistic priori distributions', *Econometric Reviews*, 3, pp. 1–100.

Dornbusch, R. (1976), 'Expectations and exchange rate dynamics', *Journal of Political Economy*, 84, pp. 1161–76.

Engle, R. and Granger, C. (1987), 'Cointegration and error-correction: representation, estimation and testing', *Econometrica*, 55, pp. 251–76.

Fair, R.C. (1993), 'Estimating event probabilities from macroeconometric models using stochastic simulation', in Stock, J.H. and Watson, M.W. (eds), *Business Cycles, Indicators, and Forecasting*, NBER Studies in Business Cycles Volume 28, Chicago, University of Chicago Press.

(1994), *Testing Macroeconometric Models*, London, Harvard University Press.

Fisher, P.G. (1992), *Rational Expectations in Macroeconomic Models*, Advanced Studies in Theoretical and Applied Econometrics 26, Dordrecht, Kluwer Academic Publishers.

Fisher, P.G., Turner, D.S. and Wallis, K.F. (1992), 'Forward unit root exchange-rate dynamics and the properties of large-scale macroeconometric models', in Hargreaves, C. (ed.), *Macroeconomic Modelling of the Long Run*, Aldershot, Edward Elgar.

Fuhrer, J.C. and Bleakley, C.H. (1996), 'Computationally efficient solution and maximum likelihood estimation of nonlinear rational expectations models', Federal Reserve Bank of Boston Working Paper no. 96-2 (http://www.std.com/frbbos/economic/wpindex.htm).

Garratt, A., Lee, K., Pesaran, M.H. and Shin, Y. (1998), 'A long run structural macroeconometric model of the UK', DAE Working Paper no. 9812, University of Cambridge.

(1999a), *A Structural Cointegrating Macroeconomic Model of the UK* (a monograph under preparation).

(1999b), 'Forecast uncertainties in macroeconometric modelling' (under preparation).

Granger, C. and Newbold, P. (1974), 'Spurious regressions in econometrics', *Journal of Econometrics*, 2, pp. 111–20.

Gredenhoff, M. and Jacobson, T. (1998), 'Bootstrap testing and approximate finite sample distributions for test of linear restrictions on cointegrating vectors', unpublished paper, Department of Economic Statistics, Stockholm School of Economics.

Hall, S.G. (1995), 'Macroeconomics and a bit more reality', *Economic Journal*, 105, pp. 974–88.

Hansen, L.P. and Sargent, T.J. (1991), 'Two difficulties in interpreting vector autoregressions', in Hansen, L.P. and Sargent, T.J. (eds), *Rational Expectations Economics*, London, Westview Press.

Hercowitz, Z. and Sampson, M. (1991), 'Output growth, the real wage, and employment fluctuations', *American Economic Review*, 81, pp. 1215–37.

Johansen, S. (1991), 'Estimation and hypothesis testing of cointegrating vectors in Gaussian vector autoregressive models', *Econometrica*, 59, pp. 1551–80.

(1995), *Likelihood-Based Inference in Cointegrated Vector Autoregressive Models*, Oxford, Oxford University Press.

Johansen, S. and Juselius, K. (1992), 'Testing structural hypotheses in a multivariate cointegration analysis of the PPP and UIP for UK', *Journal of Econometrics*, 53, pp. 211–44.

Kasa, K. (1995), 'Signal extraction and the proagation of business cycles', mimeo, Federal Reserve Bank of San Francisco.

Kim, K. and Pagan, A.R. (1995), 'The econometric analysis of calibrated macroeconomic models', Chapter 7 in Pesaran, M.H. and Wickens, M. (eds), *Handbook of Applied Econometrics: Macroeconomics*, Oxford, Basil Blackwell.

King R.G., Plosser, C.I., Stock, J.H. and Watson, M.W. (1991), 'Stochastic trends and economic fluctuations', *American Economic Review*, 81, pp. 819–40.

Koop, G., Pesaran, M.H. and Potter, S.M. (1996), 'Impulse response analysis in nonlinear multivariate models', *Journal of Econometrics*, 74, pp. 119–47.

Kydland, F. and Prescott, E. (1982), 'Time to build and aggregate fluctuations', *Econometrica*, 50, pp. 1345–70.

Levtchenkova, S., Pagan, A.R. and Robertson, J.C. (1998), 'Shocking stories', *Journal of Economic Surveys*, 12, pp. 507–32.

Litterman, R. (1986), 'Forecasting with Bayesian vector autoregressions – five years of experience', *Journal of Business and Economics Statistics*, 4, pp. 25–38.

Litterman, R. and Weiss, L. (1985), 'Money, real interest rates and output: a reinterpretation of postwar US data', *Econometrica*, 53, pp. 129–56.

Long, J.B. and Plosser, C. (1983), 'Real business cycles', *Journal of Political Economy*, 91, pp. 39–69.

Lucas, R.E. (1976), 'Econometric policy evaluation: a critique', in Brunner, K. and Meltzer, A.H. (eds), *The Phillips Curve and Labour Markets*, Carnegie-Rochester Series on Public Policy, 1, pp. 19–46.

McCallum, B.T. (1989),'Real business cycle models', Chapter 2 in Barro, R.J. (ed.), *Modern Business Cycle Theory*, Oxford, Blackwell.

Mellander, E., Vredin, A. and Warne, A. (1992), 'Stochastic trends and economic fluctuations in a small open economy', *Journal of Applied Econometrics*, 7, pp. 369–94.

Minford, P., Matthews, K. and Marwaha, S. (1979), 'Terminal conditions as a means of ensuring unique solutions for rational expectations models with forward expectations', *Economic Letters*, 4, pp. 117–20.

Murphy, C.W. (1988), 'An overview of the Murphy model', *Australian Economic Papers*, 27 (Supp.), pp. 175–99.

(1992), 'The steady-state properties of a macroeconometric model', in Hargreaves, C. (ed.), *Macroeconomic Modelling of the Long Run*, Aldershot, Edward Elgar.

Nelson, C.R. and Plosser, C.I. (1982), 'Trends and random walks in macro-economic time series', *Journal of Monetary Economics*, 10, pp. 139–62.

Pagan, A. (1987), 'Three econometric methodologies: a critical appraisal', *Journal of Economic Surveys*, 1, pp. 3–24.

Pesaran, M.H. and Pesaran, B. (1997), *Working with Microfit 4.0: Interactive Econometric Analysis*, Oxford, Oxford University Press.

Pesaran, M.H. and Shin, Y. (1996), 'Cointegration and speed of convergence to equilibrium', *Journal of Econometrics*, 71, pp. 117–43.

(1998), 'Generalized impulse response analysis in linear multivariate models', *Economics Letters*, 58, pp. 17–29.

(1999), 'Long-run structural modelling', unpublished manuscript, University of Cambridge (http://www.econ.cam.ac.uk/faculty/pesaran/).

Pesaran, M.H., Shin, Y. and Smith, R.J. (1999), 'Structural analysis of vector error correction models with exogenous I(1) variables', University of Cambridge (http://www.econ.cam.ac.uk/faculty/pesaran/).

Pesaran, M.H. and Smith, R.P. (1985), 'Evaluation of macroeconometric models', *Economic Modelling*, 2, pp. 125–34.

(1995), 'Role of theory in econometrics', *Journal of Econometrics*, 67, pp. 61–79.

(1997), 'New directions in applied dynamic macroeconomic modelling', in Dahel, R. and Sirageldin, I. (eds), *Models for Economic Policy Evaluation Theory and Practice: An International Experience*, Greenwich, Conn., JAI Press.

(1998), 'Structural analysis of cointegrating VARs', *Journal of Economic Surveys*, 12, pp. 471–505.

Phillips, P.C.B. (1991), 'Optimal inference in cointegrated systems', *Econometrica*, 59, pp. 283–306.

Plosser, C.I. (1989), 'Understanding real business cycles', *Journal of Economic Perspectives*, 3, pp. 51–77.

Poulizac, D., Weale, M. and Young. G. (1996), 'The performance of National Institute economic forecasts', *National Institute Economic Review*, 156, pp. 55–62.

Ríos-Rull, J. (1995), 'Models with heterogeneous agents', Chapter 4 in Cooley, T.F. (ed.), *Frontiers of Business Cycle Research*, Princeton, Princeton University Press.

Rogoff, K. (1996), 'The purchasing power parity puzzle', *Journal of Economic Literature*, 34, pp. 647–68.

Sims, C. (1980), 'Macroeconomics and reality', *Econometrica*, 48, pp. 1–48.

(1986), 'Are forecasting models usable for policy analysis?', *Quarterly Review*, Federal Reserve Bank of Minneapolis, 10, pp. 2–16.

Smith, R.P. (1994), 'The macromodelling industry: structure, conduct and performance', in Hall, S.G. (ed.), *Applied Economic Forecasting Techniques*, London, Harvester Wheatsheaf.

Stadler, G.W. (1990), 'Business cycle models with endogenous technology', *American Economic Review*, 80, pp. 763–78.

Turner, D.S. (1991), 'The determinants of the NAIRU response in simulations on the Treasury model', *Oxford Bulletin of Economics and Statistics*, 53, pp. 223–42.

Wallis, K.F. (1995), 'Large-scale macroeconometric modelling', Chapter 6 in Pesaran, M.H. and Wickens, M.R. (eds), *Handbook of Applied Econometrics: Macroeconomics*, Oxford, Basil Blackwell.

Wallis, K.F., Fisher, P.G., Longbottom, J.A., Turner, D.S. and Whitley, J.D. (1987),

Models of the UK Economy: A Fourth Review by the ESRC Macroeconomic Modelling Bureau, Oxford, Oxford University Press.

Wallis, K.F. and Whitley, J.D. (1987), 'Long-run properties of large-scale macroeconometric models', *Annales d'Economie et del Statistique*, 6/7, pp. 207–24.

Whitley, J.D. (1997), 'Economic models and policy-making', *Bank of England Quarterly Bulletin*, 37, 2, pp. 163–72.

Wickens, M.R. (1995), 'Real business cycle analysis: a needed revolution in macroeconometrics', *Economic Journal*, 105, pp. 1637–80.

Wren-Lewis, S., Darby, J., Ireland, J. and Ricchi, O. (1996), 'The macroeconomic effects of fiscal policy: linking an econometric model with theory', *Economic Journal*, 106, pp. 543–59.

Yule, G.U. (1926), 'Why do we sometimes get nonsense correlations between time-series?' *Journal of the Royal Statistical Society*, 60, pp. 812–54.

6 Unemployment, the natural rate and structural change

JENNIFER V. GREENSLADE, STEPHEN G. HALL,
S.G. BRIAN HENRY and JAMES NIXON

1. Introduction

The changing pattern of inflation and unemployment in the UK shown in figure 6.1 poses difficult questions about their determinants. In this chapter, we will argue that to understand and evaluate possible explanations of these changes, technical modelling matters such as the likely set of long run determinants of unemployment, the precise way expectations are incorporated, how structural change can be established, and how policy credibility can be incorporated into empirical models of inflation, each need to be addressed.

Among the alternative explanations of the changes in inflation and unemployment since 1980 the principal contenders include:

- Changes in the long-run NAIRU (Non Accelerating Inflation Rate of Unemployment) due in turn to changes in industrial relations and wage bargaining arrangements (in the standard model, a fall in the long-run NAIRU would be represented as a fall in variables responsible for wage pressure). Apart from the familiar – supply side – contenders, we add external real variables, particularly competitiveness, which could be a factor here too.

- A combination of extensive nominal inertia together with changes in weakly exogenous processes affecting UK inflation, such as world inflation or the exchange rate, could also be responsible. The behaviour of inflation and unemployment since the early 1980s could then be interpreted as movements along short-run Phillips curves.

- Extensive real inertia, produced by persistence mechanisms such as insider behaviour in wage setting, labour turnover costs, capital constraints, and so on.

132

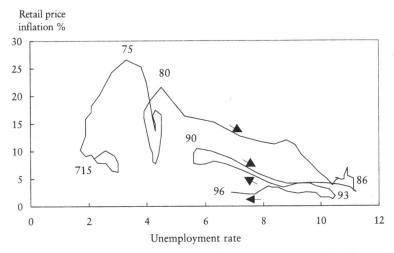

Figure 6.1 *UK price inflation and unemployment, 1971I–1996IV*

- More recently – over the 1990s – it is possible that a credible change in monetary policy regime has occurred and if so this would be a downward shift in the short run Phillips curve.

Some, or indeed all, of these could have happened simultaneously of course. It is useful at this point to recall that there are a number of stylisations which have been widely used to characterise inflation and labour market behaviour in the UK. The UK is often characterised as having low nominal wage rigidity though price inertia is possibly important (see Layard, Nickell and Jackman, 1991). It has also been widely asserted that the UK natural rate rose substantially in the 1980s before falling in the 1990s due to labour market reforms (see Minford, 1994, for the clearest statement of this view, but see also Coulton and Cromb, 1994, for an extensive survey). Lastly, although real persistence has increasingly become a major part of the research agenda (see Alogoskoufis and Manning, 1988; Bean, 1994; Nickell, 1995; and Henry and Snower, 1996), the evaluation of the *empirical* role persistence may play as opposed to movements in equilibrium unemployment itself remains an unresolved issue in that agenda.

The purpose of this chapter is to argue that empirical evidence points to a number of broad findings each of which has an important bearing on the question set out at the beginning of this chapter. These empirical findings are first that nominal inertia is probably substantial. Second, we argue that there is little evidence to support the common view that the long-run

NAIRU has changed due to changes in supply side, labour market, variables. We do conjecture that real persistence is likely to be substantial though, and we emphasise here capital accumulation as an important contributory persistence mechanism. Finally, we address the question of the credibility of monetary policy and its role in inflation performance, and to do this, we move to the complete LBS model where we incorporate policy actions *explicitly* into the analysis, using an empirical counterpart of the familiar normative policy analysis initiated by Barro and Gordon (1983) and Rogoff (1985). We conclude that credibility in monetary policy could play a part in reducing inflation, but our figuring of the time period taken for credibility gains to be achieved is of the order of five years. It thus seems premature to attribute much of an effect to this yet.

Before describing empirical results and simulation exercises, it should be emphasised that both the econometrics of estimating 'structural' models, and the methods of conducting policy analysis on empirical macroeconomic models are central to what is presented here. In terms of modelling, the empirical results reported below are derived from small *systems* of equations which are coherent with economic theory. It is only in such a framework that questions of, for example the nominal inertia in the wage-price model as a whole, can then be addressed. Similarly, the empirical policy analysis reported later incorporates the strategic methodology which underlies most of the theoretical literature. Although both the estimation and policy analysis reported later are based on new techniques, space constraints mean they cannot be fully described here. Details are given in the cited papers on which the present chapter is based, however.[1]

The contents of the rest of the chapter are a short overview of the theoretical issues followed by a review of new findings on the role of both nominal and real inertia in accounting for inflation and unemployment changes since the early 1980s in the UK. Finally, we discuss how credibility effects may be assessed in a macro framework, and conclude it has probably played a small part so far.

2. Theoretical considerations

One of the attractions of the Layard *et al.* model (1991) (hereafter referred to as the standard model) is that it provides a basic framework from which the extensions used here can be made. We note its key features first, especially those determining nominal and real inertia, before we move on to open economy extensions, additional real persistence mechanisms, and the analysis of expectations and policy credibility.

Recall that the standard model, in summary form, is a price equation

$$p - w = \beta_0 - \beta_1 u - \beta_{11}\Delta u - \beta_2 \Delta^2 p - \beta_3(k - l) \tag{6.1}$$

and a wage equation

$$w - p = \gamma_0 - \gamma_1 u - \gamma_{11}\Delta u - \gamma_2 \Delta^2 p + \beta_3(k - l) + Z_w \tag{6.2}$$

where (6.1) is a price markup depending upon (for simplicity) unemployment, changes in unemployment, price surprises $(\Delta^2 p)$ and the capital–labour ratio (productivity). The wage markup equation (6.2) then adds 'push' variables Z_w, usually taken to be real unemployment benefits, union power, mismatch and so on.

The NAIRU (u^*) derived from (6.1) and (6.2) is

$$u^* = \frac{(\beta_0 + \gamma_0) + Z_w}{\beta_1 + \gamma_1} \tag{6.3}$$

and using this definition of u^*, the unemployment–inflation trade-off is

$$\Delta^2 p = - \frac{(\beta_1 + \gamma_1)(u - u^*) - (\beta_u + \gamma_{11})\Delta u}{(\beta_2 + \gamma_2)}. \tag{6.4}$$

In these equations, expectations are formed according to $\Delta p_t = \Delta p_{t-1} + v_t$ (where v is white noise), so $\Delta^2 p$ represents inflation surprises. Equation (6.4) gives the dynamic adjustment around a constant inflation, u^* equilibrium, produced by inflation surprises. Before moving onto extensions, this simple framework is used to make some definitions used later.

First, in this simple model nominal inertia depends on the parameters on $\Delta^2 p$ in both equations (that is $(\beta_2 + \gamma_2)$). Second, real wage rigidity is given by $(\beta_2 + \gamma_1)^{-1}$, that is, the inverse of unemployment (or activity) effects on wages and prices. They determine the effect on equilibrium unemployment of a change in the exogenous variables Z_w (the only exogenous variables in this simplified version). Lastly, hysteresis effects are represented by the change in unemployment effect in both equations.

The advantage of starting with such a simple framework is that in equation (6.4) both nominal and real inertia (for example, hysteresis) affect the slope of the trade-off. In the rest of this section, we describe how this analysis can be extended, including extensions to expectations formation and credibility effects in the model.

2.1 The open economy

Although the standard model is clearly consistent with a generalised – open economy – formulation (see for example Nickell, 1988), open economy developments are often omitted in much discussion of inflation developments where the 'domestic' NAIRU is taken as a sufficient explanation for inflation. It is of course straightforward to make the open economy extension. First, the wage equation (6.2) above explicitly includes wedge terms in Z_w, specifically the tax and price wedge terms arising from the definition of the consumption real wage and the producer real wage relevant to the wage bargain. Solving for the real wage in terms of value added prices introduces a term in real import prices (as well as tax wedge terms which, since they are not the focus at present, are ignored in what follows).

$$w - p = \gamma_0 - \gamma_1 u - \gamma_{11}\Delta u - \gamma_2 \Delta^2 p + \beta_3(k - l) + \gamma_4(p_m - p) + Z_w. \quad (6.5)$$

It is then a short step to rewrite this last variable in terms of competitiveness ($P^f - P$, where P^f is foreign prices, in domestic currency).

Second, this 'internal balance' model represented by (6.1) and (6.3) is extended to incorporate 'external balance', most simply by deriving an equation between the current account balance, domestic relative to world demand, and competitiveness, that is,

$$b = - f_1 \, rxr - f_2 \, y + f_3 \, y^f + f_4 \, Z^b \quad (6.6)$$

where b is the current balance, rxr the real exchange rate, y domestic (and y^f foreign) demand, and Z^b other exogenous factors in the external sector. Setting a target for b (say b^*), provides an equation for the equilibrium real exchange rate (FEER), conditional upon overseas demand and Z^b, in terms of unemployment (by first substituting for domestic output in terms of unemployment). General equilibrium is given by the joint solution of (6.5) and (6.6). (See *inter alia* Fisher and Henry, 1992.)

2.2 Real inertia

Many economists now believe that it is difficult to account for the varied unemployment experiences in Europe since the early 1970s in terms of the magnitude of exogenous shocks. The propagation of high levels of unemployment, rather than its initiating shocks, has increasingly become the focus of attention (see Alogoskoufis and Manning, 1988; Bean, 1992;

Nickell, 1995; and Henry and Snower, 1996). The discussion of the standard model above introduced a simple persistence mechanism through its use of change in unemployment effect. (The empirical results below actually use the ratio of long-term to actual unemployment, on the grounds that the long-term unemployed have a weaker effect on wage bargains.) There are obviously many other sources of real inertia in the macro economy. Such additional persistence mechanisms include insider membership effects (pioneered by Lindbeck and Snower, 1988), outsider effects (Phelps, 1968; and Pissarides, 1990), adjustment costs on labour (Henry, 1981; and Bentolila and Bertola, 1990), and capital shortage effects (Dreze and Bean, 1990).

Much of the material here is familiar, and it is not our intention to provide a review. Two points are important, and the rest of this section is devoted to them. First, the persistence mechanisms noted above are likely to be mutually re-enforcing, a point made repeatedly by Dennis Snower (see Karanassou and Snower, 1998, for example). Hence such mechanisms acting in concert are likely to produce very persistent responses. Second, the importance of the capital stock persistence mechanism appears to us to have been under emphasised. It is this point which the rest of our discussion, and the latter empirical results, are principally concerned with.

It is a central tenet of the 'LSE' approach that neutrality of long-run unemployment with respect to productivity holds (see LNJ, 1991). This condition can be expressed in a number of ways. For our purposes it is most simply seen as the between-equation condition applied to the 'standard' wage–price model (6.1) and (6.2) above, that is, $(k - l)$ has equal and offsetting coefficients. Then both the equilibrium real wage and level of unemployment are independent of the capital–labour ratio $(k - l)$. What this means is that equilibrium unemployment is independent of the capital stock, the labour force and technical progress. Hence, as noted in Rowthorn (1996), according to this model, when there is additional investment, unions force up wages to where the loss of jobs on existing equipment exactly offsets the new jobs created by the new capacity. The same wage responses are true if there is a change in labour supply or technical progress. As Hall and Nixon (1997), and Rowthorn (1996) have noted, this result requires restrictive conditions including a CD technology – so the elasticity of substitution is unity – and a constant replacement ratio. In section 3.2 below the empirical results reject these restrictive theoretical assumptions. Before moving to that, we note here that the above restrictions arise because it is often asserted that as the unemployment rate shows no obvious trend over the centuries and as capital intensity and productivity have been rising steadily since the industrial revolution, they cannot be related to unemployment, that is, 'It does not require any formal statistical analysis to confirm that the unemployment rate and capital intensity cannot be related in the long run' (Bean, 1989).

It is strange that this 'justification' for applying a restriction to a *short-run model* (that is, the standard model above is one in which capital is fixed) is based on a centuries-long observation. What is evident is that over a long period of actual data, unemployment both can, and does, appear non-stationary, and so *prima facie* it may be correlated with the capital–labour ratio.

2.3 Expectations and credibility

Rational expectations offer the tempting possibility that inflation can be brought down with little output loss, if monetary policy is credible. This is most evident where the rate of inflation is independent of the past rate of inflation, so is given by the basic expectations augmented Phillips curve, with forward looking expectations,

$$\Delta P_t = E_t \Delta P_{t+1} + \gamma u_t .$$

Inflation is then free to jump to any value set by future expected inflation. A zero output loss, or costless disinflation, path (CIP) for inflation can be obtained from a more general inflation equation

$$\Delta P_t = \delta E_t \Delta P_{t+1} + (1 - \delta) \Delta P_{t-1} + \alpha u_t + \beta \Delta u_t$$

or

$$\Delta^2 P_{t+1} = ((1 - \delta) / \delta) \Delta^2 P_t - (\alpha / \delta) u_t - (\beta / \delta) \Delta u_t .$$

The CIP is then obtained from this last equation by setting $u = 0$, giving an equation for inflation in terms of the initial disinflation ($\Delta^2 P$ in period zero), which converges to zero providing $(1 - \delta) / \delta < 1$, since under this condition the fall in inflation today is offset by the expected fall in the next period (see Chadha, Masson and Meredith, 1992).

But it is not plausible to assume rational expectations as is done in this model. Also an explicit treatment of policy making is necessary. In such an explicit framework the way the authorities can best respond to a temporary inflation shock – the 'flexibility' of monetary policy – can be defined (see King, 1996). What is of central importance in this framework is the formation of expectations, and how this affects the credibility of monetary policy. Some of the essentials are described next.

2.3.1 The simple analysis of credibility

A simple model can be used to illustrate the basic concepts. It is as follows

$$y_t = \bar{y}_t + b\,(\Delta P_t - \Delta \hat{P}_t) + \varepsilon_t \tag{6.7}$$

$$y_t = c\,(M_t - P_t) + d\Delta P_t \tag{6.8}$$

$$M_t = \lambda_1 + \lambda_2 \varepsilon_t\,. \tag{6.9}$$

Here, (6.7) is a simple supply function, where $\bar{y}$ is the natural rate and $\Delta \hat{P}$ is the expectation of the central bank's target. (6.8) is an aggregate demand function and (6.9) a linear rule for monetary policy.

Solutions for y and P from the model are:

$$y_t = \bar{y}_t + b\alpha_t + \left(\frac{b(d-c)}{b+c}\right)\Delta \hat{P}_t + \beta_t \varepsilon_t \tag{6.10}$$

$$\Delta P_t = \alpha_t + \left(\frac{b+d}{b+c}\right)\Delta \hat{P}_t + \left(\frac{\beta_t - 1}{b}\right)\varepsilon_t \tag{6.11}$$

where α_t and β_t are functions of model parameters (including the policy rule). (See Briault et al., 1996, and King, 1996, for details.)

The inflation target is then defined using the rational expectation of ΔP *before* ε_t is realised:

$$\Delta \bar{P}_t = E\,(\Delta P_t) = \alpha_t + \left(\frac{b+d}{b+c}\right)\Delta \hat{P}\,. \tag{6.12}$$

Putting this into (6.10) and (6.11) gives

$$y_t = \bar{y}_t + b\,(\Delta \bar{P}_t - \Delta \hat{P}_t) + \beta_t + \varepsilon_t \tag{6.13}$$

$$\Delta \hat{P}_t = \Delta \bar{P}_t + \left(\frac{\beta_t - 1}{b}\right)\varepsilon_t\,. \tag{6.14}$$

Monetary policy is therefore a choice of an *ex ante* inflation target, and a response to stochastic shocks described by the choice of β_t. Two important – polar – cases now follow.

2.3.2 Fully credible regime switch

In this case expected inflation equals the target, that is, $\Delta \overline{P}_t = \Delta \hat{P}_t$. Hence

$$y_t = \overline{y} + \beta_t \varepsilon_t \tag{6.15}$$

$$\Delta \hat{P}_t = \Delta \overline{P}_t + \left(\frac{\beta_t - 2}{b} \right) \varepsilon_t . \tag{6.16}$$

So the output level is independent of the inflation target $\hat{\Pi}$ which can be set to achieve price stability without incurring an expected output loss. The optimal policy is to move immediately to a zero inflation target. In practical terms this result is of little relevance to the real world since it implies that all the central bank has to do in order to control inflation is announce a credible inflation target. This result, for example, carries over to large-scale macro models, which with rational expectations, often seem to imply that inflation control is very easy in terms of output cost and speed of pass through of policy effects (see Church *et al.*, 1997). This is clearly unrealistic. In general, much of the output cost of a deflation arises precisely because expectations do not adjust immediately. The only realistic way of assessing central bank credibility and the performance of inflation targeting regimes is to tackle the issue of the acquisition of information, and the adjustment of expectations head on. In particular, we need to assume that agents adjust their expectations over time but still do not make systematic errors in the limit: that is, expectations converge asymptotically to the rational expectation. This leads naturally to the concept of endogenous learning, where past inflation is used by agents to form their expectations of future inflation.

2.3.3 Endogenous learning

In general then, an announcement by the central bank of a future inflation target does not command immediate credibility. It takes time for the private sector to be convinced that the target will be adhered to, during which time the private sector is effectively learning about the preferences of the central bank. Formally, the learning function used here takes the form:

$$\Delta \hat{P}_t = \rho \Delta \hat{P}_{t-1} + (1 - \rho) \Delta \overline{P}_{t-1} \tag{6.17}$$

where $\rho(>0)$ is a time varying, updating parameter. For a positive value of

ρ, expected inflation converges to the inflation target, while if the inflation target were fully credible, and agents had rational expectations for example, ρ would be zero.

Policy analysis in this case takes the intertemporal loss function

$$L = \Sigma(1 + \theta)^t \left(aE(\Delta P_t)^2 + E(y - \overline{y})^2\right) \tag{6.18}$$

where θ is the discount rate. It can be shown that in this case the optimal inflation target is

$$\Delta \overline{P_t} = A\Delta \overline{P}_{t-1} - B\Delta \overline{P}_{t-2} \tag{6.19}$$

where

$$A = 2(a\rho + b^2)/(a + b^2), \text{ and } B = (a\rho^2 + b^2)/(a + b^2) \tag{6.20}$$

and the optimal degree of flexibility of monetary policy in response to shocks is:

$$\beta_t = \frac{a}{a + b^2}. \tag{6.21}$$

(See Hall, Henry and Nixon, 1997.)

The optimal degree of flexibility is independent of the learning parameter because the model assumes agents can infer last period's inflation target by adjusting *ex post* for the effect of the previous period's shock on inflation. If agents are not able to infer the effect of shocks on inflation then learning will take place over the actual (observed) inflation rate. Accommodating temporary shocks may now increase expected inflation by affecting the learning parameter ρ. Hence the output costs of a deflation will depend on how quickly the learning parameter adjusts to the new regime. The central bank therefore has an incentive to refrain from stabilisation in order to invest in credibility – that is, in a lower ρ.

3. Empirical results

The rest of this chapter summaries empirical results which arise from our earlier theoretical discussion of nominal rigidity, evidence for structural change, real persistence, and the possible effects of policy credibility. As these results are discussed in detail elsewhere, only an outline is given here.[2]

3.1 Nominal rigidity

This section considers the effects of structural change, changes in exogenous variables including world inflation effects, the degree of nominal inertia in the economy, and expectations effects on wage and price behaviour. It uses a model appropriate to a small open economy, which is a price taker in world markets, so faster world commodity price inflation can play a role in the domestic inflation rate of the country concerned. The model comprises three equations; a nominal wage, an economy-wide consumption price deflator, and a manufacturing import price deflator. The exchange rate is treated as weakly exogenous. Two versions of the model are reported, including one which embodies fully rational expectations formation. The empirical tests allow for changes in the equilibrium of the model, as well as enabling the estimated degree of nominal rigidity in the system as a whole to be calculated. Conventional Phillips curves have often been used to provide information about the immediate impact of unemployment on wage settlements and the degree of nominal inertia. However, if there is no direct attempt at 'error correction' they can give misleading results for the longer term when the influence of the error correction term becomes more important. The model that we use contains no such pitfalls. Views on the degree of nominal inertia appear to vary widely. Nominal inertia in wage setting is thought to be limited (see Layard, Nickell and Jackman [LNJ], 1991). There may be more inertia in the pricing side (see Martin, 1997). At the complete macromodel level, however, estimates of nominal inertia suggest it could be very considerable (see Church *et al.*, 1996; Turner *et al.*, 1996).

The model is actually an extension of the standard model, building on previous studies including that by Layard, Nickell and Jackman (1991), and Henry, Nixon and Williams (1997). There are three equations in the model, one for aggregate wages (W), the second is for the consumer price (P_c) and the third is for import prices (P_m). The long-run form of the equations are (variables in logs, except for the unemployment variable).

$$W = \alpha_0 + \alpha_1 P_c + \alpha_2 \Pi + \alpha_3 u + \alpha_4 u^L + \alpha_5 (P_m - P) + Z_w \qquad (6.22)$$

$$P_c = \beta_0 + (\beta_1 - 1)W - \beta_1 \Pi + (1 - \beta_1)(P_m - P) + Z_{pc} \qquad (6.23)$$

$$P_m = \gamma_0 + \gamma_1 E + \gamma_2 PW + Z_{pm}. \qquad (6.24)$$

Equation (6.22) is a familiar wage equation, depending upon consumer price (P_c), productivity, (Π), unemployment (u), the ratio of long and medium duration unemployed to total unemployment (u^L), real import prices and Z_w includes such variables as unionisation, unemployment benefits, and tax wedges. Empirical tests, however, show that unionisation and unemployment benefits can be excluded as they are insignificant (benefits) or incorrectly signed (unionisation) (see Greenslade *et al.*, 1998, for details). In what follows, the wage equation is thus this simpler – data preferred – version. Consumer prices (6.23) depend upon unit labour costs and import costs, and import prices (6.24) depend upon the nominal effective exchange rate (E) and world prices (PW). Each price equation allows for additional factors, such as demand effects in both price equations, and possible currency of invoicing effects in the import price equation. The nominal exchange rate is treated as exogenous.[3]

The model so far is static, so represents the long-run equilibrium of the system. Dynamic adjustment to these long-run equilibria is determined by lags in each equation, and in wages these are due to non synchronised wage contracts, and in prices it is assumed that changing prices can be costly. Details of the theory behind these dynamic extensions are familiar, and are not repeated here. Suffice to note that they provide a general case for there being lagged adjustment, and we will largely let the empirical form of these dynamics be freely determined.

The model is as follows

$$\Delta W_t = \sum_1^6 a_{1j} \Delta W_{t-j} + \sum_1^6 a_{2j} \Delta P_{c_{t-j}} + \sum_1^6 a_{3j} \Delta P_{m_{t-j}}$$

$$+ \sum_1^6 a_{4j} \Delta X_{t-j} + \beta_{11} e_{1_{t-1}} + \beta_{12} e_{2t-1} + \beta_{13} e_{3_{t-1}}$$

$$\Delta P_{c_t} = \sum_1^6 b_{1j} \Delta W_{t-j} + \sum_1^6 b_{2j} \Delta P_{c_{t-j}} + \sum_1^6 b_{3j} \Delta P_{m_{t-j}}$$

$$+ \sum_1^6 b_{4j} \Delta X_{t-j} + \beta_{21} e_{1_{t-1}} + \beta_{22} e_{2_{t-1}} + \beta_{23} e_{3_{t-1}} \qquad (6.25)$$

$$\Delta P_{m_t} = \sum_1^6 c_{1j} \Delta P_{m_{t-j}} + \sum_1^6 c_{2j} \Delta X_{t-j}$$

$$+ \beta_{31} e_{1_{t-1}} + \beta_{32} e_{2_{t-1}} + \beta_{33} e_{3_{t-1}}$$

X refers to the weakly exogenous variables, u, u^L, Π, E and PW. All of the cointegrating vectors (e_i) enter each equation, where e_i is of the form given in the ith equation in table 6.2 ($i = 1, 2, 3$). The lags in the dynamic equation are up to j ($j = 1...6$).

We proceed to estimate the model by first testing for cointegration, before identifying the model. When the eight variables (W, P_c, P_m, u, u^L, Π, E, PW), are tested for the presence of cointegrating vectors there appears to be at least three when unemployment, long-term unemployment, the exchange rate, world prices and productivity are treated as weakly exogenous. (Johansen Maximal Eigenvalue statistic of 33.18, 95 per cent critical value is 25.70.)

To proceed with estimating the dynamic model (6.25), the set of I(1) variables are partitioned into 3 sets: one a 'wage' equation consistent with (6.22), a 'consumer price' equation (6.23) and an 'import price'-like equation (6.24), and these are then used to estimate a general version of (6.25).

The full dynamic model is of the Vector Error Correction Model (VECM) form. To estimate it involves a number of distinct steps. First tests for the lag length of the model were done, which implied lags of up to 6 quarters. Second the weak exogeneity status of unemployment, long-run unemployment, productivity, and the nominal exchange rate was supported by LR tests (19.58 for χ^2 (12)). We treat world prices as weakly exogenous, without testing for obvious reasons. Lastly, and least familiarly, we are implicitly applying over-identifying restrictions on the model. Thus for the long- run equations given by (6.22)–(6.24) above, there are implicitly four exclusion restrictions in the wage equation, five in the price and six exclusion restrictions in the import price equation respectively. These restrictions are applied in all three equations which with levels homogeneity, and the dynamic restrictions, give a total of 46 in all. We test these by comparing the just identified estimates with the restricted, overidentified estimates of the three-equation model. The QLR statistic gave 51.3 (χ^2 (46)), so the exclusion restrictions are easily upheld. It is these non-linear estimates which are shown in table 6.1.

The model is also tested for derivative homogeneity. Again, the results support homogeneity (see Greenslade et al., 1998). Although a simplified model, estimated on restricted assumptions, this version is broadly consistent with theoretical requirements, and appears reasonably well specified.

Expected variables, of course, can play a crucial role in the dynamics of the model. With forward looking agents, wage inflation may depend on expected price (and wage) inflation, price inflation upon expected wage and cost inflation. To consider this further, an alternative version of the fully dynamic model, simultaneously allowing for both lagged adjustment and forward looking expectations, was estimated, and tested against the model shown in table 6.1.

A set of non-nested tests on the wage and price equations from the two versions – backward and forward looking – suggested that a lagged model

Table 6.1 *Restricted levels model*

	$\Delta W(-1)$	$\Delta W(-4)$	$\Delta P_c(-1)$	$\Delta P_c(-2)$	$\Delta WPC(-4)$	$RWW(-1)$	$\Pi(-1)$	$u(-1)$	$u^L(-1)$	R^2	DW
ΔW	0.23	0.17	0.23	0.19	0.21	–0.06	0.06	–0.12	0.02	0.6	2.1
	(2.8)	(1.97)	(2.1)	(1.6)	(1.7)	(–3.2)	(3.2)	(–2.2)	(1.7)		

	$\Delta W^*(-1)$		$\Delta P_c(-1)$		$\Delta P_m^*(-1)$	$PC(-1)$	$W(-1)$	$P_m(-1)$	$\Pi(-1)$	R^2	DW
ΔP_c	0.38		0.28		0.15	–0.08	0.06	0.02	–0.06	0.7	2.0
	(3.4)		(3.1)		(2.0)	(–2.2)	(2.0)	(2.4)	(–2.0)		

	$\Delta P_m(-3)$	$\Delta P_m(-4)$	$\Delta P_m(-5)$	ΔE	$\Delta E(-1)$	$\Delta PW(-1)$	$\Delta P_m(-1)$	$E(-1)$	$PW(-1)$	R^2	DW
ΔP_m	0.07	0.07	0.06	–0.52	–0.14	0.58	–0.10	–0.10	0.10	0.7	2.3
	(1.2)	(1.2)	(1.1)	(–7.4)	(–2.0)	(2.9)	(–3.1)	(–3.1)	(3.1)		

Notes: t-ratios are given in parentheses.
ΔW^* refers to a 4 quarter moving average lagged wage inflation.
ΔWPC refers to the important price wedge.
ΔP_m^* refers to an 8 quarter moving average of lagged import price inflation.

was preferred for wages, although the results were mixed for the price equation. The tests were the familiar J (Davidson and MacKinnon, 1981), JA (Fisher and McAleer, 1981), N and NT (the Cox and adjusted Cox Test respectively, Godfrey and Pesaran, 1983), Wald tests, encompassing information criterion tests. For the consumer price equation, according to the Akaike information criterion the forward looking model was preferred, although the Schwarz Bayesian criterion did not support this. For wages, it appeared that the lagged version was preferred on all the tests. Overall, it was concluded that the evidence supports the backward representation.

We finally report two further things from this wage–price model: evidence on its structural stability and its implied nominal inertia. Table 6.2 shows the results for parameter stability, with the associated probabilities given in parentheses.

The tests of parameter stability each show there is little evidence of instability in the equations. This is true of the recursive tests, residual based tests (CUSUM, CUSUMSQ tests), predictive failure and Chow tests.

These results generally show little significant evidence of parameter change for the model. Specifically, in the post-1990 period there appears no significant evidence that the model for wages and prices has changed. So on the basis of this evidence, we discount the possibility that inflation in the 1990s is lower than, say, in the 1980s because the underlying behaviour of wages and prices has changed.

The complete model is then used to calculate the extent of nominal iner-

Table 6.2 *Stability tests*

Sample	1967Q3–1984Q4		1967Q3–1990Q4	
	Predictive failure	Chow test	Predictive failure	Chow test
Distribution of test statistic	$\chi^2(46)$	$\chi^2(9)$	$\chi^2(22)$	$\chi^2(9)$
ΔW	11.0 [1.00]	6.1 [0.734]	6.2 [1.00]	4.3 [0.893]
ΔP_c	20.3 [1.00]	13.4 [0.999]	10.8 [0.985]	7.5 [0.489]
ΔP_m	10.1 [1.00]	8.0 [0.627]	4.9 [1.00]	3.1 [0.979]

tia. We create a 'base' solution using an historical database for 1968 to 1996 which is then shocked by increasing the world price level. Wage inflation initially increases by about 0.7 per cent per quarter, or about 2.5 per cent in annual terms. Since the system is homogeneous in both levels and derivative terms, wage inflation should return to base, but it takes over fifteen years to do so, with the half life response to the shock being about 5–6 years (see Greenslade, Henry and Jackman, 1998, for details).

Redoing the simulation with an endogenous nominal exchange rate (so as to keep the real exchange rate constant), results in wage inflation rising by slightly less then previously, at 0.6 per cent per quarter initially. The half life of the shock now falls to 4–5 years. Nominal rigidity thus seems to be considerable in this model.

3.2 Short and long-term distinctions in the NAIRU

Although the previous empirical results point to the probable importance of nominal rigidity, it also shows that unemployment effects on wages weaken as unemployment spells lengthen. This in turn suggests that unemployment may well be slow to return to equilibrium. As emphasised already, this is but one of the many sources of real persistence in the economy: where temporary real shocks exert long lasting effects on the level of unemployment.

One persistence mechanism in particular stands out for further consideration and that is capital accumulation for the reasons set out earlier.

It has become increasingly fashionable to refer to short-run and long-run NAIRUs. A variety of definitions and empirical practices are used however. For example, in a wage inflation model with hysteresis given by Δu, such as used earlier, we may define the 'long-run NAIRU' as occurring when $\Delta^2 P = \Delta u = 0$ (see Mellis and Webb, 1997).

It is more theoretically attractive to reserve the term 'short-run' for situations where the capital stock is given. This is the basis on which the wage and price equations in the standard model ((6.1)–(6.2) above) were derived. But it is clear that, in general, the short run NAIRU will depend upon the capital–labour ratio, and hence upon the capital stock, as well as other hysteresis-type variables such as changes in unemployment, insider effects and employment adjustment lags. The short-run NAIRU then depends upon past unemployment and the capital stock, and attempts to push the economy towards the long-run NAIRU faster than these short-run dynamics allow would lead to increasing inflation. Expressed in another way, faster capital accumulation in particular would facilitate more rapid increases in employment, without inflation accelerating, than could otherwise be achieved. But, without capital accumulation, decreases in unemployment will rapidly produce increases in inflation; hence limited or slow capital accumulation is an additional reason why high levels of unemployment may persist. The standard model outlined earlier limits persistence mechanisms by imposing the capital–labour neutrality condition: wage and price setting move in offsetting ways when additional capital accumulation occurs, so that equilibrium unemployment is left unchanged. This feature of the standard model – which depends on a unit elasticity of substitution – is rejectable empirically, as we show below. (See Rowthorn, 1996, for an extensive survey, which also rejects the standard approach.) A further question is the implication of neutrality in the long-run case when the capital stock decision is treated endogenously. We turn to this next, and present empirical results which suggest there is a dependence between the capital stock and equilibrium unemployment in the long run too.

To investigate this proposition further, a joint model of factor demands and technology is used. As it is dynamic, it incorporates other persistence mechanisms such as costly employment adjustment. Specifically the model is a consistent model of factor shares in a general model of capital, labour, energy and materials (KLEM), and as it uses a translog flexible form, it does not impose restrictions on elasticities of substitution. The share equations for this model are then

$$S^* = \alpha_I + \sum_{j=n}^{n} \alpha_{ij} \ln p_j + \alpha_{iy} \ln y + \alpha_{it} t \tag{6.26}$$

where

$$S_i^* = \frac{p_i X_i}{\sum_{j=1}^{n} p_f X_j}$$

and X_i is the quantity demanded of imput I.

Table 6.3 *Levels and dynamic estimates of the supply side model*

α_0	α_1	α_2	α_3	α_{11}	α_{12}
-0.46543	-0.212794	1.24868	-0.063788	0.163842	-0.145369
(-0.91175)	(-0.987472)	(30.9058)	(-3.94799)	(4.18784)	(-5.22424)

α_{13}	α_{22}	α_{23}	α_{33}	V	β_0
-8.45225E-03	0.165077	-0.010561	0.018169	-0.005578E-02	0.538740E-02
(-0.258361)	(5.31508)	(-3.98151)	(2.89945)	(18.5859)	(1.85901)

β_1	β_2	β_3	β_4	ΔN_{-1}	ΔN_{-2}
-0.221817	-0.491001E-02	-4.39729	-3.14291	0.323493	0.165658
(-2.93514)	(2.38615)	(2.62236)	(2.21445)	(4.03552)	(2.17369)

ΔK_{-4}	ΔE_{-1}	ΔE_{-1}	ΔM_{-1}		
0.486817	-0.299425	-0.261300	-0.217297		
(7.0986)	(-4.15931)	(-3.62754)	(2.88183)		

Notes: where α_{ij} are production coefficients, where 1 = labour (N), 2 = capital (K), 3=fuels (E) and 4-non-fuels (M).

These levels equations are estimated subject to linear homogeneity, symmetry and homotheticity, when put in dynamic equations as follows.

$$\Delta \ln(X)_{i,t} = \gamma_{i,t} \cdot \Delta \ln(X)_{i,t-1} + \beta_i \left(\frac{P_{it-1} \cdot X_{i,t-1}}{C(P_{i,t-1}, Y_{i,t-1})} - S^*_{i,t-1} \right) \qquad (6.27)$$

where X is the level of the factor. Equation (6.27) together with the generalised cost function

$$\ln C_t = \alpha_0 + \alpha_y \ln y_t = \alpha_t t + \Sigma \alpha_i \ln P_{it}$$
$$+ 1/2 \Sigma \Sigma \alpha_{ij} \ln P_{it} P_{jt}$$
$$+ \Sigma \alpha_{iy} \ln y_t \ln P_t + \Sigma \alpha_{it} t \ln P_t$$
$$+ \alpha \ln y_t + 1/2 \alpha_{yy} (\ln y_t)^2 + 1/2 \alpha_{tt} t^2$$

then comprises the general form of the model which is estimated (see Hall and Nixon, 1997, for details).

Table 6.3 above shows the full estimated non-linear system with error correction in factor shares. In the table, the dynamic model is simplified version of that shown by equation (6.27), allowing for single equation autoregressive adjustment in each of the factor demands (with no cross factor dynamic adjustment). The full model is estimated by FIML. All of the error correction terms are significant and the system is well specified, passing diagnostic tests for autocorrelation and heteroscedasticity. In terms of individual coefficients, we find that the necessary concavity conditions are global and that the estimated Allen elasticities are consistent with previous studies. Importantly, even in this – properly defined – long-run model, the elasticity of substitution between capital and labour is 0.42.

In this model, the long-run NAIRU is a positive function of the cost of capital (as well as relative material and energy prices). The reasons for this dependence on the cost of capital are easy to discern. Thus an increase in the cost of capital shifts down the price mark-up equation in the familiar 'battle of the mark ups' diagram. In other words, the price mark-up equation in this case may be written (in logs, and where we exclude other factor prices for convenience), $p - w = \xi + \alpha (\rho - w)$ where ξ is the mark-up (assumed constant for simplicity), and ρ is the cost of capital. As written this equation resembles a distribution equation: it is a relationship between achievable real wages and real rentals in the long run. Given an increase in ρ, equilibrium in wage and price setting requires a lower real wage. Assuming, as we do here, that there is real wage resistance, then this is achieved by an increase in unemployment (see Allen and Nixon, 1997).

The next question is how important quantitatively this effect may be. To investigate this, we run a simulation of the model in table 6.3, including a wage equation similar to that discussed in the previous section together with a reduced form equation for demand. This simulation demonstrates the dependence of equilibrium unemployment on capital and ultimately on factor prices. Figure 6.2, reports the response of the unemployment rate to a permanent 10 per cent increase in the nominal cost of capital. As capital and labour are substitutes in the model, an increase in the cost of capital first lowers the labour share, increasing employment via a substitution effect. As time progresses, however, unemployment then needs to rise in order to ensure that wage inflation does not increase.

The implication of the preceding discussion is that the capital stock has effects on the short-run NAIRU and our (and others') empirical results suggest that the standard approach is misleading on this score. Moving to the long run, there is likely to be a correlation between increases in unemployment and reductions in capital accumulation, as higher costs of capital will both reduce accumulation and raise unemployment, providing there is real wage resistance. Our simulation suggests this effect may be substantial. More generally the presence of these effects from capital accumulation

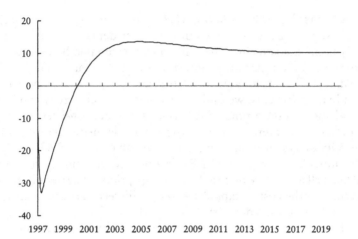

Figure 6.2 *Unemployment rate – per cent deviation from base after a 10 per cent increase in the cost of capital*

means that when looking for 'explanations' of high unemployment, these are *not* found exclusively in the labour market. The assumptions made in the standard model in effect hermetically seal off the labour market from the rest of the macroeconomy. Once an effect from capital is allowed for, as in our approach, then factors influencing capital accumulation, including real interest rates but also capital market imperfections, can have a putative effect on unemployment.

3.3 Inflation expectations and the credibility issue

To implement the normative policy analysis described earlier, we use the full LBS model, and allow for endogenous – boundedly rational – learning in the exchange rate.

We model macroeconomic policy in terms of two simple closed loop feedback rules: one determining the short-run interest rate in response to an inflation target and one determining the standard rate of income tax in response to a target debt to GDP ratio. These contain a proportional, integral and derivative control element. Thus for monetary policy

$$i = i_{-1} + \beta_1 \Delta^2 (\Pi_t - \overline{\Pi}_t) + \beta_2 \Delta (\Pi_t - \overline{\Pi}_t) + \beta_3 (\Pi_t - \overline{\Pi}_t) \qquad (6.28)$$

where i is the short-term interest rate, Π is inflation, and $\overline{\Pi}$ its target rate, while for fiscal policy:

$$T = T_{t-1} + \delta_1 + V_2 \Delta (d_t - \overline{d}_t) + V_3 (d_t - \overline{d}_t) \qquad (6.29)$$

where T is the average personal tax rate, d is the debt-GDP ratio and $\overline{d_t}$ the target.[4]

In keeping with the original Barro–Gordon model, the desired level of growth is taken to be above the estimated non accelerating inflation rate of growth (or productive potential), and to implement this we use a rate of 5 per cent per annum – well above estimated potential growth rates of 2–3 per cent. The objective function for the government is then of the basic quadratic form,

$$V = \sum_{i=1}^{N} \left[\frac{\beta_1}{2} (\Pi - \overline{\Pi}^*)^2 + \frac{\beta_2}{2} (D/Y - (D/Y)^*)^2 + \frac{\beta_2}{2} (\dot{y} - k)^2 \right] \qquad (6.30)$$

where $k = 5$ per cent, D/Y is the ratio of the debt to income, Π is price inflation and N is the time horizon of the policymaker. Clearly, in a natural rate model, the inflation term will increasingly dominate as the time horizon increases.

3.4 The time taken to achieve credibility

We start from the position that it is not possible to consider inflation targeting empirically with a rational expectations assumption. Rather we must allow expectations to evolve over time, and implement a boundedly rational form of learning. Here agents are assumed to use some 'reasonable' rule of learning such as equation (6.17) above, to form expectations where the form of the rule remains constant over time. (More generally, this rule might be the reduced form of the whole system.) This form of bounded rationality entails that even in the absence of regime changes the reduced form of the model is a combination of the stable structural equations and the changing parameters of the expectations rule, so that it is *time-varying*. It is this form of learning – which we refer to as 'adaptive learning' – which is applied in the solutions described here.

The method we use is based on Kalman filtering methods for updating the parameters in the learning function. In short, the method can be described by letting the estimated structural model, which includes expectations for all endogenous variables, be the set of n equations

$$Y_{it} = F_i (Y, X, Y^e_{t,t+1}) \quad i=1,\ldots n \; ; \quad t=1,\ldots T \qquad (6.31)$$

where Y is a vector of current and lagged values of the n endogenous variables, X is a vector of exogenous variables over all time periods, $Y^e_{t,t+1}$ is the expectation based on information available at time t of Y in period $t+1$ and Y_{it} represents the specific endogenous variable which appears only in lagged form on the right hand side of the equations. Next assume that agents, at time t, have the expectations rule of the following form:

$$Y_{t,t+1}^e = D_t Z + e_{1t} \quad \text{where } e_{1t} \sim N(0, W) \tag{6.32}$$

which they use to form the current period's expectations of next period's value of Y. The vector Z is the information set which can consist of a subset of the matrices Y and X over all current and lagged time periods and D is a time-varying matrix of parameters which evolves according to the following process:

$$D_t = D_{t-1} + e_{2t} \quad \text{where } e_{2t} \sim N(0, Q). \tag{6.33}$$

The change in the learning parameters is therefore determined by the value of the Q matrix, the hyper parameters of the state equation (6.33).

To focus on the issue in hand – the size of the parameter ρ in the learning function (6.17) – we first solve the familiar Rogoffian problem of reducing the inflation bias in single policy market case, by delegating to a conservative central banker. To implement the inflation aversion of the conservative central banker, we consider the effects of extending the period over which the optimisation is done: going from five to ten and then fifteen years. Recall that from the objective function (equation (6.30)) the authority has an incentive to push output growth above the natural rate. The results show, as expected, that as we extend the long run from five to ten and then to fifteen years, in each case the monetary authority is unable to generate a permanent increase in growth (see Hall, Henry and Nixon, 1997).

Growth picks up for a few years but ultimately has to return to the natural rate if the government is to avoid a persistent inflationary spiral, and ignore its inflation objective completely. However, the average inflation rate associated with the government's attempts to increase growth is reduced as the time horizon is lengthened. This empirically illustrates Rogoff's argument, that delegating policy to an alternative authority with a lower discount rate or a greater aversion to inflation, reduces the inflationary bias in the setting of macroeconomic policy without fundamentally affecting the path of output growth.

Meanwhile, from this exercise we are able to form a view about the time over which expectations adjust. Expectations are boundedly rational. In the simulation, agents form expectations based on the learning rule (6.17).[5] We can thus take the difference between the expected and actual inflation rate as the expectation error $(\Pi^e - \Pi)$. Over time, on our assumption that expectations are boundedly rational, expected inflation (Π^e) approaches the inflation target $(\overline{\Pi})$, since eventually this is what actual inflation converges to. The question then is how long does it take for expected inflation to converge to the target. The present exercise shows that it takes about five

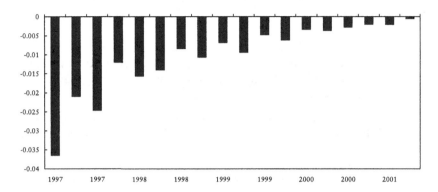

Figure 6.3 *Difference between expected exchange rate and actual outturn*

years (figure 6.3 above). But, as the monetary authority is assumed to respond optimally throughout this exercise, this is almost certainly an over
estimate.

What this exercise illustrates is how expectations adjust to fully rational
expectations, and as part of this adjustment, the time scale of the acquisition of credibility in a Rogoff-type delegation exercise. The quantification
is illustrative: we do not *estimate* the adjustment parameter. Nonetheless,
the underlying analysis is quantitative, being based on a fully estimated
model, so is an advance over previous theoretical and calibrated exercises
(see King, 1996).

Given these results, what bearing does it have on the present inflation
outturns? If we take the existing monetary framework as starting from the
granting of independence to the Bank of England to set monetary policy
in May 1997, then clearly the sort of 'ball park' figure we describe would
say that the recent inflation performance has little do to with the credibility of the Bank's anti-inflation stance. This would be too narrow an
interpretation in our view. From the time of the UK exit from the ERM (September 1992), the monetary policy arrangements have established a new
transparent, and forward looking regime. On this basis, it is possible that
policy credibility is already having *some* effect on inflation expectations
and hence inflation performance, but bearing in mind our caveat about the
assumption of optimal monetary policy in our exercise, there is considerable doubt that this could be significant.

4. Conclusions

In searching for clues to account for the changes in the level of unemployment and inflation rate shown in Figure 6.1, we have considered the possible role of nominal inertia, structural change and the capital constraint, and credibility. Our results show:

- There is considerable nominal rigidity in the UK. Thus nominal demand shocks can be expected to have long-lasting real effects. So part of the 'explanation' for the rise and the fall in unemployment in the 1980s, and again in the 1990s, is due to variations in monetary policy – the exchange rate overshooting in the early 1980s, the Lawson runaway boom with loose monetary conditions in the mid to late 1980s, and the monetary tightening followed by its abrupt relaxation in the UK's abortive attempt to join, and stay with, the ERM. All play an important part in explaining the movements in unemployment (and of course inflation) over the period.

- Has the equilibrium (NAIRU) rate of unemployment shifted inwards? The standard model links equilibrium unemployment to supply-side variables such as real out-of-work benefits and union power. To reconcile models of this sort to the events of the last decade, recourse needs be made to the assumption that there has been structural change, due for example to the labour market reforms of the 1980s. An alternative explanation, and one we prefer, is that these models do not satisfactorily account for what has happened. In short, they are misspecified, and for this reason will appear to show 'structural' change. Our models do not condition upon these supply-side variables because we do not find they are significant or/and correctly signed.

- We argue that real inertia is important, and empirical results suggest that capital accumulation is probably an important contribution to unemployment developments in unemployment models conditioned on the capital stock. Moreover, even in a properly derived long-run model we have presented results which suggest that unemployment and capital accumulation are inversely related.

- Finally, the *empirical* issue of the role of credibility gains in bringing down measured inflation we believe is still unresolved. We have indicated a way of inferring a time period over which these effects could operate, and it is possible that some credibility effect has had time to come through, although we are not in a position to say how big it might be.

Notes

1   The material presented here brings together a number of threads in research at the CEF, including that reported in Greenslade, Hall and Henry (1998); Greenslade, Henry and Jackman (1998); Hall and Nixon (1997); and Hall, Henry and Nixon (1997).
2   See note 1.
3   Identification is a well known issue here. It is discussed in detail in Henry and Lee (1996), and in Greenslade, Hall and Henry (1998).
4   This rule excludes the derivative control element as we have found this to be the best way in practice to penalise fiscal instrument instability.
5   Recall that it is the expected exchange rate which is the expectation variable in this exercise. But this can be re-expressed as an expectation for inflation using the model itself of course.

References

Allen, C., and Nixon, J. (1997), 'Two concepts of the NAIRU', in Allen, C. and Hall, S. (eds), *Macroeconomic Modelling in a Changing World*, New York, Wiley.
Alogoskoufis, G. and Manning, A. (1988), 'Unemployment persistence', *Economic Policy*, October.
Barro, R.J. and Gordon, D.B. (1983), 'Rules discretion and reputation in monetary policy', *Journal of Monetary Economics*, 12, pp. 1901–121.
Bean, C. (1989), 'Capital shortages and persistent unemployment', *Economic Policy*, 8, pp. 11–53.
  (1992), 'Some thoughts on modelling supply', paper presented to the ESRC conference 'The future of macromodelling in the UK', November.
  (1994), 'European unemployment: a survey', *Journal of Economic Literature*, 32, pp. 573–619.
Bentolila, S. and Bertola, G. (1990), 'Firing costs and labour demand: how bad is Eurosclerosis?', *Review of Economic Studies*, 57, 3, pp. 381–462.
Blanchard, O. and Muet, P. (1993), 'Competitiveness through disinflation: an assessment of the French macroeconomic strategy', *Economic Policy*, 16, April.
Briault, C.B., Haldane, A.G. and King, M.A. (1996), 'Independence and accountability', Bank of England Discussion Paper, No. 49.
Bryant, R.C. and Zhang, L. (1996), 'Inter-temporal fiscal policy in macroeconomic models: introduction and major alternatives', Brooking Discussion Papers in Economics, No. 123.
Chadha, B., Masson, P.R. and Meredith, G. (1992), 'Models of inflation and the costs of disinflation', *IMF Staff Papers*, 39, 2, pp. 395–431.
Church, K.B., Mitchell, P., Sault, J. and Wallis, K. (1997), 'Comparative properties of models of the UK economy', *National Institute Economic Review*, 161, pp. 91–100.
Church, K.B., Mitchell, P.R. and Wallis, K.F. (1996), 'Short-run rigidities and long-run equilibrium in large-scale macroeconometric models', ESRC Macroeconomic

Modelling Bureau, mimeo.

Coulton, B. and Cromb, R. (1994), 'The UK NAIRU', Government Economic Service Working Paper, No. 124.

Davidson, R. and MacKinnon, J.G. (1981) 'Several tests for model specification in the presence of alternative hypothesis', *Econometrica*, 49, pp. 781–93.

Dreze, J. and Bean, C. (1990), *Europe's Unemployment Problem*, Cambridge, Mass., MIT Press.

Fisher, G.R. and McAleer, M. (1981), 'Alternative procedures and associated tests of significance for non-nested hypotheses', *Journal of Econometrics*, 16, pp. 103–19.

Fisher, P. and Henry, S.G.B. (1992), 'Inflation and unemployment in the UK', mimeo. Bank of England.

Godfrey, L.G. and Pesaran, M.H. (1983), 'Test of non-nested regression models: small sample adjustments and Monte Carlo evidence', *Journal of Econometrics*, 21, pp. 133–54.

Greenslade, J.V., Hall, S.G. and Henry, S.G.B. (1998), 'On the identification of cointegrated systems in small samples: practical procedures with an application to UK wages and prices', Centre for Economic Forecasting, London Business School, mimeo.

Greenslade, J.V., Henry, S.G.B. and Jackman, R. (1998), 'A dynamic wage–price model for the UK', Centre for Economic Forecasting, London Business School, Discussion Paper No. 10-98.

Hall, S.G. and Nixon, J. (1997), 'Modelling wages and the supply-side of the UK economy', Centre for Economic Forecasting, London Business School, mimeo.

Hall, S.G., Henry, S.G.B. and Nixon, J. (1997), 'Inflation targeting: The delegation and coordination of monetary policy', Centre for Economic Forecasting, London Business School, mimeo.

Henry, S.G.B. (1981), 'Forecasting employment and unemployment' in Hornstein, Z., Grice, J. and Webb, A. (eds), *The Economics of the Labour Market*, London, HMSO.

Henry, S.G.B. and Lee, K. (1996), 'Identification and estimation of wage and employment equations: An application of the structural VAR modelling approach', Department of Applied Economics, mimeo.

Henry, S.G.B., Nixon, J. and Williams, G. (1997), 'Pricing behaviour in the UK', Centre for Economic Forecasting, London Business School Discussion Paper No. 05-97.

Henry, S.G.B. and Snower, D. (eds) (1996), 'Economic policies and unemployment dynamics in Europe', International Monetary Fund.

Johansen, S. (1988), 'Statistical analysis of cointegration vectors', *Journal of Economic Dynamics and Control*, 12, pp. 231–54.

Johansen, S. and Juselius, K. (1990), 'Maximal likelihood estimation and inference on cointegration – with applications to the demand for money', *Oxford Bulletin of Economics and Statistics*, 52, 2, pp. 169–210.

Karanassou, M. and Snower, D.J. (1998), 'How labour market flexibility affects unemployment: long term implications of the chain reaction theory', *Economic Journal*, 108, May, pp. 1–18.

King, M. (1996), 'How should central banks reduce inflation: conceptual issues', in *Achieving Price Stability, a symposium sponsored by the Federal Reserve Bank of Kansas*, Jackson Hole, Wyoming.

(1997), 'Monetary stability: rhyme or reason', *Bank of England Quarterly Bulletin*, 37, 1, pp. 88–96.

Kydland, F.E. and Prescott, E.C. (1977), 'Rules rather than discretion: the inconsistency of optimal plans', *Journal of Political Economy*, 85, 3, pp. 473–91.

Layard, R., Nickell, S. and Jackman, R. (1991), *Unemployment: Macroeconomic Performance and the Labour Market*, Oxford, Oxford University Press.

Lindbeck, A. and Snower, D.J. (1988), *The Insider–Outsider Theory of Employment and Unemployment*, Cambridge, Mass., MIT Press.

Lucas, R. (1976), 'Economic policy evaluations: a critique' in Brummer, K. and Meltzer, A. (eds), *Phillips Curve and Labour Markets*, Amsterdam, North-Holland.

Manning, A. (1993), 'Wage bargaining and the Phillips Curve: the identification and specification of aggregate wage equations', *Economic Journal*, 103, 416, pp. 98–118.

Martin, C. (1997), 'Price formation in an open economy: theory and evidence for the United Kingdom', *Economic Journal*, 107, pp. 1391–404.

Mellis, C. and Webb, A. (1997), 'The United Kingdom NAIRU: concepts, measurement and policy implications', OECD Working Paper No. 182. Paris.

Minford, P. (1994), 'Deregulation and unemployment – The UK experience', *Swedish Economic Policy Review*, 1, 1–2, Autumn, pp. 113–49.

Nickell, S. (1988), 'The NAIRU: some theory and statistical facts', in Cross, R. (ed.), *Unemployment, Hysteresis and the Natural Rate*, Oxford, Blackwell.

(1995), 'Labour market dynamics in OECD countries', Centre for Economic Performance, Discussion Paper No. 255, London School of Economics.

Nixon, J. and Urga, G. (1997), 'Unemployment and the capital stock: modelling the supply side of the UK economy', Centre for Economic Forecasting, London Business School, Discussion Paper No. 18-97.

Phelps, E. (1968), 'Money wage dynamics and labour market equilibrium', *Journal of Political Economy*, 76, 4, pp. 678–711.

Phillips, A. (1958), 'The relation between unemployment and the rate of change of money wages in the United Kingdom 1862–1957', *Economica*, 25, pp. 283–99.

Pissarides, C. (1990), *Equilibrium Unemployment Theory*, Oxford, Blackwell.

Rogoff, K. (1985), 'The optimal degree of commitment to an intermediate monetary target', *Quarterly Journal of Economics*, 100, pp. 1169–89.

Rowthorn, R. (1996), 'Unemployment and capital–labour substitution', University of Cambridge, paper presented to the CEPR/ESRC Workshop on Unemployment Dynamics.

Smith, P. N. and Wallis, K.F. (1994), 'Policy simulation and long run sustainability in forward looking macro econometric models', ESRC Macroeconomic Modelling Bureau Discussion Paper, No. 34.

Turner, D., Richardson, P. and Rauffet, S. (1996), 'Modelling the supply side of the seven major OECD economies', OECD Economics Department Working Paper No. 167.

7 Macroeconomic models at the Bank of England

PAUL FISHER and JOHN WHITLEY

1. Introduction[1]

Policy background to the models

The first core purpose of the Bank of England is to maintain the integrity and value of the currency. Since May 1997, the Bank's Monetary Policy Committee (MPC) has been required to set interest rates to hit the Government's inflation target (see the August 1998 *Inflation Report*, pp. 75–6). The Bank of England Act (1998) gives a statutory basis for the MPC and its role. The MPC's policy decisions are supported by a continuous research programme on macro and microeconomic features of the UK economy. The development of macroeconomic models forms part of this programme.

The role of macroeconomic models is to encapsulate in quantitative form a description of the economy that can be used as a basis for discussion and analysis of policy issues. Macroeconomic models are inevitably approximations. For one thing, there are serious difficulties in measuring macroeconomic variables (see, for example, Cunningham, 1996). More fundamentally, it is simply not possible to capture more than a few of the myriad aspects of economic behaviour in a single model. And even on those few aspects, economists will have divergent views on the appropriate theory. But models can play a very useful role in explaining the reasons for alternative judgments on economic policy, ensuring consistency over time and forcing debate to be as rigorous as possible.

The models described here were first built before the MPC was established. Discussion with MPC members is leading to revision of some of the models, and that process is likely to be continuous. This chapter therefore provides a historical snapshot of the models used in the Bank.

It cannot, however, be assumed that they provide a complete representation of the Bank's views at the time the snapshot was taken. Moreover, the models cannot be taken to represent the current views of all or any members of the MPC, and the contents of the chapter are without prejudice to future developments that the MPC may wish to promote.

The Bank uses a variety of models for policy analysis, rather than a single model (see Whitley, 1997); no individual model can be said to encapsulate 'a Bank view'. As noted above, models are, at best, only a rough approximation to the workings of a modern economy. Individual models are designed to address a fairly limited set of issues. So no one model is likely to be adequate for analysing the entire range of possible exogenous and policy shocks. Different models then answer different questions. In addition, one can never be entirely sure about the accuracy of a particular representation of the economy and so, on any one issue, one may want to gather the evidence from a variety of models to establish sensitivity. In particular, when forecasting, a set of central assumptions is unavoidable – but it is important to assess the risks that arise from choosing one assumption rather than another (see Britton, Fisher and Whitley, 1998).

The models presented here attempt to cover the aggregate macro economy. Other partial models are also used as part of the information set and can be combined with complete models, but are too numerous to cover in one paper. In addition to macromodels and partial models, the Bank's forecasting process also uses other techniques, such as spreadsheet calculations, quantification of survey results (for example, Cunningham, 1997), information from the Bank's regional agents and other calibration exercises.

The point of using all these models is to improve the Bank's forward assessments of the economy, as published in the *Inflation Reports*. But those assessments are not based on a mechanical model-led extrapolation from past and current data sets. They include judgments based not only on a variety of models, but also on other evidence about the current state and likely future development of the economy. All forecasters use evidence from several sources; some place more emphasis on their econometric model than others.

This chapter contains only a brief summary of how the different models are used to generate forecasts. But in the forecast context the econometric model has particular importance since it plays a unifying role in bringing together information from the various models and off-model sources into a quantitative framework.

The next part of this introduction sets out the underlying economic paradigm and describes how different styles of model fit into the general framework. Sections 2–6 describe the models under five broad headings; section 7 compares them and Section 8 describes how the multi-model approach is used in the forecasting process. Section 9 contains concluding comments.

1.1 The underlying economic paradigm

The *Inflation Report* forecasts and analysis are underpinned by a general view of the transmission mechanism of monetary policy that is quite widely shared. In the long run, the price level must be determined by the stock of money, given a real equilibrum for velocity and activity. However, the monetary policy instrument is a short-term interest rate and, in the short to medium run, price stickiness leads to the following effects: changes in nominal short rates of interest affect short real rates, and so the real demand for goods and services, through income, intertemporal substitution and wealth effects. Fluctuations in demand cause temporary fluctuations in output, for example through inventory accelerator-type mechanisms. Real output determines employment and so, through labour market pressure, real wages. Real activity affects inflation through real wage and price mark-up behaviour, which depend on labour market tightness and capacity utilisation respectively. This can be simplified as a short-run Phillips curve. In an open economy, changes in interest rates will typically indicate a change in the exchange rate. Two consequences follow: a change in import prices, leading to a change in domestic prices, and a temporary change in the real exchange rate, which changes net export demand and so output. Interest rates additionally affect inflation via other asset prices and via direct effects on inflation expectations. Money growth will also act on inflation in the long term via three channels – nominal demand, asset prices and inflation expectations. The speed of response to a monetary shock will depend on many factors, but particularly on how rapidly and how far expectations adjust.

Monetary policy also requires an assessment of how the many and varied shocks observed in practice affect economic activity and inflation. The Bank's approach assumes that no single model is likely to be capable of analysing all these influences. In analysing any economic shock, the natural instinct is to simplify the problem as far as possible, at least initially. This is where the strength of the multi-model approach lies. Its components can be considered as differing simplifications of the same large and complex economy, depending on the issue being considered. Clearly there is a trade-off between models that emphasise detail (typically large models) and models that concentrate on broad analysis (small models), and between models that emphasise empirical observations and those that emphasise theory. But each model should be capable of explaining key features of the UK economy.

2. Analytical optimising models: the 'small analytical model' project

2.1 Introduction

The objective of this project was to assemble a set of theoretical models from the academic literature in a form that allows them to be easily combined, solved and simulated. These are models of economic agents engaged in optimising behaviour subject to constraints, in which the basic utility functions and preferences are clearly specified. That allows the analysis to develop with reference to the deep structural parameters.

These models need to be calibrated and tested against the data – usually by means of 'stylised fact analysis'. This involves establishing key features of economic behaviour and then trying to replicate them using the various models. Unlike econometric models – which if fitted properly to the data must account for their features by construction, at least retrospectively – basic theoretical models often fail to account for the observed 'facts' in the data.

The models that have been developed so far are variants of the Real Business Cycle (RBC) model of Kydland and Prescott (1982), where cycles are explained as the equilibrium responses of agents to shocks. The basic RBC model assumes an infinitely lived representative agent maximising utility, subject to a resource constraint.

This can be expressed as:

$$\text{Maximise } E_0 \sum_{t=0}^{\infty} \beta^t U(C_t) \tag{7.1}$$

$$\text{subject to } C_t + I_t = F(K_{t-1}, A_t) \tag{7.2}$$

$$\text{where } K_t = (1-\delta)K_{t-1} + I_t \tag{7.3}$$

where β is the discount factor; $U(C)$ is the representative agent's utility function; C is consumption; I is investment; $F(K,A)$ is the economy's production function; K is end-of-period capital stock; δ is the depreciation rate; and A represents a technology parameter subject to shocks. The various extensions to this basic model described below allow for labour market behaviour, a government sector, money, sticky prices, and an open economy. These extensions are not intended to produce a general model: a model containing all these extensions would be extremely difficult to solve analytically, and would not necessarily provide additional insights.

2.2 Summary of models

The basic RBC model
The basic RBC model was used by Holland and Scott (1997) to explain some 'stylised facts' of the UK economy. Their paper examines the correlation between fluctuations in activity and 'shocks' to the economy. In this basic model the labour market is perfectly competitive. Holland and Scott show that there are significant movements in employment that are uncorrelated with real wages, but are predictable by variables such as money. There are also fluctuations in UK activity that are not predicted by demand-side variables, or fluctuations in factor inputs. Similar approaches have been applied by others to different economies.

These results are consistent with the idea common in much of the RBC literature that supply-side disturbances are an original cause of business cycles. At the same time, the basic RBC stochastic growth model cannot be said to explain UK business cycle fluctuations fully.

Labour market models
The starting-point and motivation for developing the labour market specification within the stochastic RBC model is to explain several key 'stylised facts' for the UK economy. These are as follows:

(i)   Total hours worked are at least as volatile as GDP.
(ii) Changes in total hours are split approximately equally between average hours worked and employment.
(iii) Unemployment and vacancies both vary considerably over the cycle.
(iv) Employment tends to lag, but average hours lead, output.
(v)   Unemployment is strongly countercyclical and tends to lag output, whereas vacancies are procyclical and lead output. In consequence, there is a strong negative relationship between unemployment and vacancies over the cycle (the so-called 'Beveridge curve').

A variety of models have been developed in the literature, reflecting a broad spectrum of views about how the labour market operates: simple market-clearing models; labour hoarding models; and models with Keynesian unemployment. Extensions of the basic RBC approach that reflect this divergence of views are surveyed and evaluated in Millard, Scott and Sensier (1997), and are briefly summarised below.

The first extension is to include total hours negatively in a utility function to reflect agents' preferences for leisure, and to include total hours in the production function constraint (King, Plosser and Rebelo, 1988). The basic utility function can be rewritten as:

$$\max \ E_0 \sum_{t=0}^{\infty} \beta^t U(C_t, (1 - h_t))$$

where h denotes hours worked as a fraction of the day. In this model, the sources of economic fluctuations are technology shocks, affecting the marginal product of labour and labour demand. The response of wages and/or employment depends on the degree of intertemporal substitution of labour supply. With a high degree of intertemporal substitution, productivity shocks will bring about large changes in employment, but relatively small changes in wages (an elastic labour supply curve). In contrast, a low degree of intertemporal substitution implies that wages rather than employment will adjust to changes in labour demand. High substitution is necessary to explain the observed cyclical behaviour of employment and wages, but empirical evidence suggests that labour supply is relatively inelastic (Altonji, 1986).

The model of Hansen (1985) addresses this problem by generating a highly elastic aggregate labour supply curve, irrespective of the labour supply elasticity of individual agents. All individuals choose between either working a fixed number of hours, or not working. This 'indivisible' labour market model therefore assumes that employment fluctuations occur from changes in the number of people employed, rather than from variations in average hours worked. Individuals may have a highly inelastic labour supply curve but, because there is enormous variability at the extensive margin, the aggregate labour supply curve can be highly elastic. A further extension allows a choice between hours and employment (Cho and Cooley, 1994), and for labour hoarding (Burnside, Eichenbaum and Rebelo, 1993). Errors in expectations explain why the labour market does not adjust immediately to productivity shocks. A further modification is the Gali (1995) model, in which Keynesian 'involuntary unemployment' can emerge by allowing for imperfect competition in both product and labour markets – wages are not necessarily equal to the marginal product of labour.

The set of small analytical models also includes labour market models that abandon the Walrasian approach in favour of search models. In these models, it takes time to match up unemployed workers and firms with vacancies, and so employment adjusts slowly to any shock. The key concept is the matching function, which translates the search efforts of firms and workers into new jobs. There is bargaining between firms and workers over any supply that exists relative to an already-formed job match. In the Mortensen and Pissarides (1994) model, jobs are destroyed as a result of idiosyncratic shocks that change their productivity. We have also implemented the model of Merz (1995), who combines a search model with a more sophisticated representation of the production sector.

Government sector
The basic RBC model is an aggregate model. But models such as those of Aiyagari, Christiano and Eichenbaum (1988) allow that government spending may be treated as an exogenous shock that changes the amount of resources that can be devoted to personal consumption and investment. Also included in the suite is another variant of RBC models with a government sector, the model of Braun (1994). In that model, government spending also enters the utility function, and the model allows for distortionary taxes on labour and capital income. So business cycle fluctuations may be caused by changes in labour taxes affecting the labour supply curve, as well as by productivity shocks shifting the labour demand curve.

Money
The small analytical models that include a role for money are concerned with two key questions:
(i)   why do people hold money?
(ii) what is the mechanism through which money affects output in the short run?
    The first question is addressed by 'cash-in-advance' models, as in Cooley and Hansen (1989). In this model, all consumption must be financed out of holdings of money, hence the term 'cash-in-advance'. The second question – that of the monetary transmission mechanism itself – is tackled by introducing some form of wage or price stickiness. The flexible price models are unable to produce any substantial non-neutralities. The approach that we have adopted is to introduce a 'Calvo' pricing rule, under which not all firms change prices each period, into an RBC model with a cash-in-advance approach to money, following Yun (1996).

Open economy
An important part of the monetary transmission mechanism is the exchange rate. In order to allow for this, models have been developed that extend the RBC model to an open economy. This has been achieved by using the model of Schlagenhauf and Wrase (1995). In turn, this model is

based on 'liquidity effects' models of Christiano and Eichenbaum (1992). The basic idea of the liquidity effects model is an attempt to explain the observation that an unexpected monetary expansion is usually associated with a fall in interest rates below their expected level. The open-economy version of this model distinguishes between domestic and foreign goods for consumption and money holdings, and allows for both domestic and foreign money shocks.

2.3 Solving and simulating the models

The issues to be faced in building these small theoretical models are best described with reference to the standard consumption problem.

In the simple consumption model, the representative consumer supplies labour and makes decisions about consumption and savings (purchases of capital) in order to maximise the present discounted value of future consumption (utility) subject to an aggregate resource constraint. Following the general problem stated in equations (7.1)–(7.3) and an assumption about the process governing the productivity shock, we can solve the intertemporal Euler equation as

$$C_t^{-\tau} = \beta E_t \left\{ C_{t+1}^{-\tau} (\alpha \theta_{t+1} K_t^{\alpha-1} + \mu) \right\} \tag{7.4}$$

where $C_t^{-\tau}$ is the marginal utility of current consumption; τ is the coefficient of relative risk aversion; α is the return to capital; $(\alpha \theta_{t+1} K_{t-1}^{\alpha-1} + \mu)$ is the gross return on capital in the current period; $\mu = 1 - \delta$; and where the productivity shock is given by:

$$\ln(\theta_t) = \ln(\theta_{t-1}) + g + \varepsilon_t \tag{7.5}$$

where ε_t is white noise with variance σ_ε^2; and g is the average rate of technical progress.

To solve for the steady-state values of consumption and capital stock, one needs variables to be stationary, which can be done by detrending. The Euler equation can be rewritten in detrended variables $\tilde{C}$ and $\tilde{K}$:

$$\tilde{C}_t^{-\tau} = \beta E_t \left\{ \tilde{C}_{t+1}^{-\tau} \exp\left(\frac{-\tau(g+\varepsilon_t)}{1-\alpha} \right) \left(\alpha \exp(g + \varepsilon_t) \tilde{K}_t^{\alpha-1} + \mu \right) \right\}. \tag{7.6}$$

This Euler equation is non-linear and involves expectations. Methods of solving models of this type by making linear quadratic approximations lose the crucial non-linearity. So, the Bank has adopted the method of parameterised expectations to solve the models, using the technique developed by den Haan and Marcet (1990, 1994). This involves replacing the expectations term with a simple polynomial of the state variables. The accuracy of the solutions is tested by seeing whether the expectational errors are unpredictable, as required by rational expectations models.

In these models, the decision rule depends on the underlying parameters of the utility function. So the effect of changes in those parameters can be simulated only once the optimisation process has been recalculated for new parameter values.

3. Stylised macro models

3.1 Introduction

The small analytical models described in section 2 are based on the optimising behaviour of individual agents. There has been a considerable debate as to whether these individual responses can be aggregated to give overall macroeconomic behaviour. As an alternative, models can be constructed at the aggregate level. These latter models correspond to macro theory as expressed in standard texts such as Begg, Dornbusch and Fischer (1991), rather than the new macroeconomics of Sargent (1987) or Blanchard and Fischer (1990). Aggregate macroeconomic models lack the theoretical microeconomic rigour of the small analytical models, but can nevertheless provide insights into particular problems or issues. For example, we have addressed the consequences of exchange rate movements partly on a simple version of the overshooting model of Dornbusch (1976).

3.2 Summary of the models

In forecasting and analysing an open economy, the behaviour of the exchange rate can play an important role in explaining the dynamics of output and price fluctuations.

The general paradigm is that of the Dornbusch-Buiter-Miller models (Dornbusch, 1976; Buiter and Miller, 1981), in which a system is constructed using uncovered interest parity, a demand curve for output, a Phillips curve and a money demand function to determine the exchange rate, prices, output and one of either money or the interest rate.

The stylised Dornbusch-Buiter-Miller (DBM) is as follows:

$$d_t = y_t - \beta(e_t + p_t - p_t^*) - \alpha r_t + g_t + x_t \tag{7.7}$$

$$m_t - p_t = d_t - i_t \tag{7.8}$$

$$r_t = i_t - E_t p_{t+1} + p_t \tag{7.9}$$

$$E_t e_{t+1} - e_t = i_t^* - i_t + \varsigma_t \tag{7.10}$$

$$\Delta p_t = \Delta p_{t+1}^e + \gamma(d_t - y_t) \tag{7.11}$$

$$\Delta p_{t+1}^e = \mu \Pi + (1 - \mu)\Delta p_{t-1} \tag{7.12}$$

where variables are in logs, Greek letters denote parameters and * represents 'rest of the world' variables. The first equation is the IS curve relating the output gap (demand, d, less potential output, y) to the real exchange rate ($e + p - p^*$; where e is the nominal exchange rate and p, p^* the respective price levels), the real interest rate (r), government spending (g) and a foreign demand shock (x). The second equation is an LM curve relating real money balances ($m - p$) to output and the nominal interest rate (i). The third equation is the Fisher identity defining the relationship between real and nominal interest rates. The fourth equation is the uncovered interest parity condition, where ς is a (relative) risk premium on UK assets. The fifth equation is an expectations-augmented Phillips curve, and the final equation defines price expectations, allowing for some inertia in expectations adjustment and a 'core' rate of inflation (P).

The specification of the price adjustment mechanism varies across applications. Some versions of the models (for some examples, see papers by Buiter and Miller) set Δp_{t+1}^e equal to zero, some to the 'core' rate of inflation and others to the expected growth of the money stock. Variations of (7.11) and (7.12) allow us to accommodate all of these alternatives (e.g. by setting $\Pi = \Delta(m - d)$). A 'perfect foresight' solution can also be generated by deleting (7.12) and setting Δp_{t+1}^e to be model-consistent, as discussed below. In the framework of the Dornbusch model, the policy instrument is the nominal stock of money (m) – although any path for m maps onto a path for nominal interest rates and vice versa.

Following a monetary shock, the nominal exchange rate will need to jump to a new stable path, before depreciating or appreciating to its new level. Given that prices are sticky, the real exchange rate will jump as well.

We have constructed Dornbusch-style models using both stylised and estimated parameter values. In common with the small analytical models, the DBM model contains forward-looking (rational) expectations given by the conditional expectations of the model. In a linear system, this is equivalent to the model's own forecast (model-consistent expectations). A general solution can be obtained by expressing the model as a first-order linear difference equation. (See Blanchard and Kahn, 1980; Buiter, 1984, for the continuous time case.) These methods rely on finding a unique and stable solution ('saddlepoint path'). The DBM model can be solved analytically using the Blanchard and Kahn method, but we have also applied the method of parameterised expectations described earlier, which allows for non-linearity. An alternative method used for the empirical version of the DBM model is through iterative techniques (Fisher, 1992). Here, terminal values are required for the forward-looking variables. These terminal values can be set either in reference to a steady-state solution, or as growth or level restrictions consistent with the saddlepoint path.

One application of the overshooting model is in analysing exchange rate fluctuations. The exchange rate is an endogenous variable, which fluctuates in response to particular shocks. The response will depend on the nature of the shocks. Having identified the shock(s) to the exchange rate, we then need to trace their effects on UK output and prices. For this purpose, a relatively small model gives a sensible starting-point for assessing the speed and scale of the effects. The Dornbusch model is a well-established tool for doing this. This stylised treatment was examined in the Bank of England *Inflation Report* for May 1995, and was used in analysing the appreciation of sterling from August 1996 (see section 8 for further discussion).

A second use of the Dornbusch-style model has been in comparative analysis of the transmission mechanism. A paper by Britton and Whitley (1997) estimates small overshooting models for France, Germany and the United Kingdom, with the aim of trying to identify any important aggregate differences in the transmission mechanism. This approach enables direct testing of the key parameters, so that any differences observed can be tested for significance.

4. Small macroeconometric models

4.1 Introduction

The Bank's macroeconometric modelling is based on the Dornbusch/Fleming-Mundell macroeconomic approach, originating from the extensions of the original IS/LM analysis in the 'systems of econometric equations' approach to applied policy analysis and forecasting.

The Medium Term Econometric Model (MTEM) was initially built in early 1994, since when it has been – and continues to be – revised and updated. The MTEM is used to help produce each of the forecasts of inflation that appear in the Bank's quarterly *Inflation Report*, and its design and construction reflect that priority. The MTEM is not a fixed specification; rather, it describes an approach that is designed to be flexible in use. Here we describe the broad approach.

For the purposes of monetary policy analysis, the Bank's models are designed according to three main criteria:

(i)   they should be small, avoiding unnecessary complexity;
(ii) they should be theoretically well-specified;
(iii) they should pay equal attention to the determination of prices and output.

The first criterion was intended to make model properties, and so forecasts, as transparent to the user as possible. The models are small and can be summarised in around twenty behavioural relationships, although other variables, identities, and exogenous variables bring total size up to nearly 150 variables.

The models all have a well-determined real equilibrium, based on supply driven by Cobb-Douglas technology, which determines output, employment, investment and prices consistently. Real wages are determined in a conventional bargaining framework (see Jackman, Layard and Nickell, 1991). In the long run, real unit labour costs (real wages less productivity), unemployment (or inactivity), and the capital–output ratio tend to predetermined constants that are independent of nominal outcomes under conditions of static and dynamic homogeneity. However, dynamic homogeneity is often found to be inconsistent with the data. One then has to choose whether or not to impose the relevant restrictions on theoretical grounds, or whether it is more important to fit the data. The price level responds to short-run changes in real variables, and the relationship can be expressed by a short-run Phillips curve. The Phillips curve implicit in MTEM is only vertical in the long run if dynamic homogeneity is imposed and expectations are fulfilled on average in the long run.

4.2 A summary of MTEM

The models shown below are meant to be a reasonably complete aggregate account of a one-sector economy under Cobb-Douglas technology. The main features described in this section correspond to the various versions of the model used between 1994 and 1997. But the model is under constant development and review.

Firms are assumed to set prices, given output and the capital stock. They bargain with workers over wages and choose employment. Consumer demand is broadly consistent with modern theories of consumer spending, in which variables such as wealth play an important role.

We are in the process of addressing a number of aspects of the model, mainly related to intertemporal issues. These include the lack of explicit forward-looking behaviour in price determination, and the absence of a government budget constraint (and so the role for government debt accumulation improving the demand side of the model in the light of recent theoretical advances).

The core of the model is very simple, and consistent with the underlying paradigm described in section 1.1. Output is described by a production function exhibiting diminishing returns to each factor. We have chosen a relatively unsophisticated description of technology: a Cobb-Douglas production function with constant returns to scale and disembodied technical progress. The implied marginal product of labour yields a labour demand function. Given a fixed labour supply, the intersection of demand and supply yields the equilibrium real wage consistent with no involuntary unemployment and normal (or potential) output.

In the short run, however, relatively rigid *real* wages generate involuntary unemployment, while *nominal* inertia determines the short-run relationship between real wages and the price level. Short-run changes in labour demand then trace out a positively sloped short-run aggregate supply curve, ensuring that changes in aggregate demand, as derived from an IS-LM system, translate into short-run changes in prices and output. In the long run, real wages adjust to clear involuntary unemployment, and a shift in aggregate demand has no effect on the level of output, only on prices.

A representative example of the MTEM
The representative model is set out in terms of its long-run structure, omitting most of the dynamics. This facilitates the understanding of the basic features of the model. This representation also simplifies by aggregating private sector demand components.

Goods market [(lower case denotes variables in logs; upper case denotes levels; Greek letters are the key parameters)]

(a)   *Demand and output*

(7.13) $q = a_1 n + (1-a_1)k + a_2 t = a_1(n-k) + k + a_2 t$ (production function determining potential output)

(7.14) $d-g = -\alpha_3 r + \alpha_4 a - \alpha_5 y$ (private sector aggregate domestic demand curve)

(7.15) $x = \alpha_6 z - \alpha_7(px - p^f + e)$ (exports)

(7.16) $m = \alpha_8 d + \alpha_9 (p - pm^f + e)$ (imports)

(7.17) $Y \equiv D + X - M$ (GDP identity)

(b) *Prices and costs*

(7.18) $p = w_t + [(1-\alpha_1)/\alpha_1](q-k) + \tau t$ (domestic price; supply curve)

(7.19) $pc = \alpha_{10} p + (1-\alpha_{10}) pm + ti$ (retail price mark-up over producer and import prices)

(7.20) $px = \alpha_{11} p + \alpha_{12}(p^f - e)$ (export price; export supply)

(7.21) $pm = \alpha_{14} p^f + \alpha_{15} e + \alpha_{16} d$ (import price; import supply)

(c) *Labour market*

(7.22) $n = q - (w-p)$ (labour demand curve)

(7.23) $rw = q - n - s(u - \bar{u})$ (real wage; bargaining model)

(7.24) $rw \equiv w - p + te$ (real product wage)

(7.25) $u \equiv (L-N)/L$ (unemployment rate)

Money market/policy

(7.26) $e = e_{+1} + (i - i^f) + \text{risk}$ (exchange rate arbitrage)

(7.27) $m^d - p = \alpha_{17}(y) - \alpha_{18} i - \alpha_{19}(Dp^e_{+1})$ (money demand)

(7.28) $i = Dp^* - \alpha(Dp - Dp^e_{p+1})$ (interest rate reaction function)

(7.29) $A = K + M^d/P + A^f E/P$ (real private wealth)

Overseas sector

(7.30) $B = PX.X - PM.M$ (balance of payments)

(7.31) $A^f = (E/E_{-1}) A^f_{-1} + B$ (net foreign assets)

Glossary

a	-	outside wealth	A^f	-	net foreign assets
B	-	balance of payments	d	-	domestic demand
e	-	nominal effective exchange rate	g	-	government spending
r	-	real interest rate			(exogenous)
u	-	unemployment rate	$\bar{u}$		equilibrium unemploy-
k	-	capital stock			ment rate
L	-	population of working age	m^d	-	money stock
m	-	real imports	n	-	employees in employment
p	-	GDP deflator	pc	-	retail prices
p^f	-	foreign GDP deflator	pm	-	import price
px	-	export prices	q	-	total output (GDP at
i	-	nominal interest rate			factor cost)
i^f	-	foreign interest rate	risk	-	exchange market risk
rw	-	real product wage			premium
t	-	time trend	te	-	employer's labour tax
ti	-	indirect tax			rate
tax	-	tax rate direct on person	w	-	nominal wage
x	-	real exports	y	-	demand for domestic
z	-	world trade/world demand			output

Trade and the exchange rate

The highly aggregate approach taken to the MTEM extends to international trade. The underlying paradigm is one of imperfect competition in world markets. As a result, the export demand and import supply curves faced by the United Kingdom are not perfectly elastic. Export demand (the volumes equation) is a function of overseas demand and relative prices. Export supply (the export price equation) is a function of domestic output and relative prices. Import volumes depend on domestic demand and relative prices; import prices are a function of world prices.

Money and the exchange rate

The nominal exchange rate is determined by an uncovered interest parity (equation (7.26)), in an arbitrage condition of the form:

$$e = E\,(e_{+1}) + (i - i') + \text{risk} \tag{7.26a}$$

The 'risk' variable can be interpreted as a risk premium, which plays a key equilibrating role in the system when the interest rate is held fixed. It is a function of relative prices, inflation rates and the current account ratio. It ensures that the real exchange rate evolves according to real interest rate differentials and, given that real interest rates at home and abroad converge, solves for the equilibrium current account balance consistent with the long-run real exchange rate and NAIRU. In forecasting, the exchange rate is not normally allowed to 'jump' from its starting value, and we assume that markets learn only slowly about deviations between their forecast of interest rates and the Bank's assumptions.

There are a variety of choices for the interest rate path. In forecasting, the Bank has typically assumed unchanged nominal interest rates up to the forecast horizon. However, model simulations are potentially unstable if this condition prevails indefinitely. The model currently allows the use of Taylor rules to provide a monetary policy closure. Alternatively, market forward interest rates can be imposed.

Fiscal sector

The fiscal sector of the model has few estimated equations – it is composed mostly of identities. Expenditure-based taxes create a wedge between the different measures of RPI. Detailed disaggregation on the fiscal side is assumed to be unnecessary. Clearly there is a trade-off here, between the desire for parsimony on the one hand, and the improvement in fit that would derive from the inclusion of extra, more finely differentiated tax terms on the other. We have opted for parsimony; this means that we have implicitly assumed that the marginal propensity to consume does not vary by income group, or at least that it does not vary so much that we should include terms in the marginal tax rates for different income groups in our domestic demand equation.

The absence from the current version of the model of any government budget constraint means potential fiscal instability in the long run (though of course the model is primarily used for forecasting in the short to medium term). The default choice in the model assumes that the real value of total government expenditure is exogenous but, over any forecast period, the cash total expenditure is taken from Treasury projections and that profile is held fixed so as to be consistent with the policy of cash limits. Tax rates are fixed, but the total tax take depends upon what happens to nominal GDP, which is endogenous.

4.3 Solving and simulating the small econometric models

These models are non-linear (principally log-linear), so that they are routinely solved by iterative methods such as Gauss-Seidel. But when forward-looking variants are chosen, modifications to the iterative methods have to be made and terminal conditions specified (see Fisher, 1992).

As noted above, the absence of rules to tie down the level of government debt in the long run makes the long-run properties of the model somewhat less robust, and its main use is in forecasting up to a two to three year horizon and in simulating interest rate, demand and cost shocks.

5. Output gap – Phillips curve models

The purpose of the output gap models is to provide a simple, coherent framework to evaluate how policy changes affect current and expected inflation to address issues such as credibility. These models are typically based around three equations. First, there is a Phillips curve:

$$\Delta p = \phi \Delta p_{+1}^e + (1 - \phi)\Delta p_{-1} + A(L)(y - d)_t \qquad (7.32)$$

where p is the price level, $(y - d)_t$ is the output gap, Δp_{+1}^e is expected inflation and $A(L)$ is a polynomial in the lag operator, with all variables in logs. This formulation allows for stickiness in price-setting due to contractual arrangements, while $A(L)$ allows sufficient flexibility in the dynamics to reflect realistic adjustment speeds. The degree of forward-looking behaviour is given by the parameter ϕ.

There are many possible alternative treatments of inflation expectations, ranging from simple adaptive rules to model consistent forward expectations. The key benefit from using a general form of model is that one can easily vary such assumptions.

We have found the following formulation particularly useful for approximating recent behaviour:

$$\Delta p_{+1}^e = (1-\mu)\Delta p_{-1} + \mu \Delta p^* \tag{7.33}$$

where Δp^* is the inflation target and μ is a parameter measuring the credibility of monetary policy. For a perfectly credible policy, μ will equal unity.

The reduced form is then:

$$\Delta p = \alpha + \beta \Delta p_{-1} + A(L)(y-d) \tag{7.34}$$

where $\alpha = \phi\mu$ and $\beta = \phi(1-\mu) + (1-\phi)$.

With low policy credibility and a high degree of price stickiness ($\mu \to 0$, $\phi \to 0$) so $\alpha \to 0$ and $\beta \to 1$.

So in the limit, (7.34) becomes:

$$\Delta p_t = \Delta p_{-1} + A(L)(y-d). \tag{7.35}$$

In the case of a high degree of credibility and a low degree of price stickiness ($\mu \to 1$, $\phi \to 1$) then $\alpha \to 1$ and $\beta \to 0$ and (7.34) becomes in the limit:

$$\Delta p = \Delta p^* + A(L)(y-d). \tag{7.36}$$

Next, we need to specify where the output gap comes from. A general approach to output gap models is spelt out in Fisher, Mahadeva and Whitley (1997), who estimate a variety of output gaps and derive a measure of uncertainty around the output gap. Their preferred measure uses a production function consistent with that in the econometric model. They estimate the Phillips curve (7.32) using an explicit measure of expectations derived from the Gallup/GFK survey of consumer expectations. The empirical results support some mild asymmetry in the relationship between the output gap and inflation (as in Clark et al., 1995) and some role for sector bottlenecks. However, the testing of 'speed limit' effects – that is, whether the speed at which the output gap is closed has any bearing on the inflation rate – is more complicated. The Phillips curve itself is not a reduced form of the system as a whole, and to understand speed limit effects, one needs to consider the endogeneity of inflation expectations and the output gap itself.

The three-equation model containing the Phillips curve, output gap and inflation expectations formation is set up in both stylised and empirical form, and solved under a variety of assumptions about expectations, using both analytical and iterative methods. The model is useful in describing how different Phillips curve loops may be generated, and in calculating the implicit level of inflation expectations in models where there is no direct measure of expectations. It is not used directly to produce forecasts.

6. Vector autoregressive models

The simplest way of forecasting a variable is to rely solely on its own past values. In particular, suppose that the time series for variable x_t follows the process:

$$\phi(L)\Delta^d x_t = \theta(L)\varepsilon_t \qquad (7.37)$$

where $\phi(L)$ is a pth order lag polynomial, $\theta(L)$ is a qth order lag polynomial, Δ is the difference operator and ε is a white-noise process. In this case, x_t is said to follow an ARMA(p,d,q) process. Using standard techniques, these processes can be estimated and used to produce forecasts. Another use of ARMA models is for stochastic simulation with simple models. In these models, the endogenous variables x_t will depend on some driving processes, ε_t. To run a stochastic simulation requires simulating these processes. One way of doing this is to assume that the driving processes can be represented by ARMA models and to simulate these.

Vector autoregressive models (VAR) use information from more than one variable. In generalising (6.1) to a multivariate framework, we need to impose some basic identification condition – otherwise every variable is a function of every other, and all equations are identical. The simplest VAR excludes all right hand side contemporaneous values, so that each variable is only dependent on lagged information. In fact, this is sufficient but not necessary. VARs can be identified by ordering the equations in some sensible sequence and excluding the first $(n-1)$ contemporaneous terms from the nth equation: this is the approach taken by Sims (1980).

So-called 'structural' VARs place identification conditions on the variance–covariance matrix. This is usually done in a similar 'ordering' or triangularisation, to ensure that certain residuals only affect certain variables in the long run (see Blanchard and Quah, 1989). In fact, there is no unique way of identifying a VAR – at one extreme, one can actually interpret the macroeconometric model as a restricted VAR: the difference is the over-identifying restrictions in the macroeconometric model.

In addition to different identification conditions, there are alternative estimation procedures. Bayesian VAR models (BVARs) take account of one's prior view on coefficients to help 'shrink' the distribution of parameter estimates. Usually, this means guiding the model towards a first-difference specification.

VAR models are designed to capture correlations in the time-series data with a minimum of theory-based restrictions. They therefore 'let the data speak'. The received wisdom is that VAR models provide 'reasonable' forecasts over the short to medium term.

The absence of detailed economic structure makes VAR forecasts and simulations more difficult to interpret and adjust than projections based on a macroeconomic model. Since monetary policy is as much concerned with understanding inflationary pressures as producing the best point forecast, a VAR cannot entirely substitute for the macroeconometric model for forecasting. The lack of structure in a VAR means that it is also not easily amended using results from other models. Nevertheless, VAR model forecasts may be a useful benchmark against which one can compare the more sophisticated forecast based on other approaches. If they are very different, then it may lead one to question the assumptions surrounding the more sophisticated forecast.

Simple VAR models have been estimated at the Bank for forecasting inflation (Henry and Pesaran, 1993) and ordered VARs for analysing monetary shocks (Ganley and Salmon, 1997). The Bank has also constructed some structural VARs (e.g. Quah and Vahey, 1995), and Astley and Garratt, 1996).

The Henry and Pesaran VARs for monthly and quarterly RPIX inflation have been regularly re-estimated and re-specified. These models are made parsimonious by testing down from a general specification. The original monthly VAR (January 1974 to December 1992) produced a five-variable model estimated involving the following variables with a 13-lag distribution.

- RPIX inflation
- Changes in M0
- Producer output prices
- Retail sales
- Industrial production.

The quarterly VAR contained only three variables estimated over 1974 Q1 to 1992 Q4 with a lag length of nine quarters.

- Inflation
- Changes in M0
- Consumer confidence.

The Henry and Pesaran study has been updated in the Bank with quite different results using quarterly data for 1964 Q1–96 Q4, and January 1975–July 1997 for the monthly model. The most recent specification of the monthly model (12 lags) contains inflation, manufacturing unit labour costs, the unemployment rate and retail sales. The quarterly model (9 lags) now includes only whole-economy unit labour costs and producer output prices, in addition to RPIX inflation. No additional role could be found for the exchange rate or the rate of interest. M0 no longer enters the model. The lack of structure in VAR makes them prone to a lack of robustness, and these changes in specification are neither surprising nor unusual. The practical use of these VARs has been limited. That partly reflects the conflicting results from forecasting with the quarterly and monthly equation.

The 'structural' VARs have been somewhat more successful. In particular, the predictions from SVARs can be useful to identify shocks hitting the economy. Astley and Garratt (1996) used a SVAR to identify real and nominal shocks to the exchange rate, and their consequences for UK output and inflation.

7. Cross-model comparisons

There are various criteria that can be used to compare the different models: their theoretical features; their degree of empirical support; their method of solution; how they are simulated and so on. They can also be judged by which type of issue they are best suited to analyse. Table 7.1 below gives a broad summary of the characteristics of the five classes of model.

The *small analytical models* stand out by their explicit dependence on optimising behaviour by individual agents under rational expectations. They can therefore be used to simulate the effects of changes in underlying behavioural parameters, such as risk aversion, discount rates and so on. They usually (but not invariably) assume perfectly competitive markets. They are based on calibrated parameters, and assessed on their ability to explain stylised facts such as correlations and variance of key macrovariables. Solution of these models requires the data to be stationary, which can be done by de-trending. We then apply the parameterised expectations technique of den Haan and Marcet (1990). The small analytical models can produce quantitative impulse response functions, but are more regularly used to generate correlations between economic variables.

The *stylised macro models* have a less rigorous underlying theory, but are based on standard macro analysis (extended open-economy IS/LM). They usually assume rational expectations, and can be solved analytically or by numerical methods, giving either qualitative or quantitative responses to shocks. The standard Dornbusch analytical models contain dynamic features through price stickiness, but we have also constructed empirical models. The Dornbusch models do not contain explicit wealth effects and intertemporal effects, and have been more commonly applied to demand shocks.

The *output gap models* are reduced-form models that emphasise the dynamic response of output and inflation to demand shocks under different assumptions about expectations. Both empirical and stylised parameter versions have been constructed in the Bank. A feature of these models is the statistical mechanism to generate uncertainty around measures of the output gap, and an explicit mechanism to generate inflation expectations. Since these models summarise the effects of changes in the output gap on inflation, they are designed mainly to explain the response of simple aggregate demand and supply shocks.

The *VAR models* emphasise empirical correlations and variances in the data, but do not usually have an explicit underlying theory, although structural VARs contain restrictions on impulse responses. Expectations and intertemporal considerations are implicit. There are no exogenous variables in these models, so that simulations involve shocking the innovation terms in the model. Their main uses are in short-term predictions, and inferring the nature of shocks from empirical data.

We now turn to the *econometric* models. These are the unifying models in the model suite, because they provide the main empirical framework. Because they identify all the major simultaneous feedbacks, cover most aspects of the transmission mechanism, and provide dynamic, quantitative responses, they can be used for analysing several different types of shock. But they often treat key variables such as asset prices as exogenous, or do not otherwise distinguish between different sources of shock. Since they are based on empirical correlations in the data and are not derived specifically from rigorous theory, they may be mis-specified for a particular shock. They therefore cannot be used mechanically in many situations, and have to be supplemented by information from other models. The next section describes practical examples of this.

Table 7.1 *Characteristics of the different model types*

	Small analytical models	Stylised macro	Econometric	Output gap	VAR
Theory					
Source of behaviour	Individual agent optimising	Aggregate macro	Aggregate macro	Reduced-form	Reduced-form
Static or dynamic	Both	Both	Dynamic	Dynamic	Dynamic
Expect-ations	Rational	Rational	Can be implicit, extra-polative or model consistent	Adaptive or rational	Implicit
Inter-temporal	Yes	No	Partial	No	No
Supply side	Production function, discretionary taxes	Some	Production function; labour market	No	N/A
Construct-ion	Calibrated	Stylised/ calibrated/ estimated	Estimated (long-run may be calibrated)	Stylised/ estimated	Estimated
Method of solution	Parameter-ised expect-ations	Analytic/ parameter-ised expect-ations/ numerical methods	Numerical methods	Analytic/ numerical methods	Numerical methods
Validation	Match to stylised facts	Implied responses	Econometric criteria, implied responses	Match to stylised	Goodness of fit
Simulation	Stochastic	Stochastic or deter-ministic	Usually determin-istic	Determin-istic	Stochastic/ determin-istic
Main types of shock	Productivity, preference, fiscal, foreign	Money, labour market, foreign	Interest rates, fiscal, demand, cost, foreign	Credibility, demand	Depends on formulation

The principal advantage of the macroeconometric approach is that models such as MTEM provide a forecasting tool, as well as a tool for policy analysis. While the analysis may be less theoretically rigorous than in general equilibrium models, the econometric model is necessary to generate quantitative dynamic forecasts. The best possible tool for minimising prediction error might be a VAR, or even a univariate ARMA model, but these are not useful for discussing forecast issues and uncertainties. The econometric model is therefore 'Jack-of-all-trades', combining numerical forecasts with reasonably well-founded analysis and, as pointed out above, it is only one of a suite of models that the Bank uses for a variety of purposes. It is not always the 'best' model for any particular issue, nor is it intended as the 'best' econometric model in the sense of encompassing all other econometric models or having the best fit. Rather, the design reflects flexibility and adaptability in practical forecasting.

8. Using the models together: an illustration

This section discusses how the multi-model framework is used in practice (see also Whitley, 1997). We present an example of how results from various models in the suite have been used to address one particular issue. Different models addressed to a single question will often yield different answers. These different insights and implications need to be combined, though not by simple averaging. Rather, the process requires an input of judgment in weighing the separate pieces of evidence.

A forecast is usually built around a particular default macroeconomic model. The other models can be used in a variety of ways:

(1) to prepare the input assumptions (for example, for the world economy)
(2) to amend the equations or parameters in the default model
(3) to make direct adjustments to a projection or simulation to allow for effects not incorporated in the default model
(4) to act as a check on the overall properties of the projection or simulation
(5) to assess the risks around a projection, or the sensitivity of a simulation response where it is a known way that the default model is mis-specified.

In forecasting, one is often faced with a situation where the data have been observed, and the first step is to identify what shocks have occurred. Since different shocks have different implications for output, inflation and employment, it is necessary to take a view on the source of any shock. Alternative models can be used to predict correlations between macro variables for different shocks, which can then be contrasted with the observed correlations in the data. Once the source of a shock is known, models can again be used to predict its consequences, whether qualitative or quantitative. Often the same model can be used to analyse both the source of a shock and its consequences.

Shocks may be classified in many ways: demand or supply in origin; domestic or foreign; fiscal or monetary; real or nominal. Different models may be appropriate, depending on the nature of the shocks. For example, intertemporal models may be more appropriate when considering wealth or asset shocks; simple output gap models may be more useful in considering shifts in expectations, perhaps as policy credibility changes; and explicit open-economy models may be more useful where the exchange rate is a key part of the transmission of a shock.

As noted in the previous section, the econometric models can be regarded as the unifying mechanisms and the channel through which results with other models are translated into forecasts or simulations. Despite this role, knowledge of the econometric model(s) alone cannot be used to infer changes to the forecast in response to new information, or to evaluate *ex post* forecast error.

The Bank regularly produces projections of inflation, which are published in the *Inflation Report* in the form of a probability distribution (see Britton, Fisher and Whitley, 1998). More recently, projections of GDP growth have also been published. Our models are therefore used both to produce the central projection and to analyse the risks around it.

The preparation of assessment and forecasts for the Bank of England's *Inflation Report*, following the appreciation of sterling from August 1996, gives a practical example of how the models have been used in combination.

For modelling and forecasting purposes, the exchange rate is regarded as an endogenous variable in the macroeconomy, which fluctuates in response to particular shocks: the source of the shock will have different implications for the responses of key macro variables. The first stage in evaluating the impact of the appreciation was therefore to identify the nature of the shock(s). That was not straightforward.

A variety of possible shocks were candidates for explaining the appreciation: foreign and domestic monetary news; foreign and domestic fiscal news; productivity shocks; preference shocks; oil price effects; risk premia or general portfolio shocks (possibly euro-related).

With some auxiliary assumptions, the UIP model can be used to identify exchange rate news relating to expected changes in interest rates (see Brigden *et al.*, 1997). Identifying real shocks is harder. We used the Dornbusch and Obstfeld/Rogoff (1995) models to assess the possible effect of fiscal shocks, and fundamental equilibrium exchange rate (FEER) analysis to consider the role of oil prices. The basic real business-cycle model was used to look at the possibility that there had been a shift in productivity (through the Solow residual) and information from structural VARs developed by Astley and Garratt (1996) was used to identify the relative scale of real and nominal shocks. Using all this information, together with other pieces of analysis (for example, the probability distribution of future expected exchange rates, to throw light on a portfolio shift arising from uncertainties related to EMU enabled a rough weighting on the different sources of shock with no shock seeming to dominate). Even after all this model-based analysis, there remained a significant unexplained component of the appreciation about which a judgment had to be made.

Having thus analysed the possible sources of the exchange rate shock, we then needed to map these shocks through to UK output and prices. The Dornbusch model provided a useful guide. For example, a positive productivity shock will permanently raise UK output and lower the price level; a positive foreign money shock will raise the exchange rate and temporarily lower UK prices, but with no long-run effect; and an upward oil price shock will temporarily raise the real exchange rate and lower output and prices. In this way, and using the estimated real exchange rate elasticities in the econometric forecasting model, the implications of the exchange rate appreciation for UK exports and imports, and for UK output as a whole, were assessed. The analysis incorporated assumptions about temporary margins adjustment by exporters and importers. It also took account of the fact that the estimated elasticities are based on a sample where changes in the real exchange rate have been a mixture of perceived temporary and persistent change.

In practice, the Bank had to take a view as to how much of the appreciation could be explained by monetary and fiscal factors that might only have a transitory effect on the real exchange rate, and how much reflected other factors that might have a more persistent effect (see *Inflation Report*, February 1997, pages 43–5). Whether the effect on the exchange rate was temporary or persistent would also influence the response of export and import prices and volumes, so judgments had to be made about whether the responses allowed for were in the trade price and volume equations in the model, and whether the lags were appropriate.

In order to quantify all of these effects, the model was adjusted in a variety of ways. The parameters of the export demand equation were changed to allow for any improvement in non-price competitiveness that might have partially explained the appreciation. The 'exogenous' rate of technical progress or labour productivity in the econometric model would have been adjusted had it been judged that there had been a change which made a significant contribution to explaining sterling appreciation. Judgments about the future path of the exchange rate were made, based on UIP considerations, but also reflecting an assessment of how far any unexplained element of the exchange rate appreciation would persist (see for example, *Inflation Report*, November 1997, p. 46). The estimated impact of the exchange rate on export and import prices and volumes was derived from external trade equations modified to incorporate other evidence on the speed of response or ultimate degree of impact.

The result was a blend of analysis that is consistent with theory models and empirical regularities. Clearly a great deal of judgment was required in this process. But mechanical use of econometric models by shifting an 'exogenous' exchange rate would be misleading. The procedures are time-consuming and require considerable thought. But this is seen as a virtue rather than a cost.

The treatment of the exchange rate is just one forecast issue where many models have been used to inform the Bank's judgment. Other examples are where the use of sectoral money demand models have been used (Thomas, 1997a,b) to consider the possible effects of the strong rise in broad money growth since 1995. Forward-looking models of consumption have been used together with survey and *ad hoc* evidence to analyse the consequences of windfall payments from the conversion of friendly societies to publicly quoted companies (see *Inflation Report*, February 1997, page 22). Small analytical models of the labour market have been used to consider whether possible changes in job uncertainty might change the level of consumption and employment. The output gap/Phillips curve models have been used to consider the possible effect on inflation of changes in the credibility of the inflation target; to check the consistency of the implied level of inflation expectations in forecasts; dynamic (speed limit) and asymmetric effects associated with changes in the output gap; and possible implications from sector output gaps. Both sectoral money models and other consumption models have been used to evaluate possible consequences of the rise in equity prices, and the RBC model has been used to evaluate the claim that trend productivity growth has recently shifted.

All these examples have one common feature: the default macroeconomic model (section 4.2) was not the best vehicle for analysing the issue.

The strength of the macroeconomic model is in bringing the analyses to bear on a forecast in a quantitatively systematic manner.

9. Summary

This chapter has set out a description of the various macroeconomic models that have been used at the Bank of England. These are being reviewed and augmented as research continues, and as the Monetary Policy Committee expands its demands for alternative ways of thinking about key issues. The approach formalises what many economists do already when faced with a particular issue – that is, find the most relevant simplification in the 'tool kit' and then add the necessary complications. The most relevant simplification is often a standard piece of micro or macro theory, which explains the emphasis on building up a portfolio of such models. But empirical models matter as well, if forecasts are to have some consistency with past UK data. No single model or approach is likely to be fully adequate to the task. For any single forecast, an econometric forecasting model plays a central role in the process. The Bank's approach has been to keep the size of this model small, to focus on the important issues. The need for detail and complexity is best served by specific models, according to the particular question at hand. But the debate is not just about model size. There is a case for maintaining a cross-section of models to capture some of the inherent uncertainty around views as to how the economy behaves and responds to shocks, thus enabling the Bank to evaluate the risks to any forecast.

Note

1 The models described in this paper were developed by Bank staff largely before the establishment of the new Monetary Policy Committee (MPC). No model presented here should therefore be represented as the MPC's views of the transmission mechanism. The views expressed are those of the authors and do not necessarily reflect those of the Bank of England. The Small Analytical Model (SAM) project was commissioned by Mervyn King in 1993, with the appointment of Andrew Scott as an academic consultant. The models described have been developed principally in the Conjunctural Assessment and Projections Division of the Bank. Significant contributions have been made at various stages by (in roughly chronological order): Andrew Scott, Allison Holland, Shamik Dhar, Danny Quah, Stephen Millard, John Lumsden, Marianne Sensier, Tony Garratt, Jason Dowson and Martin

Ellison. Significant contributions to the other models have been made by Erik Britton, John Butler, Alastair Cunningham, Shamik Dhar, Allison Holland, Lavan Mahadeva, Stephen Millard, Meghan Quinn, Ryland Thomas and David Tinsley. The authors are grateful for the original research contributions of many colleagues and especially to Bill Allen and John Vickers for helpful comments. Any errors in this chapter are the responsibility of the authors alone. Further developments are described in two special reports published by the Bank of England (1999) and the Monetary Policy Committee (1999). [©Bank of England 1998]

References

Aiyagari, S., Christiano, L.J. and Eichenbaum, M. (1988), 'The output and employment effects of government purchases', mimeo.

Altonji, J.G. (1986), 'Intertemporal substitution in labour supply: evidence from micro data', *Journal of Political Economy*, 94, 3, pp. 5176–215.

Astley, M. S. and Garratt, A. (1996), 'Interpreting sterling exchange rate movements', *Bank of England Quarterly Bulletin,* November, pp. 394–404.

Bank of England (1999), *Economic Models at the Bank of England*, London, Bank of England.

Begg, D., Dornbusch, R. and Fischer, S. (1991), *Macroeconomics*, London, McGraw-Hill.

Blanchard, O. and Fischer, S. (1990), *Lectures in Macroeconomics*, Cambridge, Mass, MIT Press.

Blanchard, O.J. and Kahn, C.M. (1980), 'The solution of linear difference models under rational expectations', *Econometrica*, 48, pp. 1305–11.

Blanchard, O. and Quah, D. (1989), 'The dynamic effect of aggregate demand and supply disturbances', *American Economic Review*, 79, pp. 655–73.

Braun, R.A. (1994), 'Tax disturbances and real economic activity in the post-war US economy', *Journal of Monetary Economics*, 33, pp. 441–62.

Brigden, A., Martin, B. and Salmon, C. (1997), 'Decomposing exchange rate movements according to the uncovered interest rate parity condition', *Bank of England Quarterly Bulletin*, November, pp. 377–89.

Britton, E.M., Fisher, P.G. and Whitley, J.D. (1998), *Bank of England Quarterly Bulletin*, February, pp. 30–7.

Britton, E.M. and Whitley, J.D. (1997), 'Comparing the monetary transmission mechanism in France, Germany and the United Kingdom: some issues and results', *Bank of England Quarterly Bulletin*, May, pp. 152–62.

Buiter, W.A. (1984), 'Saddlepoint problems in continuous time rational expectations models: a general method and some macroeconomic examples', *Econometrica*, 52, pp. 665–80.

Buiter, W.A. and Miller, M. (1981), 'The Thatcher experiment: the first two years', *Brookings Papers on Economic Activity*, 2, pp. 315–67.

Burnside, C., Eichenbaum, M. and Rebelo, S.T. (1993), 'Labour hoarding and the business cycle', *Journal of Political Economy*, 101, pp. 411–43.

Cho, J.O. and Cooley, T.F. (1994), 'Employment and hours over the business cycle' *Journal of Economic Dynamics and Control*, 18, pp. 411–32.

Christiano and Eichenbaum, M. (1992), 'Current real business cycle theory and aggregate labour market fluctuations', *American Economic Review*, 87, pp. 430–50.

Clark, P., Laxton, D. and Rose, S. (1995), 'Asymmetric effects of economic activity on inflation: evidence and policy implications', *IMF Staff Papers*, 42, pp. 344–74.

Cooley, T.F. and Hansen, G.D. (1989), 'The inflation tax in a real business cycle model', *American Economic Review*, 79, pp. 733–48.

Cunningham, A.W.F. (1996), 'Measurement bias in price indices: an application to the UK's RPI', Bank of England Working Paper No.47.

(1997), 'Quantifying survey data', *Bank of England Quarterly Bulletin*, August, pp. 292–300.

den Haan, W.J. and Marcet, A. (1990), 'Solving the stochastic growth model by parameterising expectations', *Journal of Business and Economic Statistics*, 8, pp. 31–4.

(1994), 'Accuracy in simulations', *Review of Economic Studies*, 61, pp. 3–18.

Dornbusch, R. (1976), 'Expectations and exchange rate dynamics', *Journal of Political Economy*, 84, pp. 161–76.

Fisher, P.G. (1992), *Rational Expectations in Macroeconomic Models*, London, Kluwer Academic Publishers.

Fisher, P.G., Mahadeva, L. and Whitley, J.D. (1997), 'Utiliser l'écart de production pour prévoir l'inflation: l'éxpérience de la Banque d'Angleterre', *Economie Internationale*, 69, pp. 135–52.

Gali, J. (1995), 'Real business cycles with involuntary unemployment', CEPR mimeo.

Ganley, J. and Salmon, C.K. (1997), 'The industrial impact of monetary policy shocks: some stylised facts', Bank of England Working Paper No. 77.

Hansen, G.D. (1985), 'Indivisible labor and the business cycle', *Journal of Monetary Economics*, 16, pp. 309–27.

Henry, S.G.B. and Pesaran, B. (1993), 'VAR models of inflation', *Bank of England Quarterly Bulletin*, May, pp. 231–9.

Holland, A. and Scott, A. (1997), 'The determinants of UK business cycles', Bank of England Working Paper No. 58.

Jackman, R., Layard, R. and Nickell, S. (1991), *Unemployment*, Oxford: Oxford University Press

King, R.G., Plosser, C.I. and Rebelo, S.T. (1988), 'Production, growth and business cycles: I. The basic neoclassical model', *Journal of Monetary Economics*, 21, pp. 195–232.

Kydland, F.E. and Prescott, E.C. (1982), 'Time to build and aggregate fluctuations', *Econometrica*, 50, pp. 1345–70.

Merz, M. (1995), 'Search in the labour market and the real business cycle', *Journal of Monetary Economics*, 36, pp. 269–300.

Millard, S.P., Scott, A. and Sensier, M. (1997), 'The labour market over the business cycle: Can theory fit the facts?', *Oxford Review of Economic Policy*, 13, 3, pp. 70–91.

Monetary Policy Committee (1999), *The Transmission Mechanism of Monetary Policy*, London, Bank of England.

Mortensen, D.T. and Pissarides, C.A. (1994), 'Job creation and job destruction in the theory of unemployment', *Review of Economic Studies*, 61, pp. 397–416.

Obstfeld, M. and Rogoff, K. (1995), 'Exchange rate dynamics redux', *Journal of Political Economy*, 103, pp. 524–60.

Quah, D. and Vahey, S.P. (1995), 'Measuring core inflation', *Economic Journal*, 105, 432, September, pp. 1130–44.

Sargent, T. (1987), *Macroeconomic Theory*, 2nd edn, London, Academic Press.

Schlagenhauf, D.E. and Wrase, J.M. (1995), 'Liquidity and real activity in a simple open economy model', *Journal of Monetary Economics*, 35, pp. 431–61.

Sims, C.A. (1980), 'Macroeconomics and reality', *Econometrica*, 48, pp. 1–48.

Thomas, R. (1997a), 'The demand for M4: a sector analysis. Part 1 – the personal sector', Bank of England Working Paper No. 61.

(1997b), 'The demand for M4: a sector analysis. Part 2 – the corporate sector', Bank of England Working Paper No. 62.

Whitley, J.D. (1997), 'Economic models and policy-making', *Bank of England Quarterly Bulletin*, May, pp. 163–73.

Yun, T. (1996), 'Nominal price rigidity, money supply endogeneity and business cycles', *Journal of Monetary Economics*, 37, pp. 345–70.

8 Estimated stabilisation costs of the EMU

RAY C. FAIR

1. Introduction

When different countries adopt a common currency, each gives up its own monetary policy. In the common-currency regime monetary policy responds to a shock in a particular country only to the extent that the common monetary authority responds to the shock. If this response is less than the response that the own country's monetary authority would have made in the pre-common-currency regime, there are stabilisation costs of moving to a common currency. This chapter estimates the stabilisation costs to European countries of adopting a common currency. The multicountry econometric (MC) model in Fair (1994) and stochastic simulation are used for this purpose. Variability estimates are computed for the current regime and for the regime that is assumed to exist if a common currency is adopted.[1]

The question that this chapter attempts to answer is a huge one, and the present results are at best exploratory. In order to answer this question one needs, first, an estimate of how the current world economy operates, second, an estimate of how it would operate if the European countries adopted a common currency, and third, an estimate of the likely shocks to the world economy. Each of these estimates in this chapter is only an approximation, and work with other approximations is needed before much confidence can be placed on the current conclusions. The main aim here, aside from presenting some initial cost estimates, is to propose a methodology for answering this question.

There is a rapidly growing literature on analysing the economic consequences of a common European currency. Wyploz (1997) provides a useful recent review. Much of this literature is in the Mundell (1961), McKinnon

(1963), and Kenen (1969) framework and asks whether Europe meets the standards for an optimum currency area. The questions asked include how open the countries are, how correlated individual shocks are across countries, and the degree of labour mobility. There is also recent work examining real exchange rate variances. The smaller are these variances, the smaller are the likely costs of moving to a common currency. In a recent study von Hagen and Neumann (1994) compare variances of price levels within West German regions with variances of real exchange rates between the regions and other European countries.

The MC model that is used for the results here contains estimates of how open countries are in that there are estimated import demand equations and estimated trade-share equations in the model. The model also contains estimates of the correlation of individual shocks across countries through the estimated error terms in the individual equations. Real exchange rates are endogenous because there are estimated equations for nominal exchange rates and individual country price levels. The coefficients of all these equations are estimated in traditional ways (by 2SLS or OLS); no calibration is done.[2] The MC model thus has embedded in it estimates of a number of the features of the world economy that are needed to analyse optimum-currency-area questions. The degree of labour mobility among countries, however, is not estimated: the specification of the model is based on the assumption of no labour mobility among countries. To the extent that there is labour mobility, the present stabilisation-cost estimates are likely to be too high.

A key feature of the MC model for present purposes is that there are estimated monetary policy rules for each of the main countries. These take the form of estimated interest rate reaction functions. In the EMU regime these rules for the European countries are replaced with one rule – one interest rate reaction function for all of Europe. There are also estimated exchange rate equations for each of the main countries in the model (except for the United States, which is the base country). In the EMU regime these equations for the European countries are replaced with one equation – the exchange rate equation for the common European currency vis-à-vis the US dollar.

Section 2 briefly outlines the MC model, and section 3 explains the stochastic simulation experiments. The variability estimates are then presented in section 4 for the regular version of the model – the 'current' regime. Section 5 discusses the changes that were made to the MC model to set up the 'EMU' regime. This is the least data-determined part of the chapter. Assumptions have to be made about the characteristics of the EMU regime, and many choices are possible. As a first cut it is assumed that all European countries join the EMU, and so the present estimates are conditional on this assumption. In future work it would be easy to use different subsets of countries, depending on what seemed most likely to happen. The general methodology is not restricted to using all the countries. The variability estimates are then presented in section 6 for the EMU regime, and they are compared with the estimates in section 4. Section 7 concludes with a discussion of some possible biases of the estimates.

Some of the results here are also related to the literature on policy co-ordination across countries. Using the methodology of this chapter it is possible to examine the effects of one country's policy behaviour on other countries, and this is briefly discussed at the end of section 4.

2. The MC model

There are 33 countries in the MC model.[3] There are 31 stochastic equations for the United States and up to 15 each for the other countries. The total number of stochastic equations is 328, and the total number of estimated coefficients is 1442. In addition, there are 1041 estimated trade-share equations. The total number of endogenous and exogenous variables, not counting the trade shares, is about 4000. Trade-share data were collected for 45 countries, and so the trade-share matrix is 45 × 45.[4] An updated version of this model has been used for the present work.

The estimation periods begin in 1954Q1 for the United States and as soon after 1960 as data permit for the other countries. They end between 1992 and 1994 except for the United States, where they end in 1997Q1. The estimation technique is 2SLS except when there are too few observations to make the technique practical, where OLS is used. The estimation accounts for possible serial correlation of the error terms. The variables used for the first stage regressors for a country are the main predetermined variables in the model for the country. A list of these variables is available from the website. Since the MC model is discussed in detail in Fair (1994) and on the website, it will be only briefly outlined here.[5]

The estimated equations

On the demand side, there are estimated equations for consumption, fixed investment, inventory investment, and imports for each country. Consumption depends on income, wealth, and an interest rate. Fixed investment depends on output and an interest rate. Inventory investment depends on the level of sales and the lagged stock of inventories. The level of imports depends on income, wealth, the relative price of imported versus domestically produced goods, and an interest rate. The interest rate used for a given country and equation is either a short-term rate or a long-term rate, depending on which is more significant. The long-term rate is related to the short-term rate in each country through a standard term structure equation, where the long-term rate depends on the current value and lagged values of the short-term rate. A decrease in the short-term interest rate in a country leads to a decrease in the long-term rate, and interest-rate decreases have a positive effect on consumption, fixed investment, and imports.

There are estimated price and wage equations per country. A recent discussion of these equations can be found in Fair (1997a, 1997b). The domestic price level in a country depends, among other things, on a measure of demand pressure (usually an output-gap variable) and the price of imports.

As noted in section 1, there is an estimated interest-rate reaction function for each country. The short-term interest rate depends on inflation, demand pressure, and the balance of payments. These are 'leaning against the wind' equations of the monetary authorities. The monetary authorities are estimated to raise short-term interest rates in response to increases in inflation and demand pressure and decreases in the balance of payments. The US short-term interest rate is an explanatory variable in a number of the other countries' reaction functions. This means that the United States is assumed to play a leadership role in setting monetary policy. Also, the German short-term interest rate is an explanatory variable in a number of the other European countries' reaction functions.

The variables that were chosen as explanatory variables in the interest rate reaction function for a given country were those whose coefficient estimates were of the expected sign and were statistically significant or close to being significant. The variables that were tried included current and past values of inflation, of various measures of demand pressure, and of the balance of payments. For some countries none of these variables were significant, which means that no evidence could be found that the monetary authority of that country leaned against the wind with respect to domestic variables. The four key European countries in this regard are Austria, France, Belgium, and Spain. Aside from the constant term and the lagged dependent variable, the only explanatory variable in the Austrian interest rate reaction function is the German short-term interest rate. For France and Belgium the only two additional explanatory variables are the German and US interest rates, and for Spain the only additional variable is the US interest rate. More will be said about the use of the interest rate reaction functions in section 4.

There is an estimated exchange rate equation per country. For Germany and all the non-European countries, the dependent variable is the exchange rate vis-à-vis the US dollar. For these countries, the exchange rate depends on the price level of the country relative to the US price level and the short-term interest rate of the country relative to the US interest rate. For the European countries except Germany, the dependent variable is the exchange rate vis-à-vis the Deutschmark. For these countries the exchange rate depends on the price level of the country relative to the German price level and the short-term interest rate of the country relative to the German interest rate.

There are also estimated equations explaining the demand for money, the forward exchange rate, employment, the labour force of men, and the labour force of women. These will not be discussed here.

In a given trade-share equation, the share of country i's total imports imported from country j depends on the price of country j's exports relative to a price index of all the other countries' export prices. The trade-share equations are in US dollars, and all export prices are converted to dollar prices using the exchange rates. The restriction that the sum of all exports equals the sum of all imports is imposed in the model.

The effects of an interest rate decrease

To help in understanding the results, it will be useful to discuss the effects of a decrease in the short-term interest rate in a country. A decrease in the short-term rate leads to a decrease in the long-term rate through the term structure equation. A decrease in the short-term rate also leads to a depreciation of the country's currency (assuming that the interest rate decrease is relative to other countries' interest rates). The interest rate decreases lead to an increase in consumption, investment, and imports. The depreciation of the currency leads to an increase in exports. This effect on exports works through the trade-share equations. The dollar price of the country's exports that feeds into the trade-share equations is lower because of the depreciation, and this increases the share of the other countries' total imports imported from the particular country. The effect on aggregate demand in the country from the interest rate decrease is thus positive from the increase in consumption, investment, and exports and negative from the increase in imports. The net effect could thus go either way, but it is almost always positive.

There is also a positive effect on inflation. The depreciation leads to an increase in the price of imports, and this has a positive effect on the domestic price level through the price equation. In addition, if aggregate demand increases, this increases demand pressure, which has a positive effect on the domestic price level.

There are many other effects that follow from these, including effects back on the short-term interest rate itself through the interest rate reaction function, but these are typically second order in nature, especially in the short run. The main effects are as just described.

More details on the model

There is a mixture of quarterly and annual data in the MC model. Quarterly equations are estimated for fourteen countries (the first fourteen in note 3), and annual equations are estimated for the remaining nineteen. However, all the trade-share equations are quarterly. There are quarterly data on all the variables that feed into the trade-share equations, namely the exchange rate, the local-currency price of exports, and the total value of imports per country. When the model is solved, the predicted annual values of these variables for the annual countries are converted to predicted quarterly values using a simple distribution assumption. The quarterly predicted values from the trade-share equations are converted to annual values by summation or averaging when this is needed.

There are sixteen European countries in the model, eight quarterly and eight annual. The following discussion will focus on eight of these: Germany, Italy, the Netherlands, the United Kingdom, Austria, France, Belgium, and Spain. Belgium and Spain are annual countries, and the others are quarterly. The other eight countries (Switzerland, Finland, Denmark, Norway, Sweden, Greece, Ireland, and Portugal) have very small or zero estimated interest-rate effects on aggregate demand, and so these countries are not much affected by a switch of monetary-policy regimes. The results for these eight countries are in general not as good as those for the other European countries, and so probably not much confidence should be placed on the small estimated interest-rate effects in these countries. These small effects may simply be due to poor data or too few observations. In other words, it may be that these countries would be importantly affected by the move to a common European currency, but that the econometric work is not good enough to pick this up.

Total European output as used below is denominated in Deutschmarks and is the sum of the output of all sixteen European countries. The European price level is defined to be the ratio of nominal to real European output.[6]

3. The stochastic simulation experiments

Since the main exercise here is to estimate and compare economic variability in the current regime and in the EMU regime, one needs a measure of economic variability and a way of calculating it. The approach taken is as follows.

Of the 328 stochastic equations, 189 are quarterly and 139 are annual. There is an estimated error term for each of these equations for each period. Although the equations do not all have the same estimation period, the period 1972–94 is common to almost all equations.[7] There are thus available 23 vectors of annual error terms and 92 vectors of quarterly error terms. These vectors are taken as estimates of the economic shocks, and they are drawn in the manner discussed below. Note that these vectors pick up historical correlations of the error terms. If, for example, German, French, and Italian consumption shocks are highly positively correlated, the error terms in the three consumption equations will tend to be all high together or all low together.

The period used for the variability estimates is 1989Q1–1994Q4, six years or 24 quarters. This study is concerned with stabilisation around some base path and not with the position of the base path itself, and it does not matter much which path is chosen for the base path. The choice here is simply to take as the base path the historical path. If the estimated errors for 1989Q1–1994Q4 are added to the model and taken to be exogenous, the solution of the model for this period using the actual values of all the exogenous variables is the perfect tracking solution. For all the stochastic simulations below, the estimated errors for 1989Q1–1994Q4 are added to the model and the draws are around these errors. This means that all the draws are around the historical path.

Each trial for the stochastic simulation is a dynamic deterministic simulation for 1989Q1–1994Q4 using a particular draw of the error terms. For each of the six years for a given trial an integer is drawn between 1 and 23 with probability 1/23 for each integer. This draw determines which of the 23 vectors of annual error terms is used for that year. The four vectors of quarterly error terms used are the four that correspond to that year. Each trial is thus based on drawing six integers. The solution of the model for this trial is an estimate of what the world economy would have been like had the particular drawn error terms actually occurred. (Remember that the drawn error terms are on top of the actual error terms for 1989Q1–1994Q4, which are always used.) By using the estimated error terms for the draws, the trials are consistent with the historical experience: the estimated error terms are data determined.[8] The number of trials taken is 100, so 100 world economic outcomes for 1989Q1–1994Q4 are available for analysis.[9]

Let y_t^j be the predicted value of endogenous variable y for quarter or year t on trial j, and let y_t^* be the base-path (actual) value. How best to summarise the 100×24 or 100×6 values of y_t^j? One possibility for a variability measure is to compute the variability of y_t^j around y_t^* for each t: $(1/J)\sum_{j=1}^{J}(y_t^j - y_t^*)^2$, where J is the total number of trials.[10] The problem with this measure, however, is that there are either 24 or 6 values per variable, which makes summary difficult. A more useful measure is the following. Let L^j be:

$$L^j = \frac{1}{T}\sum_{i=1}^{T}(y_t^j - y_t^*)^2 \tag{8.1}$$

where T is the length of the simulation period (24 or 6 in the present case). Then the measure is

$$L = \sqrt{\frac{1}{J}\sum_{j=1}^{J}L^j} . \tag{8.2}$$

L is a measure of the deviation of the variable from its base values over the whole period, and because the square root is taken, it is in units of the standard deviation of the variable.[11]

4. Variability estimates for the current regime

Values of L for four variables, ten countries plus total Europe, and four experiments are presented in table 8.1. The two non-European countries are the United States and Japan. The four variables are real output, inflation, the short-term interest rate, and the exchange rate per country. For inflation and the interest rate the values used in the calculation of L^j in (1) are in percentage points (a 5 per cent interest rate is 5.0). For real output and the exchange rate the calculation of L^j is

$$L^j = \frac{1}{T}\sum_{i=1}^{T}\left[100\left(y_t^j - y_t^*\right)/y_t^*\right]^2$$

where y is the level of the variable. Multiplying by 100 puts the values of

Table 8.1 *Values of L for four experiments*

	Real output Experiment						Inflation Experiment			
	1	2	3	4	(4/2)²	(4/3)²	1	2	3	4
GE	1.87	1.16	1.15	1.49	1.65	1.68	0.81	0.72	0.72	0.72
IT	2.64	2.21	2.19	2.52	1.30	1.32	2.14	2.05	2.05	1.95
NE	3.33	3.19	3.16	2.96	0.86	0.88	2.14	2.14	2.14	2.14
UK	2.32	2.11	2.10	2.11	1.00	1.01	3.89	3.88	3.88	3.86
AU	4.91	4.07	2.85	3.95	0.94	1.92	4.45	4.01	3.49	3.96
FR	1.54	1.49	1.15	1.34	0.81	1.36	1.60	1.62	1.60	1.58
BE	4.11	3.71	3.23	3.60	0.94	1.24	1.33	1.34	1.24	1.28
SP	1.66	1.61	1.35	1.62	1.01	1.44	2.44	2.20	1.93	1.99
US	1.67	1.64	1.64	1.63			1.12	1.13	1.13	1.13
JA	2.99	2.99	2.98	3.00			2.05	2.05	2.05	2.05
	Short-term interest rate						Exchange rate			
GE	0	1.26	1.27	–			3.27	2.66	2.69	–
IT	0	2.12	2.11	–			3.46	2.69	2.71	–
NE	0	1.49	1.50	–			3.35	2.70	2.73	–
UK	0	2.13	2.13	–			4.09	3.86	3.86	–
AU	0	0.70	1.45	–			3.66	3.00	2.91	–
FR	0	1.28	0.69	–			4.71	3.75	3.74	–
BE	0	1.12	1.65	–			3.25	2.72	2.74	–
SP	0	0.58	0.96	–			6.00	3.24	2.97	–
US	1.22	1.22	1.22	1.21			–	–	–	–
JA	0.70	0.70	0.70	0.69			3.29	3.31	3.31	3.29
EU	–	–	–	1.21			–	–	–	2.52

Notes:
1 = all European interest rates exogenous.
2 = estimated interest rate reaction functions used.
3 = same as 2 except the rule in (3) used for Austria, France, Belgium, and Spain.
4 = EMU regime.
GE = Germany, IT = Italy, NE = the Netherlands, UK = the United Kingdom, AU = Austria, FR = France, BE = Belgium, SP = Spain, US = the United States, JA = Japan, EU = Total Europe.

L in table 8.1 in percentage points for real output and the exchange rate. Even though results for only ten countries are presented in the table, the entire MC model is used for the experiments. The same draws were used for each experiment in order to lessen stochastic-simulation error for the comparisons between experiments. The rest of this chapter is essentially a discussion of table 8.1.

For all the experiments the drawn error terms are not used for the short-term interest rate and exchange rate equations. Since these equations are interpreted as policy reaction functions in the model, it seemed best to take them as rules with no stochastic shocks. In addition, the drawn error terms are not used for the long-term interest rate equations (the term structure equations) for the European countries. Since moving from the current regime to the EMU regime requires changing these equations for the European countries, it seemed best for comparison purposes not to complicate matters by having to make assumptions about what errors to use in the EMU regime for these equations. The variability estimates are thus based on all types of shocks except financial ones.

For the first experiment all the European interest rate reaction functions are dropped from the model, and the European short-term interest rates are taken to be exogenous. This is not meant to be a realistic case, but merely to serve as a baseline for comparison. The results are in the first column for each variable in table 8.1. The second experiment differs from the first in that the European interest rate reaction functions are added back in. Otherwise, everything else is the same. The results are presented in the second column for each variable.

Comparing columns 1 and 2 for output shows how stabilising the estimated interest rate reaction functions are. For Germany L falls from 1.87 to 1.16, and so the German interest rate reaction function is quite stabilising. L also falls for the other European countries, and so in general the reaction functions are stabilising. The fact that the reaction functions for Austria, France, Belgium, and Spain are stabilising means that the US and German reaction functions have some stabilising influence on these countries. (Remember that the only explanatory variables in these four reaction functions aside from the constant term and the lagged dependent variable are the German and/or US interest rates.) France and Spain, however, are not helped very much. For France L falls only from 1.54 to 1.49, and for Spain L falls only from 1.66 to 1.61.

Exchange rate variability falls for the European countries when the interest rate reaction functions are added. This is primarily because of Germany. The US interest rate appears in the German interest rate reaction function, and when the reaction function is dropped, the German rate less closely follows the US rate. The greater variability of the German rate relative to the US rate when the reaction function is dropped leads to greater variability of the German exchange rate because the German interest rate relative to the US interest rate is an explanatory variable in the German exchange rate equation. The greater variability of the German exchange rate then leads to greater variability of the other European exchange rates (vis-à-vis the US dollar) because the other exchange rates fairly closely follow the German exchange rate in the short run.

The differences in L for inflation in table 8.1, column 1 versus column 2, are fairly small, and it is clear that the reaction functions stabilise output much more than they do inflation. In the price equations the price responses to output changes are generally fairly small, and so making output more stable has only a small effect on making inflation more stable. There is also a stabilising effect on inflation from making the exchange rate more stable, but again this effect is fairly small. A country's exchange rate affects its domestic price level because its import price level is an explanatory variable in the domestic price equation.

Results using alternative monetary policy rules

Although experiment 2 uses the estimated interest rate reaction functions, the present methodology does not require that they be used. Alternative monetary policy rules can be substituted for the estimated rules. An interesting question in this regard is whether my inability to find significant domestic explanatory variables in the Austrian, French, Belgian, and Spanish interest rate reaction functions reflects actual behaviour of the monetary authorities or is simply due to specification error. If the estimated rules are highly mis-specified, it is of interest to examine other rules.

To examine the sensitivity of the results to the use of the estimated reaction functions for these four countries, a different function was postulated for each country:

$$R_t = R_t^* + 0.5 \text{x} 100(Y_t - Y_t^*)/Y_t^* + 0.25 \text{x} 100(\dot{P}_t - \dot{P}_t^*) \qquad (8.3)$$

where R is the short-term interest rate, Y is the level of real output, and P is the percentage change in domestic price level at an annual rate. The starred values are the base (actual) values. According to this rule, the interest rate differs from its base value as output and inflation differ from theirs. This rule, including the 0.5 and 0.25 weights, was used in Fair (1997c) for the United States, and it has been taken unchanged for use here. No experimenting was done here with different weights. Also, note that the US and German interest rates are not included in the rule, contrary to the estimated rules.

The results using the rule in (8.3) are presented in the column marked '3' in table 8.1. The third experiment differs from the second only in that the estimated interest rate reaction functions for France, Austria, Belgium, and Spain are replaced by the rule in (8.3). The results for output show that the new rules are considerably more stabilising for these four countries. For France, for example, L falls only from 1.54 to 1.49 using the estimated rule but from 1.54 to 1.15 using the new rule. The results for the third experiment thus suggest that the monetary authorities of these four countries could do better than follow the reaction function that I have estimated they follow. They may, of course, in fact do better, since the estimated reaction functions may not be good approximations of their actual behaviour. The importance of these results for present purposes is that there are two possible experiments to use for comparison with the EMU regime experiment.

One could, of course, also replace the estimated rules for Germany, Italy, the Netherlands, and the United Kingdom by the rule in (8.3). This was not done for experiment 3 because the estimated rules for these countries were stabilising (experiment 2 versus 1). Although not reported in table 8.1, the experiment was in fact run in which the estimated rules for these four countries were replaced by the rule in (8.3). Otherwise, everything was the same as for experiment 3. For Germany the value of L for output was 1.16, which compares with 1.15 for experiment 3 in table 8.1. The estimated interest rate reaction function and the rule in (8.3) for Germany thus have very similar stabilisation properties. The results were also close for the Netherlands (3.07 versus 3.16 for experiment 3) and for the United Kingdom (2.05 versus 2.10 for experiment 3). For Italy the rule in (8.3) was somewhat better (1.83 versus 2.19 for experiment 3), although both rules are considerably better than no rule for Italy (2.64 for experiment 1). These results are thus interesting in showing that the properties of the estimated rules for the four countries are similar to the properties of the rule in (8.3).

A digression on policy coordination

This article has perhaps something quantitative to contribute to the literature on international policy coordination that began with the work of Niehans (1968) and Hamada (1974). In the MC model the monetary authorities of different countries do not play games with each other, but instead follow simple rules (the estimated interest rate reaction functions). Since the US interest rate appears in a number of the other reaction functions, the United States has a leadership role. Also, Germany has a leadership role within Europe because the German interest rate appears in a number of the other European reaction functions.

The question that can be addressed using the methodology of this chapter is whether the stabilisation behaviour of one country helps or hurts the stabilisation behaviour of other countries. To check this with respect to the

United States, experiment 2 was rerun with the US interest rate reaction function dropped and the US short-term interest rate taken to be exogenous. In this case the United States does not stabilise, but all the other countries follow their estimated reaction functions. The value of L for output for the United States rose from 1.64 (column 2 in table 8.1) to 1.96 (not shown in table 8.1). This shows that the estimated US interest rate reaction function is stabilising for the United States. However, the value of L fell for Germany, from 1.16 to 1.02. Germany is thus better off when the United States does not stabilise, and one has a quantitative estimate of by how much.

Why is Germany hurt when the United States stabilises? Consider a shock (such as a positive consumption shock) in the United States that leads the US interest rate to increase when the US reaction function is in. This leads the German interest rate to increase, although not by as much as the US rate, and so the Deutschmark depreciates. German output is thus affected – positively if the effect of the depreciation outweighs the effect of the interest rate increase. German output thus responds to US shocks through US interest rate changes, and if US interest rate changes are turned off, there is less output variability from this source.

The United Kingdom is also hurt by US stabilisation, where L falls from 2.11 (column 2 in table 8.1) to 2.00 (not shown). Italy, France, Spain, and Japan are little affected. The Netherlands, Austria, and Belgium are actually helped. For the Netherlands, for example, L rises from 3.19 (column 2 in table 8.1) to 3.46 (not shown). These countries are helped basically because Germany is hurt. For example, when Germany stabilises well this hurts the Netherlands (just as when the United States stabilises well this hurts Germany), and so the Netherlands is better off when Germany does not stabilise as well, which is when the United States stabilises. Having the United States stabilise thus helps the Netherlands.

More experiments could be done, dropping different reaction functions, but this should give a flavour of the kinds of questions that can be considered using the present methodology. Note that no optimisation is going on here. Each country is merely following the reaction function that it has been estimated to follow.

5. The assumed EMU regime

As noted in section 1, there are many possible EMU regimes that could be postulated. The methodology here does not depend on any one paraticular choice. For the regime used here all sixteen European countries in the model were included. The following three changes were made to the MC model to move to the EMU regime.

First, the interest rate reaction functions for all the European countries except Germany were dropped, and their short-term interest rates were assumed to move one for one with the German rate. The domestic variable that is included in the estimated German reaction function is the German output gap, and this variable was replaced by the European output gap.[12] The coefficient estimates in this equation were not changed, and the US interest rate, which is an explanatory variable in the equation, was retained. The behaviour of the European monetary authority is thus assumed to be the same as the historically estimated behaviour of the Bundesbank except that the response is now to total European output instead of just German output.

Second, the long-term interest rate equations (the term structure equations) for all the European countries except Germany were dropped, and their long-term interest rates were assumed to move one for one with the German rate. The long-term German interest rate equation was retained as is. The only explanatory variables in this equation are the lagged value of the long-term rate and the current value and lagged values of the short-term rate.

Third, the exchange rate equations for all the European countries except Germany were dropped, and their exchange rates were fixed to the German rate. The German exchange rate equation has as explanatory variables the German price level relative to the US price level and the German short-term interest rate relative to the US short-term interest rate. This equation was used as is except that the German price level was replaced by the European price level. (The German short-term interest rate is now, of course, the European short-term interest rate, as discussed above.)

No other changes were made to the model. To summarise, then, in this assumed EMU regime, the two main changes are (1) the postulation of a European interest rate reaction function that responds to the European output gap and (2) the postulation of an exchange rate equation for the common European currency that responds to the European price level relative to the US price level and the European short-term interest rate relative to the US short-term interest rate.

6. Results for the EMU regime

The results for the EMU regime are presented in the fourth columns in table 8.1. The following conclusions can be gleaned from the results.

1. Comparing columns 1 and 4, output variability is less in the EMU regime that it would be in the regime in which there were no European interest rate reaction functions. The European interest rate reaction function in the EMU regime is thus stabilising relative to no rules at all.

2. Comparing columns 2 and 4, output variability is greater in the EMU regime than in the current regime for Germany and Italy and either essentially the same or smaller for the other European countries. To see how much each country is hurt or helped in going from columns 2–4, column 5 presents the ratio of the square of L in column 4 to the square of L in column 2. (The square of L is in units of variances, and so the ratio measures the per cent increase in a variance-like variable.)

   It is clear that Germany loses the most in moving to the EMU regime, with variability rising by 65 per cent. In the non-EMU regime the German interest rate reaction function does a fairly good job in stabilising German output, responding to the German output gap, and in the EMU regime the reaction function only responds to the German output gap to the extent that it is part of the total European output gap. The European monetary authority thus does not do as good a job at stabilising Germany as the Bundesbank does. (Does this help explain why German polls show the Germans not very favourable towards EMU?)

   The country that benefits the most from moving to the EMU regime is France, and it is easy to see why. Columns 1 and 2 show that the estimated French reaction function is a poor stabilisation rule: the French are essentially estimated not to stabilise. Thus, France gains in the EMU regime because there is a stabilisation rule that it benefits from, namely the overall European rule. If the French by themselves are not going to stabilise, they are better off joining a group that at least in part responds to French shocks. (Does this help explain why French polls show the French favourable towards EMU?)

   Except for Italy, where the Italian estimated rule does better than the EMU rule (variability is 30 per cent higher for Italy), the EMU rule does the same as or better than the country-specific estimated rules for the other European countries.

3. When the rule in (8.3) is used for Austria, France, Belgium, and Spain instead of the estimated interest rate reaction functions (columns 3 versus 4), output variability is noticeably greater in the EMU regime for all four countries. For example, the results show that if France followed the rule in (8.3) instead of its estimated rule, it would be hurt instead of helped by moving to the EMU (variability is 36 per cent

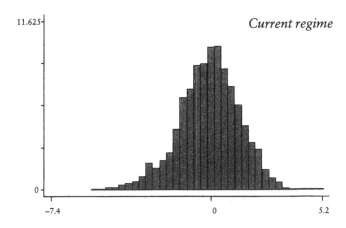

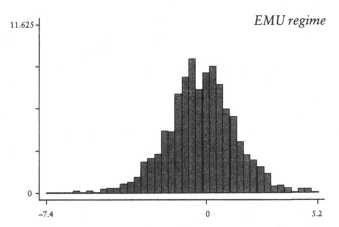

Figure 8.1 *Histograms of 2400 German output deviations*

higher). The rule in (8.3) is more stabilising for France than is the
EMU rule. Overall, experiment 3 shows that the results are clearly
sensitive to the choice of the monetary policy rule. The better is an
individual rule, the greater is the cost of moving to the EMU regime.

Figure 8.1 provides another way of looking at the differences across regimes. Consider output variability. Each experiment yields 2400 per cent
output deviations $(100(y_t^j - y_t^*)/y_t^*)$, since there are 24 quarters per trial and
100 trials, and L is one measure of variability of these values. Another

possibility is to compute a histogram of these values, and this is what is done in figure 8.1 for Germany. The first histogram is for experiment 2 (the current regime), and the second is for experiment 4 (the EMU regime). It is clear that the values are more scattered for the EMU regime, and the figure gives a visual sense of how much.

7. Conclusion

This study has presented a methodology for examining the stabilisation costs of the EMU, and table 8.1 provides quantitative estimates of these costs. These estimates are clearly preliminary, and there are a number of extensions that would be interesting to pursue in future work. First, although the estimates in table 8.1 are based on the assumption that all of Europe joins the EMU, it would be easy to examine subsets of joiners.

Second, and perhaps most important, it would be interesting to examine alternative monetary policy rules. So far only the estimated rules (the estimated interest rate reaction functions), which are just estimates of average past behaviour, and the simple rule in (8.3) have been used. One could, for example, search over different weights in (8.3) for a given country to find a good stabilising rule, and more target variables could be added if desired. The better the rule for a given country, the larger are the stabilisation costs of joining the EMU. On the other hand, one could also search for a better rule in the EMU regime. So far the only EMU rule used is the estimated German rule with European variables replacing German ones. Instead, one could try a rule like (8.3) for the EMU and search over the weights.

A third issue to consider is whether after moving to the EMU regime the policy authorities in a country would try to use fiscal policy for stabilisation purposes. For the results in this chapter fiscal policy has been taken to be exogenous. A tax-rate rule is proposed in Fair (1997c) for the United States that is an effective stabiliser, and if a rule like this were used by a European country after joining the EMU, it would lower the stabilisation costs estimated here.[13] It thus may be of interest to try some fiscal-policy rules in the EMU regime, although in doing so one would have to take into account the rather strict fiscal-policy constraints that are imposed on countries that join the EMU.

There are some possible biases in the table 8.1 estimates that are more difficult to examine. There is, for example, no labour mobility in the model, and to the extent that there is labour mobility between countries in Europe the real stabilisation costs are likely to be smaller than those in table 8.1. It would be difficult to modify the MC model to try to account for labour mobility. Also, if the change in regimes results in the shocks across countries being more highly correlated than they were historically, this is likely to bias the current cost estimates upwards. The more highly correlated are the shocks, the more is the common European monetary policy rule likely to be stabilising for the individual countries. It would be difficult to try to estimate how the historical correlations might change.

It may also be the case that the historical shocks used for the stochastic-simulation draws are too large. The shocks are estimated error terms in the stochastic equations, and they reflect both pure random shocks and possible mis-specification. However, if the shocks are too large, it is not clear how the cost estimates in table 8.1 would be affected since the values of L would go down for all experiments.

Another issue to consider is whether the EMU regime would increase credibility. If, for example, Italian long-term interest rates were lower after Italy joined the EMU (because Italian policy was then more credible), this could have a beneficial effect on Italian growth. Level effects of this sort are not taken into account in this study, since only stabilisation costs are being estimated.

Finally, it may be the case that the MC model is such a poor approximation of the world economy that no results from it are worth considering. Some people have such a low opinion of structural macroeconometric models that they put no weight on any tests of them or results using them. I find this frustrating since one of the main themes of my research has been the testing of such models, and I wish there were more interest in testing. The stochastic equations of the MC model have been extensively tested, and these tests are reported in chapter 6 of Fair (1994), in Fair (1997a, 1997b), and on the website. In addition, the accuracy of the overall model has been examined, and these results are discussed in chapter 9 of Fair (1994). Based on these results I would argue that the MC model is accurate enough to warrant taking seriously the results in table 8.1.

Notes

1   For other results using stochastic simulation to examine the EMU, see Hughes-Hallett, Minford, and Rastogi (1993), Masson and Symansky (1992), and Masson and Turtelboom (1997).
2   In a few cases a coefficient is constrained to be equal to a particular value, and in these cases the other coefficients in the equation are estimated by 2SLS or OLS subject to this constraint.
3   The 33 countries are the United States, Canada, Japan, Austria, France, Ger-

many, Italy, the Netherlands, Switzerland, the United Kingdom, Finland, Australia, South Africa, Korea, Belgium, Denmark, Norway, Sweden, Greece, Ireland, Portugal, Spain, New Zealand, Saudi Arabia, Venezuela, Colombia, Jordan, Syria, India, Malaysia, Pakistan, the Philippines, and Thailand.

4 The twelve other countries that fill out the trade-share matrix are Nigeria, Algeria, Indonesia, Iran, Iraq, Kuwait, Libya, the United Arab Emirates, Israel, Bangladesh, Singapore, and an 'all other' category.

5 All the variables and equations in the model are presented in Appendices A and B of The MC Model Workbook on our website (http://fairmodel. econ.yale.edu). All the coefficient estimates are presented in the 'Chapter 5 Tables' and 'Chapter 6 Tables' that follow the appendices. The estimated interest rate reaction function for a country is equation 7 for that country (except for the United States, where it is equation 30), and the estimated exchange rate equation is equation 9. Various test results for each equation are presented along with the coefficient estimates.

6 For a given European country i and period t, let Y_{it} be its real output, P_{it} its domestic price level, and e_{it} its exchange rate vis-à-vis the Deutschmark. Also, let e_{i90} be its exchange rate in 1990, the base year for real output. Then total European nominal output is $\sum_{i=1}^{16}(P_{it}Y_{it})/e_{it}$ and total European real output is $\sum_{i=1}^{16} y_{it}) / e_{i90}$. For the annual countries, the annual values of Y, P, and e were converted to quarterly values for these calculations, again using a simple distribution assumption.

7 For the few equations whose estimation periods began later or ended earlier than the 1972–94 period, zero errors were used for the missing observations.

8 Another way of drawing error terms would be from an estimated distribution. Let $\hat{V}$ be an estimate of the 328×328 covariance matrix V of the error terms. One could, for example, assume that the error terms are multivariate normal and draw errors from the $N(\hat{\mu}_t, \hat{V})$ distribution, where $\hat{\mu}_t$ is the vector of the historical errors for t. Because of the quarterly–annual difference, $\hat{V}$ would have to be taken to be block diagonal, one quarterly block and one annual block. Even for this matrix, however, there are not enough observations to estimate all the nonzero elements, and so many other zero restrictions would have to be imposed. The advantage of drawing the historical error vectors is that no distributional assumption has to be made and no zero restrictions have to be imposed.

9 The solution of the MC model, which is explained in Fair (1994), is a somewhat involved task, and trials are costly in terms of computer time. For a simulation period of 24 quarters, 100 trials takes about 21 minutes on a Pentium Pro 200 computer. No solution failures on any trial occurred for the stochastic simulations reported in table 8.1.

10 If y_t^* were the estimated mean of y_t, this measure would be the estimated variance of y_t. Given the J values of y_t^j, the estimated mean of y_t is $(1/J)\sum_{j=1}^{J} y_t^j$, and for a non-linear model it is not the case that this mean equals y_t^* even as J goes to infinity. As an empirical matter, however, the difference in these two values is quite small for almost all macroeconometric models, and so it is approximately

the case that the above measure of variability is the estimated variance.

11 L is, of course, not an estimated standard deviation. Aside from the fact that for a non-linear model the mean of y_t is not y_t^*, L^j is an average across a number of quarters, and variances are not in general constant across time. L is just a summary measure of variability.

12 Continuing from note 6, total European potential output is defined to be $\sum_{i=1}^{16} YS_{it}/e_{i90}$, where YS_{it} is the potential output of country i for period t. The output-gap variable used is the per cent deviation of actual European output from potential European output.

13 Regarding the policy coordination discussion at the end of section 4, the US tax-rate rule in Fair (1997c) affects other countries much less than does the US monetary-policy rule. Experiments like those in table 8.1 run with and without the US tax-rate rule (and with the US short-term interest rate exogenous) show small differences in the L values for other countries. Unless the US interest rate is changed, there are small effects on other countries' exchange rates, which lead to smaller overall effects on the other countries' output.

References

Fair, R.C. (1994), *Testing Macroeconometric Models*, Cambridge, Mass., Harvard University Press.
(1997a), 'Testing the NAIRU model for the United States', April, on website http://fairmodel.econ.yale.edu.
(1997b), 'Testing the NAIRU model for 27 Countries', April, on website http://fairmodel.econ.yale.edu..
(1997c), 'A fiscal-policy rule for stabilisation', June, on website http://fairmodel.econ.yale.edu..
Hamada, K. (1974), 'Alternative exchange rate systems and the interdependence of monetary policies', in Aliber, R.Z. (ed.), *National Monetary Policies and the International Financial System*, Chicago, University of Chicago Press, pp. 13–33.
Hughes-Hallett, A., Minford, P. and Rastogi, A. (1993), 'The European Monetary System: achievements and survival', in Bryant, R.C., Hooper, P. and Mann, C.L. (eds), *Evaluating Policy Regimes: New Research in Empirical Macroeconomics*, Washington, D.C., The Brookings Institution, pp. 617–68.
Kenen, P. B. (1969), 'The theory of optimum currency areas', in Mundell, R.A., and Swoboda, A.A. (eds), *Monetary Problems of the International Economy*, Chicago, University of Chicago Press, pp. 41–60.
Masson, P.R., and Symansky, S. (1992), 'Evaluating the EMS and EMU using stochastic simulations: some issues', in Barrell, R. and Whitley, J. (eds), *Macroeconomic Policy Coordination in Europe: The ERM and Monetary Union*, London, Sage Publications, pp. 12–34.

Masson, P.R., and Turtelboom, B.G. (1997), 'Characteristics of the Euro, the demand for reserves, and policy coordination under the EMU', in Masson, P. R., Krueger, T.H. and Turtelboom, B.G., *EMU and the International Monetary System*, Washington, D.C., International Monetary Fund, pp. 194–224.

McKinnon, R. (1963), 'Optimum currency areas', *American Economic Review*, 53, pp. 717–25.

Mundell, R.A. (1961), 'A theory of optimum currency areas', *American Economic Review*, 50, pp. 657–65.

Niehans, J. (1968), 'Monetary and fiscal policies in open economies under fixed exchange rates: an optimising approach', *Journal of Political Economy*, 76, pp. 893–920.

von Hagen, J., and Neumann, M.J.M. (1994), 'Real exchange rates within and between currency areas: how far away is the EMU?', *Review of Economics and Statistics*, 76, pp. 236–44.

Wyplosz, C. (1997), 'EMU: why and how it might happen', *Journal of Economic Perspectives*, 11, pp. 3–22.

9   Optimal monetary policy

ANDREW P. BLAKE, MARTIN WEALE and
GARRY YOUNG

1. Introduction

The new monetary arrangements have created a system where the Bank
of England sets interest rates in order to deliver an inflation target. Mr
King, the Deputy Governor, is reported to have said that eventually he
hopes markets will be surprised not by the Monetary Policy Committee's
actions but by the data.[1] If their response to the data is known then the
outcome of their meetings will be more or less predictable.

Before one can address whether a monetary policy of this sort could work
better or worse than 'judgment' it is necessary to decide what type of structure it should have. In this chapter we set out a possible structure for a
predictable monetary policy and investigate how it might be conducted in
an uncertain environment. The National Institute's model of the domestic
economy, NIDEM, provides the tool for our study.

Our basic framework is to assume that monetary policy is set by means
of a simple rule. A wide range of studies suggests that rules of this type can
do a reasonably good job of controlling inflation. However, the use of simple rules always raises the question whether one might do better in
responding to any particular shock. Or rather, how much better might one
do through choosing an optimal response to an identified shock. Thus we
look at a policy structure which is represented by optimal deviations from
a simple rule.

Such a policy has obvious advantages on the one hand for the Monetary
Policy Committee and on the other hand for the Treasury Select Commit-
tee which has the job of holding the Monetary Policy Committee to account.
The simple rule would define what normally happens and the Monetary
Policy Committee would explain its policy not as a justification for a rise

or fall in interest rates but as a deviation from the outcome dictated by the simple rule. Even if the markets were not fully apprised of the optimisation exercises undertaken by the Committee, policy would immediately become much more transparent.

The chapter is set out as follows. Firstly, we describe the modelling of monetary policy in macromodels together with the same problem faced in the real world by a monetary authority. Secondly, we briefly outline a simple model and how that fits into the policy frameworks proposed by various authors. Thirdly, we describe our approach and the advantages it offers both as a modelling solution and as a guide to real world policymakers. Fourthly, we describe the stochastic simulations and control outcomes. Our conclusions also make clear the further work we see as necessary to make our policy proposals operational.

2. Modelling monetary policy

It is generally agreed that models need a well defined set of financial policies in order to function as forecasting and analytical tools. Using constant interest rates and tax rates makes no sense because any well-specified model will be unstable with such policies (Weale *et al.*, 1989). However, it is often difficult to decide on the appropriate form of policy rules. This is partly because the objectives of policy are seldom disclosed in sufficient detail to enable modellers to implement a representative policy in their models. With the UK's entry into the exchange rate mechanism the policy framework was easy to model. Its abandonment for an explicit inflation targeting regime presented a new set of problems.

Whilst the target is well defined (the retail price index excluding mortgage costs) and the instrument to control it (short-term interest rates), how the instrument should be moved in response to deviations from the target is not. Even how the policy framework should be judged to be successful used to be rather vague – although a commitment to obtaining an inflation rate of 2½ per cent or less by the end of the 1992–7 parliament was met. Since the election of a new government, a number of changes have been implemented, not the least that giving operational independence to the Bank of England. However, the target rate is set by central government. Additionally, a narrow range of 1 per cent either side of the same target is now judged to be acceptable. Operationally it seems that an assessment of inflation prospects over the next two years is used to decide whether interest rates should be changed, with the magnitude and timing of changes left to the Monetary Policy Committee at the Bank.

Macromodellers are faced with the task of reproducing such a policy regime, first to make forecasts (including of the inflation rate itself) and secondly to analyse how effective monetary policy can be. In many ways this is a problem identical to that faced by the Monetary Policy Committee. New information about the state of the economy has to be acted upon in some, presumably systematic, way.

Modellers have approached this in two basic frameworks. First, they have advocated simple policy rules that have a given structure guided by both economic and control theory. There is a huge variety of approaches to this. The argument is typically that there should be a rule which feeds back on the inflation rate deviations from target, perhaps with additional indicators or indeed targets of policy. Such policy rules may have several coefficients, which are sometimes chosen by reference to historical experience (Taylor, 1996), or by optimisation where the discounted value of expected inflation deviations is minimised by choice of coefficients given the state of the economy (Westaway, 1986), or heuristically by designing rules 'by hand' that seem to perform well in a variety of circumstances (Blake, 1997). The second framework is to use optimisation not just to choose the coefficients of a rule but to set the entire trajectory for interest rates to minimise the representative cost function. Church *et al.* (1996) compare the various approaches for recent vintages of the major macromodels.

This closely follows the rules versus discretion debate, with simple rules associated with the former and optimal control the latter. The modern twist on this is, of course, that an enforced rule can improve on the discretionary outcome because time inconsistency renders the discretionary outcome highly suboptimal. In what follows we rather sidestep the time inconsistency debate, not because we feel it is an unimportant one, but rather because we see it as an empirical issue, of which this chapter is part of the evaluation process. Indeed, we are trying to have the rule as a reference point and the discretion to depart from it. We do need to assume that the policy regime is credible for our analysis, and see this as an important extension for future investigation.

3. Inflation targeting using simple and optimal rules

It is easiest to outline the various approaches that might be used to model inflation targeting using a simple model. In doing so it is best to adopt a model where the optimal policy is able to be calculated analytically. This is usually both a function of the model and the objective function. One such combination has recently been extensively analysed. Svensson (1997) suggested that the proper target of monetary policy is *expected* rather than actual inflation. This is so whenever there is a lag in the operation of monetary policy. But in this case exact deterministic control of the inflation target is feasible after a fixed horizon. Then the optimal control reduces to a per period targeting of the h period ahead inflation rate where this is the response lag.

A simple two equation model that gives this property is

$$\pi^e_{t+1} = \phi z_{t+1} - \theta r_t$$

$$z_{t+1} = \kappa z_t$$

where π is the inflation rate, r the interest rate and z an arbitrary state variable, perhaps aggregate demand. This is a simplified version of Svensson's model.

The second part of the problem is to model the objectives of the monetary authority. An objective function that might represent the central bank's preferences is

$$\sum_{t=0}^{T} \left(\pi^e_{t+1} - \pi^d_{t+1}\right)^2.$$

The central bank has a target for the inflation rate in each period π^d_k (which may be a constant) and penalises deviations from it quadratically. This is the only object of policy.

As there are no 'instrument costs' but a transmission lag from policy to the final target of policy, the problem reduces to a series of static problems where the optimal policy is to achieve the future inflation rate exactly. Substituting the model into the objective function gives an unconstrained optimisation problem of the form

$$\sum_{t=0}^{T} \left(\phi \kappa z_t - \theta r_t - \pi^d_{t+1}\right)^2.$$

The first order conditions yield

$$-\theta\left(\phi \kappa z_t - \phi r_t - \pi^d_{t+1}\right) = 0$$

for each value of $t > 1$, which gives

$$r_t = \theta^{-1}\left(\phi \kappa z_t - \pi_{t+1}^d\right)$$

as the optimal policy. π_0 *cannot* be affected by the instrument so is irrelevant to the optimisation.

If z were to be stochastic we could modify the equation so that

$$z_{t+1} = \kappa z_t + \varepsilon_{t+1}$$

where ε is not observable when interest rates are set. This means that the forecast inflation rate still appears in the optimal rule, but is not realised. As before, controlling the forecast inflation rate is not the same as feeding back on it, as indicated by the optimal rule which includes only currently dated variables.[2]

Svensson is essentially saying that for this type of model with transmission lags one should adopt a target that one can achieve and be seen to be achieving.[3] This is in complete contrast to the alternative of a fixed simple rule for interest rates, even a well designed one. For, say, a complex model without a closed form for the optimal interest rate policy rule it may be that a given (suboptimal) rule has the drawback that there is considerable incentive to depart from it when another policy is better. In essence Svensson is saying that operationally policymakers do whatever is required to achieve the given target.

The other side of the debate can be epitomised by Taylor (1996) who proposes a specific rule. Such a rule in the context of the above model might be

$$r_t = \mu(\pi_t - \pi_t^d)$$

where μ is chosen to bring the inflation rate close to the desired rate over time. The dating we have chosen for the feedback indicates that the optimal policy is not available to the monetary authority. In general the choice of parameter can be approached using optimisation by minimising a loss function such as the one above, although Taylor favours using historical experience, and others choose parameters 'which work'.

The argument about which form of policy should be used seems clear cut. Svensson argues that optimality is attainable and therefore can be achieved by using the optimal policy. This places him firmly in the discretion camp. The Taylor approach is in the rules camp, where in complex models a simple and transparent approach that yields a sub-optimal but very good outcome is preferable because following a mechanical rule reduces uncertainty about likely actions by the monetary authority, whereas using optimality criteria it is much less clear what the authorities will do in the future or in response to shocks. Svensson's comeback is that there will come a time when it is imperative to depart from the simple rule because the outcome otherwise will be disastrous.

This suggests a synthesis. If we use a (perhaps Taylor-type) rule as our basis for monetary policy we can then consider optimal divergences from that policy, where shocks make it imperative to react in the short run to disturbances. In what follows we outline a framework which allows us to derive the optimal deviation from a rule in the face of an identified shock.

4. Our approach

The National Institute's model of the UK economy is usually operated with feedback rules for several reasons, some of them merely practical. We will cover why later in this section, but if the model operates with simple rules we can firstly ask the question are simple rules good enough? If the answer is yes, then is it worth doing something else? We will argue below that there are frequently times when departing from an announced policy rule is required.

The necessary additional step required to make our approach feasible is to modify the way that we operate monetary policy by having two elements to setting interest rates. We can apply optimal control to see if one could do better than a default policy rule, and do no harm to the process to leave that rule in place – in fact, as we argue below, the modeller is forced to use such a policy rule.[4]

Our modelling approach is the following. We 'mix up' simple and optimal rules in the sense that we wish to look at the effect of optimisation relative to the simple rule. The simple rule is one which we use routinely in forecasting. The main additional innovation is that we implement optimal control by considering optimal deviations from the simple rule over the subsequent two years from a new shock. This has two major benefits. Firstly, for a variety of reasons, it reduces the major costs of optimal control. The next subsection explains how. Secondly, it allows us to model more closely the actual policy process.

4.1 Reducing the costs of optimal control, guaranteeing model solution and modelling the decision process

We adopt the following split of the monetary instrument

$$r_t = \tilde{r}_t + \hat{r}_t$$

where we will set the two parts of the 'new' instrument in separate ways. Firstly, we will set part by a given policy rule of the form

$$\hat{r}_t = \gamma(L)\hat{r}_{t-1} + \beta(L)\pi_t$$

where $\gamma(L)$ and $\beta(L)$ are polynomials in the lag operator. This simple policy rule will usually have proportional, integral and derivative components and perhaps also indicator variables which anticipate future inflation. The precise rule used in the stochastic control exercise is given below. Secondly, $\tilde{r}_t$ will be set by explicit reference to an objective function, similar to the one above. This split serves three purposes:

- A rule may be required to give determinacy to a model which otherwise would not solve 'open loop'. In these circumstances an optimal control policy can be implemented open loop which would usually require derivatives that could not otherwise have been obtained.

- At the very least a sensible rule brings the economy closer to the final optimum, so less work has to be done in optimisation. This is particularly important in a stochastic exercise where repeated re-optimisation is required.

- Given that the 'predetermined' part of policy does put the model near its optimum, the rule can be used to provide a 'terminal condition' for the optimal policy that reduces the dimensionality of the problem significantly.

We discuss each of these in turn.

4.2 Ensuring determinacy

Price level indeterminacy (and indeed expectational indeterminacy in exchange rates) plagues models with fixed nominal interest rates. To use the interest rate as the monetary instrument means a resolution of this problem needs to be found. Splitting the instrument vector as described will provide an effective means of so doing.

Even without additional optimal control the model will then have properly articulated monetary policy which resolves the problems described. This is a simple model solution problem rather than anything else. It does not reduce the computational burden but rather makes computation possible. The National Institute's model is solved with a simple rule in place to enable us to use it properly.

As we are forced to use 'open loop' control methods it follows that without a determinate model the required derivatives would be simply unobtainable. This is because in effect we linearise the model about a reference trajectory by simulation.

Reducing computational costs by a simple rule

If the policy problem can be solved completely by the simple rule, the optimisation procedure will show just that. If the rule puts the instruments close to their final optimum without the need to move the solution this is likely to speed computation. This requires the rule to be well specified and to involve the optimal control in 'fine tuning' the policy represented by the rule. For complex objectives this is unlikely to be the case, but for simple objectives, such as inflation targeting, then a simple rule does a considerable amount of the work required. In the case where objectives are complex then a simple rule to ensure determinacy alone may be the best alternative.

The rule we use for interest rates is remarkably effective at targeting inflation. Blake (1997) shows how effective a simple rule can be in changing the inflation rate. Note that optimising a simple rule is much harder than the optimal control approach we suggest as the problem becomes highly nonlinear in the coefficient of the policy rule. It also produces a rule which is a compromise between short and long run considerations, not one that can be used to react quickly to identified disturbances.

Reducing the dimension of the control problem

We believe that a powerful advantage offered by this framework is by recognising that policy rules in conjunction with achievable objectives can be used to take care of the long run of the problem, meaning that only the immediate first few periods need to have instruments set by the control methods. This reduces the dimensionality of the problem considerably without compromising the optimal control very much. In fact, it may be an improvement on the standard procedure of attaching a 'tail' to the optimisation which fixes the instruments at the end to some value, possibly chosen endogenously. Blake and Westaway (1995) demonstrated that this was often unsatisfactory with rational expectations models.

A simple rule that does most of the long-run control can leave the optimal control to short-run control, perhaps for the first two or three years. In our example, we use a two year horizon, in common with the stated aim of the monetary authorities. The rest of the simulation is dealt with by the simple rule alone. This is a huge reduction in computing cost relative to the case where a full optimal control of, say, twenty years of interest rates is being manipulated. Whilst such problems are amenable to solution they increase the number of derivatives required from eight to eighty. This tenfold increase is pretty much reflected in the computing time required.

4.3 The role of time inconsistency

An important consideration with optimal control of the sort that we necessarily use is that optimising policy with forward expectations is usually time inconsistent. In a deterministic simulation this raises no problems in so far as the policy is inconsistent (and therefore may not be sustainable) but at least one can distinguish *ex post* whether one has reneged or not on announced policies. In a stochastic context, this is no longer true.

For a stochastic control problem solved open loop there is no policy rule to adhere to and therefore no default. A policymaker can only re-optimise, and change the path of the instruments. This is partly in response to the incoming shock, and partly a result of time inconsistency. This is not an issue that can be ducked, and it is important to adopt policies which are 'not very' time inconsistent.

The obvious way to do this is to implement time consistent policies. This has two difficulties. Firstly, time consistent policies are not uniquely defined. Secondly, they have never been calculated for complex macromodels directly. For example, Blake and Westaway (1995) proposed an algorithm but the computational requirements are very high and it has yet to be implemented. Note that the proposed policy regime deviates from the principle of optimality both by violating the time consistency constraint and by eschewing the full dynamic control solution by truncating the time horizon artificially.

This reinforces the result that the other way to ensure time consistency is to produce a solution that cannot be bettered by reneging and re-optimising. Targeting future inflation – and achieving the target – is precisely one such mechanism. Although this runs the risk of relocating the source of time consistency to the institution that sets the target it is certainly in keeping with the UK's current policy regime.

5. Optimal stochastic control on NiDEM

The control exercise we consider is intended to show the benefits of departing from the simple rule in a variety of circumstances. In appendix

A9 we describe the method in detail. Rather than demonstrate a single, deterministic, optimal control problem which would involve reporting a welfare loss improvement for a very artificial exercise, the stochastic aspects seem to us to be the most important part of the problem faced by the monetary authorities. A full stochastic optimal control exercise, even with the computational gains that we have made by simplifying the problem in the way outlined above, is still an extraordinarily demanding exercise for a model such as ours and in many ways not as illuminating as we might hope.

Our approach is to break up the simulation exercise into three parts where we identify different sources of shocks. These are quantity, price and foreign shocks separately. This is at least partly to mimic the problem facing the monetary authorities, where at least part of the problem is to decide if there has been a change in conditions and if so what is the major source of any new disturbance. For our model we might reclassify the quantity shocks as demand shocks and the price shocks as supply ones. This is due to the particular forms of adjustment in the model, where price is adjusted by mark-up formulae as a supply response, although obviously there are elements of demand and supply in both quantity and price shocks. The foreign shocks are easier to classify, and are those variables either exogenous to most of the rest of the model and in theory determined abroad, although some behavioural equations for investment abroad and so on must at least partly depend on domestic variables, for example the cost of capital. Full details of the variables shocked are given in appendix B9.

This constitutes about a hundred equations of the model, roughly a third of which are for each set of shocks. They also account for two thirds of the model's behavioural equations, with identities, pure output variables and expectational variables numbering well over two hundred of the total four hundred. Some behavioural equations have been omitted because they are either policy variables (we do, after all, assume policymakers are acting rationally!), did not fit into any of our chosen categories or fit into too many. They do contain the most important equations of the model in the separate categories. For quantity shocks we include consumption, price shocks the major domestic price indices and for foreign shocks the exchange rate.

We then shock each of the equations for these variables by a vector of residuals taken from historical experience[5] for each of the variables in each of the three cases. The historical shocks were taken from the relatively recent past, from 1984 onwards. This is partly to address the view that the variance–covariance of shocks to the economy has changed markedly, certainly since the 1970s. This should not impact on our exercise if the model we use is a genuinely structural representation of agents' decisions, but it may be that our model better describes more recent behaviour as that accounts for the greater part of the modelling effort.

5.1 Simulation results

The stochastic exercise is set to mimic the problem faced by a monetary authority by shocking the first period and setting policy to try to improve on that outcome. We can demonstrate the impact of the different shocks by considering the forecast error variance. With our default monetary policy rule in place this is akin to a stochastic forecast. The forecast base was produced in October 1997.[6] It is important to stress that this is not the model prediction with 'fixed' monetary policy in the sense that interest rates are constant, but fixed in that it uses a feedback policy rule of

$$\hat{r}_t = \hat{r}_{t-1} + 0.125(\pi_t - 2.5) + 0.5(\pi_t - \pi_{t-1}).$$

This is the default forecasting rule and is similar to the rule used by Blake (1997) in a stochastic simulation exercise.[7]

In figure 9.1 we plot the forecast variances of inflation for the first three years. The timing of responses clearly depends on the source of the shock. The most obvious feature is that domestic price shocks impact immediately, which is to be expected given that they constitute components of the final target. Foreign shocks, which include the exchange rate and foreign prices, take longer, and peak after four quarters. This is perhaps surprisingly slow given that the exchange rate plays such a key role in determining the domestic price level. Quantity shocks peak another quarter after foreign, and also take longer to die away.

Note that these are all contemporaneous shocks, observed by all agents; it is merely their source that differs. Their varying time profile reflects that each impacts on different parts of the model and then afterwards affects the inflation rate through the rest of the model.

Welfare losses are calculated on the basis of the simple loss function

$$V = \sum_{t=0}^{80} 0.99^t \left(5(\pi_t - 2.5)^2 + 0.1\tilde{r}_t^2\right)$$

where $t = 0$ corresponds to the fourth quarter of 1997. The summation can run over all periods as the included instrument costs represent a cost of 'using discretion' relative to the rule. These are zero when only the simple rule is used and beyond two years ahead in the case where we use eight periods of active control. For the shocks from figure 9.1 we plot the

Table 9.1 *Welfare losses*

	Costs		
	Simple	Optimal	% reduction
Base	11.34	10.06	11.3
Quantity	12.64	10.24	19.0
Price	22.78	17.19	25.6
Foreign	15.04	12.40	17.5
Total	17.19	13.50	21.5

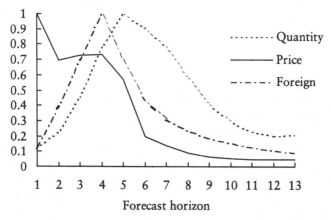

Figure 9.1 *Normalised inflation forecast error variances*

welfare losses for each case in the first column of table 9.1. Note that there is no element of optimisation here; the welfare losses are just the objective function evaluated for each realisation. This includes in the first row the cost associated with the forecast base itself.

The average difference from *target* of the inflation rate will, of course, depend on how far it is away when the simulation starts. This is reflected in the cost of the base case, a case which itself is open to optimisation. Note that it is perfectly possible that a shock *improves* the outcome relative to the case when there is none. Indeed, for the quantity shocks alone, in about a quarter of the cases the unoptimised cost is actually reduced by the shock.

The forecast with the simple rule in place necessarily depends on that simple rule. The forecast variances, of course, depend on the rule, but it

Table 9.2 *Interest-rate mark-up and cumulated output growth*

(standard errors in parenthesis)

	Average growth		Average short-run interest rate mark-up
	Simple	Optimal	
Quantity	2.22 (0.06)	2.23 (0.07)	0.740
Price	2.22 (0.03)	2.24 (0.02)	0.841
Foreign	2.15 (0.14)	2.16 (0.13)	0.911
Total	2.20 (0.09)	2.22 (0.08)	0.830

is important to recognise that the deviation from target at a fixed future date gives relatively little information about how to react with monetary policy. The price shocks die away quite quickly, but as we shall see a considerable amount can be done in the short run to reduce inflation.

The control exercise is then to take each replication and use two years of additional active interest rate movements on top of the simple rule to minimise the above loss function. As a preamble in figure 9.2 we show the simple deterministic control, essentially optimising the forecast. This leads to a reasonable 11 per cent reduction in cost.[8] Note that the base forecast is for inflation to be above target and then to fall below it for some time. Part of the control problem for this 'realisation' is to get the inflation rate up over the intermediate future.

We could, of course, do this by optimising the parameters of our simple rule.[9] We could even do this in conjunction with our proposed policy framework. This would clearly reduce the cost in so far as it is not the absolute minimum attainable by full optimal control and we would have additional degrees of freedom, but probably not by much.

The required initial reduction and then increase in inflation incorporated in the base around which the stochastic control exercise is conducted colour the optimisation exercises we conduct. The exercise will depend on the time profile of inflation that the shocks induce but very few of the shocks actually change the basic requirement of the deviations to the simple rule, even though the timing and pattern of the deviations are highly dependent.

In table 9.2 we present two illustrations of the real costs (or otherwise) of the additional interest rate rises. The most obvious of these is the average increase in the interest rate over the two years of additional active control. This ranges from 0.74 per cent to over 0.9 per cent. This not actually constant over the period, as we show in the illustrative examples in

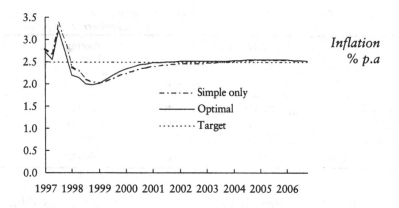

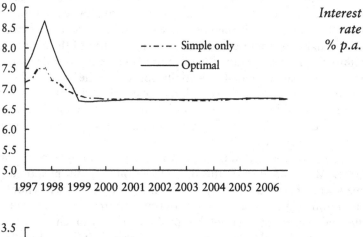

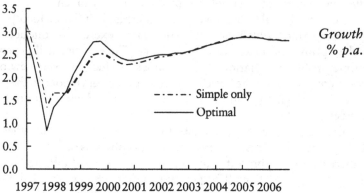

Figure 9.2 *Deterministic control solution*

the next subsection, but usually the interest rate is markedly higher over this period, reflecting the required initial deflation present in most of the simulations. A perhaps surprising result is the average growth rates with and without the optimal control. The averages are over five years, and give an indication of the 'output forgone' in each policy regime. As can be seen clearly, the benefit to the stabilised inflation rate is *more* output in the long term, although the estimates are not very different. This, of course, provides further justification for the additional policy activism.

5.2 Illustrative simulations

In figures 9.3–9.5 we plot the forecast inflation rate for each of the chosen sets of shocks before and after control together with the corresponding interest rate profiles and growth forecasts for representative shocks.

Figure 9.3 shows a quantity shock, and this is very similar to the base case in many ways. The initial reduction in the inflation rate is achieved with some loss of output growth with interest rates peaking in the short run about ¼ per cent over the simple rule. Inflation gets back to base more quickly than with the simple rule and stays on track. In table 9.1 we show that an average 19 per cent reduction in the welfare loss was achieved for all the replications. This replication gives a 21 per cent reduction, about average.

In figure 9.4, the illustrated price shock impacts much quicker, as expected. The impact on the inflation rate peaks nearly a year later at almost 5 per cent and although it quickly declines from then on it persists below base after that. An additional 3 per cent hike in interest rates in the short run reduces the inflation rate by about 1 per cent from its peak, and the inflation rate is much closer to target afterwards. The cost in the short run is a recession, but in the longer run higher growth compensates. For price shocks in general an average 25 per cent reduction in the cost function was achieved although figure 9.4 shows a replication with a 33 per cent gain.

Figure 9.5, the foreign shock, has an interesting profile. A modest decrease in inflation is followed by a too high inflation rate in the medium term. This must be a case which could be mitigated by a longer period of active control past the two year horizon. This is despite a considerable short-run increase in interest rates, and indicates how the persistent effects of the foreign shock are difficult to eradicate. A small negative growth rate for one quarter is again compensated for by later strong growth. Table 9.1 again shows a good overall gain in welfare of 17½ per cent, but less than for the other shocks.[10] The illustrated shock is actually not completely representative as it gives a 27 per cent gain, but the time profile is similar to the others.

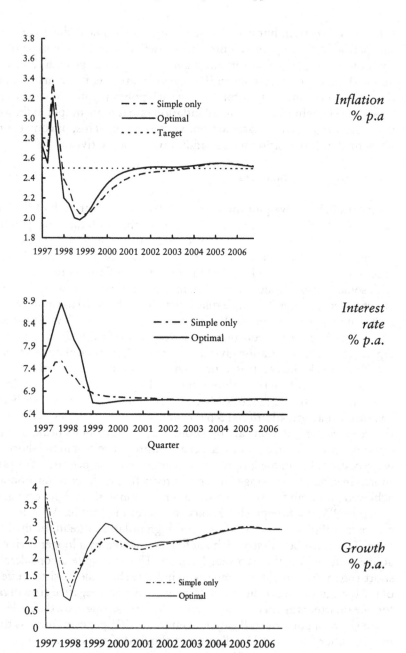

Figure 9.3 *Quantity shock*

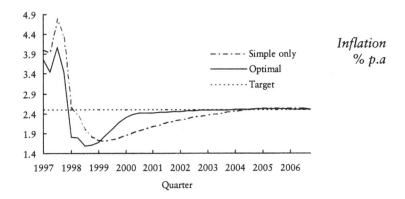

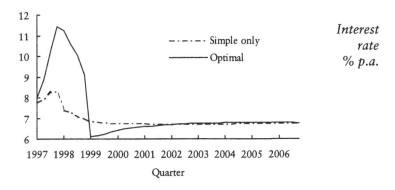

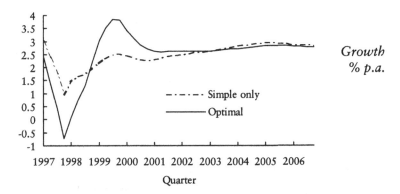

Figure 9.4 *Price shock*

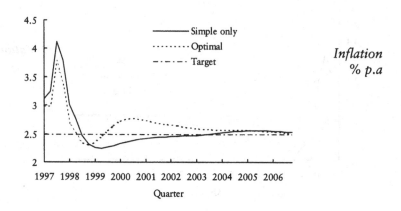

Inflation
% p.a

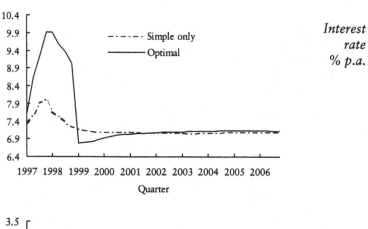

Interest
rate
% p.a.

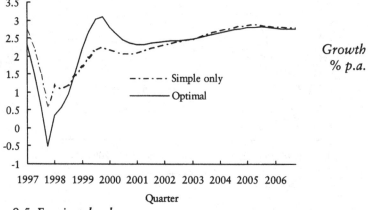

Growth
% p.a.

Figure 9.5 *Foreign shock*

It is perhaps worth while summarising the operation of the policy framework. First, a policymaker makes an inflation forecast based on the monetary policy rule and consequent interest rate forecast. It then assesses how much the policy needs to be modified to take account of any new information. Although the mechanism by which this is achieved in our model is by having a split instrument, in terms of implementing the policy it would clearly be preferable to announce the interest rate shown in the figures, as a modified policy relative to the no optimisation case.

6. Conclusions

In this chapter we have tried to marry two approaches to policy design in the very contemporary context of inflation targeting. This has been for two reasons. First, each on its own is rather inadequate. The full optimal control approach gives too few clues as to the value of revising policy in the light of new information and can appear much too opaque to policymakers to be informative. Using simple rules can also be seen as being unnecessarily restrictive, giving too little discretion when obvious policy choices ought to be made. Secondly, we aim to provide a framework that feasibly can be adopted by policymakers; it focuses on the role of new information whilst emphasising the need for a long-run policy regime that delivers the target of policy properly.

That regime is one where a policymaker uses a simple rule, designed to control the inflation rate using the base interest rate, and supplements it by using two years of deviations from that rule, designed using optimal control techniques. Using stochastic optimal control we are able to show quite considerable gains to inflation control in this way. As a additional point of interest we are also able to show that the source of the shock makes a considerable difference to the time profile of inflation responses.

Good policy advice cannot be model free although there is much to be said for choosing policies which work well on a range of models. The policy regime we have outlined is also time inconsistent in the way that both optimal and simple rules are. An analysis of the value of commitment needs to be added to this study to see how robust the framework is. This is a promising avenue for future research, combining as it does previous policy proposals with practical application to the current regime of inflation targeting.

Appendix A9: Control problem solution

In this appendix we outline how the optimal control is implemented.
We begin with a quadratic objective function of the form

$$E(V_0) = \frac{1}{2} \sum_{t=0}^{T} r^t [(y_t^e - y_t^d)' Q_t (y_t^e - y_t^d) + (u_t^e - u_t^d)' R_t (u_t^e - u_t^d)] \qquad (9.1)$$

where y_t^e is a p-vector of target variables at time t expected at $t = 0$, u_t^e a similar q-vector of instruments, y_t^d the desired values of those target variables, Q_t and R_t symmetric positive semi-definite weighting matrices and ρ the discount factor. It is convenient to write this as a stacked system

$$E(V_0) = \frac{1}{2}(\mathbf{y} - \mathbf{y}^d)' \mathbf{Q}(\mathbf{y} - \mathbf{y}^d) + \frac{1}{2}(\mathbf{u} - \mathbf{u}^d)' \mathbf{R}(\mathbf{u} - \mathbf{u}^d) \qquad (9.2)$$

where

$$\mathbf{Q} = \begin{bmatrix} Q_0 & 0 & 0 & \cdots & 0 \\ 0 & \rho Q_1 & 0 & \cdots & 0 \\ 0 & 0 & \rho^2 Q_2 & \cdots & 0 \\ \vdots & \vdots & \vdots & \ddots & \vdots \\ 0 & 0 & 0 & \cdots & \rho^T Q_T \end{bmatrix}$$

and

$$(\mathbf{y} - \mathbf{y}^d) = \begin{bmatrix} y_0 & - & y_0^d \\ y_1^e & - & y_1^d \\ y_2^e & - & y_2^d \\ & \vdots & \\ y_T^e & - & y_T^d \end{bmatrix}$$

with $\mathbf{R}$ and $(\mathbf{u} - \mathbf{u}^d)$ defined similarly. The stacked system is therefore of the order $p \times (T + 1)$.

This objective function is minimised subject to the model. Write the reduced form of the model as

$$y_t = \bar{y}_t + \sum_{i=0}^{T} J_{ti}(u_i - \bar{u}_i) \tag{9.3}$$

where $\partial y_t / \partial u_i = J_{ti}$ with u a vector of q instruments. In matrix terms this is

$$y = \bar{y} + J(u - \bar{u}) \tag{9.4}$$

where

$$J = \begin{bmatrix} J_{00} & J_{01} & \cdots & J_{0T} \\ J_{10} & J_{11} & \cdots & J_{1T} \\ \vdots & \vdots & \ddots & \vdots \\ J_{T0} & J_{T1} & \cdots & J_{TT} \end{bmatrix}.$$

If the model has no anticipatory behaviour then $J_{ti} = 0, \forall i > t$ and J collapses to

$$J = \begin{bmatrix} J_{00} & 0 & \cdots & 0 \\ J_{10} & J_{11} & \cdots & 0 \\ \vdots & \vdots & \ddots & \vdots \\ J_{T0} & J_{T1} & \cdots & J_{TT} \end{bmatrix}.$$

If additionally the model is a linear time invariant one of the form $y_t = Ay_{t-1} + Bu_t$ then $J_{ti} = A^{(t-i)}B$. A model with anticipatory behaviour will be somewhat different, but in principle having solved the model the values for J_{ij} are easily obtainable. Unless the model is linear solution will usually only be obtained by numerical methods. Then it is useful to think of (9.4) as being a local linearisation of the model. For the time being we maintain the linearity assumption.[11]

Substituting the model into the objective function and optimisation gives

$$\frac{\partial V_0}{\partial u^*} = J'Q(J(u^* - \bar{u}) + \bar{y} - y^d) + R(\bar{u} - u^d) = 0. \tag{9.5}$$

Adding and subtracting $R\bar{u}$ to the first order condition enables us to write the optimal value of the instruments as

$$u^* = \bar{u} - (J'QJ + R)^{-1}(J'Q(y^d - \bar{y}) + R(u^d - \bar{u})). \tag{9.6}$$

Control is a simple one step process.[12]

Non-linear models are a little more complex. If the objective function is still quadratic and the model 'nearly' linear then an iteration based on (9.6) can be developed. This will be of the form

$$\mathbf{u}_{k+1} = \mathbf{u}_k - \alpha_k d_k \tag{9.7}$$

where d_k is the descent direction, the parameter α is the distance travelled and k the iteration count. Note that for the linear quadratic problem above $d_k = (\mathbf{J}'\mathbf{QJ} + \mathbf{R})^{-1}(\mathbf{J}'\mathbf{Q}(\mathbf{y}^d - \overline{\mathbf{y}}) + \mathbf{R}(\mathbf{u}^d - \overline{\mathbf{u}}))$, $\alpha_\kappa = 1$ and $\mathbf{u}_k = \overline{\mathbf{u}}$. Instead, with quadratic preferences but with a non-linear model the iteration is most naturally defined as

$$\mathbf{u}_{k+1} = \mathbf{u}_k - \alpha_k (\mathbf{J}_k'\mathbf{QJ}_k)^{-1}(\mathbf{J}_k'\mathbf{Q}(\mathbf{y}^d - \mathbf{y}_k) + \mathbf{R}(\mathbf{u}^d - \mathbf{u}_k)) \tag{9.8}$$

where we index $\mathbf{J}$ by k reflecting the dependence of the derivatives on the reference point. α should be chosen to provide the maximum reduction in the objective function. In general a 'sufficient decrease' is used before calculating a new descent direction.

Potentially three considerable costs are incurred in this search. First, calculating derivatives numerically requires at least $q \times (T + 1) + 1$ simulations for every update of (9.8). Secondly, the matrix $(\mathbf{J}_k'\mathbf{QJ}_k + \mathbf{R})^{-1}$ must be calculated. Thirdly, the value of α_k must be found. This requires at each step a complete simulation to be run to evaluate the objective function for a given value.

Each of these can be reduced in turn. First, the derivatives can be re-calculated less often than at each iteration, although this can be a false economy. The most expensive in terms of computing is to evaluate the derivatives at every step by using two sided calculations, perturbing the instruments by positive and negative values of a number δ and dividing the difference in the simulation values by 2δ. For a linear model this makes no difference in evaluating J; for a non-linear model the improvement may be small relative to the increased, nearly doubled, costs. Fixing the derivatives at an initial value reduces the costs enormously, particularly if a number of control exercises are done relative to an initial point.

Secondly, the inverse Hessian can be updated by low order methods for a quasi-Newton step, such as DFP or BFGS (Press *et al.*, 1992). The Hessian is of the same dimension as $\mathbf{u}$, potentially a large matrix if instruments are used actively far into the future, but updating the matrix usually generates a need for more iterations. Inversion is usually taken to be an n^3 process (the cost goes up with the cube of the dimension) so an accurate calculation using (9.6) above but for a low order n is the most attractive option. This is generated by our proposed procedure.

Thirdly, whilst bracketing the minimum and then finding the greatest decrease in cost for any α might be a reasonable linesearch strategy this is typically not recommended, even if a single function evaluation is considerably cheaper than calculating a new descent direction. Instead, a simple choice of α can be used, such as the sequence 1, 0.1, 0.01 and then termination if no improvement is found. Note that if the problem were linear-quadratic then unity would be the correct choice, so there is a strong prior for quasi-Newton methods that unity is the best choice.

Note that our proposal is to reduce the dimension of the problem by truncating the active interest rate policy at a horizon of two years. This considerably reduces the cost of calculating derivatives, as there are only eight instruments. In experimentation we found that the biggest improvement in computational cost was actually to use central differences for the derivative calculations. This clearly reduced line search costs by requiring a single step of $\alpha = 1$ which usually gave a (near) zero gradient. Having programmed up the algorithm exactly, updating formulae are almost irrelevant as the Hessian is only 8×8, and cheap to invert. An iteration step using the most accurate model gradient with a directly calculated Hessian was then our preferred strategy. Derivatives were calculated at the point about which the step was made, rather than calculated once and stored off-line. This improved accuracy at each step, a cost that proved well worth bearing.

As the exercise is stochastic, the optimal control was calculated after each of the shocks was applied. This meant there is little benefit to storing the derivatives 'off-line' as the base about which the control is calculated is different for each replication. It should be clear from the above exposition that if the change between simulation exercises is confined to altering the objective function then an accurate set of derivatives about the base path can be used as a starting point for each exercise. For a stochastic exercise model derivatives need to be re-evaluated for each step of the algorithm. It is in these circumstances that shortening the period of active control makes the control problem much more computationally feasible.

Appendix B9: Simulations

The three sets of simulations were defined as 'quantity', 'price' and 'foreign'. The first two could perhaps have been called 'demand' and 'supply' instead, as for some the classification is arbitrary. The demand or quantity shocks include stocks and investment which might be deemed supply shocks and the supply or price shocks include in particular the price indices, which might be seen as a response to demand pressures. In the way the model is set up this is not really the case, as price adjustment is determined more as a markup. Much less uncertainty exists when classifying the foreign disturbances. The equations shocked for each were:

Demand/Quantity

DIVFI	Dividends paid by financial companies
DIVIC	Dividends paid by industrial and commercial companies
HIMPR	Real expenditure on home improvements
HSTART	Housing starts, thousands
NE	Value of net equity outstanding
NLVAL	Loan-value ratio for first time borrowers
PTRANS	Property transactions
QCE	Consumers' expenditure
QDKBS	Investment in business services, excluding leasing
QDKDST	Investment in distribution
QDKLAD	Investment, public sector dwellings
QDKMF	Investment, manufacturing
QDKOTH	Other investment
QDKPD	Investment in private dwellings, excluding home improvements
QDKPUB	Investment by public sector
QDURABLE	Consumers' expenditure on durables
QEXMF	Exports, manufactures
QEXOTH	Exports, other
QEXSER	Exports, services
QMMF	Imports, manufactures
QMOTH	Imports, other
QMSER	Imports, services
QSDT	Level of stocks, distributive trades
QSMF	Levels of stocks, manufacturing
QSRST	Stock level in the rest of industry
SCCRED	Stock of consumer credit
SLIQPE	Stock of household liquid assets
SMORTS	Stock of mortgage debt
SNCCRED	Stock of personal sector debt excluding consumer credit

Supply/Price

AHPQM	Average hours per quarter in manufacturing
AHPQS	Average hours per quarter in non manufacturing
AVEARN	Average earnings
CEDX	CPI excluding imputed rent and petrol and gas
EFEM	Female employment
EMPHBS	Total hours per quarter in business services
EMPHDST	Total hours per quarter in distribution
EMPHMF	Total hours per quarter in manufacturing
EMPHREST	Total hours per quarter for the rest of industry
EMPPUB	Employment in public services
FDIRA	Direct investment outflows
HPIMA	House prices, average in period, mix adjusted, all houses
MM	Mismatch
OBS	Output of business services
OCN	Output of construction industries
ODOTH	Other domestic output
ODST	Distribution output
OMF	Output index, manufacturing
OSERV	Output in distribution and business services
PDK	Deflator, fixed investment
PEXMF	Deflator, exports of manufactures
PEXOTH	Deflator, other exports
PEXSER	Deflator, exports of services
PMFM	Manufacturing input prices
PMMF	Deflator, imports of manufactures
PMOTH	Deflator, imports, other
PMSER	Deflator, imports of services
POP	Population of claimant age
PPAC	Deflator, public authority consumption
PWMF	Wholesale price of manufactures
RPI	Retail price index
RPIXMIP	RPI excluding mortgage interest component
SDIRA	Stock of UK direct investment overseas
TPBS	Technical progress in business services
TPDST	Technical progress in distribution
TPMF	Technical progress in manufacturing
TPOTH	Technical progress in 'other' sector

Foreign

EFFRAT	Effective exchange rate
EWIP	European industrial production
FDIRL	Direct investment inflows
FPORTA	Portfolio investment outflows
FPORTL	Portfolio investment inflows
M7GDP	Index of real GDP in the Major 7 economies
REB	US corporate bond rate
REU	Eurodollar rate
RGER	German short term interest rate
RWGT	World interest rate, trade weighted
RWIP	Non-European industrial production
RWXULC	Weighted world real unit labour costs
SDIRL	Stock of overseas direct investment in the UK
SPORTA	Stock of UK portfolio investment overseas
SPORTL	Stock of overseas portfolio investment in the UK
USW	US household sector gross financial assets
WCP	World consumer prices
WEQPR	Weighted world equity prices
WPD	Weighted world wholesale prices
WPDKD	Weighted world investment deflator
WPFB	World export price of primary products, $US
WPMF	World export price of manufactures, $US
WPO	World price of oil
WR	Weighted world interest rate
WTTOT	World trade, total

Notes

1 'The inflation target five years on', lecture given by Mr Mervyn King, Deputy Governor of the Bank of England, at the London School of Economics to mark the 10th anniversary of the Financial Markets Group at LSE.
2 In effect this in macromodelling terms is a 'type 2 fix' over time.
3 We abstract from the rather tricky problem of targeting a variable which is never *actually* hit. Bernanke and Woodford (1997) offer an interesting critique of the approach.
4 Use of a 'two part' policy rule originated in Weale *et al.* (1989) where it was

used to stabilise a model for linearisation purposes. There are similarities in that part of the necessity of the simple rule in the first place is to solve the model satisfactorily. Using a stabilising rule with optimal control was first done on the Institute's model by Westaway (1995).

5 This is an approach to stochastic simulation known as bootstrapping.

6 As an aside it gives us a certain amount of information about how uncertain our forecasts are based on current information.

7 The exercise we describe is different from that for two reasons. Firstly there was no objective function and therefore no optimisation. Secondly, here we focus on the information content of the *current* state. The forecast error variances are then a function only of current information, not the stochastic steady state as there. The object of our previous work was to evaluate an inflation targeting 'band width', to see how close one could keep inflation to target using a simple rule.

8 A full optimal control exercise does further reduce this by about another 5 per cent, a significant amount. This opens the question as to what is the appropriate active horizon to use, an important area for further research.

9 Computationally this is likely to involve much more work than optimising the value of variables as the results depend much more nonlinearly on the parameters of the simple rule and 'corner solutions' close to instability become much more likely.

10 This shock also proved to be the most troublesome to optimise, clearly reflecting the need to do more work later as the effects of the shock build up.

11 We could develop the argument by assuming a general non-linear model

$$y = \Theta(u)$$

and objective function

$$V_0 = \Omega(y) = \Omega(\Theta(u)) = \tilde{\Omega}(u)$$

where $\tilde{\Omega}(\cdot) = \Omega(\Theta(\cdot))$. Then

$$V_0 = u'\tilde{\Omega}_u + \frac{1}{2}u'\tilde{\Omega}_{uu}u$$

where we approximate by a second order Taylor approximation about zero. First order conditions for the optimisation problem given this approximate objective function require that

$$\tilde{\Omega}_{uu}u = -\tilde{\Omega}_u$$

which is equivalent to the optimisation outlined in the rest of appendix A9.

12 In deriving (9.6) we by a little sleight of hand assume that $(J'QJ + R)$ is invertible. The instrument cost term in (2), $(u^e - u^d)'R(u^e - u^d)$, will ensure this with enough restrictions, for example positive definiteness of R. We prefer to assume that such sufficient costs are included by having as outputs some part of the control inputs without such a restriction, and possibly with $R = 0$.

References

Bernanke, B.S. and Woodford, M. (1997), 'Inflation forecasts and monetary policy', NBER Working Paper 6157.

Blake, A.P. (1996), 'Forecast error bounds by stochastic simulation', *National Institute Economic Review*, 156, pp. 72–9.

(1997), 'Evaluating policy rules by stochastic simulation', mimeo, National Institute of Economic and Social Research.

Blake, A.P. and Westaway, P.F. (1995), 'An analysis of the impact of finite horizons on macro-economic control', *Oxford Economic Papers*, 47, pp. 98–116.

Church, K.B., Mitchell, P.R., Smith, P.N. and Wallis, K.F. (1996), 'Targeting inflation: comparative control exercises on models of the UK economy', *Economic Modelling*, 13, pp. 169–84.

Press, W.H., Flannery, B.P., Teukolsky, S.A. and Vetterling, W.T. (1992), *Numerical Recipes in Fortran: The Art of Scientific Computing*, Cambridge, Cambridge University Press.

Svensson, L.E.O. (1997), 'Inflation forecast targeting: implementing and monitoring inflation targets', *European Economic Review*, 41, pp. 1111–46.

Taylor, J.B. (1996), 'How should monetary policy respond to shocks while maintaining long-run price stability? – Conceptual issues', in *Achieving Price Stability*, Federal Reserve Bank of Kansas City.

Weale, M., Blake, A., Christodoulakis, N., Meade, J. and Vines, D. (1989), *Macroeconomic Policy: Inflation, Wealth and the Exchange Rate*, London, Unwin-Hyman.

Westaway, P.F. (1986), 'Some experiments with simple feedback rules on the Treasury model', GES Working Paper no. 87.

(1995), 'The role of macroeconomic models in the policy design process', *National Institute Economic Review*, 151, pp. 53–64.

10 How tough should monetary policy be if inflation is forward looking?

CAMPBELL B. LEITH and SIMON WREN-LEWIS[1]

1. Introduction

With the adoption of an explicit inflation target in the UK, there has been renewed interest in the properties of feedback rules for interest rates based on deviations from this target. This discussion has generally involved two presumptions. The first concerns policy, and assumes that the more aggressive policymakers are in reacting to deviations from the target, the closer inflation will be to that target. The restraint on being very tough, therefore, is that it may cause costly instability in output. The second is more technical, and involves the stability of macromodels. Following Sargent and Wallace (1975) it is generally presumed that when inflation is forward looking and expectations are rational, models will be unstable if nominal interest rates are fixed. In this chapter we show that neither proposition is necessarily true.

In section 2 we use the UK econometric model COMPACT to examine both issues. COMPACT solves under constant nominal interest rates, and also suggests that a more aggressive monetary policy rule could lead to periods of higher inflation following a demand shock. However we would be the first to note that these econometric macromodel simulations are not sufficient evidence on their own. One problem is that this result could reflect some unidentified anomaly in the model (in terms of either its equations or its solution), with implications for the model and nothing else. Another is that it leaves the economic reason behind the result unexplained, and simulation results that are not backed up with a convincing account in terms of economic theory are largely worthless.

In section 3, therefore, we use an extremely simple theoretical model to show why solutions are quite possible under fixed nominal interest rates. The Sargent and Wallace result does not hold once we introduce nominal government debt into the model. Section 4 examines why tougher monetary policy rules might raise inflation when inflation is forward looking. We use a simple forward looking Phillips curve to show that, if the economy contains some mechanism which returns prices to their original path, then deflation that is delayed may be more effective in correcting price disequilibria than immediate deflation. We also show that bringing forward deflation can lead to periods in which inflation is higher. Sections 3 and 4 therefore not only provide analytical foundations for COMPACT's properties, but they also suggest that the implications of COMPACT for policy may be more generally applicable. A final section concludes.

2. Alternative monetary rules in COMPACT

COMPACT is a rational expectations, intertemporal model of the UK economy. Its aim is to translate modern macroeconomic theory into an econometric model that is both consistent with past evidence and capable to producing quantitative policy advice. It attempts to bridge a gap which has developed between mainstream academic macroeconomics and econometric macromodels (see Wren-Lewis, 1993). The focus of the model is on policy analysis, and it is not used for forecasting.

In theoretical terms the model has a number of defining characteristics. It is 'New Keynesian', in the sense that traditional Keynesian nominal rigidities are combined with forward looking behaviour by price and wage setters. Put simply, contracts or other adjustment costs prevent wages or prices being changed continuously, but as a result agents attempt to anticipate future events when prices are changed. Expectations are assumed to be rational; that is, they are consistent with the structure of the model.

In the longer run, the model is an open economy version of the classical growth model with intertemporal consumers. Specifically most consumers base their spending plans on their expected discounted income and financial wealth, but the discount rate they use exceeds the market rate of interest.[2] Some consumers, however, are credit constrained, and they spend all of any additional income they receive. COMPACT is virtually unique in embodying a vintage production technology: technological advance has to be embodied in new machines, and the capital/labour mix on old machines is fixed. This, together with the extended dynamics from intertemporal consumption behaviour, means that the intermediate period between the Keynesian short run and the Classical long run is quite extended in COMPACT. The model is described in detail in Wren-Lewis *et al.* (1996) and Darby *et al.* (1999).

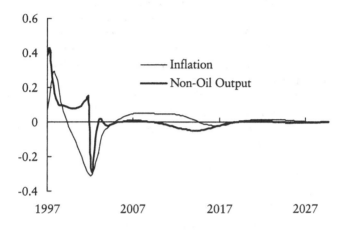

Figure 10.1 *Five-year 1 per cent world trade shock: output and inflation with fixed rates*

We now turn to the implications of different monetary policy rules in COMPACT.[3] For the sake of illustration we will consider one particular shock: a 1 per cent increase in world trade and output which lasts for five years. We assume for simplicity that both world output and investment rises in line with trade, but world prices remain unchanged.

The New Keynesian nature of the model means that this shock will raise output in the short term, which will in turn raise inflation. Higher output will also generate higher tax receipts, leading to a fall in the budget deficit. The model has a simple 'default' fiscal policy rule, which adjusts income tax allowances in a way which gradually returns the debt income ratio to its base level (that is, the level that would have occurred with no shock).

We first show that COMPACT solves when monetary policy involves a constant nominal interest rate. Figure 10.1 plots output and inflation over a 30-year period: in fact the model is solved for 70 years, but the model is clearly very close to its equilibrium over the last 30 years.

Output is higher over the period of the shock, but there is rapid crowding out in the first few periods of the simulation. After five years world trade and world output return to their pre-shock level, and accelerator effects in the model lead to a short-term decline in output at that time. Thereafter there is some prolonged but mild cycling in output, reflecting the extended dynamics implied by the vintage model.

In a forward looking rational expectations model, inflation anticipates future increases in demand. As we show formally in section 4, the current level of inflation is determined by the cumulated sum of future levels of excess demand. As a result, inflation initially jumps up, responding to the expected period of higher output: the jump is masked in figure 10.1 because inflation is defined as an annual change. As we progress through the simulation, the cumulated sum of future excess demand falls, and inflation declines to reflect this. After a couple of years output falls in the future dominate, and inflation is below base.

We now rerun this simulation with two different monetary policy rules. Both rules have the following form

$$r_t = a\pi_t + bp_t \qquad (10.1)$$

where r is the nominal interest rate, π is annual inflation, and p is the price level, where all these variables are measured in terms of deviations from the base path. The 'tough' rule sets $a = 1.2$, while the weaker rule sets $a = 1.1$. In either case the parameter b is very small, at 0.02. The b parameter, although small, is required because without it the model has difficulty solving. A non-zero value of b also ensures that prices tend to return to their base level in the long run. Fixed nominal interest rates can be thought of as a rule where $a = b = 0$.

As we would expect, tougher monetary policy rules mean that the demand shock has less effect on output. Figure 10.2 below plots output in the three simulations.

We might therefore expect inflation to be lower in the initial periods with the tougher monetary policy rule, and highest under fixed nominal interest rates. Figure 10.3 shows what actually occurs.

Inflation is in fact lowest when nominal interest rates are fixed. In the first few periods, the tougher feedback rule (0.2) does give marginally lower levels of inflation than the weaker rule (0.1), but after a year inflation is in fact higher with the tougher rule. The contrast is even more evident if we look at the price level over a longer period.

In all the runs the demand shock produces a prolonged period of negative inflation once the shock itself has disappeared. The two feedback runs gradually return the price level to its original level partly because of the 'integral control' term in the feedback rule, although its influence is very small and gradual. The price level returns to base relatively quickly under fixed nominal interest rates. As we shall see in the next section, this reflects the behaviour of the 'nominal anchor' in the model, government debt, which is not significantly changed as a result of the shock.

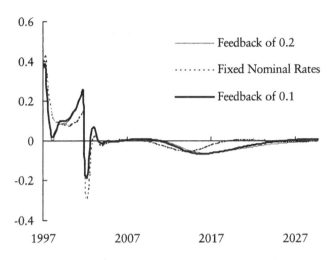

Figure 10.2 *World trade shock: output under the three rules*

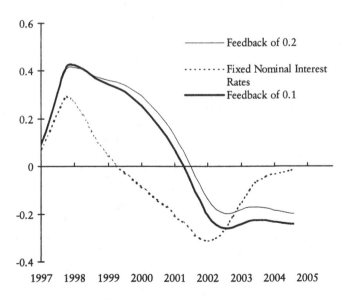

Figure 10.3 *World trade shock: inflation under the three rules*

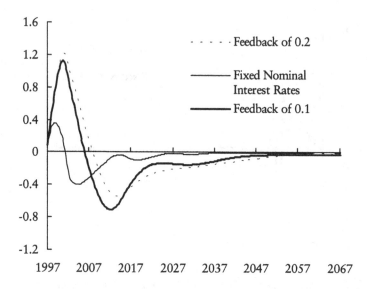

Figure 10.4 *World trade shock: the price level under the three rules*

These results are certainly puzzling at first sight. Why should a tougher rule produce a generally worse outcome for inflation, and why do constant nominal interest rates appear to generate the most stable outcome? When modellers generate results like these for the first time, their initial reaction is almost bound to be to ask what is wrong with the model. Unfortunately that is often the right question to ask, as curious results often reflect problems with the structure of the model that had not been appreciated beforehand.

A useful technique for examining model properties of this kind is 'theoretical deconstruction' (see Wren-Lewis *et al.*, 1996). Most econometric models are complex in their theoretical structure, and do not mirror some standard theoretical paradigm exactly. To understand the complete model's system properties better, it can be useful to peel away this additional complexity stage by stage, until the model has become simple enough to reflect some theoretical model in the literature. An explanation for some curiosity may emerge when the unusual property disappears at some stage of the deconstruction process. The result may reveal some fault in model design, or (occasionally) some interesting theoretical result.

In this particular case, however, the deconstruction process failed to reveal any element of model complexity that could account for the result. Although the degree and extent to which tougher rules produced higher inflation varied as the model changed, the possibility of the 'perverse' result remained even when the model was stripped down to an essential core. The model continued to solve under fixed nominal interest rates. This raised another possibility, which is that such 'odd' results might be an inherent property of the core model. To investigate this further, we examined very simple theoretical structures to see if they mimicked COMPACT's properties. In the next section we consider the issue of stability under fixed nominal rates, while in section 4 we tackle the question of why inflation might be higher under tougher rules.

3. The stability of fixed nominal interest rates

It is commonly asserted that models that embody forward looking price setting with rational expectations cannot be stable under fixed nominal interest rates. The instability of very simple forward looking inflation models was first shown by Sargent and Wallace (1975), who considered a closed economy. A similar argument for an open economy is that, under UIP, there is a unit root in the nominal exchange rate, and so some nominal anchor is required to tie down its value. COMPACT appears to provide a counter-example to both these assertions. However this could reflect a problem with COMPACT. In particular, the solution of forward looking econometric models with UIP conditions involves some difficult issues, and it is possible to get apparent solutions which are in fact spurious.[4]

In fact, the Sargent and Wallace result is not robust to a number of augmentations of their basic model. In particular, if we add nominal wealth (that is, nominal government debt) to the model, then stability is quite possible under fixed nominal interest rates. We can show this with a simple second order dynamic system in continuous time. (Woodford (1996) and Leith and Wren-Lewis (1999) demonstrate similar results in models with inter-temporal consumption which have more complex dynamic structures.) Equation (10.2) is the government's budget constraint

$$dw_t = w_t(r_t - \pi_t) - \tau y_t + g_t \qquad (10.2)$$

where $dx(t) = dx(t)/dt$, w_t is real government debt (wealth) at time t, r_t is the nominal interest rate, π_t is inflation, y_t is output, τ is the (fixed) tax rate and g_t is real government spending. Real government spending reacts negatively to the level of the real debt stock,

$$g_t = g_1 - \beta w_t \qquad (10.3)$$

where

$$g_1 = \frac{(\tau y_w - \rho)\overline{w} - \tau y_p \rho}{1 - \tau y_g} + \beta \overline{w} \, .$$

The constant, g_1, is set by the government to ensure the budget is balanced in equilibrium, where the equilibrium values of wealth and real interest rates are $\overline{w}$ and ρ, respectively. If $\beta = 0$, then the authorities fix the real value of government spending. We describe β below as the fiscal feedback parameter.

An alternative rule often used in the literature involves stabilising the debt to GDP ratio. As equilibrium output is fixed in this model, then stabilising the debt to GDP ratio and stabilising real debt are equivalent in the long run. In the short run stabilising the debt to GDP ratio can produce the undesirable property that an increase in output not matched by increases in debt will be expansionary and potentially destabilising.

Define real interest rates as

$$\rho_t = r_t - \pi_t \, . \tag{10.4}$$

The model ignores outside money, so inside money, which is not net wealth, becomes the alternative asset to government debt. Inflation is determined by a simple 'forward-looking Phillips curve':

$$d\pi_t = -\alpha y_t \tag{10.5}$$

where $d\pi$ is a right-hand-side derivative, and we set the equilibrium level of output to zero. The more conventional backward looking Phillips curve is of course the same equation with a positive coefficient on output. An equation of this form can be derived in a number of ways, as Leith and Wren-Lewis (1999) show.

Finally the demand for output depends on wealth, real interest rates and government expenditure,

$$y_y = y_w w_t - y_p (r_t - \pi_t) + y_g g_t \, . \tag{10.6}$$

Taking linear derivatives around an equilibrium at which $\rho_t = \rho$ and $w_t = \overline{w}$, this system may be simplified to:

$$dw_t' = \overline{w}(r_t' - \pi_t') - \tau y_t' + g_t' + \rho w_t' \tag{10.7}$$
$$y_t' = y_w w_t' - y_p (r_t' - \pi_t') + y_g g_t' \tag{10.8}$$
$$d\pi_t' = -\alpha y_t' \tag{10.9}$$
$$g_t' = -\beta w_t' \tag{10.10}$$

In matrix algebra form,

$$\begin{bmatrix} dw' \\ d\pi' \end{bmatrix} = \begin{bmatrix} \rho - \beta - \tau(y_w - \beta y_g) & -\tau y_p - \overline{w} \\ -\alpha(y_w - \beta y_g) & -\alpha y_p \end{bmatrix} \begin{bmatrix} w' \\ \pi' \end{bmatrix} + \begin{bmatrix} \tau y_p + \overline{w} \\ \alpha y_p \end{bmatrix} r'.$$

The determinant of the transition matrix is,

$$\begin{vmatrix} \rho - \beta - \tau(y_w - \beta y_g) & -\tau y_p - \overline{w} \\ -\alpha(y_w - \beta y_g) & -\alpha y_p \end{vmatrix} = -\rho \alpha y_p - \alpha \overline{w} y_w + \beta(\alpha y_p + \alpha \overline{w} y_g).$$

Since inflation is free to jump in this forward looking model, the requirement for stability is that there are as many unstable eigenvalues as there are 'jump' variables. Therefore, we need one positive and one negative eigenvalue – or, equivalently, we require our transition matrix to have a negative determinant. This condition is fulfilled if,

$$\beta < \frac{\rho \alpha y_p + \alpha \overline{w} y_w}{\alpha y_p + \alpha \overline{w} y_g}. \tag{10.11}$$

Note that as the RHS of (10.11) is positive, the condition is always satisfied if government spending is fixed. This in itself is surprising, because it is often asserted that the combination of fixed government spending and constant tax rates are themselves unstable, because government debt will explode once it begins to increase. However this would be inevitable only if government debt were denominated in real terms. If, as is the case here and generally in reality, it is denominated in nominal terms, then a debt interest spiral can be avoided by changes in prices, that is, the inflation tax.

This simple model is not meant to be a realistic model. One possibly unrealistic feature of the model is that it implies that inflation falls following a positive demand shock. In terms of the need for model stability this is quite understandable, as a positive demand shock will raise taxes and reduce government debt, so a negative inflation tax is required to avoid a collapse in government debt. However the real world, and COMPACT, are clearly more complex. What the model does do is illustrate that a model with nominal government debt, like COMPACT, need not be unstable under fixed nominal interest rates.

Although this model has a well defined equilibrium, the price level itself is hysteretic: its value is determined by the history of shocks to the model. Government debt provides the 'nominal anchor' that ties down the price level, but because this nominal anchor is not precisely controlled (directly or indirectly) by the authorities, there is no price level control. We might expect, however, that provided nominal debt was reasonably large, prices would not change much in response to relatively small shocks. This does seem to mirror COMPACT's behaviour, as figure 10.4 showed.

The model is for a closed economy, so it does not directly address the problem of a unit root in the nominal or real exchange rate implied by UIP. If nominal interest rates are fixed by the authorities, then, given world rates, the only movement in the nominal exchange rate that is possible following an unexpected shock is a jump in the initial period of the shock. However as long as a model has some mechanism for determining the equilibrium real exchange rate, then a determinate price level will also tie down the initial jump in the exchange rate. As an extreme example consider a model that embodied long-run PPP, but where demand was independent of the real exchange rate. We could then simply add UIP and long-run PPP to the model above, and the value of the nominal exchange rate could be calculated recursively once the path of prices had been determined by the system above. In short, whatever the long-run change in the price level implied by the shock, PPP would give us the initial jump in the nominal exchange rate. In reality real exchange rates would influence demand, but there is no reason in principle why this more complex model cannot also be stable.

COMPACT's ability to solve under constant nominal interest rates is not therefore surprising. Most UK government debt is defined in nominal terms (that is, it is not index linked), and COMPACT reflects this. As a result, provided fiscal policy does not react too strongly to excessive levels of debt, our analysis suggests that the presumption must be that stability is possible under fixed nominal interest rates.

4. The path of deflation and price path disequilibria

The previous section explained why a model could still solve under fixed nominal interest rates if inflation was forward looking, but it did nothing to explain why this policy could produce more stability in inflation in the face of shocks relative to a more active feedback rule. This result certainly appears counterintuitive. The problem with fixed nominal interest rates is that any demand shock which raises inflation will reduce real interest rates, and lower real interest rates will tend to increase rather than reduce demand.

This mechanism does indeed operate in COMPACT. Real interest rates have a powerful effect on consumption and investment. This is why output is higher after a positive demand shock for the first few years with the weaker rule, and higher still under fixed nominal rates (see figure 10.2). A tougher monetary rule does stabilise output in the short term. However this greater stability in output does not necessarily feed through to short-term inflation if inflation is forward looking.

With a forward looking Phillips curve, the impact of any expected period of excess demand is independent of how many periods into the future it is likely to occur. The analogy is with interest rates and the exchange rate: the current exchange rate reflects the undiscounted sum of future levels of the interest rate differential. Although short-term output is higher with weaker rules in COMPACT, output a few years after the shock is higher with stronger rules, and this provides a countervailing stimulus to short-term inflation.

Why do stronger rules produce more disequilibrium in output after a few years? A potential answer lies with the behaviour of intertemporal consumers and investors. In intertemporal models of consumption, the rate of growth of consumption is related to the level of real interest rates: if real interest rates are higher, the incentive to save increases. (See the discussion of the Keynes/Ramsey rule in Blanchard and Fischer (1989), chapters 2 and 3 for example.) Real interest rates are clearly higher after an inflationary shock with a tougher monetary rule. If utility is logarithmic (which is the case for Blanchard/Yaari consumers), higher real rates will depress consumption in the short term, but also increase its subsequent rate of growth, generating the possibility that consumption may be relatively higher (compared to a weaker rule) subsequently. A similar argument applies to investment. A temporary increase in real interest rates may lead firms to postpone investment, but as the long-run real interest rate is unchanged so will be the long-run capital stock, so if investment is reduced in the short term it needs to be higher at some later date.

Once the initial period of lower output under a stronger rule has passed, the period of higher output (relative to a weaker rule) will tend to raise inflation in a forward looking model. However this provides only a clue to the COMPACT results: for a complete answer we need to know what the overall size and pattern of output losses will be.

To assess what the overall size of output losses will be, we need to note that the price level always returns to something very close to its original level in the long run. In these circumstances, Leith and Wren-Lewis (1999) show deferred deflation can be more effective at reducing prices after some positive shock. The point can be illustrated by considering a discrete time version of equation (10.2):

$$\pi_t = E_t[\pi_{t+1}] + \alpha y_t \tag{10.12}$$

Suppose some shock raises the log of prices by X above their equilibrium path, so equilibrium must be restored by reducing output at some time so that (logged) prices fall by X. Let us further assume that the authorities can choose the speed at which the path for prices falls to the equilibrium price path, because they have direct control over output.

The output loss required for *immediate* restoration of equilibrium is $-X/\alpha$. Suppose, however, that the authorities decide to spread the output loss equally over two periods. In this case the cumulated output loss will only be $-2X/3\alpha$. To see this, substitute out for expected inflation in (10.12) using (10.12) led one period, taking expectations and applying the law of iterated projections:

$$\pi_t = E_t[\pi_{t+2}] + \alpha\{y_t + E_t[y_{t+1}]\}. \tag{10.13}$$

As agents know that equilibrium will be restored in period $t+2$, then expected inflation in that period will be zero. Combining (10.13) with the same equation led one period gives

$$\pi_t + \pi_{t+1} = -X = -\alpha\{y_t + 2E_t[y_{t+1}]\}. \tag{10.14}$$

The cumulated output cost of reducing inflation is therefore lowered by delaying the deflation.

This result can be generalised to a T period delay in restoring price path equilibrium. Solve the forward-looking Phillips curve forwards T periods,

$$\pi_t = \pi_{t+T} + \alpha \sum_{i=0}^{T} y_{t+i}. \tag{10.15}$$

If equilibrium has been restored by time $t+T$, then $\pi_{t+T} = 0$. If we also assume that deflationary policy smoothes the output reduction over time such that it is equal to $\bar{y}$ between t and $t+T$ then the sum of excess inflation between t and $t+T$ is given by,

$$\sum_{i=0}^{T} \pi_{t+T} = \alpha \sum_{i=1}^{T} i y = \alpha\bar{y}\frac{T(T+1)}{2}. \tag{10.16}$$

Therefore, the reduction in output required in each period to eliminate the price path disequilibrium within T periods is,

$$\bar{y} = -\frac{2X}{\alpha T(T+1)} \tag{10.17}$$

whilst the cumulated deflation is simply,

$$T\bar{y} = -\frac{2X}{\alpha(T+1)}.$$ (10.18)

It is clear that the cumulated output cost of eliminating a given price path disequilibria is decreasing in T. There is no need to invoke convex costs of output disequilibrium to justify a gradualist policy. As T tends to infinity the cumulated output cost, in fact, tends towards zero and we recover the familiar costless disinflation result (see, for example, Chadha *et al.*, 1992).

Leith and Wren-lewis (1999) also show that this result depends critically on the forward-looking nature of the Phillips curve. A more traditional backward looking Phillips curve requires the same cumulated output loss to correct price disequilibria whatever its timing.

It might be tempting to think that this result implies that the authorities can achieve the best result by deferring deflation indefinitely. There are two reasons why this would be unwise, however. The first is simply that a gradualist policy allows disequilibrium to persist, which will have costs. In the example above, where deflation occurs over two periods the price path in the second period is still X/3 above its equilibrium level. Second, this analysis assumes that the delayed deflation is credible: agents believe it will take place. The longer it is put off, the stronger this assumption becomes. At least some immediate deflation may be required to convince agents that future deflation will follow. One way the authorities might buy credibility is through the commitment to a policy rule.

We have shown that the cumulated sum of output losses required to return an economy to its desired price path is lower when these losses were spread over a longer time. Now consider how changing the timing of output losses affects the timing of the return to the equilibrium price path. Consider the solution to (10.12)

$$\pi_t = \pi_\infty + \alpha \sum_{i=0}^{\infty} y_{t+i}.$$ (10.19)

Assuming that the economy was initially in equilibrium, then the sum of excess inflation between now and infinity must equal zero in order for price path equilibrium to be restored,

$$p_\infty - p_{-1} = \sum_{i=0}^{\infty} \pi_i = \alpha \sum_{i=0}^{\infty} (1+i) y_i = 0.$$ (10.20)

This can be seen to also imply that the weighted sum of future output deviations is zero. We assume that just such a path for output exists and consider the implications for altering its timing, whilst still ensuring that any price path disequilibrium is removed.

The experiment we consider is one of bringing forward output losses. This will require the sum of output losses to increase, but when will the extra output losses that are required occur? There are two possibilities: the additional output loss takes place either during the period of redistribution, or after it. The COMPACT simulations suggest that the latter possibility is the relevant case. In COMPACT, a stronger rule appears to increase the concavity of output losses.

Our experiment therefore involves reducing output at a point in time, but increasing it at a later date by the same amount. However as we have just shown, in order to ensure that the cumulated sum of future inflation is zero and there is no long-run price path disequilibrium it is necessary to further reduce output. Formally, we shall reduce output at time j, by an amount z and increase output at time l ($l > j$) by z. This will then require us to reduce output at time m ($m > l > j$) by an amount $z(l-j)/(1+m)$ to ensure that equilibrium is restored.

Consider the price path disequilibrium at time k,

$$p_k = -\sum_{i=k+1}^{\infty}\pi_i = \sum_{i=0}^{k}\pi_i = \alpha\sum_{i=0}^{k-1}(i+1)y_i + \alpha(k+1)\sum_{i=k}^{\infty}y_i. \qquad (10.21)$$

It is now possible to examine the change in any price path disequilibria brought about by bringing forward deflation at any point in time, that is before, during and after the timing alteration. The change in the price path disequilibria in anticipation of the bringing forward of deflation is given by,

$$\Delta p_k = -\alpha(k+1)z + \alpha(k+1)z - \alpha(k+1)\frac{l-j}{1+m}z < 0. \qquad (10.22)$$

This is unambiguously negative. That is, bringing forward deflation will always reduce the price path disequilibrium at any point in time before the timing shift has taken place.

The change in the price path disequilibrium at any point in time between j and l is given by,

$$\Delta p_k = -\alpha(j+1)z + \alpha(k+1)z - \alpha(k+1)qz$$
$$= \alpha z(k-j-qk-q) \qquad (10.23)$$

The sign of this expression is ambiguous, but is more likely to be positive for values of k close to l. For example, for values of j, k, l and m of 1, 4, 5 and 6, respectively the sign of the expression is positive. This is due to the fact that prices at a time close to l are most strongly influenced by the anticipation of the additional deflation at time m relative to the effect of the reduced deflation at time l. At any point in time between l and m the change in the price path disequilibrium is given by,

$$
\begin{aligned}
\Delta p_k &= -\alpha(j+1)z + \alpha(l+1)z - \alpha(k+1)\frac{l-j}{1+m}z \\
&= \alpha(l-j)z - \alpha(k+1)\frac{l-j}{1+m}z > 0
\end{aligned}
\qquad (10.24)
$$

Therefore, at any point after the bringing forward of deflation, but before the additional deflation has been implemented, the price path disequilibrium will be greater. In this case, the deflation has been brought forwards, but afterwards prices anticipate the additional deflation at the later date. Finally, the change in the price path disequilibrium after the movement in the output path is,

$$
\Delta p_k = -\alpha(j+1)z + \alpha(l+1)z - \alpha(1+m)\frac{l-j}{1+m} = 0 .
\qquad (10.25)
$$

As would be expected, in a purely forward looking model, after the shifts in output have taken place, they have no impact on the extent of price path disequilibrium.

This analysis shows how bringing forward deflation can increase price disequilibria. The key condition for this to occur was that the additional deflation required to restore equilibrium when deflation is brought forward was, itself, delayed. This certainly appears to be a feature of the simulations in COMPACT, which is itself a function of the intertemporal nature of the model's consumption and investment equations discussed above.

The importance of the dynamic behaviour of demand is confirmed by further results in Leith and Wren-Lewis, 1999. They note that if demand is simply a linear function of real interest rates, then a tougher monetary rule will tend to place the additional deflation required in the short term, which will not generate periods of higher inflation. However using a simple third order dynamic system incorporating an intertemporal consumption function, they show that a demand shock may indeed generate the change in output pattern examined above, and that as a result a tougher monetary rule will raise inflation in all but the very short term. These results strongly suggest that the COMPACT simulation reflects an underlying property of New Keynesian macromodels rather than any embarrassing peculiarity.

5. Summary and conclusions

In this chapter we have shown that it is possible for tougher monetary rules to generate higher inflation following demand shocks when inflation is forward looking. However we should stress that we do not want to conclude from this that policy should always be 'soft', for two reasons. First, the result depends critically on the existence of forward looking behaviour with rational expectations (in both demand as well as inflation), and while we would argue that this is an important case to consider, policy should also be robust to alternatives. Second, the result requires that policy is credible, and the credibility of policy may itself be a positive function of the toughness of the policy rule.

We would want instead to draw two conclusions from our results. First, if mechanisms exist in the economy which bring prices back to some predefined path after a shock, then a more gradualist approach to controlling inflation may be relatively more advantageous if inflation is forward looking. Second, when inflation is forward looking, the relationship between policy rule parameters and inflation outcomes is complex, and may as a result be counter-intuitive in certain situations. An important topic of further research would be to examine how general the results shown here are. For example the relationship between different fiscal policy rules and price level control could be examined. Another interesting issue which arises from our results is whether the dynamic structure of the monetary policy rule could be refined to avoid some of the difficulties associated with strong reaction functions noted here.

Notes

1 We would like to thank Rebecca Driver, Ben Lockwood, Peter Sinclair and John Taylor for helpful comments. This research would not have been possible without support from ESRC Grant L116251026.
2 The underlying intertemporal model is the 'model of pepetual youth' due to Blanchard and Yaari: see Blanchard (1985) for example.
3 There is of course no reason why monetary policy has to be formulated in terms of a fixed rule. The advantages of following a rule are discussed in Taylor (1993). The simplest form of rule would be to relate the level of interest rates to deviations of inflation from the target level. Taylor has suggested a slightly more elaborate rule, where interest rates also respond to deviations in output from its 'non-inflationary' trend, but we ignore this elaboration here to focus on the issues of stability and toughness.
4 The key problem is that solutions to econometric models obtained by itera-

tive methods are only approximations, where the approximation reflects the convergence criteria used in each equation. It is possible that, if these criteria are tightened, the model will gradually iterate to a quite different solution, or may not converge at all.

References

Blanchard, O.J. (1985), 'Debt, deficits, and finite horizons', *Journal of Political Economy*, 93, pp. 223–47.

Blanchard, O. and Fischer, S. (1989), *Lectures on Macroeconomics*, Cambridge, Mass., MIT Press.

Chadha, B., Masson, P.R. and Meredith, G. (1992), 'Models of inflation and the costs of disinflation', *IMF Staff Papers*, 39, 2, pp. 395–431.

Darby, J., Ireland, J., Leith, C. and Wren-Lewis, S. (1999), 'An intertemporal rational expectations model of the UK economy', *Economic Modelling,* 16, pp. 1–52.

Leith, C. and Wren-Lewis, S. (1999), 'Interactions between monetary and fiscal policy rules', University of Exeter Discussion Paper no. 99/13.

Sargent, T. and Wallace, N. (1975), 'Rational expectations, the optimal monetary instrument, and the optimal money supply rule', *Journal of Political Economy*, 83, pp. 241–54.

Taylor, J.B. (1993), *Discretion versus policy rules in practice* , Carnegie-Rochester Series on Public Policy, 39, pp. 195–214.

Woodford, M. (1996), 'Control of the public debt: a requirement for price stability', National Bureau of Economic Research Working Paper No. 5684.

Wren-Lewis, S. (1993), 'Macroeconomic theory and UK macromodels: another failed partnership?' , International Centre for Macroeconomic Modelling Discussion Paper no. 20.

Wren-Lewis, S., Darby, J., Ireland, J. and Ricchi, O. (1996), 'The macroeconomic effects of fiscal policy: linking an econometric model with theory', *Economic Journal*, 106, pp. 543–59.

11 Technical progress and the natural rate in models of the UK economy

KEITH B. CHURCH, PETER R. MITCHELL,
JOANNE E. SAULT and KENNETH F. WALLIS

1. Introduction

What are the macroeconomic consequences of technological (or technical) change? The standard neoclassical growth model gives a clear answer. In the long run, the natural rate of growth of the economy is equal to the rate of technical progress plus the growth rate of the population. Technical progress increases the potential supply of output, and given sufficiently flexible factor and product markets this potential can be realised, resulting in increased consumption, investment and real wages. These prognostications of beneficial outcomes nevertheless may not assuage more classical concerns about the possibility of permanent technological unemployment. And even with a beneficial view of long-run equilibrium, the processes of adjustment to the introduction of new technologies may be sufficiently protracted that substantial unemployment costs are incurred.

Macroeconometric models are useful devices for quantifying some of these effects. They provide estimates of the relevant long-run responses and the nature of the intervening adjustments to a change in the rate of technical progress. This is done at a relatively high level of aggregation, and macroeconometric models are typically silent on compositional and distributional questions, such as the impact of new technologies on employment and investment in different industries. Nor is technical progress itself explained by these models, instead the rate of technical progress is exogenous and typically constant.

In this chapter we undertake simulations of changes in the rate of technical progress on three models of the UK economy in order to answer the question posed in our opening sentence. The models considered are those of Her Majesty's Treasury (HMT), the National Institute of Economic and

Social Research (NIESR), and the 'COMPACT' model group, as deposited at the ESRC Macroeconomic Modelling Bureau in late 1996; their general properties are reviewed along with those of two further models by Church *et al.* (1997). As is usual in the Bureau's research programme, our analysis focuses not only on answering the substantive economic question posed above, but also on using it as a case study for cross-model comparisons. In general the models conform to what is now the leading paradigm among both policy analyst-advisers and macroeconometric modellers in many OECD economies, in which a broadly neoclassical view of macroeconomic equilibrium coexists with a new Keynesian view of short-to-medium-term adjustment. Thus, at least in respect of the long-run equilibrium, the level of real activity is independent of the steady-state inflation rate, whereas in the short run, adjustment costs and contractual arrangements imply that markets do not clear instantaneously and there is a relatively slow process of dynamic adjustment to equilibrium. This is by no means a full-employment equilibrium, however, and an important question is what determines the non-accelerating-inflation rate of unemployment (NAIRU). The NAIRU is often independent of the steady-state inflation rate and so becomes the 'natural' rate of unemployment; it may, however, depend on the rate of productivity growth. These and other possible differences are explored in the remainder of this chapter.

A technical progress shock is essentially a supply-side shock and so draws attention to the supply-side specifications of the models. These have seen substantial developments in the last decade or two, redressing an important imbalance in the demand-oriented models of the 1970s. The forecasting failures of those models in the face of supply-side shocks, a desire for greater theoretical consistency in the models, and a shift in the emphasis of policy all pointed towards such a reorientation. However model-based analyses have addressed only a small range of the resulting issues. They have typically focused on measures that impact directly on costs, a popular simulation in the light of the experience of the 1970s being a change in the world price of oil. Relatively less attention has been given to technical progress, despite the debate about the causes and consequences of the slowdown in productivity growth in the 1970s. The OECD's INTERLINK model seems to have been the only model used to address this question (Englander and Mittelstädt, 1988; Torres and Martin, 1990; Giorno *et al.*, 1995) until a recent comparative study of Australian models (Hargreaves, 1994) and an initial investigation of two UK models (Church *et al.*, 1998). The present chapter further develops this line of research.

The chapter proceeds as follows. In section 2 we briefly describe how key features of the supply side are represented in the models, with particular attention to the production technology and the determination of the NAIRU. This provides a framework for interpreting the results of simulations of changes in technical progress, which are presented in section 3. It is seen that several of the 'natural rate' propositions are reflected in the results, although there are substantial differences in short-run dynamics and some of the unemployment responses are scarcely beneficial, if not perverse. Since these are national-economy models and the shock is applied on the same basis, terms of trade responses are also an important factor. Section 4 contains concluding comments.

2. Technical progress and the supply side of macroeconometric models

2.1 The production function and factor demands

The basic description of technology within the models is a two-factor production function with constant returns to scale, of either the Cobb-Douglas or constant elasticity of substitution (CES) form. Technical progress is assumed to be Harrod-neutral or labour-augmenting, the model's steady state then conforming to the stylised fact of a constant investment/output ratio; technical progress proceeds at a constant exponential rate. The production function thus has the general form

$$Y_t = F\left(K_t, L_t e^{\beta t}\right). \tag{11.1}$$

In none of the present models is a production function estimated as such; rather the estimated factor demand equations are based on the underlying production function, and technical progress then appears in those equations as time-trends. We now describe how this is done in the three models.

HM Treasury
In the HMT model firms are assumed to choose factor input levels to minimise current costs given the expected level of output, subject to a Cobb-Douglas production function with labour elasticity α. The first-order conditions yield log-linear equations for employment and investment each containing the trend term $\alpha\beta t$, although the implied cross-equation restriction is not imposed in estimation. Indeed, in the manufacturing employment equation this is estimated as a split time-trend, with a lower rate of growth over 1975–80. The treatment of expectations uses the CBI/NIESR series for expected manufacturing output.

NIESR

In the NIESR model the firm's objective is to maximise the present dis-counted value of future expected net cash flows, subject to a CES production function. The cash flow variable includes a quadratic cost of adjusting the capital stock. The resulting investment equation involves fu-ture expected investment, which is one of the forward-looking variables treated as 'rational' or 'model-consistent' expectations in solving this model. The analysis uses an 'effective' labour measure throughout, implicitly treat-ing the second argument of the production function (11.1) as a single variable. Technical change is thus measured as an index of labour efficiency, calculated as the residual output growth unexplained by growth in the two primary factor inputs, at an average annual rate which varies by sector.

COMPACT

Whereas the HMT and NIESR models assume that factor proportions are continuously variable, the COMPACT model adopts a vintage or 'putty-clay' model of production in which, once a new vintage of capital investment is installed, there are no factor substitution possibilities. The optimal choice of factor proportions prior to installation then depends on expected future factor prices over the equipment's entire lifetime, within an *ex ante* Cobb-Douglas technology. The age profile of the capital stock in use then determines the required labour input. Technical progress enters as in (11.1), but any change in technical progress is only gradually embodied in the capital stock as a result of its vintage structure.

2.2 Prices, wages and the NAIRU

Prices are determined as a mark-up on costs, and the wage equation is gen-erated by a bargaining model as described by Layard and Nickell (1985). Both equations are usually estimated in error correction form and exhibit static and dynamic homogeneity, and so can be solved to obtain an expres-sion for the NAIRU, as in Joyce and Wren-Lewis (1991) and Turner (1991). The long run of a typical wage equation may be written as

$$w - p + t^e = pr + \theta\left(t^i + t^e + t^d + t^m\right) - \gamma u + z^w \tag{11.2}$$

where w, p and pr are (log) nominal earnings, producer prices and average labour productivity respectively, u is the unemployment rate, t^d, t^i and t^e are the average direct, indirect and employers' tax rates (per cent) respec-tively, and t^m is the 'tax' imposed by high import prices or the real exchange rate. These four terms drive a 'wedge' between employers' real wage costs and employees' real consumption wages, whose long-run impact on the bargained wage outcome and consequently on the NAIRU is measured by the parameter θ. In the HMT model $\theta = 0.5$, whereas in the other two models $\theta = 0$ so a permanent change in any of the wedge terms has no effect on the NAIRU. Finally other wage pressure variables may be included in z^w, such as the replacement ratio and a measure of union power.

The earnings equations in the HMT and COMPACT models are statically but not dynamically homogeneous with respect to productivity. Thus in a dynamic steady state with real wage growth occurring at the rate of growth of productivity, this steady-state productivity growth rate also affects the *level* of real wages and hence the NAIRU in these models: an increase in productivity growth leads to a fall in the NAIRU. (This response is not observed in simulations of the COMPACT model, however, since in the model code a constant trend productivity growth number rather than an endogenous productivity growth variable appears at the relevant point.) The underlying effect is consistent with evidence presented by Manning (1992) that the slowdown in productivity growth is an important explanation of the increase in unemployment in many OECD countries; Turner *et al.* (1993) study the G3 economies and report a similar finding for Germany, but not for Japan or the United States. No such effect occurs in the NIESR model; on the other hand, in this model the NAIRU is a function of the *rate of change* of the wedge, together with the cost of stockholding and the proportion of long-term unemployment.

It should be noted that the average labour productivity measure considered in this section can be immediately equated to the labour efficiency measure discussed in the preceding section only in the steady state of the simple growth model. In a full-model simulation of changes in technical progress, feedbacks from the rest of the model to employment, notably from output and relative factor prices, also influence the labour productivity outcome, and the adjustment to a new steady state may be protracted.

2.3 Aggregation

In the COMPACT model the features discussed above are treated at the level of the non-oil private sector of the economy, whereas the other two models disaggregate this. In the HMT model separate factor demand equations are estimated for manufacturing and non-manufacturing, and the latter is further disaggregated in the NIESR model, into business services, distribution and 'other'. A more aggregate model is more transparent and easier to maintain, *ceteris paribus*, although information is lost whenever different components of an aggregate behave differently and these different behaviours can be successfully modelled.

The technical progress measure in the NIESR model, analogous to the parameter β in (11.1), takes different values across the four sectors, as noted above; these are, at annual rates, manufacturing 3.2 per cent, distribution 0.032 per cent, business services 0.92 per cent, other 5.92 per cent, compared with the single aggregate figure in the COMPACT model of 1.96 per cent. The corresponding estimates of productivity trends derived from the HMT model's manufacturing and non-manufacturing employment and investment equations are not directly comparable, since they are functions of movements in relative factor prices as well as technical progress. Chan *et al.* (1995, p.36) give these as, in manufacturing, 2.6 per cent over 1970–75, 2.1 per cent over 1975–80 and 3.7 per cent over 1981–92, and in non-manufacturing 1.0 per cent.

3. Simulation experiments

3.1 Experimental design

Macroeconomic responses to a technical progress shock are estimated by comparing the results of two solutions of each model, one a base run and the other a perturbed run in which the relevant technical progress variable is assigned values that deviate from its base-run values. Two shocks are considered. The first is an increase in the *level* of labour-augmenting technical progress of 1 per cent. The second is an increase in the annual *growth rate* of technical progress, analogous to the parameter β in equation (11.1), of 0.1 percentage points. This is a permanent change, and the first shock can be equivalently considered to be a temporary shock to the growth rate. In the NIESR and COMPACT models explicit labour efficiency trends appear, which can be directly perturbed. In the HMT model, equivalent perturbations are applied to the manufacturing and non-manufacturing employment and investment equations.

The base run in the NIESR model corresponds to a published forecast, extended to a horizon of 33 years for simulation purposes. The COMPACT model is not used for forecasting, and a 71-year simulation base is supplied by its proprietors. The public release of the HMT model does not include a forecast or simulation base, and we use the forecast of the Ernst and Young ITEM (Independent Treasury Economic Model) Club, kindly provided by the Club, which has a horizon of 12½ years. All three models operate at a quarterly data frequency.

The macroeconomic responses to a shock may include changes in inflation and the state of the public finances, which may in turn induce changes in monetary and fiscal policy, since the models operate in a policy framework that reflects the broad objectives of current policy, namely low inflation and sound public finances. In the NIESR and COMPACT models the monetary policy rule sets the nominal short-term interest rate as a function of the deviation of inflation from its target, which in our perturbed run is taken to be the base-run values of inflation. The fiscal closure rules adjust the direct tax rate whenever the PSBR/GDP ratio (NIESR) or debt/GDP ratio (COMPACT) deviates from its target value, again the base-run values. For the HMT model we are not able to find correspondingly simple rules that perform well in all our experiments (see also Church *et al.*, 1997), and so we apply optimal control techniques, with an objective function that reflects the same policy framework. This penalises (squared) deviations of the inflation rate and the PSBR/GDP ratio from their base-run values, together with (squared) changes in the interest rate and income tax instruments, as is conventional in this approach, in order to avoid excessive and unrealistic movements in these policy instruments.

An implication of the fiscal policy rule together with the maintenance of (exogenous) government expenditure at its base-run values is that any beneficial effect of increased technical progress on the public finances is passed on to the personal sector in the form of lower taxation. Other possibilities, such as increasing public expenditure or reducing the 'Maastricht' target ratios, remain for future study.

3.2 An increase in the level of technical progress

The economy-wide responses of output, employment, investment and productivity in the first simulation are shown in figures 11.1–11.4, where annual averages of quarterly data are presented. Only the first 40 years of the COMPACT solution are shown in the figures, the remaining 30 years exhibiting little further change in variables of interest. The results show that productivity does eventually increase by about 1 per cent in each of the models although some uncertainty remains in the case of the HMT model that this is the long-run outcome. The adjustment in the COMPACT model is protracted due in part to the vintage system, whereas the NIESR model has a slow but very smooth path to the new equilibrium.

Identical outcomes in terms of productivity behaviour can be achieved through different combinations of employment and output responses. In the HMT and COMPACT models the productivity increase is driven by an increase in output with employment returning to base, although in the case of the HMT model it seems likely that there is some cyclical behaviour still to unwind. In the COMPACT model we do see the neutrality of

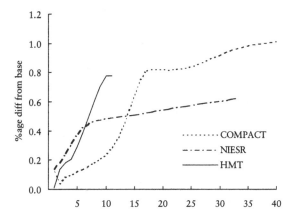

Figure 11.1 *Per cent increase in level of TP: output*

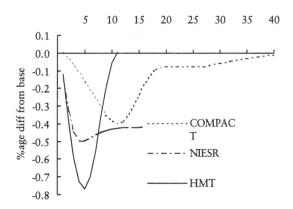

Figure 11.2 *Per cent increase in level of TP: employment*

the natural rate to changes in the level of productivity discussed above. By contrast in the NIESR model output is not a full 1 per cent higher but the productivity gain is achieved with a permanent reduction in the level of employment. Investment increases in line with output in each of the models although the determination of investment behaviour is different in each case as described below.

In the HMT model the 1 per cent increase in the level of technical progress has an immediate effect on output. Both manufacturing and non-manufac-

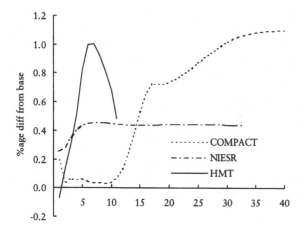

Figure 11.3 *Per cent increase in level of TP: investment*

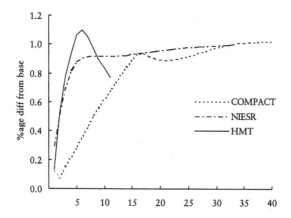

Figure 11.4 *Per cent increase in level of TP: productivity*

turing output are above base throughout the simulation period, ending at levels 1.34 per cent and 0.52 per cent above base respectively in the final quarter. Taken together with the employment responses, average labour productivity in both sectors increases, peaking in quarters 25 (manufacturing) and 21 (non-manufacturing) at values 1.18 per cent and 1.21 per cent above base, before diminishing as the reductions in employment at the beginning of the simulation are reversed. In the final quarter productivity remains 0.86 per cent (manufacturing) and 0.66 per cent (non-manufacturing) above base, employment in manufacturing being 0.47 per cent above base at this point, while in non-manufacturing employment is virtually back at base.

In the NIESR model output and investment increase sharply in the first year of the simulation while employment declines, being 0.4 per cent below base even after 33 years. This means that average productivity increases by 1 per cent, although the employment/output mix that achieves this is different from the other models. This result can in part be explained by looking at the results at the sectoral level. In the NIESR model the determination of public sector employment differs from that in other parts of the economy. For manufacturing, distribution, business services and 'other' sectors the effective labour input is determined by inverting the production function where actual hours worked adjust only slowly towards target hours, hence after 33 years employment is still 0.2–0.3 per cent below base. Employment in public services falls equiproportionately with increases in technology and rises in line with output. In this simulation public sector employment falls about 0.9 per cent below base whereas output in this sector increases by 0.1 per cent in the long run producing a 1 per cent increase in public sector productivity.

The results from the COMPACT model are dominated by the properties of the vintage system of production. The responses of output, investment and employment are notably slower than in the other models, reflecting the fact that the improvement in technical progress gradually increases the level of the capital stock over a long period of time. Firms are faced with a choice between investing in the new more productive machinery which requires shifting forward capital expenditure or continuing to produce output using old machines. Wages depend on average output per head and thus increase as the new machinery is introduced. When firms decide on the current investment mix the expectation of higher future wage rates is an important influence. This gives a lower labour to capital ratio in current investment and hence employment falls below base for ten years before recovering back towards its original values as marginal costs finally reflect the improvement in technical progress. After about 30 years output has risen by 1 per cent reflecting the 20 years it takes the new technology to be embodied in all machines. However although the neutrality of the NAIRU with respect to a change in the level of productivity appears to hold eventually, there is a substantial 'cost' arising from the incorporation of new technology as it is fifty years before the unemployment rate returns to its baseline level.

Figures 11.5 and 11.6 show the impact of an increase in the level of technical progress on unemployment and real wage behaviour allowing

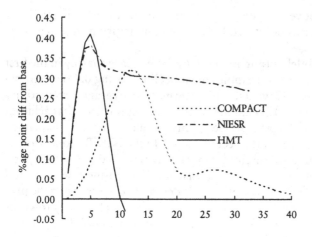

Figure 11.5 *Per cent increase in level of TP: unemployment rate*

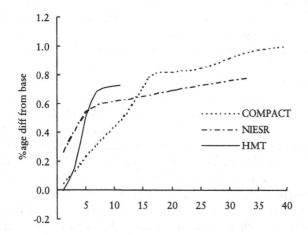

Figure 11.6 *Per cent increase in level of TP: real wage*

comparisons across models with our *a priori* expectation that the level of
the real wage should fully reflect the improvement in technical progress
and that the NAIRU is invariant to the increase in the level of technical
progress, although the shock may affect tax rates and the terms of trade
which in the HMT model in turn affect the NAIRU.

Falling prices along with a higher unemployment level in the HMT
model counter any positive effects that the increase in productivity has on

average earnings during the first 3 years of the simulation. As the productivity increase feeds through, average earnings rise slightly above base for around 2 years before declining back below base for the remainder of the simulation, finishing 0.64 per cent below base in both the manufacturing and non-manufacturing sectors. The RPI falls by 1.3 per cent, giving an increase in real wages of 0.66 per cent, although these quantities have not settled down by this time.

Relative factor prices are an important determinant of employment levels in the HMT model. As prices change the interest rate adjusts in order to target inflation, and these interest rate changes have implications for the cost of capital in both sectors. An initial fall is reversed after about 5 years, the cost of capital peaking at 3.36 per cent (manufacturing) and 2.88 per cent (non-manufacturing) above base after about 7½ years. The cost of capital response dominates that of wage costs, which explains the employment dynamics in figure 11.2, the positive output effect only beginning to emerge at the end of the simulation period. The unemployment rate in figure 11.5 is almost a mirror image. In the HMT model the NAIRU is affected by the wedge, in particular its income tax rate and real exchange rate components in this simulation. The income tax rate falls in order to target the deficit ratio back to base, while rising export prices and falling import prices worsen the terms of trade; these two effects offset one another throughout the simulation.

The unemployment rate in the NIESR model also peaks in year 5 at about the same rate as in the HMT model. Thereafter a small and protracted decline occurs with the unemployment rate still about 0.3 percentage points higher by the end of the simulation. The effect of the increase in the level of technical progress on the wage bargain is an increase in the real wage of around 0.6 per cent in the first six years of the simulation followed by a period of slower growth, such that the increase is just 0.8 per cent by the end of the simulation compared with the 1 per cent increase expected from the core supply-side framework.

3.3 An increase in the growth rate of technical progress

The results of a 0.1 percentage point increase in the growth rate of technical progress for output, employment, investment and productivity growth are shown in figures 11.7–11.10. The rate of technical progress determines the overall growth of the economy so we would expect to see the economy move to a new steady state at a higher growth rate.

In the HMT model the growth rates of output, employment, investment and in turn productivity, fluctuate for the first 5 years of the simulation

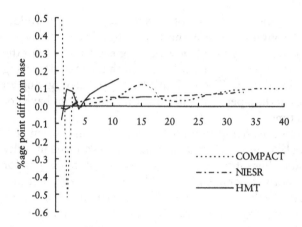

Figure 11.7 *0.1 percentage point increase in growth of TP: output growth*

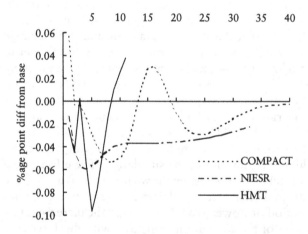

Figure 11.8 *0.1 percentage point increase in growth of TP: employment growth*

before reaching relatively stable paths. In the final quarter the productivity growth rate is 0.13 percentage points above base (manufacturing) and 0.09 percentage points above base (non-manufacturing). The increase in the growth rate of technical progress is more than fully reflected by investment decisions in both sectors, although the growth rate responses do not seem to have settled down at constant levels by the end of the simulation period. The improvement in the growth rate of output in the manufacturing sector reaches a similar level to that of investment, 0.27 percentage

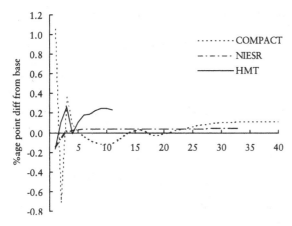

Figure 11.9 *0.1 percentage point increase in growth of TP: investment growth*

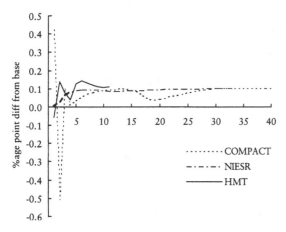

Figure 11.10 *0.1 percentage point increase in growth of TP: productivity growth*

points above base in the final quarter, although in the non-manufacturing sector the output growth response is only half of this. Changes in the growth rate of employment are much smaller than those of output and investment. In the non-manufacturing sector the growth rate falls and then slowly returns back towards base. The lost growth is never recouped during the course of the simulation, leaving employment levels around 0.5 per cent below base during the second half of the simulation.

In the NIESR model employment and output growth decline in the first two years although productivity growth increases as the fall in output is less than that in employment. From year 3 output growth climbs above base but the employment growth rate remains below. By the end of the simulation output growth is about 0.08 percentage points higher and still increasing very gradually towards equality with the increment in the growth rate of technical progress. Employment growth also appears to be adjusting back towards base at the end of the simulation. As in the previous simulation the explanation of the aggregate employment response is found in the behaviour of the public sector where employment growth declines throughout the simulation ending up at a constant difference from base of around −0.08 percentage points, in contrast to the other sectors where employment growth returns to base in the long run, leaving 'effective labour' growth increased by 0.1 percentage points.

In the COMPACT model the longer simulation horizon does allow the improvement in the growth rate of technical progress to manifest itself completely in the behaviour of output and investment, both of which show the full 0.1 percentage point increase in growth. Although the growth rate of employment returns to its base-run value, the level of employment never returns to its original values and instead settles down some 0.5 per cent lower. As in the first experiment the adjustment of the COMPACT model to the new equilibrium is protracted, with large short-run fluctuations occurring before equilibrium is reached. The growth rates of output and investment both jump sharply in the first quarter by 0.53 per cent and 1.04 per cent respectively, increase again in the second quarter but then fall back for the following year. Both increase steadily for the rest of the simulation. By contrast employment changes very little, increasing to a maximum response 0.07 per cent above base after three quarters. This small employment gain is eliminated by the end of year 5. The initial volatility of output is reflected in productivity growth itself, before the model starts to settle down.

The increase in the growth rate of technical progress is assumed to be confined to the UK economy. In each of the models the level of employment is lower as a result of the shift in technology, but output is higher, its level continuously diverging from base-run values. Clearly this extra output has to be consumed either by the domestic market or overseas, and these compositional effects differ across the models, as shown in figure 11.11.

In the HMT model lower prices and higher interest rates lead to initial nominal and real appreciations of the exchange rate. The real appreciation

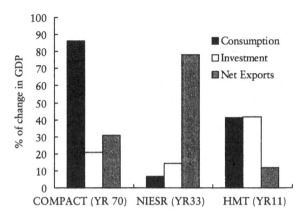

Figure 11.11 *0.1 percentage point increase in growth of TP: contributions to long-run rise in GDP*

worsens competitiveness stimulating imports and depressing exports. This has an adverse effect on the terms of trade, pushing up unemployment. However, the interest rate falls below base in quarter 5, so the nominal exchange rate depreciates. Prices fall by less, giving a real depreciation. The increase in competitiveness which results helps exports recover quickly, and the improvement in the terms of trade position helps dampen unemployment.

The income tax rate moves to target the deficit ratio, with a downward trend in the basic rate during the second part of the simulation, corresponding to the increase in the tax base. This gives higher real personal disposable income and hence increases in consumers' expenditure, which is 0.66 per cent above base in the final quarter. The lower income tax rate assists in dampening unemployment through its role in the wedge variable.

In the NIESR model interest rates are 0.1 percentage points higher in each of the first three years of the simulation, then continue to rise very gradually, being 0.2 percentage points higher by the end of the simulation. This ensures that the small initial increase in inflation is eliminated by the fifth year. Although this interest rate profile might lead us to expect a slight appreciation of the nominal exchange rate, both nominal and real rates decline, ending up 5 per cent and 2 per cent lower respectively in the final period. This exchange rate response accounts for the behaviour of net export demand, which increases steadily as a proportion of the increase in GDP, accounting for 78 per cent of this by the end of the simulation compared with 14 per cent and 7 per cent for investment and consumption, as shown in figure 11.11. The contribution of consumption is negative for the first fourteen years of the simulation, while that for investment is virtually zero.

Consumption growth is 0.1 percentage points higher by the end of the simulation as higher real personal disposable income and wealth offset the depressing effect on consumers' expenditure of increased unemployment. The rise in disposable income is enhanced by the fiscal solvency rule which, after a short-lived increase in the basic rate of income tax of about 0.1 pence, reduces the tax rate to 0.3 pence below base by the end of the simulation. The fiscal policy rule aims to hold the PSBR/GDP ratio at its base-run values, and higher GDP growth not only improves the public finances, *ceteris paribus*, as noted above, but also reduces the ratio, *ceteris paribus*.

In the COMPACT model a long-run depreciation of the real exchange rate is required to bridge the gap between domestic demand and output. Immediately after the shock is implemented there is a large fall in the nominal exchange rate and a corresponding jump in prices and hence the inflation rate. Interest rates increase in line with inflation and this moderates and then reverses the depreciation. The inflation rate falls below base in the thirteenth year, but finally returns to its original level at the very end of the simulation horizon. Both the nominal exchange rate and the price level eventually reach new lower levels just below base, giving a long-run real depreciation of about 4.3 per cent.

This improvement in competitiveness ensures that the increase in technical progress is fully reflected in output as exports increase throughout the simulation. In the HMT and COMPACT export equations the presence of a term in cumulated investment of the UK relative to the rest of the world, representing 'quality' (Owen and Wren-Lewis, 1993), reinforces the competitiveness effect. In the COMPACT model non-oil exports increase by 3.85 per cent by the final quarter of the simulation. Despite both competitiveness and cumulated investment terms working in the opposite direction and the absence of any improvement in technical progress elsewhere, non-oil imports also increase in the COMPACT model.

The increase in the growth rate of output expands the tax base and in order to satisfy the debt ratio target the basic rate of income tax has to fall. By the end of the simulation the basic rate is 3.63 percentage points lower in the COMPACT model. The combined impact of this tax cut and the increase in real wages described above stimulates domestic demand ensuring that most of the increase in output is consumed at home. Consumers' expenditure is below base for the first thirteen years reflect-

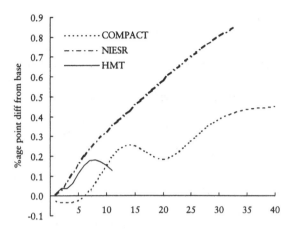

Figure 11.12 *0.1 percentage point increase in growth of TP: unemployment rate*

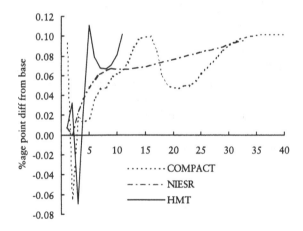

Figure 11.13 *0.1 percentage point increase in growth of TP: real wage growth*

ing both initial higher interest and tax rates, but once the interest rate returns to base and the tax rate starts falling, consumers' expenditure increases steadily, finishing 7.44 per cent higher at the end of the simulation. This increase in domestic demand combined with the real exchange rate depreciation sucks in imports which are eventually 2.15 per cent higher. However, the response of exports ensures improvement in the domestic trading position.

The responses of unemployment and real wages are shown in figures 11.12 and 11.13. In the NIESR model the level of the real wage increases steadily throughout the simulation as does real wage growth which ends up around 0.1 percentage points higher by the last year of the simulation. The unemployment rate and the 'population needing work' ratio increase throughout the simulation without appearing to stabilize at a new higher level.

For the first eleven years of the COMPACT simulation wages and prices rise in line with each other. They then decline, but wages lag behind prices and finish permanently higher giving a final increase in average real wages of 5.92 per cent. The level of the wage bargain achieved reflects the level of average productivity while the price level depends on the change in marginal productivity. The increase in the NAIRU in this simulation mirrors the increase in the ratio of average to marginal productivity, this worsening occurring despite a reduction in the maximum vintage of machinery in use which by itself would tend to reduce marginal costs and hence the natural rate. With lower employment fewer people enjoy the increased real wage or the reduction in the basic rate of income tax that also occurs in this simulation.

For the HMT model average earnings fall during the initial stages of the simulation, but this is soon reversed and average earnings rise throughout the remainder of the simulation, stimulated by the continual increase in the level of productivity. The growth rate exceeds that of prices, hence real wage growth is increased, by an amount which matches the increase in technical progress at the end of the simulation. The unemployment profile in figure 11.12 suggests that the beneficial effect on the NAIRU in this model of an increase in productivity growth is beginning to appear by the end of the simulation.

4. Conclusion

In the textbook neoclassical growth model it is the growth rate of technical progress, together with that of the population, that determines the overall rate of economic growth. Our conclusion from the results presented in this chapter is that this is also broadly true of three economy-wide empirical models of the UK economy. Increases in technical progress are fully reflected by increases in productivity and hence by increases in the real wage received by workers. However the models also suggest that the transition to a new equilibrium following a technology shock is protracted and may possibly result in permanent technological unemployment.

An increase of 1 per cent in the level of technical progress is expected to leave the natural rate of unemployment unchanged. Only in the COM-PACT model is this clearly the case, where employment does eventually recover to its original level and the 1 per cent increase in productivity is achieved through an equivalent increase in output. The NIESR model suggests that the same productivity increase is achieved with a smaller workforce and an increase in output of less than 1 per cent, a result which is due to the reaction of the public sector. An increase in the growth rate of technical progress results in an increase in the growth rate of output in each of the models. However it is only in the HMT model that this change might reduce the NAIRU. The other two models show a substantial permanent increase in the unemployment rate although those remaining in work enjoy increased growth in their real wages.

Macroeconometric models provide an internally consistent account of the main macroeconomic responses to an external shock. Their system-wide perspective is their main distinguishing feature from partial empirical analyses that focus more sharply on specific questions, but difficulties of measurement and explanation are common to both modes of analysis. For the technical progress question, a key measurement issue is that of accurately recording and evaluating improvements in the quality of output, which assumes particular importance in parts of the public sector and the services sector where output measurement is based on measures of labour input. Whereas an economy-wide aggregate treatment might mask distortions of this kind, a more disaggregated treatment that attempts to distinguish possibly different behaviour in these sectors is potentially at risk from the mismeasurement of the contribution of technical progress. Some of the model-based results reported above are no more nor less at risk from this issue than other kinds of analysis. Explanations of technical progress at the macroeconomic level are similarly difficult to obtain, hence in model-based analysis it is treated as an exogenous variable. Attempts to explain it by relating it to such variables as research and development expenditure or indicators of patenting activity at levels of aggregation much beyond individual case studies have not proved successful, and endogenising it in this way in an economy-wide model would in turn require explanations of those 'explanatory' variables.

The models considered here are national-economy models, with the rest of the world treated as exogenous, and the changes in technical progress that are implemented in the models apply only to the UK economy. These exercises provide useful insights into the supply-side responses of the models, but to the extent that technological change is a global phenomenon, with innovation being rapidly transmitted among the industrialised nations, our results do not represent accurate forecasts. Equivalent technical progress shocks in the UK's trading partners might be expected to produce similar supply responses, but demand might respond more quickly thanks to the trade mechanism. Nevertheless single-country competitiveness gains should no longer be a feature, hence the export share of growth might be expected to be less than that shown in our results. Findings along these lines are reported by Giorno et al. (1995), who compare the results of single-economy and area-wide changes in trend productivity using the OECD's INTERLINK model and show that overall adjustment towards long-run equilibrium is significantly speeded up in the case of an area-wide shock. The extension of our analysis to the domestic effects of global technological changes is a future research task.

References

Chan, A., Savage, D. and Whittaker, R. (1995), 'The new Treasury model', Government Economic Service Working Paper no. 128 (Treasury Working Paper no. 70), London, HM Treasury.

Church, K.B., Mitchell, P.R., Sault, J.E. and Wallis, K.F. (1997), 'Comparative properties of models of the UK economy', *National Institute Economic Review*, 161, pp. 91–100.

Church, K.B., Mitchell, P.R. and Wallis, K.F. (1998), 'Short-run rigidities and long-run equilibrium in large-scale macroeconometric models', in Brakman, S., van Ees, H. and Kuipers, S.K. (eds), *Market Behaviour and Macroeconomic Modelling*, London, Macmillan, pp. 221–41.

Englander, A.S. and Mittelstädt, A. (1988), 'Total factor productivity: macroeconomic and structural aspects of the slowdown', *OECD Economic Studies*, 10, pp. 7–56.

Giorno, C., Richardson, P. and Suyker, W. (1995), 'Technical progress, factor productivity and macroeconomic performance in the medium term', *OECD Economic Studies*, 25, pp. 153–77.

Hargreaves, C.P. (Ed.) (1994), *A Comparison of Economy-Wide Models of Australia: Responses to a Rise in Labour Productivity*, Commission Paper no. 2, Economic Planning Advisory Commission, Commonwealth of Australia.

Joyce, M. and Wren-Lewis, S. (1991), 'The role of the real exchange rate and capacity utilisation in convergence to the NAIRU', *Economic Journal*, 101, pp. 497–507.

Layard, P.R.G. and Nickell, S.J. (1985), 'The causes of British unemployment', *National Institute Economic Review*, 111, pp. 62–85.

Manning, A. (1992), 'Productivity growth, wage setting and the equilibrium rate of unemployment', Centre for Economic Performance Discussion Paper no. 63, London School of Economics.

Owen, C. and Wren-Lewis, S. (1993), 'Variety, quality and U.K. manufacturing exports', Discussion Paper no. 14, International Centre for Macroeconomic

Modelling, University of Strathclyde.

Torres, R. and Martin, J.P. (1990), 'Measuring potential output in the seven major OECD economies', *OECD Economic Studies*, 14, pp. 127–49.

Turner, D.S. (1991), 'The determinants of the NAIRU response in simulations on the Treasury model', *Oxford Bulletin of Economics and Statistics*, 53, pp. 225–42.

Turner, D.S., Richardson, P. and Rauffet, S. (1993), 'The role of real and nominal rigidities in macroeconomic adjustment: a comparative study of the G3 economies', *OECD Economic Studies*, 21, pp. 90–137.

12 The conduct of monetary policy when the business cycle is non-linear

STEVEN COOK, SEAN HOLLY and PAUL TURNER[1]

1. Introduction

In the UK, as in a number of other industrialised economies, there have been significant changes to the way in which monetary and fiscal policy is conducted. The adoption of inflation targets in 1992 and the granting of operational independence to the Bank of England in May 1997 has been followed by an intense debate about how the Bank should conduct monetary policy and how it should be accountable to the Government, parliament and the public. There has also been a debate about the conduct of fiscal policy with the Government recently committing itself to a Code for Fiscal Stability based on strict fiscal rules.

There is a strong presumption in discussions of the conduct of monetary policy that stability is desirable and that the short-run benefits for output and employment of a monetary stimulus are more than counteracted by the output losses resulting from the need to bring inflation back under control. However, there is also a strong presumption that the trade-off between inflation and economic activity in the short run is linear.[2] This means that the effect of a given excess demand on inflation is the same whether it is negative or positive.

Yet there is now an extensive theoretical literature which suggests that adjusting asymmetrically to negative and positive shocks on the part of firms may be an optimal thing to do. Moreover, when there are costs to adjusting, there may be a range of inaction within which little adjustment takes place. A good example of this class of models is that of Ball and Mankiw (1994).[3] They show that when there are 'menu' costs of changing prices there will be a range of inaction where the costs of changing prices will exceed the benefits. However, with positive trend inflation the costs are asymmetric. If a firm experiences a negative shock which requires a cut in its relative price some of the work can be done by general inflation, the necessary cut in nominal prices will therefore be less than that for relative prices. When the shock is positive requiring the firm to raise prices, a larger nominal price rise will be required to compensate for the effect of general inflation. Ball and Mankiw also show that this process reverses itself when inflation is negative. Firms lower their prices more quickly than they raise them. Only at zero trend inflation is adjustment symmetrical.

Despite the attractions of the Ball–Mankiw model as an explanation for nominal inertia and asymmetric adjustment, making it operational presents a number of difficulties (see Arden *et al.*, 1997a). There is also the problem that the evidence for convexities in price adjustment is decidedly mixed. However, we have found that it can be very difficult to detect asymmetric adjustment using conventional tests of significance even when it is there by construction. In Cook *et al.* (1997) we provide Monte-Carlo evidence on the power of tests to reject the null of linearity even when the true model is of the piecewise linear form of Granger and Lee (1989). We have repeated similar experiments in which the adjustment function takes the cubic form and again we find that, for reasonably sized samples, there is considerable lack of power.

If there is a presumption in favour of non-linearity rather than linearity, there is a potentially important policy implication. In the standard literature on the optimal rate of inflation, if there is downwards rigidity in nominal prices, a low rate of inflation may help to lubricate the process of relative price adjustment. However, when price adjustment is asymmetric as in the BM model, the optimal rate of inflation is zero. This arises because the output costs of getting inflation back under control outweigh the benefits. This point has some relevance for recent discussions of the best way in which the Bank of England should conduct monetary policy.

The most recent discussion of the mechanisms by which an operationally independent central bank should conduct monetary policy is to be found in Mervyn King (1997). King argues that monetary policy should be expressed as a 'monetary policy reaction function' that describes policy in terms of two variables. The first is an *ex ante* inflation target defined as the desired inflation rate in a world without shocks. The second is the discretionary response by the central bank to shocks. This last element is by far and away the most important, but at the moment the most unclear, aspect of the conduct of monetary policy. How is the Bank to respond to (large) shocks as they occur? It seems that the Bank wishes to retain discretion not in the setting of the goals of monetary policy but in the horizon over which the inflation target is to be achieved. The argument is that this horizon will vary with the nature and size of the shock. If a horizon of eighteen months to two years is observed strictly so that current interest rates are set in order to achieve the inflation target by that time, a large (supply) shock which raises inflation in the short run will require a monetary tightening which will exacerbate the associated contraction in output. With demand shocks that raise output and inflation simultaneously there is no need to vary the horizon for policy. A tightening of monetary policy will simultaneously rein in output and inflation.

Despite King's description of policy in terms of a reaction function, the Bank still rejects the explicit use of simple feedback rules of the kind associated with John Taylor (1985), which set interest rates according to deviations of output and inflation from their desired levels. One possible reason for this is that simple interest rate rules are likely to perform badly when the underlying structure of the economy is non-linear. For example, Laxton, Rose and Tetlow (1993) show that welfare costs increase sharply if the true non-linear economy is controlled as if it were linear. However, there is also the issue as to whether the Bank can afford to be more circumspect in responding to a large supply shock if price adjustment is asymmetric.

In this paper we take up a number of issues. We investigate the relationship between the performance of simple interest rate feedback rules and the underlying structure of the economy, notwithstanding the general desirability of a fully optimal rule. This investigation is conducted by use of simulations on the Cambridge University Small UK Model (CUSUM) which is a small model of the UK economy emphasising non-linearities in certain critical economic relationships. We demonstrate that the performance of interest rate rules changes significantly when we allow for the presence of such non-linearities, particularly when the economy is subjected to continuous stochastic disturbances. The plan of the chapter is as follows. In section 2 we discuss the relationship between simple rules and optimal monetary policy. This is followed in section 3 by a discussion of the non-linearities in the price and investment functions which are a major feature of CUSUM. In section 4 we present simulation results for the economy and demonstrate the effects of its underlying non-linear structure. Finally, in section 5, we present our conclusions and suggest some directions for future research.

2. Simple rules and optimal monetary policy

Despite the fact that explicit interest rate feedback rules are not a feature of actual monetary policy, there has been an increasing tendency for these to be built into macroeconometric models of the economy. A number of possible rationales for their use can be put forward:

- They are intended as a description of actual central bank behaviour. By doing this they help to improve the forecasting ability of the model and to improve the quality of dynamic policy simulations.
- They are intended to capture the way in which a consistent central bank with a set of well defined preferences would behave. We may acknowledge that the monetary authority might frequently override the decisions implied by a simple policy rule but nevertheless believe it to be important to analyse how a rational policy maker would behave and what would be the implications for the economy.
- Such rules have nothing to do with describing the behaviour of central banks but are placed in the model simply in order that it should have certain desirable long-run properties. For example, we may wish to constrain the model to produce a constant long-run rate of inflation or to avoid a situation in which the level of national debt grows uncontrollably through time.

The current literature on inflation targeting emphasises the difference between *fully optimal* solutions – derived from a full inter-temporal optimisation problem – and *simple* rules – based on traditional engineering concepts such as proportional, integral and derivative control. The alleged benefits of employing simple rules are that they are more easily understood and more robust to changes in model specification than fully optimal rules (see Nixon and Hall, 1996, for a review of the arguments).

In this paper we make use of simple rules since they seem to capture the actual behaviour of policymakers more accurately than fully optimal rules. However, we motivate the simple rules we use by means of an admittedly *ad hoc* economic model. This is helpful in that it emphasises that even the simplest rules can be interpreted as arising from some sort of optimisation procedure. To see this consider the following model:

$$\Delta p_t = \theta_1 (y_t - y^*) + \Delta p_{t-1} \tag{12.1}$$

$$y_t = \beta_1 - \beta_2 (i_t - \Delta p_t) \tag{12.2}$$

$$y^* = \beta_1 - \beta_2 \rho . \tag{12.3}$$

Equation (12.1) is a standard backwards looking Phillips curve, equation (12.2) is the short run IS curve and equation (1a2.3) specifies the long-run relationship between equilibrium output and an exogenous real interest rate ρ. Now suppose the policy authorities have a loss function of the form:

$$V = \frac{\phi_1}{2} (\Delta p_t - \pi)^2 + \frac{\phi_2}{2} (y_t - y^*)^2 + \frac{\phi_3}{2} (i_t - i_{t-1})^2 . \tag{12.4}$$

The first term penalises deviations of inflation from a target value π, the second penalises deviations of output from capacity – either because the authorities care about this *per se* or because it is regarded as a leading indicator of future inflationary pressure – and the third term penalises changes in the policy instrument, the rate of interest. Minimising (12.4) subject to the constraint set defined by (12.1)–(12.3) yields the following first order condition:

$$-\theta_1\beta_2\phi_1\left(\Delta p_t - \pi\right) + \beta_2^2\phi_2\left(i_t - \Delta p_t - \rho\right) + \phi_3\left(i_t - i_{t-1}\right) = 0. \tag{12.5}$$

If $\phi_2 = 0$ then this reduces to the following expression:

$$\Delta i_t = \frac{\theta_1\beta_2\phi_1}{\phi_3}\left(\Delta p_t - \pi\right) \tag{12.6}$$

which constitutes integral control. Alternatively we might set $\phi_3 = 0$ which would yield the proportional control rule given in equation (12.7):

$$i_t = \rho + \Delta p_t + \frac{\theta_1\phi_1}{\beta_2\phi_2}\left(\Delta p_t - \pi\right). \tag{12.7}$$

This indicates that the policy parameter on deviations of inflation from target depends positively on the ratio of the weights on inflation and output control in the authorities' loss function, positively on the short-run impact of output on inflation and negatively on the short-run effects of changes in the real interest rate on output.

More generally we have the case in which all the weights in the loss function are non-zero. In this case we obtain a linear combination of the integral and proportional control rules as shown in equation (12.8):

$$\Delta i_t = \frac{\theta_1\beta_2\phi_1}{\phi_3}\left(\Delta p_t - \pi\right) - \frac{\beta_2^2\phi_2}{\phi_3}\left(i_t - \Delta p_t - \rho\right). \tag{12.8}$$

3. Non-linear models of pricing and investment

In order to justify considering non-linear or asymmetric adjustment of prices we can appeal to the models of Ball and Mankiw (1994) and Tsiddon (1993) in which menu costs lead to the conclusion that it is optimal for firms not to respond to small shocks very quickly. However, when the shocks are such as to require prices to rise, firms will do so more quickly the higher the rate of inflation. For investment, modern theorising emphasises the option value of an investment when there are irreversibilities (Dixit, 1992). As Gale (1996) shows, this may induce an asymmetry over the business cycle. During downturns firms may delay investment while in the upturn there will be a burst of investment as profitable opportunities present themselves.

The method we use to detect asymmetries empirically is to posit models in which the equilibrium relationships derived from economic theory provide the dynamic attractors for prices and investment. We then try to establish whether adjustment on each side of the attractor is non-linear or asymmetric. The first stage is to identify cointegrating vectors for prices and investment by estimating general models and deriving the implicit cointegrating vectors along the lines suggested by Stock and Watson. We then fit a variety of functions to deviations from the attractors in an error correction form.

The derivation of the equilibrium price relationship is described in Arden, Holly and Turner (1997). It is based on the profit maximisation problem facing an imperfectly competitive firm with a Cobb-Douglas production function defined over labour, capital and raw material inputs. The equilibrium relationship is given in equation (12.9):

$$p = \gamma_0 + \frac{\beta}{1-\alpha}(w - y - l) + \frac{1-\alpha-\beta}{1-\alpha}p^m + \frac{\alpha}{1-\alpha}(y - k) \qquad (12.9)$$

where p is the price level, w is the wage rate, y is real output, l is employment, p^m is the price of raw materials and k is the capital stock. All variables are in natural logarithms. α and β are the shares of capital and labour in output and γ_0 is an intercept term.

Using (12.9) as the equilibrium relationship we estimated an error correction model for prices by use of the Stock and Watson (1993) methodology. This yielded estimates of the α and β parameters equal to 0.295 and 0.518 respectively. We then constructed a disequilibrium term based on these parameter estimates and re-estimated the model, replacing the lagged levels terms with our error correction term. This yields the linear model given below:

Linear price equation sample period 1970Q1 to 1996Q4

$$\Delta p_t = 0.0122 + 0.3145\ \Delta tx_t + 0.0440\ \Delta p^m_{t-1} + 0.0777\ \Delta p^m_{t-4}$$
$$(8.53)\quad (4.41)\qquad\quad (1.62)\qquad\qquad (2.73)$$

$$+\ 0.2187\ \Delta(w+l-y)_t + 0.0826\ \Delta(w+l-y)_{t-1} - 0.1846\ \varepsilon_{t-1}$$
$$(5.78)\qquad\qquad\quad (2.08)\qquad\qquad\qquad (5.86)$$

$R^2 = 0.76$ SEE = 0.0072 DW = 1.74
LM(4) = 0.76 ARCH(1) = 0.53 NORM = 0.54

where $tx = ln(1+itr)$; itr is the indirect tax rate. LM(4) and ARCH(1) are the F-forms of the Lagrange Multiplier tests for fourth order serial correlation and a first order autoregressive conditional heteroscedasticity in the residuals. NORM is the Jarque-Bera test for normality of the residuals asymptotically distributed as $\chi^2(2)$ under the null of normality.

To investigate the possibility of non-linearities in the model we then added quadratic and cubic error correction terms to the above specification. The resulting equation is shown below:

Non-linear price equation sample period 1970Q1 to 1996Q4

$$\Delta p_t = 0.0119 + 0.3497\,\Delta tx_t + 0.0179\,\Delta p^m_{t-1} + 0.0692\,\Delta p^m_{t-4}$$
$$\quad (8.53) \quad (5.15) \qquad (0.67) \qquad\qquad (2.53)$$

$$+ 0.2113\,\Delta(w+l-y)_t + 0.0417\,\Delta(w+l-y)_{t-1} - 0.2520\,\varepsilon_{t-1}$$
$$\quad (5.92) \qquad\qquad (1.04) \qquad\qquad\qquad (5.02)$$

$$+ 1.9865\,\varepsilon^2_{t-1} + 5.8592\,\varepsilon^3_{t-1}$$
$$\quad (2.63) \qquad (0.36)$$

$R^2 = 0.79$ SEE = 0.0067   DW = 1.82
LM(4) = 0.30   ARCH(1) = 0.79   NORM = 0.38

The two non-linear error correction terms are jointly significant and, though the cubic term is not significant, we retain it because it marginally improves some of the simulations.

The equilibrium investment relationship relates the investment–capital ratio to the real price of equity and the level of output. Again we estimate a general model and derive the implicit relationship between the levels of the variables. This equation is listed below:

$$\varepsilon_t = (i-k)_t + 14.4298 - 0.08259\,y_t - 0.1135\,(pe-pk)_t$$

where i is private sector non-residential investment, k is the OECD measure of the business sector capital stock, y is non-oil Gross Domestic Product, pe is the FT ordinary share price index and pk is the price deflator for investment goods. All variables are in natural logarithms. This relationship is then used as the error correction term in the following linear model:

Linear investment equation sample period 1965Q4 to 1996Q1

$\Delta(i-k)_t = -0.0012 + 0.1223\ DDV85Q1 + 0.8000\ \Delta y_t - 0.1172\ D^2(i-k)_{t-1}$
            (0.32)   (4.66)   (2.90)   (2.07)
            $- 0.2865\ \varepsilon_{t-1}$
            (5.79)

R² = 0.42   SEE = 0.0364   DW = 2.04
LM(4) = 0.12   ARCH(1) = 0.02   NORM = 0.04

This equation has reasonable statistical properties with a significant error correction term. Again we allow for the presence of non-linearities by including higher powers of the error correction term. The results are reported in the equation below:

Non-linear investment equation sample period 1965Q4 to 1996Q1

$\Delta(i-k)_t = -0.0068 + 0.1329\ DDV85Q1 + 0.7805\Delta y_t - 0.08180\ \Delta^2(i-k)_{t-1}$
            (1.48)   (4.99)   (2.83)   (1.38)

            $- 0.2799\ \varepsilon_{t-1} + 1.4059\ \varepsilon^2_{t-1} - 4.2380\ \varepsilon^3_{t-1}$
            (3.87)   (1.82)   (0.96)

R² = 0.44   SEE = 0.0361   DW = 1.99
LM(4) = 0.05   ARCH(1) = 0.01   NORM = 0.37

In this case the evidence for significant non-linearities is somewhat weaker. The quadratic term is only marginally significant and again the cubic term is insignificant. However, since our Monte-Carlo experiments[4] indicate that the power of conventional tests to identify asymmetries is likely to be low in these cases we retain the non-linear terms for the model simulations.

4. Model simulations

In this section we turn to a variety of simulations based on CUSUM. In order to investigate the way in which non-linearities interact with interest rate rules, we carry out both deterministic and stochastic simulations. Our focus is on two main issues. The first is the asymmetric effects of large, relative to small shocks, deriving from both the demand and supply sides of the economy. The second is the effects on the stochastic distribution of output and inflation resulting from the non-linearities in the underlying behavioural relationships.

4.1. Differences between 'large' and 'small' shocks

The first set of simulations which we report concerns the effect on inflation and growth of shocks on both the supply side of the model and the demand side. We also explore the effects of 'small' shocks and 'large' shocks. The version of the model used here has forward-looking expectations for the exchange rate, the long-term interest rate and equity prices. In figures 12.1 and 12.2 we show the effect on inflation and output growth of four shocks to world trade in manufactures: a 5 per cent rise in world trade and a 5 per cent fall, and a 20 per cent rise and a 20 per cent fall.

Figure 12.2 illustrates the effects on output. For the small shock the effect on output of the trade shock is more or less symmetric. For the large shock there is some evidence of asymmetries, though they are not especially large. The negative shock depresses output more than the positive shock raises it. These results are mirrored for inflation in figure 12.1. The small shocks to demand have symmetric effects while again there are differences between the large negative and positive shocks.

The shock to the labour market was simulated by exogenising nominal wages and raising and lowering them by first 3 per cent and then 9 per cent. This should be thought of an experiment on the model, and not necessarily a realistic economic example. It is clear from figures 12.3 and 12.4 that when the labour market shock is 'small' the response of inflation and output growth to negative and positive shocks is broadly symmetrical. We appear to be operating in a linear region for the economy. However, when the shock is 'large', a quite different response is observed. The positive shock has a much larger effect in raising inflation than the negative shock reduces inflation. Moreover, the positive wage shock lowers output more than the negative shock raises it. It is also clear that while the effect on inflation dies out after two years, the output effects are much more persistent and the path for output is more volatile with the larger shock.

4.2 Stochastic simulations

Although the simulations reported in the previous section point to some significant asymmetries in the response of inflation and output, especially with the supply side shock, they do not show the complete picture. As it is well known that the expected value of a non-linear function is not in general equal to the non-linear function of the expected value of random

Effects of demand shocks on inflation and GDP growth

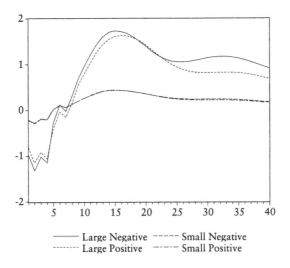

Figure 12.1 *Effects of demand shocks on inflation*

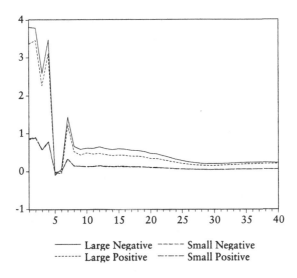

Figure 12.2 *Effects of demand shocks on GDP growth*

Effects of supply shocks on inflation and GDP growth

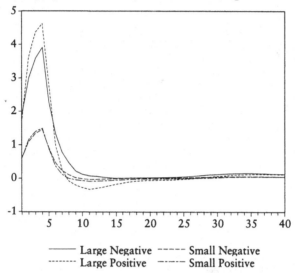

Figure 12.3 *Effects of wage shocks on inflation*

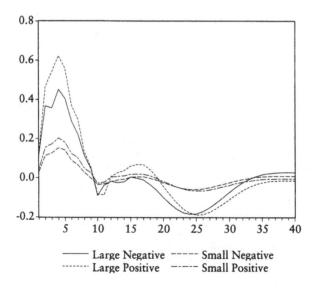

Figure 12.4 *Effects of wage shocks on output growth*

disturbances, we turn in this section to stochastic simulations (see Fisher and Salmon (1986) for an extensive discussion of the issues). One of the roles of stochastic simulation of macroeconomic models is to explore the uncertainties associated with forecasting with non-linear models. However, they can also be thought of as a generalisation of simple shocks and a way of exploring model properties. In our case it is arguable that it is through stochastic simulation that the non-linearities built into the model become most evident. Stochastic simulation is also of interest to us because it provides a useful diagnostic tool for the evaluation of economic policy. For example, we may be interested in establishing how robust a particular rule for policy is in an uncertain environment.

There is, however, an immediate problem of how to conduct stochastic simulations with forward looking expectations. One approach is to stochastically simulate the model over time and solve for the expectations as well. This involves the following stages. From a base path for the model with consistent expectations introduce a set of random shocks in the first period while setting shocks in all remaining periods to zero. Then solve the model under consistent expectations. Then move forward one period and add another set of shocks, setting all subsequent periods to zero and solve the model again under consistent expectations. Do this to the end of the simulation and then start again in period one. Although this is very expensive computationally, there is no technical obstacle to this procedure. However, it is not clear that this is what we would want to do. Solving the model in this way assumes that the shocks to the exchange rate, for example, are unanticipated and transitory. This means that the arbitrage relationship will largely discount the effects of the one-off, transitory shock However, shocks can be anticipated in part, persistent and sometimes permanent. So in order to approximate this situation we carried out the replications under an adaptive mechanism for the three expectational variables, with 80 per cent of a change in asset prices being factored into expectations immediately.

To produce the stochastic simulations reported in this section we added random error terms to 23 of the model equations, 16 of which are behavioural relationships and 7 of which are exogenous variables. We then solved the model 100 times for different realisations of the random variables. In designing our stochastic experiments we use what Fisher and Salmon (1986) describe as the 'naïve' method. That is to say we use the standard errors of each of the behavioural equations, and estimate ARIMA models for 'exogenous' variables in order to provide standard errors for these variables. We assume that the covariance matrix of the errors is diagonal. We also use antithetic variates (Calzolari, 1979) in order to improve the efficiency of the experiments. This effectively means that the model is solved 50 times using alternative sets of seeded random variables and then another 50 times using the negative of the first set. This is an extremely efficient way of exploring the probability distribution while economising on the number of replications necessary. We also carried out 100 replications for each reported case. The period over which we conducted the exercises was from 1994Q1 to 2005Q4. Up until 1993Q4 the data are historical. Thereafter, the model is allowed to run on its own. We confine our attentions to just inflation and output growth.

Our initial simulations assume fixed interest rates. However, we did not set the interest rate arbitrarily. Instead we experimented to find that fixed rate of interest which generates inflation equal to the target value of 2.5 per cent by the end of our simulation period. In order to control for the general forms of non-linearity in the model we first simulated a version of the model which uses the symmetric version of the price and investment equations. For the symmetric model a fixed nominal rate of interest of 6.75 per cent is required to achieve the target rate of inflation by the end of the simulation period. Therefore the equilibrium real rate of interest is equal to 4.25 per cent in this case. In figure 12.5 we show the solution for inflation in the symmetric model. The solid line is the solution path for the deterministic model while the broken line is the mean of 100 stochastic replications. As can be seen these are very close together. We find something similar for output growth in figure 12.6.

When we turn to the asymmetric version of the model we find that a slightly higher interest rate is necessary to achieve the inflation target by the end of the simulation period. The nominal rate required is now 7.5 per cent implying an equilibrium real rate of interest of 5 per cent. Using this value we computed solution paths for output and inflation in the deterministic case along with the average of 100 stochastic replications of the model. The results, which are shown in figures 12.7 and 12.8, are striking. The main feature is that there is a clear upward bias in the stochastic path for inflation.[5] Although it is less marked for output growth there is some suggestion that the solution path is slightly higher. The intuition for this result is that the shocks hitting the system mean that the error correction term in the price equation becomes more or less evenly distributed around zero. However, the non-linearity of the pricing equation means that a negative error correction term produces upward pressure on prices much stronger than an equivalent positive term leads to downward pressure. The net effect is to increase the mean inflation rate. Similar effects apply to the non-linear investment function but the overall impact of this appears to be rather weaker than for the price equation.

Symmetric model: fixed interest rate simulations

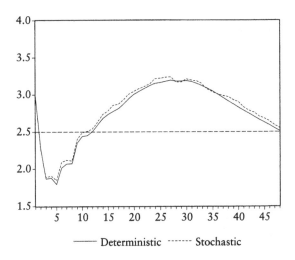

Figure 12.5 *Inflation*

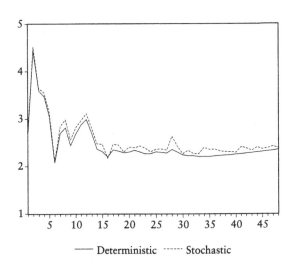

Figure 12.6 *GDP growth*

Asymmetric model: fixed interest rate simulations

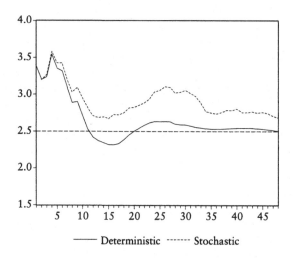

Figure 12.7 *Inflation*

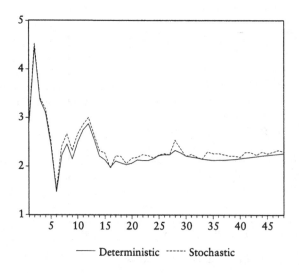

Figure 12.8 *GDP growth*

One notable feature of the stochastic simulations is that, even in the long run, the equilibrium inflation rate is slightly higher than in the deterministic case. This in turn means that the equilibrium real interest rate is rather lower, which may help account for the higher output growth path in the stochastic case. If the authorities wish to meet the inflation target in a stochastic environment then it becomes necessary to set nominal interest rates at a higher level. This in turn will mean that equilibrium real interest rates will be higher than in the deterministic case.

The simulations with fixed interest rates make it clear that, in the absence of a policy response, non-linearities in the adjustment of prices generate a higher average path for inflation. The question is whether if monetary policy were responsive it would help to lower the mean path for inflation. Following on from the discussion in section 2 we assessed the performance of two feedback rules. These are the straight proportional control rule and the proportional plus derivative control rule.

To derive the proportional control rule we assume the following values for the parameters of the monetary authorities' loss function and for equations (12.1) and (12.2): $\phi_1 = 0.8$, $\phi_2 = 1.0$, $\phi_3 = 0$, $\theta_1 = 0.5$, $\beta_2 = 0.5$. We also set target values for the inflation rate and real interest rate of 2.5 and 5 per cent respectively. These imply an interest rate rule of the form

$$i_t = 5 + \Delta p_t + 0.8\,(\Delta p_t - 2.5).$$

To derive the proportional plus integral control rule we place a non-zero weight on changes in the rate of interest. The following parameter values are chosen: $\phi_1 = 0.8$, $\phi_2 = 1.0$, $\phi_3 = 0.5$, $\theta_1 = 0.5$, $\beta_2 = 0.5$. Again we set target values for the inflation rate and real interest rate of 2.5 and 5 per cent respectively. These imply an interest rate rule of the form:

$$i_t = 0.67\,i_{t-1} + 0.27\,(\Delta p_t - 2.5) + 0.33\,(\Delta p_t + 5).$$

Before we assess the performance of these alternative control rules in a stochastic setting, we first illustrate their implications for the deterministic version of the model. The time paths for inflation for the fixed interest rate rule and the two feedback control rules are shown in figure 12.9. These simulations give rise to a rather surprising result; the most effective way of bringing inflation down to its target value appears to be to simply fix the nominal rate at the appropriate level rather than to make use of any sort of feedback mechanism. However, such a conclusion is premature. The success of the fixed rate rule depends critically on choosing the 'correct' equilibrium real interest rate to aim for. If the authorities mistakenly set

Inflation and interest rates under alternative control rules

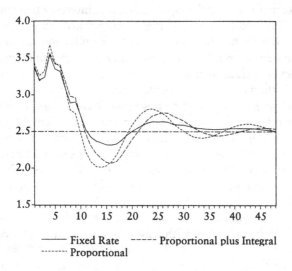

Figure 12.9 *Inflation*

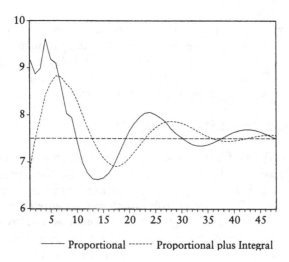

Figure 12.10 *Short-term interest rates*

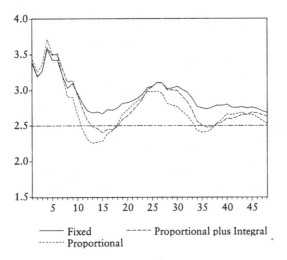

Figure 12.11 *Inflation under alternative control rules with stochastic disturbances*

too low a rate then inflation will overshoot its target in both the short and the long run. The feedback rules are less sensitive to the choice of equilibrium real interest rate because they incorporate specific terms in the deviation of inflation from target. Another factor which must also be taken into account is that feedback rules are likely to be more effective in a stochastic setting since they enable the authorities to respond systematically to shocks which move inflation away from its target path.

If we compare the two feedback rules we see that the initial fall in inflation is much steeper under proportional control relative to proportional plus integral control. To understand the reasons for this we must look in more detail at the behaviour of interest rates. Figure 12.10 shows the time paths of the short-term interest rate under proportional and proportional plus integral control. The horizontal line through 7.5 shows both the fixed rate case and the equilibrium for the other two cases. The reason for the difference in adjustment speeds between the two feedback rules can be seen in this diagram. With proportional control the immediate policy reaction is to increase interest rates sharply to deal with the fact that inflation is above target. However, when we have proportional plus integral control then the initial increase is rather smaller because we put a positive weight in the loss function on interest rate changes. This initial difference produces a phase shift in the subsequent adjustment path which is mirrored in the inflation solution paths.

Finally, we compare the behaviour of inflation under the alternative control rules when the economy is subject to stochastic disturbances. Figure 12.11 shows the average inflation rate from 100 stochastic replications of the model under the three policy regimes discussed. We have already shown that the effect of stochastic disturbances is to increase the average inflation rate relative to the deterministic case and this is again clearly evident in the figure. The interesting question here is whether the feedback control rules perform any better in steering the economy towards its target inflation rate. figure 12.11 indicates that this is indeed the case. The average inflation paths for both control rules lie systematically below that for the fixed interest rate rule with the proportional rule keeping inflation closer to target than either fixed rates of proportional plus integral control.

5. Conclusions

The results here indicate that the inclusion of non-linear relationships for prices and investment in our macroeconomic model changes its behaviour in ways which are important for the purposes of monetary policy. Three main conclusions stand out with regard to the conduct of monetary policy:

- Positive and negative shocks have different effects on inflation and output growth. The most pronounced example of this is the asymmetric effect of wage shocks in which positive shocks to wages raise inflation more than negative shocks reduce it. The obvious policy conclusion is that that the monetary authorities can improve performance if they can vary their response to match the type and sign of the disturbance they wish to respond to.
- The price equation asymmetry produces a significant upward bias in the time path of inflation under a fixed interest rate rule when we consider the case in which the economy is subjected to continuous stochastic disturbances. In order to achieve any given inflation target the monetary authorities must set a higher interest rate than the deterministic model would suggest is necessary.
- Feedback control rules provide one mechanism through which the upward bias in the inflation rate can be offset. By incorporating deviations of inflation from target explicitly into the control rule, the time path for inflation is tied more closely to its desired value than if interest rates are set at the level indicated by the deterministic model.

In future work we intend to extend the results presented in this chapter in a number of ways. These include the extension of the non-linear adjustment specification to other equations in the model and the analysis of the performance of feedback control rules under alternative types of stochastic disturbance.

Notes

1 The authors would like to acknowledge financial support from ESRC Award No. L116251017.
2 However, it is also widely agreed that Phillips' original relationship between inflation and unemployment was convex.
3 Tsiddon (1993) arrives at similar conclusions with a more complex model.
4 Using the parameters of the asymmetric investment equation given above, along with the variance of the error correction term and the standard error of the equation, we ran Monte-Carlo experiments to evaluate the frequency with which we could reject the false null of a linear model in favour of the true alternative of the cubic model. With a sample size of 100 we found that we could only reject the false null in 30 per cent of replications.
5 It might be argued that, if the mean path for inflation is higher, nominal interest rates should also be higher over the solution path, since otherwise the real interest rate on average is lower.

References

Ammer, J. and Freeman, R.T. (1995), 'Inflation targeting in the 1990s: the experiences of New Zealand, Canada, and the United Kingdom', *Journal of Economics and Business*, 47, 2, May, pp. 165–92.
Arden, R., Holly, S, and Turner, P. (1997a), 'The asymmetric adjustment of prices: theory and evidence from UK manufacturing', Department of Applied Economics Discussion Paper No. 9715, University of Cambridge.
(1997b), 'Asymmetries in private sector investment expenditure: an empirical investigation', Department of Applied Economics Discussion Paper No. 9716, University of Cambridge.
(1997c), 'Asymmetric adjustment costs, asymmetric pricing and employment: evidence from the UK', Department of Applied Economics Discussion Paper No. 9717, University of Cambridge.
(1997d), 'Production smoothing, inventory investment and asymmetric adjustment', Department of Applied Economics Discussion Paper No. 9719, University of Cambridge.
Ball L. and Mankiw, G. (1994), 'Asymmetric price adjustment and economic fluctuations', *Economic Journal*, 104, pp. 247–61.
Calzolari G. (1979), 'Antithetic variates to estimate the simulation bias in nonlinear

models', *Economic Letters*, 4, pp. 323–38.

Cook, S., Holly, S. and Turner, P. (1997), 'Investigating the power of tests for asymmetries in macroeconomic relationships', mimeo, University of Cambridge.

Dixit, A. (1992), 'Investment and hysteresis', *Journal of Economic Perspectives*, 6, pp. 107–32.

Fisher, P.G. and Salmon, M.H. (1986), 'On evaluating the importance of nonlinearity in large macroeconometric models', *International Economic Review*, 27, pp. 625–46.

Gale, D. (1996), 'Delay and cycles', *Review of Economic Studies*, 63, April, pp. 169–98.

Granger, C.W.J. and Lee, T.H. (1989), 'Investigation of production, sales and inventory relationships using multicointegration and non-symmetric error correction models', *Journal of Applied Econometrics,* 4, pp. 145–59.

King, M. (1997), 'The inflation target five years on', Lecture given at the London School of Economics, 29th October.

Laxton, D., Rose, D. and Tetlow, R. (1993), 'Monetary policy, uncertainty and the presumption of linearity', Bank of Canada Technical Report No. 63.

Stock, J.H., and Watson, M.W. (1993), 'A simple estimator of cointegrating vectors in higher order integrated systems', *Econometrica*, 61, pp. 783–820.

Taylor, J.B. (1985), *What Would Nominal GDP Targeting Do to the Business Cycle?*, Carnegie-Rochester Series on Public Policy, 22, pp. 61–84.

Tsiddon, D. (1993), 'The (mis)behaviour of the aggregate price level', *Review of Economic Studies,* 60, October, pp. 889–902.